• Al-Arish

SINAI AND
THE RED SEA
COAST

• Sharm el-Sheikh

• Hurghada

• Luxor

• Aswan

AROUND CAIRO
See pp158–169

**SINAI AND THE RED
SEA COAST**
See pp216–233

CAIRO AREA BY AREA

CENTRAL CAIRO
See pp68–85

ISLAMIC CAIRO
See pp86–111

**RHODA ISLAND
AND OLD CAIRO**
See pp112–125

GIZA AND HELIOPOLIS
See pp126–139

| 0 kilometres | 140 |
| 0 miles | 75 |

EYEWITNESS TRAVEL
EGYPT

EYEWITNESS TRAVEL

EGYPT

LONDON, NEW YORK,
MELBOURNE, MUNICH AND DELHI
www.dk.com

PROJECT ART EDITOR Jo Doran
PROJECT EDITORS Hugh Thompson, Claire Folkard
EDITORS Liz Atherton, Irene Lyford,
Ferdie McDonald, Marianne Petrou, Martin Redfern
DESIGNERS Emma Rose, Rebecca Milner, Ian Midson,
Sue Megginson, Anthony Limerick
PICTURE RESEARCHERS Monica Allende, Cynthia Frazer,
Katherine Mesquita
MAP CO-ORDINATORS David Pugh, Casper Morris
DTP DESIGNER Maite Lantaron

MAIN CONTRIBUTORS
Jane Dunford, Dr Joann Fletcher, Carole French, Robin Gauldie,
Andrew Humphreys, Kyle Pakka, Richard Williams

MAPS
ERA-Maptec Ltd

PHOTOGRAPHERS
Max Alexander, Jon Spaull,
Peter Wilson

ILLUSTRATORS
Gary Cross, Richard Draper, Claire Littlejohn, Maltings Partnership,
Chris Orr & Associates, John Woodcock

Reproduced by Colourscan, Singapore
Printed and bound by South China Printing Co., Ltd, China

First published in Great Britain in 2001
by Dorling Kindersley Limited
80 Strand, London WC2R 0RL
A Penguin Company
Reprinted with revisions 2003, 2005, 2007

Copyright 2001, 2007 © Dorling Kindersley Limited, London

A CIP CATALOGUE RECORD IS AVAILABLE FROM THE BRITISH LIBRARY.

ISBN 978 1 40532 093 1

THROUGHOUT THIS BOOK, FLOORS ARE REFERRED TO IN ACCORDANCE
WITH EUROPEAN USAGE: THE "FIRST FLOOR" IS THE FLOOR ABOVE GROUND LEVEL

*Front cover main image: Sphinx and the
Pyramid of Khafre, Giza*

**The information in this
DK Eyewitness Travel Guide is checked regularly.**
Every effort has been made to ensure that this book is as up-to-date
as possible at the time of going to press. Some details, however,
such as telephone numbers, opening hours, prices, gallery hanging
arrangements and travel information are liable to change. The
publishers cannot accept responsibility for any consequences arising
from the use of this book, nor for any material on third party websites,
and cannot guarantee that any website address in this book will be
a suitable source of travel information. We value the views and
suggestions of our readers very highly. Please write to: Publisher,
DK Eyewitness Travel Guides, Dorling Kindersley, 80 Strand,
London WC2R 0RL, Great Britain.

Fertile fields watered by the Nile at Luxor

CONTENTS

View from the Cairo Tower looking
at the Radio and TV Union Building

◁ A local guide keeping out of the heat of the sun at Luxor Temple in the Nile Valley

Camel trekking in the desert

TRAVELLERS' NEEDS

SURVIVAL GUIDE

CAIRO AREA BY AREA

Fruit stall at Dakhla Oasis showing
the wide variety of produce grown

Colossal foot at the Ramesseum

Ancient Egyptian frieze of lotus
blooms, symbolic of rebirth

SHOPPING AND ENTERTAINMENT IN CAIRO **150**

EGYPT AREA BY AREA

Hanging Church in Coptic Cairo

HOW TO USE THIS GUIDE

This guide helps you to get the most from your visit to Egypt by providing detailed practical information and expert recommendations. *Introducing Egypt* maps the country and sets it in its historical and cultural context. The Cairo section and the five area chapters describe important sights using maps, photographs and illustrations. Features cover topics from food and wildlife to hieroglyphics and mythology. Restaurants and hotel recommendations can be found in *Travellers' Needs*, while the *Survival Guide* has tips on everything from making a telephone call to using local transportation, as well as information on money and other practical matters.

CAIRO AREA BY AREA

The city is divided into three areas, each with its own chapter. A fourth chapter covers the peripheral areas of Giza and Heliopolis. All sights are numbered and plotted on each chapter's area map. Information on each sight is easy to locate as the entries follow the numbering used on the map.

A locator map shows where you are in relation to other areas in the city centre.

All pages relating to Cairo have red thumb tabs.

Sights at a Glance lists the chapter's sights by category: Streets and Squares, Holy Places, Museums, Historic Buildings and Mosques.

1 Area Map
For easy reference, sights are numbered and located on a map. The central sights are also marked on the Street Finder *maps on pages 140–49.*

Street-by-Street: Fatimid Cairo

2 Street-by-Street Map
This gives a bird's-eye view of the key area in each chapter.

Stars indicate the sights that no visitor should miss.

Walking routes, in red, take in the area's most interesting streets.

3 Detailed information
City sights are described individually. Addresses and opening hours are given, as well as information on admission charges, guided tours, photography, wheelchair access and public transport.

EGYPT AREA BY AREA

1 Introduction

The landscape, history and character of each area is described here, along with an account of how the area has developed over the centuries and what it has to offer the visitor today.

EGYPT AREA BY AREA

Apart from Cairo, the country has been divided into five areas, each of which has a separate chapter. The most interesting cities, towns, ancient and religious sites, and other places of interest are located on a *Regional Map*.

2 Regional Map

This shows the road network and gives an illustrated overview of each area. Interesting places to visit are numbered, and there are useful tips on getting to and around the region by car and public transport.

Each area of Egypt can be quickly identified by its colour-coded thumb tabs *(see inside front cover).*

3 Detailed information

All the important towns and other places to visit are described individually. They are listed in order and follow the numbering on the Regional Map. Within each town or city there is detailed information on important buildings and other sights.

For all major sights, a *Visitors' Checklist* provides the practical information you will need to plan your visit.

4 Egypt's Top Sights

These are given two or more pages. Historic buildings are reconstructed, or dissected to reveal their interiors. Other interesting sights are shown in bird's-eye view, with important features highlighted.

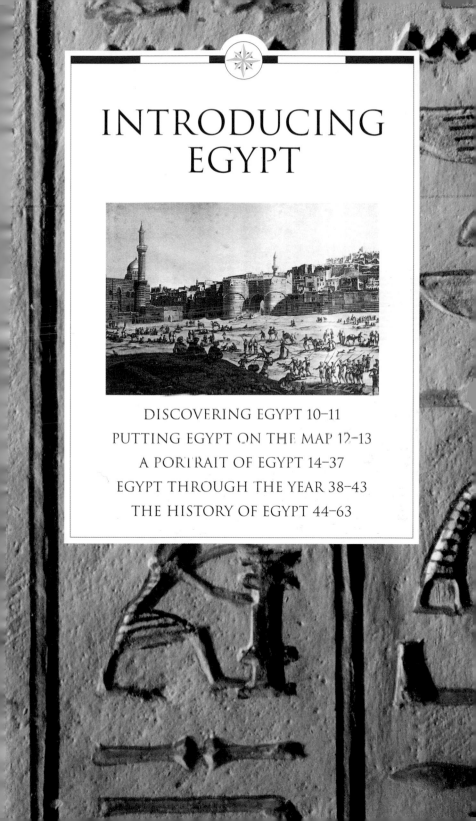

INTRODUCING
EGYPT

DISCOVERING EGYPT

Few countries can match Egypt's wealth of ancient monuments and temples; the relics of Pharaonic culture have been drawing visitors for centuries. The geographical variety of Egypt means that visitors are spoiled for choice: from the bustle of Cairo to the austere adventure of the Western Desert; from the coral of the Red Sea to the cultural wealth of the Nile Valley temples; from the lush Delta region with its cosmopolitan, cultured city of Alexandria to the endlessly fascinating pyramid fields around Cairo. These pages offer a brief overiew of each region.

Tutankhamun's gilded fan, Egyptian Museum

The majestic Sphinx on the Giza Plateau, in the suburbs of Cairo

CAIRO

- **Mosques and museums**
- **Wondrous pyramids**
- **Shopping in the souqs**
- **Buzzing nightlife**

Cairo is a city where ancient and modern are intertwined. As well as the **Pyramids** *(see pp128–35)*, the **Sphinx** at Giza *(see p135)* and the fabulous **Egyptian Museum** *(see pp74–7)*, there are early Christian churches and Ottoman and Mamluk mosques. The old souqs, alleys and houses are clustered together with modern five-star hotels, shopping malls, restaurants, cinemas and theatres. **The Citadel** (Al-Qalaa) *(see pp104–7)*, dating from the 12th century, contains fascinating mosques, museums and battlements which reflect a diverse heritage. Nearby is one of the largest and oldest mosques in Egypt, the

Mosque of Ibn Tulun *(see pp110-11)*, built entirely of mud brick.

The world's oldest bazaar, **Khan al-Khalili** *(see p90)*, is the place to go for antiques, textiles and handicrafts. The city's restaurants offer all types of cuisine and there is a great selection of bars, nightclubs and *sheesha* cafés.

For classical and Arabic music head to the beautiful domed **Opera House** *(see p84)*, a cultural centre with galleries and concert halls.

AROUND CAIRO

- **The pyramids at Saqqara**
- **Lakes and oases**
- **Ancient Memphis**
- **Carpet schools**

For a day or two's excursion out of Cairo, visitors can take a felucca up the Nile to the **Nile Barrages** at **Qanater** *(see p169)*, a good picnic spot. Heading south out of Cairo, the road leads to **Saqqara** *(see pp162–4)*, the site of the Pyramid of Djoser, which is much older than the Great Pyramids and less crowded. Further down the road are the even more isolated pyramid site of **Dahshur** *(see p165)* and **Fayoum Oasis** *(see p168)*, Egypt's largest oasis, with its lush vegetation. Closer at hand are the three pyramids of **Abusir** *(see p162)* and the site of the ancient city of **Memphis** *(see p165)*, with a small museum. After a guided tour around one of the many carpet schools in this area, you might not be able to resist buying a rug.

Camels riding past verdant Fayoum, Egypt's largest oasis

◁ Hieroglyphics on tomb in the Valley of the Kings

THE NILE VALLEY

- **Theban tombs**
- **Luxor and Karnak**
- **The lazy Nile**
- **The dams at Aswan**

For an abundance of tombs and temples, head to **Luxor** *(see pp184–90)* and **Thebes** *(see pp192–203)*. No one can fail to be impressed by the Valley of the Kings, the temples at Karnak and Luxor and the Luxor Museum.

A cruise down the Nile allows you to take in various temples, including **Edfu** *(see pp204–5)*, **Kom Ombo** *(see p205)* and, eventually, **Abu Simbel** *(see pp214–15)*.

Most cruises stop at **Aswan** *(see pp208–11)*, whose two famous dams (Aswan Dam and High Dam) are extraordinary feats of engineering.

The unmistakable sail of a felucca slowly gliding along the Nile

SINAI AND THE RED SEA COAST

- **Beautiful beaches**
- **Spectacular diving**
- **Monasteries and castles**
- **Watersports and golf**

Sun, sea, diving and good food can all be found here. **Sharm el-Sheikh** *(see p226)*, at the southern tip of the Sinai peninsula, has the best choice of hotels, restaurants and nightlife. Naama Bay is good for snorkelling and also boasts many *sheesha* cafés, bars and clubs.

Sinai has much more to offer, however. The Greek

The extraordinary colours of the Red Sea coral reef

Orthodox **Monastery of St Catherine** *(see pp222–5)* has a fabulous collection of religious icons, while those venturing further up the coast will enjoy the 12th-century Crusader castle on **Pharaoh's Island** *(see p231)*. **Dahab** *(see p230)* is great for diving, sailing and wind-surfing, as is **Hurghada** *(see pp232–3)*, on the west coast of the Red Sea. **Soma Bay** *(see p233)* and **El-Gouna** *(see p233)* offer a tranquil setting, plus top-class spas and golf.

THE DELTA AND THE NORTH COAST

- **Alexandria**
- **Ottoman architecture**
- **Important battlegrounds**
- **Historic Rosetta**

The second city in Egypt, **Alexandria** *(see pp240–47)* was founded by Alexander the Great in the 4th century BC. Little remains of the city's Graeco-Roman architecture, but there are a Mamluk fortress and some Ottoman mosques in the Anfushi area. Although a busy port, the city has a more laid-back Mediterranean feel than Cairo.

To the west of Alexandria is the town of **El-Alamein** *(see p251)*, with its World War II cemeteries and museum. To the east lie **Abu Qir** *(see p250)*, site of Nelson's victory at the 1798 Battle of the Nile, and **Rosetta** (Rashid) *(see p239)*, where the Rosetta Stone was discovered.

THE WESTERN DESERT

- **Verdant oases**
- **Desert treasures**
- **Safari adventure**
- **Berber culture**

A vast expanse of sand and rock, the Western Desert stretches from the Nile west towards the Libyan border. Apart from a few Bedouin desert-dwellers, the area is uninhabited, except for **Kharga** *(see p256)*, **Dakhla** *(see p256)*, **Farafra** *(see p257)*, **Bahariyya** *(see p257)* and **Siwa** *(see p260)* oases, which house a surprising number of ancient Egyptian and Roman temples and medieval forts. Four of these oases are reachable by a looping desert road from Cairo to Asyut and are the main stopping-off points for desert safaris. Siwa, the most remote oasis, offers a great insight into Berber culture.

Ancient ruins in Siwa, a remote oasis in the Western Desert

Putting Egypt on the Map

Sitting on the northeast corner of Africa, with coastlines along the Mediterranean and Red seas, Egypt borders Libya to the west, Israel to the east and Sudan to the south. Over 90 per cent of the country is desert and most of the 74 million population live along the Nile Valley and in the Nile Delta, with a small percentage living in the oases that dot the barren interior.

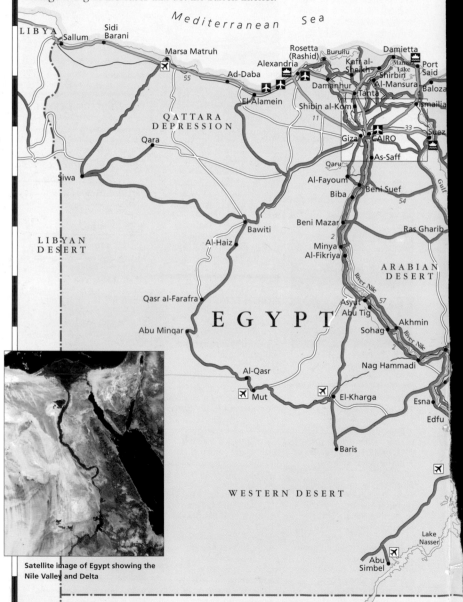

Mediterranean Sea

LIBYA

Sidi
Barani

Sallum

Marsa Matruh

Ad-Daba

55

QATTARA
DEPRESSION

Qara

Siwa

LIBYAN
DESERT

Bawiti

Al-Haiz

Qasr al-Farafra

Abu Minqar

Al-Qasr

Mut

Alexandria

El-Alamein

Rosetta
(Rashid)   Burullu   Damietta

Kafr al-   Manzala
Sheikh   Lake   Port
Shirbin   Said

Damanhur   Al-Mansura   Baloza

Tanta   Ismailia

Shibin al-Kom

11

Giza   CAIRO   33   Suez

As-Saff

Qaru

Al-Fayoum

Biba   Beni Suef   54

Beni Mazar   Ras Gharib

2

Minya
Al-Fikriya

ARABIAN
DESERT

River Nile

Asyut   57
Abu Tig

Sohag   Akhmin

2

Nag Hammadi

El-Kharga   Esna

Edfu

Baris

E G Y P T

WESTERN DESERT

Lake
Nasser

Abu
Simbel

*Satellite image of Egypt showing the
Nile Valley and Delta*

SUDAN

EUROPE, THE MIDDLE EAST AND NORTH AFRICA

REP. OF IRELAND
UNITED KINGDOM
DENMARK
RUSSIAN FEDERATION
POLAND
BELARUS
GERMANY
UKRAINE
KAZAKHSTAN
FRANCE
ROMANIA
ITALY
BULGARIA
GEORGIA
SPAIN
GREECE
TURKEY
TUNISIA
SYRIA
IRAQ
IRAN
MOROCCO
JORDAN
ALGERIA
LIBYA
EGYPT
U.A.E
MAURITANIA
SAUDI ARABIA
MALI
NIGER
CHAD
SUDAN

Beirut
Sidon
Tyre
Haifa
Sea of Galilee
Tel Aviv
Jerusalem
Ashdod
Gaza
Dead Sea
Bardaw Al-Arish
ISRAEL
55
Nakhl
Maan
Al-Thamad
SINAI
Taba
Aqaba
JORDAN
Abu Zenima
Haql
66
Nuweiba
Dahab
Al-Tur
Sharm el-Sheikh
Strait of Tiran
Strait of Gabal
Suez
Gulf of Aqaba
44
Hurghada
Duba
Port Safaga
Red Sea
77
Qena
Al-Quesir
Luxor
EASTERN DESERT
Marsa Alam
2
Kom Ombo
44
Aswan
Berenice
Halaib

CAIRO AND ENVIRONS

Zagazig
Ismailia
Quweima
Shibin al-Kom
Benha
Al-Bagur
Tukh
Bilbeis
Great Bitter Lake
1
44
Shubra al-Khaima
11
Kerdassa
33
CAIRO
see next page
Giza
Maadi
Saqqara
Helwan
As-Saff

0 kilometres 35
0 miles 20

Gulf of Suez

SAUDI ARABIA

KEY

✈	International airport
✈	Domestic airport
⛴	Ferry port
	Motorway
	Major road
	Railway line
	International border
xxxx	Disputed border

0 kilometres 140
0 miles 60

Dahaban

A PORTRAIT OF EGYPT

*S*ettling along the fertile banks of the Nile, the ancient Egyptians established a magnificent and enduring civilization whose achievements have captured the imagination of the world ever since. Although looking to the future, modern Egypt cannot ignore its glorious past, but the resulting contrasts make it a uniquely fascinating place to visit.

The world's fascination with this country centres on the civilization of ancient Egypt that flourished from around 3000 BC to 30 BC, ruled by approximately 30 dynasties. The river Nile was the powerful force that enabled the ancient Egyptian kingdom to develop. The river's annual cycle of inundation watered the land and replenished the fertile topsoil. This resulted in an agricultural abundance that allowed them to concentrate on developing the knowledge and culture that formed their unique and sophisticated civilization. Over the succeeding millennia, waves of foreign conquerors passed through

Pectoral of Tutankhamun (1336–1327 BC)

the country – Persians, Greeks, Romans, crusaders, Arabs and Turks – leaving traces behind in their descendants. Today most Egyptians are classified as being of Eastern Hamitic descent. The once nomadic Bedouin and Berber tribes of the desert are of Arab descent and the third major racial grouping (less than 200,000) is the Nubian community in the south.

DAILY LIFE

Even today, the river Nile remains the lifeblood of Egypt, with around 96 per cent of the population forced by the harsh environment to live in the Nile Delta or Nile Valley.

The fertile Nile Delta, one of the most intensely cultivated areas of the world

◁ Traders negotiating at one of Egypt's lively and fascinating camel markets

Solitary felucca sailing serenely down the tranquil waters of the Nile

The ancient cycle of flooding ended with the completion of the High Dam at Aswan in 1971, forcing the Egyptian *fellaheen* (farmers) to resort to artificial fertilizers. However, it is easy to imagine that life today along the river's edge remains just as it has for thousands of years.

The typical Egyptian rural settlement is a village of between 500 and 10,000 people set amid intensely cultivated fields. Houses are often no more than one or two storeys high and each village also has a mosque or church, and perhaps a colourful pigeoncote, a few shops and an official government building. Most of the inhabitants of

Men chatting in a Cairo coffee house, a popular male Egyptian pastime

smaller villages work in agriculture and the landscape is usually dotted with farmers, wearing the traditional *galabiyya* (long smock), working the green fields or tending their precious animals – buffalo, sheep and goats.

The urban population has been expanding rapidly since the 1980s. Increasing pressure on agricultural land and the growth of city-based service industries have led to large numbers of Egyptians moving from the country to urban areas. The buildings in towns and cities are predominantly two-storey houses or higher apartment blocks with flat roofs and balconies, often built close together. The high population density in cities also leads to problems of traffic congestion. Nowhere is this more evident than in Cairo, where there is a constant cacophony of car engines and horns.

Throughout Egypt the family has remained the most significant unit of a patriarchal society. Traditionally, an individual's social identity was closely linked to his or her status in the network of relations. Today families are far more likely to disperse and the ideal of an extended family that lives together is less frequent. However, strong ties with in-laws, grandparents, nieces and nephews and the rest of the family still create a strong social fabric that binds the whole community together.

The *hegab* or headscarf, increasingly worn by Egyptian women

RELIGION AND CULTURE

Underpinning all levels of Egyptian society is a powerful religious faith. Islam is constitutionally established as the official religion and around 90 per cent of the population are Sunni Muslim *(see p91)*, the rest being Christian, mainly of the Coptic church *(see p122)*. However, say to an Egyptian of either faith "I'll see you tomorrow" and the answer will be the same – "Inshallah", which means "if God is willing". For the casual tourist, the many casinos, bars, nightclubs and beach resorts can disguise the fact that Egyptians uphold a fairly conservative mix of traditional and religious values, particularly outside the main cities. Gambling or drinking alcohol in public is frowned upon and Egyptian men rarely wear shorts, except maybe at the beach.

Women, too, are almost always well-covered. In the 1970s, as women gained greater independence and access to education, they swelled the

Umm Kolthum in concert

numbers of the non-agricultural workforce and many Muslim women chose to discard their *hegab* (headscarf). With the wide appeal of Islamist conservatives in the 1990s, women started dressing more modestly and, even in Cairo, increasing numbers are once again covering their heads and wearing loose-fitting clothes. However, the numbers of women in employment have remained at a high level.

Egyptians, governed by outsiders for thousands of years, have only been truly independent since 1952 when Gamal Abdel Nasser removed the last foreign royal and forged a truly Egyptian identity for his people. Despite a climate of political turmoil, this period of Egypt's history was a time of cultural vitality, when Umm Kolthum, the diva of the Arab world, gave concerts for the masses and Naguib

Modern Cairo with the Pyramids of Giza just visible through the evening haze

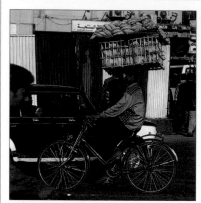

Negotiating the streets around Midan Ataba in Cairo on a daily bread round

Egypt's cinema had its heyday in the 1940s and 50s when its studios made films for the whole Arab world. Apart from a few independent films which gain a wider exposure during international film festivals, little of merit emerges these days.

POLITICS AND ECONOMICS

After the abolition of the monarchy in 1952, Nasser went on to dissolve all political parties and introduce a new constitution in 1956, declaring the Republic of Egypt. Led by Nasser, the National Union, later the Arab Socialist Union (ASU), became the sole party. In 1971 a new constitution declared Egypt to

Nasser, President of Egypt 1956–70

Mahfouz penned his most famous novels. Awarded a Nobel Prize in 1988, Mahfouz single-handedly rejuvenated the Egyptian literary scene. However, few other Egyptian writers have managed to emulate his success. Today, as a result of Egypt's population boom and greater exposure to western music, there is a ready market for home-grown modern pop music. Nevertheless Umm Kolthum's soulful music is as all-pervasive as ever, constantly played in shops and taxis throughout Egypt.

be "a democratic, socialist state". But it was not until 1977 that the formation of other political parties was allowed. Three years later the ASU was abolished. The current ruling party, the National Democratic Party (NDP) led by Hosni Mubarak, is a direct descendant of Nasser's ASU. Egypt's

Highrise blocks of modern Cairo overlooking the Nile

"dominant party system" allows a large ruling party to straddle the centre of the ideological spectrum, surrounded by small pressure parties. This has limited the possibility for radical reform, but allowed the government to proceed in a slow and cautious manner.

Over the past ten years, the national debt has been reduced, but it is still twice the size of the national budget.

Ancient tombs lying in the path of a motorway

Agriculture is the most important industry. Employing a large amount of the workforce, it feeds much of the country and provides valuable exports, especially the cotton crop. The High Dam project increased arable land by hundreds of thousands of acres and provided a much needed boost to the power supply. However, in the same period, just as much land was swallowed up by industrial and urban development, constantly building over Egypt's celebrated past. Although slowing down, population growth undermines all efforts to foster the economy. Other important sources of income are oil, gas, mining, and of course, the tourist industry. The brutal murder of 58 tourists in 1997 *(see p176)* rocked the country, causing the number of visitors to plummet. While the tourist figures are only now getting back to their former levels, the government is fully aware of the instability and problems that would be caused by further unrest.

A visitor at a Red Sea resort, enjoying Egypt's beautiful beaches and all-year round sun

EGYPT TODAY

Given the importance of tradition and religion to Egyptian daily life, it is perhaps surprising that Western technology and lifestyles have steadily gained influence over the past decade. International fast-food franchises are now found all over the country. However, the "benefits" of this most recent cultural invasion are available only to the select few, due to the seemingly unbridgeable gap between the rich and poor. To make matters worse, television programmes and films from the West have had a huge impact on Egyptian perceptions, raising expectations and creating resentment among the less well-off. This situation is not always helped by the sight of tourists enjoying luxuries beyond the reach of many Egyptians. Even so, the fascinating mix of ancient monuments, modern culture and the natural hospitality of its people ensure that Egypt's popularity continues to grow.

Discovering Ancient Egypt

Greek historian Herodotus

The magnificence and longevity of the ancient Egyptian civilization has always held a timeless fascination. As early as 1400 BC, King Tuthmosis IV undertook excavations at Giza, and the Greek historian Herodotus left a detailed account of his tour of Egypt in 450 BC. However, modern Egyptology really started with the study of the country commissioned in 1798 by Napoleon. Since then the subject has developed rapidly. In the last 20 years, computers and electron microscopes have begun to replace the pickaxe and shovel.

Napoleon's scholars *amassed the material for the authoritative work* Description de l'Egypte *during the French occupation (1798–1802).*

Jean-François Champollion
(1790–1832), was a French linguist whose brilliant work in deciphering the hieroglyphic script was the single most important event in the development of Egyptology.

Hieroglyphs *were used as early as 3200 BC and are the oldest known writing system. Used primarily in religious contexts, their last datable use was in AD 394 at the Temple of Philae when the script numbered over 6,000 characters.*

Howard Carter *had to carefully remove many layers of solidified perfumes and resins covering Tutankhamun's innermost coffin. The body was protected by several layers of coffins, the last one of solid gold.*

HOWARD CARTER (1873–1939)

Carter trained as an artist and joined the Archaeological Survey of Egypt in 1891. In 1922, he achieved fame when he found King Tutankhamun's tomb, virtually untouched, in the Valley of the Kings.

The treasures *Carter found on opening the tomb were abundant. Most items are on display in the Egyptian Museum (see* pp74–7).

RELOCATION OF ANCIENT TEMPLES

The construction of the Aswan High Dam and Lake Nasser (1960–71) threatened many temples and rock tombs along the Nile with total submersion. Concern over the loss of such archaeological treasures led UNESCO to promote an international relief campaign. Three stages of operations were necessary: a survey of the area, the excavation of sites, and the final movement of as many endangered monuments as was possible. Twenty monuments from Egyptian Nubia and four from the Sudan were carefully dismantled, then reassembled at safe distances from their original sites. The two largest operations involved the Great Temple at Abu Simbel *(see pp214–15)* and the temple complex at Philae *(see p212)*.

Trajan's Kiosk (also known as the Pharaoh's Bedstead) before relocation at Philae

UNDERWATER DISCOVERIES

In 1996, a team led by the French marine archaeologist, Franck Goddio, began to explore the submerged Royal City of Alexandria, where Egypt's last pharaoh, Cleopatra, held court. The finds so far include statues, sphinxes and ceramics.

Tutankhamun's death mask, *shown here at the British Museum with Queen Elizabeth II in 1972, was the top exhibit in a display of Carter's finds that toured the major museums of the world rekindling interest in Egypt's rich history.*

ARCHAEOLOGY AND TECHNOLOGY

Egyptology is a relatively young science, but huge advances have been made since Champollion's work opened the door on ancient Egyptian history. Today, Egyptologists are greatly assisted by new technologies, both in the laboratory and in the field – and even under water.

Restoration and preservation work *on ancient artifacts involves skilled and painstaking processes, which have to be conducted in a strictly controlled environment.*

Modern technologies, *such as CAT scanning, radio-carbon dating, DNA and trace element analysis, endoscopy and electron microscopy have all contributed to more accurate dating and a deeper understanding of archaeological finds.*

Hieroglyphics

Hieroglyph for motion or "to go"

Dating from around 3200 BC, ancient Egyptian hieroglyphics are the world's oldest known writing system. The word "hieroglyph" means "sacred carved letter" and refers to the beautiful pictorial script used by ancient Egyptians to express their religious beliefs and engraved onto nearly every available surface of their monuments. Although pictorial, hieroglyphs convey extremely complex semantic information; they could be read from left to right, right to left or top to bottom. However, when writing on papyrus, the hieroglyphic system was too slow and impractical for everyday use and over the centuries more easily written scripts were developed with the last datable hieroglyphic inscription being at Hadrian's Gate at Philae in AD 394.

Thoth, *the ibis-headed god of wisdom and patron deity of scribes, is here portrayed holding his sceptre of power or was.*

Egyptian scribes, *in a virtually illiterate population, were part of society's elite. It took many years to learn the art of hieroglyphics but the rewards could be high – King Horemheb started off his career as a scribe.*

THE ROSETTA STONE – CRACKING THE CODE

Until 1822, the ability to read hieroglyphic inscriptions had been lost. It was a black granite stele, discovered in 1799 in Rosetta by Napoleon's army, that held the key. It contained a text in three scripts: hieroglyphic, demotic and Greek. The two main contestants in the race to decipher the symbols were Thomas Young, a British physician and Jean-François Champollion, a gifted French linguist. By 1819, Young was ahead of the Frenchman, translating the demotic text as well as identifying the cartouches of Ptolemy and Cleopatra. However, Champollion was also able to decipher these names and others, compiling an extensive list of symbols. Using this list, he realised that there were separate types of hieroglyphs with different functions and therefore discovered the basis of the writing system used in hieroglyphic texts.

The Rosetta Stone, inscribed by the priests of Ptolemy V (196 BC)

Ptolemaic scribes *raised the number of hieroglyphic symbols from 700 to 6000, in an attempt to keep their knowledge exclusive.*

THE IMPORTANCE OF NAMES

Ancient Egyptians believed that names were as vital to one's existence as the soul. Names held great power and speaking the name of the dead could bring them to life. Therefore, funerary texts often included spells to cause the name of the deceased to be remembered in the afterlife and so ensure eternal life.

The oval cartouche forms a protective wall or enclosure.

Hieroglyphs give the name, "Ramses, beloved of Amun".

Egyptian kings *protected their names within cartouches and increased their chances of eternal life by the sheer number of epithets they possessed.*

This detail of the King List *found at Abydos gives some of Ramses II's names, including "the king of Upper and Lower Egypt, Usermaatre Setepenre, son of Ra, and Ramses, beloved of Amun".*

HIEROGLYPHIC TEXT

Hieroglyphs were a decorative art and ritual pictures, combined with texts, played a vital part in religious ceremonies. Funerary texts were designed to protect the dead and help guide their passage to the underworld. This detail from the funeral texts of the scribe Nebked (c.1400 BC), shows the deceased (his writing kit tucked into his belt) worshipping the god Osiris with his wife and mother.

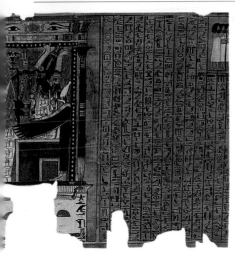

Hieratic script *was a faster way of writing. Dating from c.2600 BC, it was used for everyday communications until c.600 BC when it was superseded by the even faster demotic or "popular" script.*

TRANSLATING HIEROGLYPHS

Put simply, there are three main types of hieroglyphs. "Phonograms" convey the sounds of the syllables, for example the ancient Egyptian for "son" was spoken *sa* and this is denoted by the duck. "Ideograms" portray the actual object or action, such as a sun on the horizon to indicate "appearance". The final type is "determinatives" which indicate, confirm or modify the meaning of the word to which they are attached, for example, three bars denote a plural. To further complicate matters, many symbols can be either ideograms, phonograms or determinatives. The basket symbol, *neb*, can be a phonogram for "Lord" or simply represent a "basket". Symbols of humans and animals always face the start of the text, indicating the direction the text runs.

Ra
ra

Son
sa

Lord
neb

Appearance
kha

Determinative plural symbol

Hieroglyphs for "Son of Ra, Lord of Appearances"

Temples and Religious Life

For the ancient Egyptians, the universe was composed of dualities – fertile and barren, life and death, order and chaos – held in a state of equilibrium by the goddess Maat. To maintain this balance, they built enormous temples dedicated to the gods. At the centre of every settlement and devoted to a particular god or set of gods, the "cult" temple served as a storehouse of divine power, maintained by the priesthood for the benefit of all. The temple was also an economic and political centre employing large numbers of the local community and serving as a town hall, medical centre and college.

Statue of a priest praying

Goddess Maat, *the personification of cosmic order and harmony, set the rules by which all kings must govern. Her power regulated the stars, the seasons and humans' relationship with the gods.*

Funerary priest in a leopard skin, performing sacred rituals

A DAY IN THE LIFE OF A TEMPLE PRIEST

Egyptian priests were literally "servants of the god or goddess", responsible for performing the daily rituals that regulated the workings of the universe. The king, although the intermediary between the mortal and the divine, delegated his duties to the high priest of the temple. This priest was then responsible for the most important of the temple rituals – the honouring of the god within its shrine. Twice daily the "cult" statue was bathed and clothed before receiving offerings of food and drink. Incense was burnt and holy water from the sacred lake scattered to show the purity of the offerings. After the essence of the food had been consumed by the gods, the priests were able to eat the actual offerings.

CULT TEMPLE RECONSTRUCTION

As well as housing the deity, the temple complex symbolized the universe. Its architecture represented the fundamental elements of water, sunlight, stars, forests and, inside the depths of the temple, darkness.

Covered colonnade

Flagstaffs

Entrance to enclosure

Processional route

Pylons, or monumental gateways, had vast towers decorated with giant reliefs of the king warding off his enemies.

The central court, *as depicted in this 19th-century reconstruction of the court at Philae (see p212), was a colonnaded courtyard brightly decorated with reliefs showing the king making offerings to the temple's deities.*

Tomb decorations, *such as this detail from Luxor* (see pp184–5) *illustrating the offering of ducks, depicted typical ritual ceremonies. Reliefs and paintings of rituals ensured that these important ceremonies were continually enacted.*

The shrine, *like this one from Edfu temple* (see pp204–5), *was the most essential part of the Egyptian temple. Located in the innermost sanctuary, it housed the statue of the temple god. Daily offerings were made to persuade the divinity's beneficial essence to reside in the statue.*

Small hypostyle hall

Outer temple wall

Inner chambers were dimly lit and marked the approach to the sacred inner sanctuary. They were used for storing valuables or worshipping subsidiary deities.

Priests' houses

The hypostyle hall's ceiling was usually painted with constellations of stars, while its great columns were decorated with plant reliefs. It was meant to resemble a primeval forest with the stars and sky overhead.

Sacred lakes, *like this one at Karnak* (see pp188–9), *were an important feature of "cult" temples and were used by religious personnel, who bathed in the lake to ensure ritual purity.*

The Ramesseum in Thebes *(see pp200–1),* **the mortuary temple of Ramses II**

MORTUARY TEMPLES

In addition to the local "cult" temples, each king built a mortuary temple to serve as a place where, following his death, offerings could be made for his soul. The temples were originally attached to the royal tombs of the Old and Middle Kingdoms but by around 1500 BC they had developed into vast, elaborate complexes built at separate locations to the tombs which were now hidden away in secluded desert valleys. The great temples on the West Bank at Luxor *(see pp184–5)* are fine examples of New Kingdom mortuary temples. The magnificent Temple of Queen Hatshepsut *(see pp196–7)* at Deir al-Bahri has one of the most original mortuary temple designs.

Mythology

Ancient Egyptian religion was a highly complex belief system involving a great number of deities originally based on aspects of the natural world. As these evolved into more cohesive "personalities", each locality developed myths relating to their own particular deities. These myths were many and varied, with even the story of creation having at least three different versions, based on the belief that life first emerged from the waters of chaos as a mound of earth. A number of places claimed to be the original site of this primeval mound and that the first life was created by the gods associated with that particular place, be they the 9 gods of Heliopolis, the 8 gods of Hermopolis or the one god of Memphis.

Household god Bes

Amun, *whose name means "the hidden one", became a national deity when Thebes ruled Egypt, in an attempt to unify the country.*

CREATION MYTH

This detail from a popular creation myth shows the Egyptian gods in relation to the world. In the beginning there was nothing but the sea of chaos, Nun. Then Atum thought himself into being, sneezing to create Shu and then Tefnut. He caused the seas to recede and called forth all the plants and animals. Shu and Tefnut gave birth to two children: Geb, the earth, and Nut, the sky, who in turn gave birth to the stars.

Nephthys pours the waters of fruitfulness over the earth, where men hoe the land.

Nut, mother of all, swallows the sun each night, giving birth to it again in the morning.

Geb, god of the earth; his bent leg represents the mountains.

OSIRIS, ISIS AND HORUS

One of the most universal Egyptian myths is that of Osiris and Isis. The story has it that Osiris was a king who taught the Egyptians how to live, worship and grow corn. He was murdered by his jealous brother Seth, who cut up the body, scattering it over Egypt. Osiris's beloved wife Isis and her sister Nephthys collected up all the pieces and, with the help of the gods Anubis and Thoth, they put him back together as the first mummy. Isis used her magic to revive him and at the same time conceived a son, Horus, who would avenge his father. Osiris, brought back to life, went down to the underworld to be the lord and judge of the dead.

Statuette of Osiris (centre) with his son Horus and loyal wife Isis

Osiris in a typical pose

THE SUN

Fundamental to the Egyptians, the sun was regarded as the source of all life, conquering the forces of darkness each night before emerging victorious at dawn to repeat the eternal cycle. Worshipped under a variety of names and guises, the sun was most often represented by the falcon-headed god Ra, as well as Atum, Khepri, Harakhty and the Aten sun-disk. The sun god's representative on earth, the king was hailed as the "Son of Ra". When Amun was elevated to supreme deity, for political reasons, his status was validated by linking him with Ra's supremacy to create Amun-Ra, the "King of the Gods".

Khepri was represented as a dung beetle or scarab. Identified with the sun god Ra, he was said to roll the sun across the sky like a ball of dung.

Ra-Harakhty was the combination of two gods: the sky god Horus, whose right eye was the sun and left eye the moon, and the all-powerful sun god Ra.

Ra, creator of the universe, wears the sun on his brow.

Maat keeps the world in balance.

Shu, jealous of Geb and Nut, stands keeping them apart.

MAJOR GODS

- **Amun**: powerful local Theban deity.
- **Anubis**: jackal-headed god of embalmers.
- **Atum**: creator aspect of the sun god.
- **Bes**: household god of women in childbirth.
- **Geb**: god of the earth.
- **Hathor**: goddess of love, pleasure and beauty.
- **Horus**: falcon-headed god closely identified with each pharaoh.
- **Isis**: goddess of magic.
- **Khepri**: a sun god as a scarab beetle.
- **Maat**: goddess of truth and universal balance.
- **Nekhbet**: vulture goddess of Upper Egypt.
- **Nephthys**: with Isis, protector of the dead.
- **Nut**: goddess of the sky.
- **Osiris**: god of the underworld.
- **Ptah**: creator god and patron of craftsmen.
- **Ra**: pre-eminent form of the sun god.
- **Sekhmet**: lioness goddess of destruction.
- **Seth**: god of chaos.
- **Shu**: god of the air.
- **Tefnut**: goddess of moisture.
- **Thoth**: the ibis-headed god of wisdom.
- **Wadjet**: cobra goddess of Lower Egypt.

THE BENU BIRD

The Benu bird flew across the waters of Nun at the dawn of creation and saw land first break the water's surface. The Benu bird was identified with the sun and the primeval mound was symbolized by the Benben stone at Heliopolis, thought to be where the sun's first rays touched land. It was the prototype for obelisks whose tips were gold plated – to catch the first rays of the sun.

Tomb painting showing the worship of the Benu bird

Obelisk, symbol of first land

Burial Traditions

Wedjat "eye of Horus" amulet

The ancient Egyptians believed in an eternal afterlife and they developed a complex funerary cult aimed at maintaining their life after death. This involved preserving the body of the dead person through a process of mummification so that their soul would live on their embalmed corpse. The deceased were then supplied with everything they might need in the afterlife before being launched into eternity via a set of elaborate funeral rituals.

Anubis, *the jackal-headed god of embalming, is shown putting the finishing touches to a mummy in this 19th-Dynasty tomb relief.*

MUMMIFICATION TECHNIQUES

The earliest mummies from prehistoric times were probably accidental. True mummification began in the Fourth Dynasty with the development of artificial embalming techniques. Special priests first removed the internal organs of the deceased, leaving only the heart, to be weighed in the afterlife. Then the corpse was dried out with natron and finally wrapped in linen.

Natural mummification *occurred when dead bodies were placed in simple sand graves. The sand absorbed the body's moisture, drying out the corpse and preserving soft tissue.*

Natron, *a naturally occurring mixture of sodium salts, was packed in and around the body to dry it out artificially. This took 40 days.*

Canopic jars *stored the embalmed internal organs of the deceased. The intestines, stomach, liver and lungs had separate jars, which were buried alongside the coffin in the tomb.*

Ramses III, *one of the best preserved of the royal mummies, was discovered in 1881 at Deir al-Bahri. The mummy is now on display in the Egyptian Museum (see* pp74–7).

The mummified body *was stuffed with linen and sawdust before being wrapped in tight linen bandages. Finally the wrapped mummy was placed in its painted wooden coffin.*

ANIMAL MUMMIES

The ancient Egyptians believed that all living things contained the divine essence and were, therefore, worthy of respect. In sharing the attributes of the gods they symbolized, animals were venerated as the gods' representatives on earth and mummified after their death. By the Late Period (664–332 BC), animals of all kinds were being mummified and buried in catacombs, from literally millions of ibises and cats to bulls and lions, shrews, snakes and crocodiles.

Ibis mummy

Cat mummy

MUMMY MASKS

A mask was fitted over the head of the mummy to help the dead person's spirit to recognize its body. From the glittering gold masks of pharaohs such as Tutankhamun to the more common painted masks made of *cartonnage* (a sort of papier-mâché), mummy masks were idealized portraits of the deceased.

A mummy mask *showed the face framed by a stylized wig and wide collar.*

Roman portrait masks, *painted on flat wooden panels, were laid over the face of the mummy. The portraits were often painted during the lifetime of the deceased and were more realistic than earlier masks (see p165).*

ACCESSORIES

In addition to significant worldly possessions, the mummy was usually buried with funerary items, including amulets, a set of shabti figures, and a model boat to transport the mummy to Abydos.

Amulets *were worn by Egyptians in life and in death to protect the body from evil and to bring good luck.*

Shabti figures *were models of workers placed in the tomb to carry out manual work on behalf of the deceased in the afterlife.*

A model funerary boat *symbolized the mummy's journey to Abydos, home of Osiris, god of the dead (see p26).*

FUNERARY RITES AND CEREMONIES

At the funeral, relatives left offerings of food and priests performed special funerary rites. These ceremonies and rituals were meant to protect the deceased, ensure a successful journey into the afterlife and sustain them on their way. As further protection, ritual images and texts were placed with the body or used to decorate the tomb.

The Book of the Dead *was a guide through the underworld. The deceased is portrayed here crossing the Lake of Offerings with his gifts.*

The Opening of the Mouth *ritual was performed to the body prior to burial in the belief that this would reactivate the senses, so the deceased would function in the afterlife.*

The Weighing of the Heart *was the final stage in the journey to the afterlife. A jury of gods presided over the ceremony to decide whether the deceased deserved eternal life. The jackal god Anubis weighed the heart against the feather of truth. If the heart was too heavy, it was given to the monster Ammut, who devoured it; only if it balances will the dead live forever.*

Daily Life in Ancient Egypt

Tomb model of man ploughing with oxen

In the hierarchical society of ancient Egypt, the importance of the family was fundamental. Early marriages were encouraged, with the hope of producing children to continue the family line and, importantly, to organize a proper burial. Marriage seems to have required no religious or civil ceremony, but simply involved one partner moving into the home of the other. Youngsters enjoyed a brief period of childhood before taking on adult responsibilities. Education was mainly vocational, with boys often being apprenticed to their fathers.

This family group *comprises husband and wife* (centre), *their son* (right) *and older male* (left).

EGYPTIAN HOUSING

Egyptian houses were built of sun-baked mudbricks and so have not survived well. From the evidence that has been preserved it seems that houses were typically square with a central living room, bedrooms and storerooms and sometimes stairs leading to the roof or to an upper floor. Some even had primitive bathroom suites.

Egyptian houses *had basic air-conditioning, provided by small windows and roof vents as shown in this painting from the tomb of 18th-Dynasty scribe Nakht.*

The roof vent is designed to catch the cool north breezes.

Soul houses, *such as this terracotta example, were included in tombs to house the soul of the deceased. The models demonstrate many features of ancient Egyptian housing and even mirror houses in rural Egypt today.*

Small, high windows let in light and breezes, but not the sun.

Cooking would take place outside or in outbuildings.

More complex housing, *such as this model townhouse, reflected the higher status of the owner.*

WORKERS' VILLAGE AT DEIR AL-MEDINA

In a secluded valley on the west bank of the Nile opposite Luxor are the excavated foundations of a village that was inhabited by the craftsmen and labourers who constructed the tombs in the Valley of the Kings. In this early example of urban planning, the houses, arranged in rows, all opened off one central street and were enclosed within an outer wall. A typical house in Deir al-Medina had between 4 and 6 rooms plus a cellar or two for storage. Around the village are the chapels and tombs of the government-employed workers.

The village at Deir al-Medina, founded in the 16th century BC for those working in the Valley of the Kings

Women *often worked and looked after the children. In this 26th-Dynasty tomb relief, a mother with her child sorts fruit in an orchard.*

WOMEN IN SOCIETY

Although their status generally derived from that of their fathers or husbands, women in ancient Egypt enjoyed a relatively high profile. Equal to men before the law, they could own or rent property, engage in business, receive an equal share of inheritances and, in some cases, even rule as pharaoh. Divorce and remarriage were available to them, and if a man divorced his wife, she was entitled to maintenance. Women were expected to manage the household and family, and the poorer ones had to work alongside the men too.

Two women *are depicted in this 30th-Dynasty relief using a tourniquet press to extract the essential oils of lilies for perfume.*

Three noble-women *are seen in this 18th-Dynasty detail, sharing their pleasure in the perfume of lotus blossoms and mandrake fruit.*

WORKING LIFE IN ANCIENT EGYPT

Most of the farmland was owned by the king, the temples and rich individuals. This was farmed by the bulk of the population, who worked either directly for the owner or as a tenant farmer paying large amounts of rent and tax. Slightly better off were the skilled craftsmen, many of whom worked for the pharaoh, the temples or rich nobles. Their crafts included carpentry, jewellery and stone-working. Near the top of the hierarchy was an elite of professionals who ran the country – the scribes *(see p22)*, the priests *(see p24)* and top-ranking officials.

Nile-style farming *is depicted in this painting from the 19th-Dynasty tomb of Sennedjem and Iyneferti. Although portraying the idealized afterlife, it shows the methods used to reap grain, plough and harvest flax.*

The Nile *may have provided fish and fertile soil, but it had its share of risks as well as its rewards. As depicted in this Old Kingdom tomb relief scene, herdsmen had to be mindful of the danger posed to livestock from crocodiles.*

Dairy produce, *as depicted in this tomb relief, played an important part in the diet. Other livestock reared by ancient Egyptian farmers included sheep, goats and even pigs.*

Skilled craftsmen *were usually employed in large workshops or in special communities such as Deir al-Medina.*

Peasant farmers *also supplied most of the labour for large building projects. This was a requirement for everybody except officials. In this tomb painting a team of unskilled workers are making mudbricks.*

Islamic Egypt

Islam was founded by Mohammed, a merchant who was born in around AD 570 in Mecca. At the age of 40 he began to receive revelations of the word of Allah (God) and these were transcribed as the Quran. Mohammed's preachings were not well received in Mecca and, in AD 622, he and his followers fled to Medina. This flight *(hejira)* constitutes year zero in the Islamic calendar. Before he died in AD 632, Mohammed returned to conquer Mecca. The armies of Islam swept through the Byzantine provinces of the eastern Mediterranean, arriving in Egypt in AD 640.

The crescent moon, *a familiar symbol of Islam, has resonances with the lunar calendar, which orders Muslim religious life.*

The Quran, *the holy book of Islam, is regarded as the direct word of Allah. Muslims believe that it can only be fully understood if read in Arabic. It is divided into 114 chapters, or suras, which cover many topics, including matters relating to the family, marriage, and legal and ethical concerns.*

This house *is decorated with pilgrimage scenes, which include a depiction of the great mosque in Mecca. The picture indicates that the house-owner has made the pilgrimage to Mecca.*

Muslims praying outside the Mosque of Sayyidna al-Hussein

THE FIVE PILLARS OF FAITH

Islam rests on the "five pillars of faith". The first of these, the *Shahada*, is a simple declaration that "there is no God but Allah and Mohammed is his Prophet". The second is the set of daily prayers that are supposed to be performed five times a day, facing in the direction of Mecca. The third is fasting during the daylight hours of the holy month of Ramadan. The fourth is the giving of alms. The fifth is *Haj*: at least once in their lifetime all Muslims must, if they are able, make the pilgrimage to Mecca, the birthplace of Mohammed.

VISITING A MOSQUE

Apart from at prayer times and during the Friday congregation, most mosques in Egypt are open to visitors. As well as paying a small entrance fee, it is customary to give a tip to the guardian and to the person who looks after your shoes or provides a scarf to cover your head during your visit. Mosques are open 24 hours, but only open to visitors from 9am–7pm. They close earlier in winter and during the month of Ramadan *(see also p330)*.

Arcaded courtyard of the Mosque of al-Azhar, Cairo

Muslim festivals *are relatively infrequent, with just four major dates in the calendar* (see p41). *The most important of these are* Eid al-Adha, *marking the time of the pilgrimage* (Haj), *and* Eid al-Fitr, *which is held at the end of Ramadan. Islamic celebrations tend to be communal affairs and usually take the form of great feasts, often held outdoors.*

THE CALL TO PRAYER

A *muezzin* traditionally makes the call to prayer five times each day from the balcony of a mosque's minaret. Today, microphones and loudspeakers are used to allow the *muezzin* to be heard from afar.

Mosques *have been built in a variety of styles but they all share some common features. Chief of these is the* mihrab, *the niche that indicates the direction of Mecca. Most mosques also have a* minbar, *from which the* imam *delivers his Friday sermon.*

Balcony, from where the call to prayer is traditionally made

Minaret

Crescent-shaped finial

Prayer hall entrance, where footwear must be removed

Islamic Architecture

Roof detail on a *madrassa*

The term Islamic architecture refers not only to mosques but also to a wide range of interesting buildings. The styles used were developed primarily under the early Islamic dynasties (the Tulunids, Fatimids and Ayyubids) and reached the height of creativity during the Mamluk era *(see p57)*. Craftsmen from all over the Near East were brought to Egypt to build palaces and mausoleums for rich and vainglorious sultans. They also created public institutions such as hospitals, schools and street fountains, many of which are still in use. The last great period of Islamic architecture in Egypt was under the Ottoman Turks *(see p58)*. Although reserving their best work for the imperial city of Istanbul, the Ottoman legacy includes some impressive structures.

Typical mosque-style building with domes and minarets *(see p93)*

DOMESTIC ARCHITECTURE

Private houses (called *beit* in Arabic) owed their design to both climatic and social conditions. Certain features, such as small windows covered with wooden screens, large airy rooms, shady arcades and fountains, kept the rooms cool. Typically these houses would be partitioned into separate male and female zones, known as the *salamlek* and *haramlek* respectively.

Mashrabiyya screens allowed the women of the house to look out without being seen.

Rooftop wind catchers channelled cool breezes into the rooms below.

The grandest private houses *could rise as high as three or four storeys. They used recurring features such as* ablaq *(striped layers of stone), arcades and fountains.*

Indoor fountains were built into the homes of the wealthy to keep the room temperature down.

The House of Amasyali *is one of numerous examples of the exquisite Ottoman merchants' houses that have survived in the town of Rosetta (see p237).*

Wooden ceilings *were often carved with beautifully intricate geometric patterns and then painted in rich colours.*

A qaa or reception **room** *typically formed the sumptuous centrepiece of the wealthy merchants' houses.*

SABIL-KUTTAB (FOUNTAIN AND SCHOOL)

Sabils (public fountains) are a typical element of Islamic architecture – some no more than a tap and a trough, some grand like the Sabil-Kuttab of Abdel Katkhuda. The *kuttab* was an open loggia or gallery where teachings of the Quran took place.

Tiles painted *with scenes from Mecca were used to decorate some* sabil-kuttabs *in keeping with the religious nature of these buildings.*

Sabil-Kuttab of Abdel Katkhuda *(see p98)*

MADRASSA (LAW SCHOOL)

A *madrassa* is a Quranic school, where law and theology are taught. Usually a mosque and *madrassa* are one and the same building. Sunni Islam, the variant of Islam followed in Egypt, has four schools of law (Hanafi, Malaki, Shafii and Hanbali), and so typically a *madrassa* will have four separate teaching areas, one for each. These often take the form of *iwans*, which are large arched spaces arranged around a central courtyard.

Fountains existed for the ablutions that had to be carried out before prayer.

Madrassa of Sultan Barquq *(see p97)*

WIKALA (HOTEL)

Also known as a caravanserai, the *wikala* is the precursor of the modern inn. It provided hospitality to the travelling merchant caravans that brought such great wealth to medieval Egypt. Animals were kept on the ground floor, along with goods placed in storage, while upstairs were the lodgings. At night, the whole building was sealed behind a sole gate for security purposes.

The rooms for the travellers overlooked the tiled central courtyard of the *wikala*.

Fountains provided water for the animals.

The Wikala of al-Ghouri *(see p92)*

MAUSOLEUM (TOMB)

Some of the most splendid pieces of architecture in Egypt are mausoleums. Just like the pharaohs before them with their pyramids and immense mortuary temples, medieval sultans sought to glorify themselves in death. This they did by spending lavish amounts on enormous funerary complexes that often incorporated mosques and *madrassas* beside a domed tomb chamber. Inside, the bodies of the dead were laid above ground in a cenotaph marked by a pillar-like headstone. During Ottoman times, soldiers' headstones were frequently decorated with a carved turban.

Elaborate wrought-iron decoration was used to adorn the tomb.

The crescent moon symbol of Islam was an essential component of any Islamic mortuary structure.

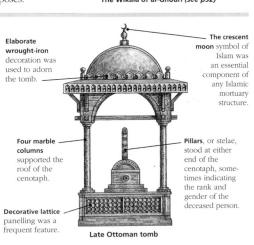

Four marble columns supported the roof of the cenotaph.

Pillars, or stelae, stood at either end of the cenotaph, sometimes indicating the rank and gender of the deceased person.

Decorative lattice panelling was a frequent feature.

Late Ottoman tomb

The Landscape and Wildlife of Egypt

Although Egypt comprises over 90 per cent desert, it is not a totally barren landscape. A number of plants and animals have developed strategies to cope with extreme temperatures and long periods of drought. Humans, however, are less adaptable and while a tiny percentage lives in desert oases *(see p261)*, 96 per cent live close to water in the green Delta or along the Nile Valley. However, despite plentiful water and rich soil, this land struggles to provide enough food for the rapidly growing population. Around Egypt's coastline the seas teem with marine life and the colourful coral reefs of the Red Sea *(see p227)* are probably the one of the richest natural environments on the planet.

Desert travel, reliant on camels and date palms

DESERTS

The popular image of deserts is of endless seas of sand. However, the rocky interior of Sinai also counts as a desert – strictly defined as an area with less than 25 cm (10 inches) of rainfall a year. Strong winds are also characteristic of the desert, eroding the rocks into bizarre shapes and creating sand which accumulates as slowly moving sand dunes.

Agriculture *in the desert oases is vital to the economy of the country, providing large quantities of sugar cane, dates, figs and other fruit and vegetables.*

Scorpions *are perfectly adapted to the desert environment: they rarely need to drink, as they obtain their fluids from a diet of insects.*

Fennec foxes *sleep during the day, only leaving their burrows in the cool dusk. Exceptional hearing enables them to catch insects and small mammals in the dark.*

Date palms *thrive in the rocky desert environment. Growing "with their head in fire and feet in water", they are a sure sign of a hidden water source.*

Sinai's red massif *rises in places to over 2,000 m (6,700 ft). Criss-crossed with wadis (dry river beds), the area is brought to life by sporadic flooding.*

NILE VALLEY AND DELTA

The Nile creates a habitable tract of land never more than 20 km (13 miles) wide from Lake Nasser to the Delta. In the past, floods replenished the soil with rich silt deposits which enabled the land to support a wide range of flora and fauna. The Aswan Dam *(see p211)* ended the floods, making farmers reliant on chemical fertilizers. Today, the Delta is one of the most intensely farmed areas.

Farmland *is irrigated by a complicated system of canals and dykes. The resulting wet croplands provide the ideal environment for cattle egrets, which hunt for frogs, insects and small rodents.*

Acacia *is easily identified along the banks of the Nile by its eye-catching balls of yellow flowers.*

Papyrus, *widely used in ancient times, was all but extinct by the 19th century. It is only grown in a few select areas.*

The Purple Gallinule *is a colourful duck-sized water bird found the length of the Nile. Its long, slender toes enable it to walk on lily pads.*

The Spitting Cobra, *a symbol of Lower Egypt in Pharaonic times, hunts its prey at night in crop fields. It is not usually a danger to humans, but it might attack if threatened, spitting venom accurately at its attacker's eyes.*

COASTAL REGIONS

Egypt's northern coastline is on the Mediterranean Sea where fishing is a key industry. While Egypt's Red Sea and Sinai coastlines also maintain fishing communities, they are far more important as a resource for the tourist industry. These coastlines support several large strips of coral reef *(see p227)* which attract divers from all over the world. A fragile environment, the reefs are under serious threat from overdevelopment of the coastline.

Coral reefs *provide a colourful environment for an equally spectacular array of marine life.*

MANGROVE SWAMPS

The mangrove swamps of the Sinai Peninsula perform an important function protecting the shoreline against erosion and filtering pollutants from the water. The mudflats they create provide a vital environment for crabs and wading birds. Mangroves are able to live in salt water by excreting excess salt via their leaves.

Mangrove swamps fringing the Sinai coastline

EGYPT THROUGH THE YEAR

The Egyptian calendar is crowded with Muslim, Christian, national and local festivals. The dates of these events can be difficult to predict as they are often calculated in different ways. The Islamic calendar is based on twelve 29- or 30-day lunar months, while Egypt's Christian Coptic church uses the Julian calendar and the solar Coptic calendar. Extra confusion is caused by the frequently changing dates of non-religious events or festivals.

Making sweets in the market

Visitors should confirm the date of the event locally. Whatever the calendar, these are mostly joyous events and a great way to experience Egyptian culture at close hand as both Muslims and Copts often enjoy celebrating *moulids* or festivals together. A wide range of esoteric sports events is staged throughout the year which range from the interesting to the bizarre, from camel racing to long-distance swimming in the Nile at Cairo.

SPRING

Springtime is a pleasant time to visit Egypt. The main visitor attractions such as the Pyramids at Giza, Luxor and Aswan are not too crowded and the temperature has yet to reach the scorching highs of summer. One weather phenomenon that can cause problems is the *khamseen*, a hot, dry wind that blows up from the Sahara Desert in the south. This can turn the air orange with dust and drive everyone indoors.

The main spring festivals are the beginning of the Egyptian New Year in March and the Christian festival of Easter. On the Monday after Easter Sunday, all Egyptians celebrate Sham an-Nessim or the "sniffing the breeze". They go on picnics or hold events outdoors to take in the fresh spring air.

MARCH

Flower Show at the Orman Gardens, Sharia Giza, Giza.
Feast of the Annunciation *(Mar 23)*. This Coptic feast celebrates the announcement to the Holy Virgin that she was to give birth to Jesus.
Easter is the most important date on the Coptic calendar. The Coptic Pope celebrates Easter Mass at St Mark's Cathedral in Cairo.
Sham an-Nessim, celebrated by both Copts and Muslims, is a day when families enjoy outdoor pursuits and reputed to date from Pharaonic times.

APRIL

International Camel Race Competition. The bumpiest race in the world takes place around Sharm el-Sheikh.
Sinai Liberation Day *(Apr 25)*, celebrates Israel's withdrawal from Sinai in 1982.

Coptic Christians celebrating Palm Sunday, a week before Easter

MAY

Labour Day *(May 1)* is a public holiday when most businesses will be closed.
Moulid of St Damyanah *(May 15–20)*, a Coptic festival celebrating one of their important saints.
National Fishing Competition, Sharm el-Sheikh. These events take place regularly at Red Sea resorts.
Nile Swimming Race, Zamalek, Cairo. Amazingly an international field swims the murky waters of the Nile in the popular Egyptian sport of long-distance swimming.
Ragabiyya is a local festival in Tanta, Egypt's fifth-largest city. The festival lasts for three days in celebration of the Sufi saint, Sayyid Ahmad al-Badawi, and is held when the Nile rises in late spring.

Families celebrating the arrival of spring on Sham an-Nessim

MUSLIM FESTIVALS

Celebrated with great feasts, family gatherings, music and street processions, Muslim festivals are joyous occasions. The largest of the festivals are Eid al-Fitr, which takes place at the end of Ramadan, the month of ritual fasting, and Eid al-Adha, which marks the time of the pilgrimage to Mecca. Other Muslim festivals include the Moulid an-Nabi which celebrates the birth of the Prophet Mohammed, Ras as-Sana, the Islamic New Year, and various saints' name days known as *moulids.*

Cookies for Eid al-Fitr *are traditionally baked in preparation for the three-day feast that marks the end of Ramadan. Food plays an important part of Muslim festivals and preparing it is often a social affair.*

Sufi dancers *are a feature at moulids. Wearing brightly coloured outfits, they chant and sway for hours in an effort to achieve unity with God. The dancers may also be led on a procession through the town.*

ISLAMIC CALENDAR

The Islamic calendar has twelve months, each with 29 or 30 days. Purely lunar based, the Islamic year is around 11 days shorter than that of the Western calendar. Because Islam relies on actual sightings of the crescent moon at a given place, it is difficult to give dates in advance. Local Islamic centres will be able to provide the dates for the current year.

Eid al-Adha This four-day festival marks the time of the *Haj,* or pilgrimage to Mecca.

Ras as-Sana The Islamic equivalent of New Year's Day and quite a low-key affair.

Moulid an-Nabi Birth of the Prophet and one of the major holidays of the year. The streets burst into colour and noise with the celebrations.

Ramadan The ninth month of the Muslim calendar when most Muslims observe a degree of fasting and abstinence. The *iftar,* or breaking of the fast, occurs every evening when the sun sets.

Eid al-Fitr The end of Ramadan and the signal for a joyous, three-day feast.

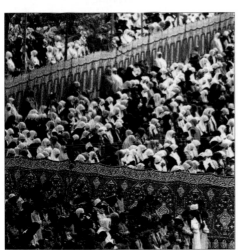

Eid al-Fitr *is a happy celebration marking the end of Ramadan. During the festivities, which usually last for three days, new clothes are worn and gifts are exchanged.*

Religious holidays *provide the perfect opportunity for family gatherings. Muslim celebrations often centre around the enjoyment and sharing of food and picnics are therefore a popular choice.*

Donkey trekking in the heat of summer, Valley of the Kings, Luxor

SUMMER

From June to August the temperature in Egypt climbs to unbearable levels in Upper Egypt, although the sites are often less crowded and hotel accommodation is plentiful. Many Egyptians choose to holiday on the North Coast where the temperature is slightly cooler. The Red Sea coastal resorts, although also very hot, have beautiful, clear water in which visitors can keep themselves cool. In the summer heat and smog, Cairo can get very uncomfortable and there are fewer interesting festivals.

JUNE

Al-Ahram International Squash Competition, Giza, attracts large audiences and an international field. It takes place in floodlit, glass courts against the spectacular backdrop of the Pyramids.
Evacuation Day *(Jun 18)* celebrates the departure of the British Forces from the Canal Zone in 1956 and the start of the Egyptian Republic.

JULY

Revolution Day *(Jul 23)* commemorates the 1952 coup which toppled the puppet monarchy *(see p62)*.

Shopping and Tourism Festival, Cairo *(Jul–Aug)*.

AUGUST

International Folk Festival, Ismailia, attracts folk groups from all over the world.
International Song Festival, Cairo, often features an interesting range of artists.

AUTUMN

Autumn brings cooler weather to Egypt and a proliferation of events and festivals. While some of these are obvious attempts to boost tourist revenues, the best can be truly magical events that are well worth making the effort to go to. However, it is worth noting that the time of year some of these events take place is liable to change at the whim of the Egyptian authorities.

SEPTEMBER

Nile Festival Day or Wafaa an-Nil, Cairo. This is a series of processions, parades and sporting competitions which take place on the Nile.

COPTIC FESTIVALS

Christmas, Epiphany, Easter and the Annunciation are the main Christian festivals of the year and all are celebrated by Copts, with Easter being the most important. Saints' days also feature strongly and, as with Islamic feasts, they are usually celebrated with a lively moulid. The main saints' days include the Moulid of St Damyanah, the Feast of the Apostles Peter and Paul and various moulids of the Virgin and St George which take place throughout August. The spring festival of Sham an-Nessim is celebrated by both Muslims and Christians with family picnics of painted eggs and salted fish.

Pope Shenouda III, *the patriarch of the Coptic Christian church, presides over important religious ceremonies and events.*

COPTIC CALENDAR

While some Coptic festivals correspond to the Julian calendar, others rely on the solar Coptic one. This calendar has 13 months, 12 of 30 days each and an intercalary month at the end of the year of 5 or 6 days, depending whether it is a leap year or not.

Easter This is the most important date in the Coptic calendar. However, it can differ by up to a month from the date of the Orthodox church's festival.

Coptic festivals *are primarily religious affairs with celebrations centred around church services for the young and old.*

A colourful pageant at the Arabian Horse Festival, Az-Zahraa

International Cinema Festival, Alexandria. The Egyptians pride themselves on their cinema. This festival features more home produced films than the very popular Cairo festival in December.

OCTOBER

Aida Opera, Giza. This spectacular Egyptian-themed extravaganza was written by Verdi for the opening of the Suez Canal. Performed in front of the pyramids, this is a very popular production.
Alexandria Mediterranean Biennale (for artists) brings Mediterranean artists together for an exchange of cultural and artistic ideas.

National Day (Armed Forces Day) *(Oct 6)* is a day of parades, fly-bys and non-stop patriotic songs and films.
The Battle of El-Alamein Commemoration, with services conducted by former Allied and Axis countries, remembers those that died in the campaigns in North Africa during World War II.
Ramses Festival, Abu Simbel *(Oct 22)*. On this day, and again in February, the sun reaches 55 m (183 ft) into the inner chamber of the Temple of Ramses and illuminates the statues inside.
Moulid of Sayyid Ahmed al-Badawi, Tanta. Egypt's largest festival, up to two million revellers attend this

week-long celebration at the end of the cotton harvest.
National Liberation Day *(Oct 23)* and the **Suez Victory Day** *(Oct 24)* are popular celebrations of Egypt's martial past.
Pharaoh's Rally (International Egypt Rally), is a gruelling 12-day, 6,400-km (4,000-mile) motor vehicle race through the Egyptian deserts. Major car manufacturers and competitors come from all over the world to participate in this event.

NOVEMBER

Arabian Horse Festival, Az-Zahraa. Proud of its Arabian horses, Egypt holds two festivals for displaying these beautiful animals. The other is held at Sharkeya in the Delta during May.
International Fishing Competition, Sharm el-Sheikh. These competitions are staged at several of the Red Sea resorts and attract international competitors.
Luxor National Festival *(Nov 4)* is combined with a commemoration of the discovery of the Tomb of Tutankhamun in 1922.
World Bowling Championship, Cairo. Tenpin bowls, which claims its origins in ancient Egypt, is rapidly growing in popularity in the modern country.

One of the cultural highlights of the Egyptian calendar, Verdi's spectacular opera, Aida

WINTER

Winter brings some slight relief from the heat and, in Cairo and Alexandria and along the North Coast, even the odd shower of rain. The days are still sunny and warm but the nights can be quite cold, especially in desert areas. It also brings the start of the tourist season and a large influx of foreign visitors seeking winter sun and a glimpse into the fascinating, civilization of ancient Egypt. Cruise tours and hotels in Upper Egypt tend to get busy during this period and prices increase accordingly.

The organized chaos of the International Book Fair, Cairo

DECEMBER

The International Nile Regatta is organized by the Egyptian Rowing Federation, this event attracts teams of young and more experienced rowers from all over the world. The Regatta takes place in Luxor and Cairo.
The International Cinema Festival, Cairo, is an often chaotic festival which brings the very best of world cinema to Egypt. However, the event's popularity is partly due to the fact that it is the only time of the year that Egyptians get to see uncensored films. While films notorious for sex or nudity are well-attended and lively affairs, there are a lot of other good films to see.

JANUARY

International Sailing Championship, Port Safaga. This event is best viewed from the shore, watching the colourful sails gliding across the usually calm sea.
New Year's Day *(1 Jan)* is a public holiday.
Coptic Christmas *(7 Jan)*. On this day, Copts throughout Egypt dress up in their Sunday best, visit their relatives and feast together. It is not an official public holiday, but many Egyptian Copts take this day off.
International Egyptian Marathon, Luxor. As many as 2,000 competitors brave the heat to take part in this run around Luxor. As well as the marathon there is also a

Windsurfing on the Red Sea

"Pharaonic Race". This 100-km (62-mile) run started in 1977 supposedly after an archaeologist found an inscription describing a similar length race run by royal soldiers in the 7th century BC.
International Windsurfing Competition, Hurghada. The Red Sea provides ideal conditions for such watersport competitions and similar events are held around the year.
Epiphany *(19 Jan)*, a Coptic celebration of the revelation of Jesus's divinity after his baptism by John.
The Paris-Dakar-Cairo Rally is one of the most famous rallies in the world. A brave field of competitors traverse Africa from West to East finishing the 11,000-km (7,000 mile) race in front of the Pyramids at Giza, in clouds of fumes and dust.
Cairo International Book Fair, Nasr City. Ostensibly for the book trade, this event also attracts regular book lovers and Cairenes simply looking for a day out among the fast food stalls. During the event a bus service departs for Nasr City from Midan Tahrir.

FEBRUARY

Abu Simbel Festival *(22 Feb)*. This festival celebrates one of the two days in the year (the other is in October) when the sun's rays penetrate the sanctuary of Ramses's Great Temple at Abu Simbel.

A competitor in the motorcycle class of the Paris-Dakar-Cairo Rally

The Climate of Egypt

Snorkelling in the Red Sea

Egypt's weather is predominantly hot, sunny and very dry. The only rain that falls regularly is on the North Coast during winter, but this is under 100 mm (4 inches) a year. There are two seasons – May to October, the hot season, and November to April, the cool season. In general, it is warm all the year round, although the deserts can get cold during winter nights. The most striking meteorological phenomenon is the *khamseen*, a dry wind during April and May that causes sandstorms.

THE DELTA AND THE NORTH COAST

°C	Apr	Jul	Oct	Jan
	23	30	28	
	15	23	20	18
				11
☀	10	12	9	7
☂ mm	3	-	5	48
month	Apr	Jul	Oct	Jan

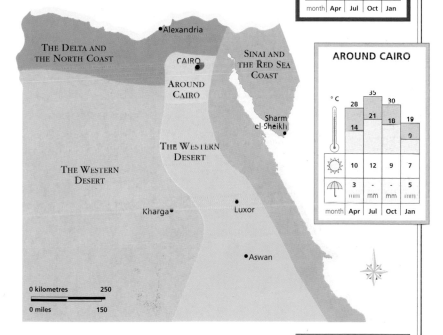

Alexandria

THE DELTA AND THE NORTH COAST

CAIRO

SINAI AND THE RED SEA COAST

AROUND CAIRO

Sharm el Sheikh

THE WESTERN DESERT

THE WESTERN DESERT

Kharga

Luxor

Aswan

0 kilometres 250
0 miles 150

AROUND CAIRO

°C	Apr	Jul	Oct	Jan
	28	35	30	
	14	21	18	19
				9
☀	10	12	9	7
☂ mm	3	-	-	5
month	Apr	Jul	Oct	Jan

THE WESTERN DESERT

°C	Apr	Jul	Oct	Jan
	37	42	37	
	20	23	21	21
				5
☀	11	12	11	10
☂ mm	-	-	-	-
month	Apr	Jul	Oct	Jan

THE NILE VALLEY

°C	Apr	Jul	Oct	Jan
	34	40	35	
	18	25	19	24
				8
☀	9	10	8	7
☂ mm	-	-	-	-
month	Apr	Jul	Oct	Jan

SINAI AND THE RED SEA COAST

°C	Apr	Jul	Oct	Jan
	26	32	30	
	16	25	23	21
				10
☀	11	12	11	10
☂ mm	-	-	-	-
month	Apr	Jul	Oct	Jan

ΚΡΟΚΟΔΙΛΟΠΑΡΔΑΛΙϹ

THE HISTORY OF EGYPT

Egypt's history has been crucially influenced by its environment. When lack of rain forced the early nomadic inhabitants to migrate towards the Nile Valley, the fertile floodplain gave birth to a nation that produced some of the most important achievements in human history and established a culture that would remain largely unchanged for over 3000 years.

Although the beginning of Egyptian history is generally given as 3100 BC, human activity in the Predynastic Period can be traced back many thousands of years before this date. The Sahara Desert used to be a green and fertile savannah, home to a nomadic population who hunted the wildlife they portrayed in rock drawings (petroglyphs). Archaeologists have also discovered that cattle-herders in Nabta Playa in the Western Desert built stone-circle calendars dating from 8000 BC.

The way of life of these early peoples remained much the same for around 4000 years, but as the climate became increasingly arid, the population left the growing areas of desert (*deshret* or red land) for the banks of the river Nile where the annual flooding sustained a region of great fertility (*kemet* or black land). The excavation of their settlements has revealed the rapid development of a sophisticated culture of mud-brick houses and workshops, together with primitive temple structures.

King Narmer's Palette c.3100 BC

The need to organize these settlements led to the invention of the world's first form of writing – hieroglyphs. Excavations at Abydos have shown that this script was in use from around 3250 BC, several centuries before the earliest writing in Mesopotamia. Further expansion meant settlements inevitably came into conflict with each other. The country polarized into two opposing kingdoms of north (Lower Egypt) and south (Upper Egypt). Around 3100 BC, the two were unified for the first time into a single state. This event was commemorated on the cosmetic slate palette of King Narmer (sometimes known as Menes), found at Hierakonpolis. The palette is possibly the most important historical document from the whole of Egyptian history, recording the creation of the world's first nation state. The dramatic pose as he is about to smash the skull of his defeated foe became the standard way to portray Egypt's kings throughout the next 3,000 years.

TIMELINE

8000 BC Early human settlement of Nabta Playa in Western Desert builds huge sculptures and a stone-circle calendar

Pots from 4000–3000 BC

3400 BC Egypt's oldest temple built at Hierakonpolis

3250 BC Invention of hieroglyphs – world's first script

10,000 BC	5000 BC	4500 BC	4000 BC	3500 BC	3000 BC

10,000 BC Nomadic population of Sahara draw petroglyphs of the animals they hunt

Earliest known human sculpture

c. 4000 BC Earliest known human figure sculpted in Africa, at Neolithic settlement in western Delta

3100 BC Political unification of Egypt by King Narmer. Memphis becomes the capital city

◁ **Graeco-Roman mosaic showing the flooding of the Nile, Egypt's temples and its fabled wildlife**

THE OLD KINGDOM
(3100–2180 BC)

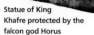

The power base of the Old Kingdom was established at Memphis, the first capital of a united Egypt. This was strategically located where Upper Egypt meets Lower Egypt at the apex of the Delta close to modern Cairo. Whereas the earliest kings chose Abydos as their funeral site to reflect their southern origins, later rulers preferred to be buried close to their new capital in its necropolis, Saqqara. The site of Egypt's earliest pyramid (c.2650 BC), Saqqara is also home to many stone *mastaba* (bench-shaped) tombs built for members of the royal court and beautifully decorated. The king was seen as the living incarnation of the god Horus and his court sought to be buried close to his divine power.

Statue of King Khafre protected by the falcon god Horus

King Narmer's successors managed to suppress any outside threat to Egypt's stability whilst organizing the country into 42 provinces or *nomes*. These were administered by means of a highly efficient bureaucracy of officials. The great wealth created through a carefully organized system of taxation – based on the collection and redistribution of Egypt's abundant grain supplies – was also used to fund ambitious building schemes. This culminated in the massive pyramid complexes of the Old Kingdom god-kings such as Djoser, Sneferu, Khufu and Khafre. The organization required for such huge projects helped to unify the nation, while the vast numbers of skilled craftsmen involved meant that art and technology developed at a rapid pace.

Of all the pyramid-building pharaohs, Sneferu was the greatest, building three such structures, including the first true pyramid at Dahshur. It was only with techniques perfected by Sneferu that his son Khufu was able to construct the largest of all Egypt's pyramids at Giza around 2589 BC.

Eventually centuries of pyramid-building, together with a series of poor harvests, severely depleted the economy. This led to a decline in royal power, which was reflected in the small size of the later pyramids built at Abusir and Saqqara. The incredibly long reign of Pepi II (2278–2184 BC), only added to the problem and with the pharaoh seen as a feeble old man, royal authority was further undermined. After an incredible

The Pyramids at Giza, magnificent symbols of the divine power of the early Egyptian kings

TIMELINE

2665 BC The world's oldest stone monument, the step Pyramid of King Djoser, built at Saqqara

2613–2589 BC Reign of King Sneferu, builder of 3 pyramids at Dashur and Meidum

2900 BC	2800 BC	2700 BC	2600 BC	2500 BC

Figurine from a unified Egypt fashioned in c.2900 BC

2686 BC Oldest surviving mudbrick building built by King Khasekhemwy at Hierakonpolis

c.2589 BC The Great Pyramid of Khufu (Cheops) built at Giza

c.2558 BC Pyramid of Khafre (Chephren) built at Giza. Its complex includes the oldest surviving temple in Egypt

THE HISTORY OF EGYPT

94 years on the throne Pepi II was succeeded by Egypt's first female pharaoh Nitocris, but despite being remembered as "the bravest and most beautiful" of her time, it was too late to reverse the decline in royal fortunes.

FIRST INTERMEDIATE PERIOD, MIDDLE KINGDOM AND SECOND INTERMEDIATE PERIOD (2180–1550 BC)

As royal power declined, officials began to relocate to their home provinces. No longer reliant on the king, they created their own small kingdoms maintained with private armies. As the country gradually fragmented, central authority finally broke down into anarchy and the First Intermediate Period began c.2180 BC.

The lack of overall authority is clearly expressed in provincial and rather "idiosyncratic" art styles typical of local trends. The breakdown of social order is also reflected in the literature – "All is ruin...men kill their brothers...blood is everywhere".

The remnants of royal power relocated to Herakleopolis, at the entrance to the Fayoum Oasis, and attempted to rule through the forging of alliances with the southern regions. However, any temporary unity was shattered when Thebes formed an independent monarchy. Civil war and fierce fighting between neighbouring tribes tore the whole country apart.

Statue of Montuhotep II, Theban founder of the 11th Dynasty

After a long and bitter struggle the powerful Theban warlord Montuhotep II conquered the north to reunite the country under the 11th Dynasty. His reign took Egypt from the chaos of the First Intermediate Period into the stability of the Middle Kingdom (c.2055 BC). Thebes now grew into a major metropolis, home to skilled craftsmen who created new art styles at a rate not seen since the Age of the Pyramids. The old trade routes and mines were reopened and expansionist policies prevailed. Although the office of pharaoh would never again reach the absolute divinity of earlier times, the Theban monarchy restored royal power as growth in revenue led to a resumption of building projects. The greatest new structure was Montuhotep's imposing funerary complex built at Deir al-Bahri which, 500 years later, would serve as the prototype for Hatshepsut's temple.

Model of the private army of the Governor of Asyut (c.2000 BC)

Teams of workers dragging a huge stone statue, from the Middle Kingdom tomb of Djehutyhotep (c.1850 BC)

The kings of the 12th Dynasty, which lasted from c.1985–1795 BC, moved the royal residence back to the traditional capital, Memphis, in order to be closer to the centre of the country. They continued with ambitious building projects, and the art and literature of this time is regarded as the "classic" period of Egyptian culture. Pharaohs such as Senusret III and Amenemhat III constructed impressive pyramids at Saqqara, Dahshur, Lahun and Hawara, where they were buried alongside their relatives with beautiful jewellery made of gold, amethyst, carnelian and lapis lazuli.

Successful military campaigns expanded Egypt's borders, whilst at home the crown centralized its authority by removing power from provincial governors and replacing these governors with a vast bureaucracy of loyal officials. Many of these officials were migrants from nearby Palestine

Sphinx bearing the face of Amenemhat III

who had settled peacefully in northern Egypt and had been gradually absorbed into Egyptian society over a period of about 150 years. By infiltrating the government they took advantage of the instability caused by a series of short-lived rulers during the 13th and 14th Dynasties. In 1650 BC, these settlers, referred to as the Hyksos (Rulers of Foreign Lands), finally assumed control.

This marks the beginning of the Second Intermediate Period, when Egypt was once again divided geographically. Based in their northern capital Avaris, the Hyksos formed an alliance with Nubia to help them to control southern Egypt, where the native Egyptian opposition to foreign rule had organized itself in Thebes. The country was once again subject to intermittent civil war until the Theban warlord Seqenenre Taa II and his sons Kamose and Ahmose finally drove the Hyksos out of Egypt to re-unite the Two Lands.

TIMELINE

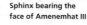

1965 BC Assassination of Amenemhat I and accession of his son Senusret I	*Statue of Senusret III*	**1795–1725 BC** Unstable 13th Dynasty of 70 kings	**1750–1650 BC** Minor rulers of the 14th Dynasty
1900 BC		**1800 BC**	**1700 BC**
1874–1855 BC Reign of Senusret III		**1799–1795 BC** Reign of Egypt's second female ruler Sobekneferu	
1855 BC Senusret III and his family buried at Dahshur		*Middle Kingdom Horus head pendant*	

THE NEW KINGDOM
(1550–1070 BC)

With the reunification of north and south, the New Kingdom began. This is Egypt's "Golden Age", when a series of unrelenting warrior pharaohs turned the country into the most powerful empire in the ancient world. The expulsion of the Hyksos was followed by vigorous military campaigns as far north as the river Euphrates and as far south as Nubia. The enormous wealth amassed from foreign tribute was channelled into massive building projects in and around Thebes, with successive monarchs trying to outdo their predecessors. The magnificent temple of Karnak – the cult centre of the local Theban deity Amun – was embellished by successive pharaohs, as Amun was linked with the sun-god Ra to create Amun-Ra, "King of the Gods". Meanwhile, pharaohs built huge funerary temples for themselves on the west bank of the Nile, and were buried in spectacular rock-cut tombs in the Valley of the Kings, designed to ensure their eternal afterlife.

As the first king of the New Kingdom, Ahmose continued his family's military successes and established a pattern for his successors. His son Amenhotep I followed in his father's footsteps by pacifying Nubia. He also founded a village for royal tomb builders at Deir al-Medina,

Statue of Hatshepsut as a bearded pharaoh

where both he and his mother and co-ruler Ahmose-Nofretari were worshipped long after their deaths.

Then began the succession of the Tuthmosis pharaohs: men born to minor wives of the king who strengthened their claims to the throne by marrying into the female royal line. Tuthmosis II was succeeded by his wife and half-sister Hatshepsut, the most familiar of Egypt's female pharaohs, who is often portrayed in statues as a bearded pharaoh. Her successor, Tuthmosis III, the so-called "Napoleon of Ancient Egypt", expanded the Egyptian Empire into Asia Minor and as far as the Euphrates. His son Amenhotep II, a great warrior like his father and an accomplished athlete, consolidated Egypt's control over the vassal states of Asia Minor. Their foreign conquests created the wealth used so wisely by the greatest of all the pharaohs, Amenhotep III. Known as "the Magnificent", his peaceful 38-year reign marks the height of Egypt's cultural and artistic achievement.

Tuthmosis III making offerings to Amun-Ra, the national deity during the New Kingdom

1650 BC Palestinian Hyksos take power	**c.1560 BC** Theban warlord Seqenenre Taa II killed fighting the Hyksos	**c.1500 BC** Valley of the Kings becomes royal burial ground	*Head of Tuthmosis III*	**1458–1425 BC** Tuthmosis III campaigns as far as the Euphrates
	1600 BC		**1500 BC**	**1400 BC**
	1550 BC Seqenenre Taa II's younger son Ahmose drives the Hyksos out of Egypt and becomes the first ruler of the 18th Dynasty	**1525 BC** Amenhotep I founds royal tomb builders' village of Deir al-Medina	**1473–1458 BC** Reign of Hatshepsut	**1390–1352 BC** Peaceful reign of Amenhotep III, "the Magnificent"

The Egyptian Pharaohs

The ancient Egyptians dated events to the particular year in the reign of a king or pharaoh (regnal dating). It was a Ptolemaic scholar, Manetho, who later sorted the kings into dynasties, a system still used today along with ancient king lists, astronomical records and modern archaeological dating methods. The resulting chronology is, however, neither fixed nor complete and liable to change.

EARLY DYNASTIC PERIOD

3100–2890 BC		2890–2686 BC	
IST DYNASTY		**2ND DYNASTY**	
Narmer	3100	Hetepsekhemwy	2890
Aha	3100	Raneb	2865
Djer	3000	Nynetjer	
Djet	2980	Weneg	
Den	2950	Sened	
Anedjib	2925	Peribsen	2700
Semerkhet	2900	Khasekhemwy	2686
Qaa	2890		

aka Amenhotep IV (see p175)   † aka Amenophis
* denotes female pharaoh   ‡ aka Sesostris

FIRST INTERMEDIATE PERIOD

2181–2125 BC	2160–2055 BC
7TH & 8TH DYNASTIES	**9TH & 10TH DYNASTIES**
	HERAKLEOPOLITAN
During this unstable period of ancient Egyptian history there were numerous ephemeral kings. The weakening of centralized power led to the establishment of local dynasties.	Kheti
	Merykare
	Ity
	11TH DYNASTY
	(THEBES ONLY)
	Intef I 2125–2112
	Intef II 2112–2063
	Intef III 2063–2055

MIDDLE KINGDOM

2055–1985 BC	1985–1795 BC	
11TH DYNASTY	**12TH DYNASTY**	
ALL EGYPT	Amenemhat I	1985–1955
Montuhotep II 2055–2004	Senusret I ‡	1965–1920
Montuhotep III 2004–1992	Amenemhat II	1922–1878
Montuhotep IV 1992–1985	Senusret II ‡	1880–1874
	Senusret III ‡	1874–1855
	Amenemhat III	1855–1808
	Amenemhat IV	1808–1799
	Sobekneferu*	1799–1795
	Overlaps in dates indicate periods of co-regency	

"Block" statue from the 12th Dynasty

NEW KINGDOM

	1550–1295 BC		1295–1186 BC		1186–1069 BC	
	18TH DYNASTY		**19TH DYNASTY**		**20TH DYNASTY**	
	Ahmose	1550–1525	Ramses I	1295–1294	Sethnakhte	1186–1184
	Amenhotep I †	1525–1504	Seti I	1294–1279	Ramses III	1184–1153
	Tuthmosis I	1504–1492	Ramses II	1279–1213	Ramses IV	1153–1147
	Tuthmosis II	1492–1479	Merneptah	1213–1203	Ramses V	1147–1143
	Tuthmosis III	1479–1425	Amenmessu	1203–1200	Ramses VI	1143–1136
	Hatshepsut*	1473–1458	Seti II	1200–1194	Ramses VII	1136–1129
	Amenhotep II †	1427–1400	Siptah	1194–1188	Ramses VIII	1129–1126
	Tuthmosis IV	1400–1390	Tawosret*	1188–1186	Ramses IX	1126–1108
	Amenhotep III †	1390–1352			Ramses X	1108–1099
	Akhenaten #	1352–1336			Ramses XI	1099–1069
	Nefertiti					
	Smenkhkare*	1338–1336				
	Tutankhamun	1336–1327				
	Ay	1327–1323				
	Horemheb	1323–1295				

Bracelet of Queen Ahotep, mother of Ahmose, first king of the 18th Dynasty

Head of Ramses III, who built the great mortuary Temple at Medinat Habu

LATE PERIOD

672–525 BC		525–359 BC		404–c.380 BC		380–343 BC	
26TH DYNASTY		**27TH DYNASTY**		**28TH DYNASTY**		**30TH DYNASTY**	
(Saite)		(Persian Period 1)		Amyrtaios	404–399	Nectanebo I	380–362
						Teos	362–360
Necho I	672–664	Cambyses	525–522	**29TH DYNASTY**		Nectanebo II	360–343
Psamtek I	664–610	Darius I	522–486	Nepherites I	399–393		
Necho II	610–595	Xerxes I	486–465	Hakor	393–380		
Psamtek II	595–589	Artaxerxes I	465–424	Nepherites II	c.380		
Apries	589–570	Darius II	424–405				
Ahmose II	570–526	Artaxerxes II	405–359				
Psamtek III	526–525						

One of the stone sphinxes from Luxor Temple, carved with the face of Nectanebo I

OLD KINGDOM

2686–2613	2613–2498 BC	2494–2345 BC	2345–2181 BC
3RD DYNASTY	**4TH DYNASTY**	**5TH DYNASTY**	**6TH DYNASTY**
Sanakht 2686–2667	Sneferu 2613–2589	Userkaf 2494–2487	Teti 2345–2323
Djoser 2667–2648	Khufu 2589–2566	Sahure 2487–2475	Userkare 2323–2321
Sekhemkhet 2648–2640	Djedefre 2566–2558	Neferirkare 2475–2455	Pepi I 2321–2287
Khaba 2640–2637	Khafre 2558–2532	Shepseskare 2455–2448	Merenre 2287–2278
Huni 2637–2613	Menkaure 2532–2503	Raneferef 2448–2445	Pepi II 2278–2184
	Shepseskaf 2503–2498	Nyuserre 2445–2421	Nitocris* 2184–2181
		Menkauhor 2421–2414	
		Djedkare 2414–2375	
		Unas 2375–2345	

The Pyramids at Giza, built in the 4th Dynasty

	1795–1650 BC	SECOND INTERMEDIATE PERIOD	
		1650–1550 BC	1650–1550 BC
	13TH DYNASTY	**15TH DYNASTY**	**17TH DYNASTY**
	1795–c.1725	**(HYKSOS)**	In addition, several kings ruled from Thebes including the following:
	14TH DYNASTY	Salitis	
	1750–1650	Khyan c.1600	Intef
	Minor rulers probably contemporaneous with the previous dynasty.	Apepi c.1555	Ta I
		Khamudi	Seqenenre Taa II c.1560
		16TH DYNASTY	Kamose 1555–1550
		1650–1550	
		Minor Hyksos rulers contemporary with the 15th Dynasty.	

Limestone relief of Senusret I from the Temple at Karnak

THIRD INTERMEDIATE PERIOD · LATE PERIOD

1069–945 BC	945–715 BC	818–715 BC	747–656 BC
21ST DYNASTY	**22ND DYNASTY**	**23RD DYNASTY**	**25TH DYNASTY**
Smendes 1069–1043	Sheshonq I 945–924	Several continuous lines of rulers at Herakleopolis Magna, Hermopolis Magna, Leontopolis and Tanis including the following:	Piy 747–716
Amenemnisu 1043–1039	Osorkon I 924–889		Shabaqo 716–702
Psusennes I 1039–991	Sheshonq II c.890		Shabitqo 702–690
Amenemope 993–984	Takelot I 889–874		Taharqo 690–664
Osorkon the Elder 984–978	Osorkon II 874–850		Tanutamani 664–656
Siamun 978–959	Takelot II 850–825	Pedubastis I 818–793	
Psusennes II 959–945	Sheshonq III 825–773	Sheshonq IV c.780	
	Pimay 773–767	Osorkon III 777–749	
	Sheshonq V 767–730		
	Osorkon IV 730–715	**24TH DYNASTY**	
		Bakenrenef 727–715	

Silver coffin of Psusennes I from Tanis

PTOLEMAIC PERIOD

343–332 BC	332–305 BC	305–80 BC	80–30 BC
PERSIAN PERIOD 2	**MACEDONIAN DYNASTY**	**PTOLEMAIC DYNASTY**	**PTOLEMAIC DYNASTY (CONT.)**
Artaxerxes III	Alexander	Ptolemy I 305–285	Ptolemy XI 80
Ochus 343–333	the Great 332–323	Ptolemy II 285–246	Ptolemy XII 80–51
Arses 338–336	Philip Arrhidaeus 323–317	Ptolemy III 246–221	Cleopatra VII* 51–30
Darius III	Alexander IV 317–305	Ptolemy IV 221–205	Ptolemy XIII 51–47
Codoman 336–332		Ptolemy V 205–180	Ptolemy XIV 47–44
		Ptolemy VI 180–145	Ptolemy XV 44–30
		Ptolemy VII 145	
		Ptolemy VIII 170–116	
		Ptolemy IX 116–107	
		& (second reign) 88–80	Egypt becomes part of the Roman Empire in 30 BC (*see pp56–7*)
		Ptolemy X 107–88	

Alexander the Great in Egyptian headgear

Philistines, one of the "Peoples of the Sea", being taken prisoner by Egyptians, from Ramses III's mortuary temple at Medinat Habu

With the death of Amenhotep III in 1352 BC, the succession passed to his son Akhenaten *(see p175)*. His mismanagement of the political situation, relocation of the capital to Akhetaten (modern Tell al-Amarna) and attempts to overturn the traditional religious hierarchy destabilized Egypt and brought the country close to ruin. Akhenaten's successor, probably his wife Nefertiti, restored order by returning the seat of power to Thebes and re-establishing the traditional religion. The reign of Akhenaten's son Tutankhamun was largely devoted to restoring internal stability before trying to reverse Egypt's fortunes abroad. But it took the military prowess of Horemheb, who had worked his way up from scribe to general and finally king, to restore the country to its former greatness. The last king of the 18th Dynasty, he soon began recovering Egypt's empire. This military policy was continued by the rulers of the 19th Dynasty, which began in 1295 BC. Under Seti I, Egypt regained much of her prestige abroad, whilst at home the monarchy's reputation was consolidated and enhanced by

Bust of Queen Nefertiti, 18th Dynasty

great new building projects such as Karnak's hypostyle hall *(see pp188–9)* and Seti's temple at Abydos. Seti was succeeded by his son Ramses II – also known as Ramses the Great – whose 66-year reign saw royal construction on a massive scale. Huge monuments, including the awesome Great Temple of Abu Simbel *(see pp214–15)*, were erected in a deliberate effort by Ramses to impress his subjects and preserve his reputation for posterity.

Ramses was succeeded by his son Merneptah, and four more pharaohs in less than 20 years. In c.1186 BC, Sethnakhte inaugurated the 20th Dynasty; nine kings followed, all named Ramses. The greatest of these was Ramses III, who successfully defended Egypt's northern borders against repeated invasions by Libyans and settlers from the Mediterranean region – the so-called "Peoples of the Sea". But his weak successors could not sustain his victories, and foreign infiltration grew rapidly. With internal disorder and social unrest, even the royal tombs were ransacked. The New Kingdom finally collapsed in 1070 BC.

TIMELINE

1279–1213 BC Reign of Ramses II	**c.1274 BC** Ramses II claims victory over the Hittites at the Battle of Qadesh	**1070 BC** Fall of New Kingdom. Egypt divided between north and south		**747–656 BC** Nubians conquer Egypt and rule as 25th Dynasty

1300 BC	**1150 BC**	**1000 BC**	**850 BC**

1352–1336 BC Reign of Akhenaten. Relocation of capital to Akhetaten		**1070 BC** Kings rule from Tanis in the Delta, with Theban priests in control of the south	**945–924 BC** Sheshonq I, thought to be "Shishak" from the Old Testament, invades Israel

Collar of Tutankhamun

THIRD INTERMEDIATE PERIOD, LATE PERIOD AND PTOLEMAIC PERIOD (1070–30 BC)

The New Kingdom gave way to four centuries of disunity and foreign infiltration, known as the Third Intermediate Period. Egypt was again divided between north and south: the south remained under the control of the semi-royal high priests of Thebes, while the monarchy was located in the north and ruled from Tanis in the eastern Delta.

Alexander the Great

Egypt was further fragmented by the Libyan invasion of the western Delta, but in 747 BC the country was united by the Nubians, who managed to hold onto power for over a century, ruling as the 25th Dynasty.

Ptolemy V, wearing traditional Pharaonic clothing, making offerings to the sacred Buchis bull

The Late Period began with the Assyrian invasion of Egypt in 669 BC. The Assyrians meant to rule the country through their vassal king Nekau then Psamtek of the western Delta city Sais, but Psamtek outmanoeuvred his former masters and the 26th "Saite" Dynasty saw a brief flowering of native Egyptian culture.

Hopes of a permanent revival were, however, cut short by the Persians' invasion in 525 BC. Two hundred years of Persian domination was only interrupted by the short-lived 30th Dynasty – the last native Egyptian rulers. Finally the Macedonian king Alexander the Great "liberated" Egypt from the Persians and founded his new capital Alexandria on the Mediterranean coast, followed by the Ptolemaic Period.

On Alexander's death in 323 BC, his most trusted general assumed power, and over the next three centuries (305–30 BC) 14 of Ptolemy's successors and namesakes ruled from their capital Alexandria. The Ptolemies were accepted by the native Egyptians because they ruled as traditional pharaohs and built temples, such as Edfu, Dendara and Philae, in deliberate imitation of ancient Egyptian design. They also embellished Alexandria, which became the most important city of the ancient world. The last of the Ptolemies, Cleopatra VII, inherited the throne in 51 BC. Her 21-year reign briefly restored Egyptian greatness in the face of the expansionist ambitions of Rome. Her suicide marks the notional end of ancient Egypt, as the country finally became a Roman province.

---

669 BC Ashurbanipal of Assyria invades Egypt

Female mummy head from Late Period

332 BC Alexander the Great conquers Egypt and founds Alexandria

323 BC Death of Alexander in Babylon and burial of his body in Egypt

30 BC Egypt becomes Roman province

51–30 BC Reign of Cleopatra VII

700 BC	550 BC	400 BC	250 BC	100 BC

664–525 BC Native Egyptian renaissance under 26th "Saite" Dynasty

525 BC Invasion by Persian King Cambyses

380–343 BC 30th Dynasty, the last native Egyptian rulers

305 BC Ptolemy I establishes Ptolemaic dynasty, ruling from Alexandria

Coin of Cleopatra

Cleopatra VII (69 BC–30 BC)

Cleopatra's cartouche

Perhaps the most familiar of ancient Egyptian figures, the real Cleopatra is hidden beneath centuries of misinformation. Most of the detail about her is supplied by Roman sources who waged a propaganda war against her. To them she was the ruler of a decadent eastern culture who seduced two of Rome's generals in order to sieze the Roman Empire. In fact, Cleopatra was an educated Macedonian Greek, who had one child with Julius Caesar and three during her 11 years with Mark Antony. These two men used Egypt's wealth for their imperial ambitions as much as she used their military might to assure her position.

Ptolemy I (305–285 BC) *ruled Egypt after his close friend Alexander the Great died, founding a dynasty that lasted nearly 300 years.*

ORIENTALIST PAINTING OF CLEOPATRA

Part inspired by reliefs on temple walls, part by a confusion of the exotic and the erotic, this painting by Alexandre Cabanel (1823-89) misrepresents Cleopatra in seductive Pharaonic attire.

This Classical bust *is probably a more realistic representation of Cleopatra. She was portrayed in Pharaonic dress on the walls of temples such as Dendera (see p179) to re-inforce her position in the eyes of her subjects as the rightful heir to the great pharaohs.*

This Ptolemaic papyrus *bears Cleopatra's signature. Although fluent in seven languages, including Egyptian, she used Greek for official documents.*

EGYPT AND ROMAN EXPANSION

Rome's expansion from the 4th to the 1st century BC was fuelled in part by the need for ever-increasing quantities of grain. Grain's importance to the ancient economies is somewhat analogous to the value of oil to modern economies. Thanks to its efficient Greek administration, Egypt's vast grain harvests made it incredibly wealthy and a threat to Rome, if the country fell into the wrong hands. Therefore the Romans knew they had either to ensure Egypt's ruler was sympathetic towards them, or annex the country. At first, Egypt avoided being absorbed by Rome through a skilful combination of bribery and diplomacy – on different occasions, Julius Caesar and Mark Antony were paid large sums of money to restore the throne of Egypt to Cleopatra's father, Ptolemy XII. When Cleopatra and her brother were installed on the throne in 51 BC, Rome expected simply to add Egypt to their empire.

KEY
- Rome 300 BC
- Rome 51 BC
- Ptolemaic Kingdom 51 BC

CLEOPATRA AND ROME

In 51 BC, Cleopatra and Ptolemy XIII, her brother, were named co-rulers of Egypt. When they fought for sole control, Rome sent Julius Caesar to settle the dispute. He put Cleopatra on the throne and formed a close relationship with her. Three years after Caesar's murder, Mark Antony paid a visit to Cleopatra seeking funding for his expeditions. They became lovers and when Antony handed Roman territories over to Egypt in 34 BC, Rome, at Octavian's urging, declared war on Cleopatra.

Julius Caesar, *after moving Cleopatra to Rome, was killed by Republicans who feared that, under her evil influence, he wanted to return Rome to monarchy.*

Mark Antony *was derided by Rome for his lack of self control towards Cleopatra. Forced to marry the sister of Octavian, he later returned to his Egyptian lover.*

Octavian, *with the prize of the Roman Empire at stake, decided to fight Antony at sea near Actium, off the coast of Greece.*

At the Battle of Actium (31 BC) *the two fleets quickly clashed, opening up a gap in Octavian's formation. Seeing her chance, Cleopatra headed for Egypt closely followed by Antony. His men, thinking him a deserter, defected to Octavian. A year later Octavian's army routed Antony's troops and marched on Alexandria.*

The African asp *is a cobra, which, as the uraeus snake, protected the pharaoh in this world and the next. It is possible, therefore, that Cleopatra did in fact choose to die by snake bite.*

THE ENDURING APPEAL OF CLEOPATRA

The appeal of Cleopatra's story is magnified by her tragic death: defeated by Octavian and believing reports that Cleopatra was dead, Antony committed suicide; Cleopatra realising all was lost then took her own life. As told by Roman writers, this tale of sex, power, greed and ultimately tragedy proved irresistible for artists from the Renaissance, Shakespeare and Hollywood.

Shakespeare's play *was based on Plutarch's* Lives *(c.AD 75), the Roman account most sympathetic to Cleopatra.*

Hollywood films *such as* Cleopatra, *starring Liz Taylor and Richard Burton used grand sets and outrageous outfits and did not let historical accuracy ruin a good story.*

Eye makeup *was one detail Hollywood did not get wrong, except that it was worn by both sexes. Ancient Egyptians used ground minerals mixed with water and stored in tubes.*

FROM CHRIST TO MOHAMMED

Egypt was now a province of mighty Rome, whose emperors established themselves as the successors of the pharaohs. As Christianity spread throughout the Roman Empire, its Egyptian adherents, known as Copts, came into conflict with the Roman authorities. Even when Christianity was adopted

Salah ad-Din al-Ayyubi (1138–93), the scourge of the European Crusaders

as the official religion of the Eastern half of the now divided Roman Empire in 323 AD, there were differences in theology, and the Copts were mercilessly persecuted.

The Eastern Romans, later known as Byzantines, remained largely unchallenged in power until in the 7th century they were confronted by a new force sweeping up from Arabia. Following the teachings of the Prophet Mohammed, the army of Islam defeated the Byzantines in battle and entered Egypt. Ignoring Alexandria, the Arab army, led by the general Amr Ibn al-Aas, marched on the fortress of Babylon-in-Egypt near to the old capital of Memphis. After a brief siege it surrendered and Amr settled his men just to the north, where he founded a new city known as Fustat.

Egypt became a province of an already vast Islamic empire ruled first from Damascus (the Umayyad dynasty), then from Baghdad (the Abbasids). Ahmed Ibn Tulun, an administrator sent from Baghdad, decided to declare the territory independent. His mosque still stands but his dynasty did not outlive him long; his son was assassinated and rule from Baghdad reimposed.

In AD 969 Egypt was seized by the Fatimids from Tunisia. They built a new city north of Fustat, encircled by fortified walls and containing palaces, great mosques and plazas. They called their new city Al-Qahira, "The Victorious", a name later corrupted by European tongues to "Cairo". Their reign in Egypt lasted for barely more than 200 years, until it was brought to an end in 1171 by the arrival of a Syrian warrior-general, Salah ad-Din al-Ayyubi, known in English as Saladin. In Cairo, Salah ad-Din expanded the city walls and added a fortress that survives as today's Citadel (see pp104–7). A hero of the Arab world, who recaptured Jerusalem from the European Crusaders, Salah ad-Din's role in Egyptian history is, however, overshadowed by the dynasty that succeeded him, a warrior caste called the Mamluks.

Detail of a manuscript showing Mamluk cavalrymen in training (1348)

TIMELINE

30 BC–395 AD Roman Period

Roman mummy portrait from 4th century AD

451 Egypt's Coptic church splits from Eastern Christianity at the Council of Chalcedon

527 St Catherine's Monastery founded in Sinai

| AD 1 | 150 | 300 | 450 | 600 | 75 |

394 End of ancient Egypt as Roman Empire accepts Christianity as official religion and closes all temples

640 Islamic army under Amr Ibn al-Aas invades and conquers Egypt

19th-century lithograph of Sultan Baybars I (c.1265) executing Christians who refuse to convert to Islam

SLAVES AND SOLDIERS

The word "Mamluk" means "one who is owned," and reflects their origins as slaves brought to Egypt to be palace guards. Their service was rewarded by land and eventual freedom. By the middle of the 13th century the Mamluks were the most powerful force in the land, and were able to claim Egypt for themselves.

The Mamluks retained the slave system, and whoever had the largest slave army installed himself as sultan at the top. There was no hereditary lineage, instead it was succession by the strongest. Once in power, there remained constant challenges, and only the exceptionally able and ruthless survived.

The Mamluks prided themselves on their martial skills and were known particularly for their masterful horsemanship. From their base in Cairo they fought victorious campaigns throughout Palestine and Syria, completing the job begun by Salah ad-Din by finally evicting the Crusaders from the Holy Land in 1291. They governed Jerusalem and Damascus, and carved out an empire that extended north as far as eastern Turkey. With these territories came control of East-West trade. The taxes raised on spices, perfumes, silks and dyes made Cairo one of the richest cities in the world. This wealth remains evident in the legacy of superb architecture left behind from this time, built with fine marble panelling, intricate ivory-inlaid woodwork, and carved stone ornamentation.

Mamluk monopolies forced Europe to seek alternative routes to the East, and when, in 1498, Vasco da Gama rounded the Cape of Good Hope, the fortunes of Egypt were dealt a crippling blow. Worse still, the Ottoman Turks from their capital of Constantinople were eroding the Mamluks' empire from the north. Sultan Qansuh al-Ghouri (1501–16) rode out to meet this new threat. His Mamluk army was defeated, and the following year the Ottoman Turks entered Cairo to take control of Egypt.

Magnificent interior of the Mosque of Qaitbey (1475), built with money raised by taxes

	969 Fatimids found the city of Al-Qahira, forerunner of modern Cairo	1250 Mamluks accede to power		1468–96 Reign of Qaitbey, enthusiastic patron of architecture	Mamluk tile from the 15th century
900	**1050**	**1200**	**1350**	**1500**	
876–9 Construction of the Mosque of Ibn Tulun	1171 Salah ad-Din becomes ruler of Egypt	*Mamluk jacket (c.13th century)*		1516 Al-Ghouri's Mamluk army defeated by Ottomans, who take control of Egypt	

The defeat of the Mamluks by Napoleon's army during the 1798 Battle of the Pyramids

OTTOMAN RULE

Under Ottoman rule, Egypt ceased to be the centre of the Mediterranean world and Cairo became just one of numerous provincial capitals ruled from Constantinople. The Turkish sultan Selim "the Grim", so called for his habit of executing his advisers, ruled Egypt and the Mamluks lived on as lords or *beys* still wielding considerable power.

The Ottoman empire reached its peak during the reign of Suleiman the Magnificent, but his death in 1566 heralded a long era of decline for the empire. A succession of weak Ottoman sultans enabled the Mamluks to re-emerge in the mid-17th century as the most powerful force in Egyptian politics. However, internal rivalry and bloody feuding prevented them

Sultan Selim I (1467–1520), also known as Selim "the Grim"

from exploiting power to the full. At the same time, economic decline and recurrent outbreaks of plague further weakened the country.

EUROPE "DISCOVERS" EGYPT

In 1798 Egypt was invaded by a French army under the command of Napoleon Bonaparte. With France and Britain at war, Napoleon saw the occupation of Egypt as a way of threatening British rule in India. The French defeated the Mamluks at the Battle of the Pyramids but this success was short lived. Napoleon's fleet was destroyed at Abu Qir *(see p250)* by the British Navy, led by Admiral Nelson. A declaration of war by the Ottoman sultan followed, by 1801 the French expedition had come to an end. Their legacy is

TIMELINE

1520–66 Reign of Suleiman the Magnificent

1566 Death of Suleiman the Magnificent

1650 Mamluks re-emerge as a powerful force

1550   1600   1650

1528 Egypt's first Ottoman mosque (Suleiman Pasha) built at the Citadel

Suleiman the Magnificent

1623 First overt rebellions in Egypt against rule from Constantinople the *Description de l'Egypte*, an exhaustive scientific study of the country which encouraged many other writers and artists to visit Egypt.

MOHAMMED ALI AND HIS HEIRS

In the resulting power vacuum, the Mamluks, Ottoman troops and a contingent of Albanian mercenaries locked horns in a struggle for power which was won, in 1805, by Mohammed Ali, commander of the Albanians. To consolidate his position he eliminated the threat of the Mamluks by inviting the leading *amirs* to a banquet and having them massacred on the way home. He then began to transform Egypt into an industrialized nation. Bringing agriculture under state control, he built textile plants, shipyards and munitions factories to supply his new Western-style army. After a series of military victories in Greece, Arabia and the Sudan, Mohammed Ali threatened the Ottoman sultan, but was forced to back down after the British intervened and he died in 1849.

Mohammed Ali in negotiations with the British, following his threat to overthrow the Ottoman sultan

The 1811 massacre of the leading Mamluk *amirs* ordered by Viceroy Mohammed Ali

Two successors followed before Khedive Ismail acceded to power. He was determined to transform Egypt into a modern nation and introduced the first national postal service, extending railroad networks throughout the country. His greatest achievement was to preside over the opening of the

19th-century advertisement showing Europeans at Giza

Suez Canal in 1869 *(see pp60–61)*. Such projects were funded by loans from European banking houses at exorbitant rates of interest. As the national debt rose, Ismail was forced to sell the majority of Suez Canal shares to the British and the French.

In 1882, Egyptian army officers led by Colonel Ahmed Orabi staged popular uprisings in an attempt to establish a more independent regime. The breakdown in local order led the British to send in the warships, shelling Alexandria and landing an army of occupation which routed Orabi's forces at Tell al-Kebir.

1719 Plague decimates the population of Egypt

1798 Egypt invaded by Napoleon

1805 Mohammed Ali wins control of Egypt

1882 British troops occupy Egypt

| 1700 | 1750 | 1800 | 1850 |

1707 Mamluk power struggle reaches new heights in Cairo

Napoleon Bonaparte

1822 Translation of hieroglyphs by French scholar Champollion

1869 Khedive Ismail opens the Suez Canal

Khedive Ismail

The Construction of the Suez Canal

As early as the 7th century BC, the ancient Egyptians had connected the Nile and Red Sea with an east-west canal. A north-south canal, slicing through the Isthmus of Suez to connect the Mediterranean with the Red Sea was first considered in the Middle Ages by Venetian merchants. At the end of the 18th century, Napoleon's engineers took up the idea but dropped it when they mistakenly calculated that one sea was 10 m (33 ft) higher than the other. The canal project was taken up by Ferdinand de Lesseps, the French consul to Egypt, who received the go-ahead during the reign of Khedive Said. Construction began on 25 April 1859.

Statue of Ferdinand de Lesseps

This impressive *satellite picture shows how the Suez Canal separates Africa (Egypt) from Asia (Sinai).*

THE CANAL ROUTE

This 19th-century painting by Albert Rieger shows how the Suez Canal utilizes lakes as passing places for shipping – Lake Manzila at its northern end, Lake Timsah, and the Bitter Lakes at the mid-point of the canal. This route is 163 km (101 miles) in length.

Rosetta branch of the Nile

Cairo

The Bitter Lakes provided a natural passing point for shipping.

Suez remains the most important of Egypt's ports.

Ferdinand de Lesseps
(1805–94) was a French diplomat descended from a long line of civil servants. It took him 20 years to receive approval for his canal plans.

Construction *of the canal began in a manner that recalled the great building projects of ancient Egypt. Hampered by a lack of drinking water, huge numbers of labourers worked in awful conditions, aided only by camels with baskets.*

DIGGING THE SUEZ CANAL

At the outset, the building of the canal was largely carried out by hand, but acquiring the 20,000 workers needed each month proved extremely difficult. In addition, fatalities were high, running at about 200 per year, and work was periodically halted by waves of infectious diseases, such as cholera. After five years of construction, the Egyptian government discontinued its supply of unhappily drafted peasant labour and work continued with the use of mechanical diggers and a smaller number of labourers. It took ten years to plough through the 96 km (60 miles) of lake and 64 km (40 miles) of land, but finally, in March 1869, the waters of the Mediterranean flowed into the basins of the Bitter Lakes finally bringing into existence a new sea route between Europe and Asia.

The Cairo Marriott Hotel, *built along the lines of Spain's Alhambra as a palace for Empress Eugénie of France, was one of the extravagant projects designed for the opening of the canal.*

BUILDING BOOM

The construction of the Suez Canal inspired a building boom in Cairo where grand new buildings, such as the Khedival Apartments on Sharia Emad al-Din, were constructed to house the various dignitaries invited for the opening celebrations. An opera house was erected for their entertainment and a palace (now the Marriott Hotel) built for the guest of honour Empress Eugénie, wife of Napoleon III of France. A tree-lined road, still in use today, was also laid for the Empress's visit to the Pyramids. The canal also resulted in the founding of three new towns – Port Said, Ismailia and Suez.

Ismailia was the headquarters of the Suez Canal Company.

Lake Timsah

Lake Manzila

Port Said is the Mediterranean gateway to the canal.

Inaugural celebrations *for the canal began on 17 November 1869. Khedive Ismail, escorting the French Empress Eugénie and Austro-Hungarian Emperor Franz Josef in this painting by Mahmoud Said, offered weeks of lavish hospitality to visiting dignitaries.*

The opera *Aida was written by Giuseppe Verdi for the canal opening. However, it was not completed in time and another Verdi opera, Rigoletto, was performed in its place.*

THE SUEZ CRISIS

The cost of building the canal and financing the accompanying lavish celebrations bankrupted Egypt. Ismail was forced to sell his shares and full ownership passed to the French and British who kept control over the canal for the next 80 years. When, in the wake of Egyptian independence, President Nasser nationalized the canal in 1956, Britain and France, in collusion with Israel, invaded the canal zone in an attempt to take it back by force. In the face of widespread international condemnation they were forced to retreat, leaving the canal in Egyptian hands.

President Gamal Abdel Nasser (1918–70)

British troops at Port Said during the 1956 invasion

Early 20th-century photograph of members of the British elite at Shepheard's Hotel in Cairo

BRITISH OCCUPATION

When Egypt's soaring national debt rendered the country unable to repay British loans, Britain invaded. The occupation, motivated by the need to protect British interests in the Suez Canal, was intended as a temporary policing measure. Although the *khedives*, the heirs of Mohammed Ali, remained on the throne, all real power was held by the British.

With the outbreak of World War I in 1914, Britain took an even firmer hold on Egyptian affairs. The demands of the British war effort fell hard on the country's peasants and popular discontent spread. At the end of the war, Egyptian demands for autonomy, led by nationalist leader Saad Zaghloul, were curtly dismissed, causing the 1919 rebellion. The violence of the rebellion forced Britain to proclaim the end of its protectorate and recognize Egypt as an independent state with a hereditary monarch, King Fuad I, sixth son of Khedive Ismail. Despite

Nasser receives a hero's welcome after the successful coup of 1952

the king, Britain still controlled Egypt's legal system, communications, foreign policy and the Suez Canal. During World War II, Egypt was vital to British war aims. At El-Alamein the Eighth Army under Montgomery repulsed Rommel's Afrika Korps, changing the course of the war in North Africa.

1952 REVOLUTION

At the conclusion of the war, the British withdrew most of their soldiers from the country, but new forces in Egyptian politics were demanding nothing less than full independence. The disaster of the 1948 War, in which the Egyptian army was defeated by the newly-formed state of Israel, contributed to the mood for independence. Fuad's son, King Farouk, who was rumoured to have made a fortune by selling faulty equipment to Egyptian troops, was blamed for the disaster. In 1952 Egyptian anger resulted in "Black Saturday", when European businesses in central Cairo were torched by rampaging mobs. Six months of rioting and political instability followed until, on 23 July, a group calling itself the Free Officers, led by Gamal Abdel Nasser, seized power in a bloodless coup. The monarchy was deposed, King Farouk went into exile and Mohammed Neguib, an army general, became prime minister, commander-in-chief and, later, president. He was deposed in 1954 by Nasser, who succeeded him first as prime minister,

TIMELINE

Howard Carter exiting the tomb of Tutankhamun

1919 Nationwide anti-British riots

1922 King Fuad I is made king by the British

1942 Battle of El-Alamein, a turning point in Allied fortunes in WWII

1900	1920	1940

1922 Howard Carter discovers tomb of Tutankhamun

1935 King Farouk succeeds his father, King Fuad I

1952 Free Officers seize power, paving the way for an independent republic then in 1956 as president. Nasser's ideology of socialism, allied with Arab nationalism, made him a hero to the masses. During the Suez Crisis of 1956 he took on the combined forces of Britain, France and Israel, who invaded following Nasser's announcement of his intention to nationalize the Suez Canal. The invaders were forced to withdraw after intervention by the United Nations and America.

This golden era for Nasser was brought to an abrupt end in 1967, with the shattering defeat of Egypt in the Six Day War with Israel. Nasser died a broken man three years later.

Former US President Bill Clinton and President Mubarak during the Middle East peace talks in 2000

SADAT AND MUBARAK

Nasser's successor was his vice-president, Anwar Sadat. Sadat turned his back on his predecessor's socialist policies and encouraged private and foreign investment. On 6 October 1973, he launched a surprise attack on Israeli lines along the Suez. This early military success, though quickly reversed, paved the way for peace talks that culminated in the signing of the Camp David peace treaty in 1979.

Sadat was assassinated in 1981 by Islamic extremists and was succeeded by his vice-president, Hosni Mubarak. Mubarak inherited an ailing economy caused by overpopulation and lack of arable land. Economic recovery was slow and for much of Mubarak's reign Egypt was ostracized by the other Arab nations because of its peace with Israel. In 1992 Boutros Boutros-Ghali became the first African and Arab Secretary-General of the United Nations, a position he held until 1996.

During the 1990s, Egypt was rocked by Islamist-inspired violence, including fatal attacks on tourists. Visitor numbers plummeted, seriously damaging the economy. Today, however, unrest is largely confined to Middle Egypt. The country still maintains a cool peace with Israel and plays a key role as a peace broker in the Middle East crisis.

Lasers and fireworks illuminate the Giza Pyramids on Millennium night

Anwar Sadat (1918–81)

1956 Newly elected as president, Nasser provokes Suez Crisis

1981 Sadat is assassinated and succeeded by Hosni Mubarak

2000 International coverage of Millennium celebrations at the Pyramids

| 1960 | 1980 | 2000 |

1967 Defeat by Israel in the Six Day War

1970 Nasser dies and is succeeded by Anwar Sadat

1988 Egyptian novelist Naguib Mahfouz wins Nobel Prize for Literature

1999 Egyptian scientist Ahmed Zewail wins Nobel Prize in Chemistry

Naguib Mahfouz

CAIRO
AREA BY AREA

Cairo at a Glance

Cairo is one of the most densely populated cities in the world. Though its suburbs have spilled over onto the Nile's west bank, its top attractions lie on the eastern bank. Central Cairo is the heart of the modern city and boasts some fine 19th-century architecture. Gezira and Rhoda islands, cooled by the Nile, seem quieter than the centre, while Old Cairo's Roman and early Christian history predates the capital itself. Islamic Cairo is the highlight of the city; its minarets and domes, bazaars and alleyways recall scenes from *1001 Nights*. Further afield, the suburb of Heliopolis spreads northeast, while Giza and the Pyramids lie to the west.

Cairo Tower

CENTRAL CAIRO
See pp68–85

Cairo Tower (see p84) *offers the best vantage point from which to see the city, as shown above. Amid this modern cityscape, feluccas slide slowly down the Nile, as they have done for thousands of years.*

The Egyptian Museum (see pp74–7) *houses the world's largest collection of ancient Egyptian artifacts. Exhibits include ceramics like this hippopotamus and the wealth of the boy king Tutankhamun.*

The Hanging Church (see pp120–21) *is one of a cluster of churches built in the ancient fortress of Babylon in Old Cairo. This beautiful church's name derives from its position, suspended above two Roman gate towers.*

◁ Surrounded by the domes of Fatimid Cairo, the minaret of the Madrassa and Mausoleum of Sultan Qalawun

Khan al-Khalili (see pp88–90) *is an Aladdin's cave of spices, perfumes, jewellery and souvenirs. The bazaar spills over into the nearby areas which, dotted with some superb Mamluk architecture, have buzzed with similar commercial activity since the Middle Ages.*

The Mosque of al-Azhar (see p91), *at the heart of the Fatimid capital of "Al-Qahira" (Cairo), has been a centre for Islamic scholarship and teaching for more than a thousand years.*

ISLAMIC CAIRO
See pp86–111

| 0 metres | 900 |
| 0 yards | 900 |

The Citadel (see pp104–7) *was built by Salah ad-Din in the 12th century and crowned with the Mosque of Mohammed Ali 700 years later. This stone fortress dominates Cairo's eastern horizon.*

RHODA ISLAND AND OLD CAIRO
See pp112–125

The Mosque of Ibn Tulun (see pp110–11) *is said to be Cairo's oldest mosque. Its size and simple geometric shapes give it an air of tranquillity which contrasts nicely with the eclectic collection of the nearby Gayer-Anderson Museum.*

CENTRAL CAIRO

When Ismail *(see p63)* acceded to power in 1863, Cairo was an almost medieval city with a street plan little changed in 500 years. But the khedive, educated in France, set about transforming his capital into a modern, fashionable city that could compare with Paris. Rather than try to impose order on the existing city, he chose to drain the marshy flood plains between it and the Nile and start again. His creation is the heart of Central Cairo. Fine 19th-century European architecture – albeit battered and worn – is the backdrop to thoroughly Middle Eastern streetlife, with the placid Nile offering a refuge from the noise and crush of people and cars.

Sculpture outside Opera Complex

SIGHTS AT A GLANCE

Areas, Streets & Squares
Corniche el-Nil ⑬
Garden City ⑫
Midan Opera and
   Midan Ataba ⑦
Midan Ramses ⑥

Midan Tahrir ②
Sharia Qasr el-Nil ⑤
Sharia Talaat Harb ④
Zamalek ⑲

Museums & Historic Buildings
Abdeen Palace Museum ⑨
American University in Cairo ③
Beit as-Sennari ⑩
Cairo Tower ⑰
Egyptian Museum pp74–7 ①
Mahmoud Khalil Museum ⑮
Manial Palace ⑭

Mausoleum of Saad
   Zaghloul ⑪
Museum of Islamic Art ⑧
Opera House Complex ⑯

Walks
River Promenade ⑱

GETTING AROUND
Walking is the best way to experience Central Cairo. Taxis are the most convenient way to travel if it is too far to walk. The riverboat, or alternatively the Metro, with stations at Midan Tahrir (Sadat Station) and Midan Ramses (Mubarak Station), are useful for getting to Old Cairo *(see pp346–7)* and Heliopolis.

KEY
▨	Street-by-Street map *pp70–71*
⊠	Post office
Ⓜ	Metro station
⚓	Felucca hire
🚤	Riverbus terminal
🚌	Bus station
🚆	Train station

◁ **The faded grandeur of a typical apartment balcony near Midan Ataba** *(see p78)*

Street-by-Street: Around Midan Tahrir

Overrun by traffic and far from pretty, Midan Tahrir is the hub of Central Cairo. All routes lead here and within just a few days most visitors become very familiar with its Brutalist landmarks: the Nile Hilton Hotel, the Arab League Building and the Mogamma, home to 18,000 bureaucrats. Brighter spots include the dusky pink Egyptian Museum and the elegant curve of façades between Sharia Qasr el-Nil and Sharia Talaat Harb – the location of airline offices, travel agents, souvenir shops and cafés.

Ramses Station

SHARIA CHAMPOLLION

SHARIA RAMSES

Bus Station

KUBRI 6 OCTOBER

Zamalek

CORNICHE EL-NIL

Central Cairo
Cairo's bustling modern centre is flanked to the west by the tranquil waters of the Nile.

★ **Egyptian Museum**
The museum has the greatest collection of Pharaonic treasures in the world and is one of Cairo's most popular sights ❶

The Nile Hilton Hotel *(see p72)* was built in 1959 and was the first modern hotel to be erected in Egypt.

Gezira

| 0 metres | 130 |
| 0 yards | 130 |

KEY

- - - Suggested route

STAR SIGHTS

★ Egyptian Museum

Corniche el-Nil
This boat-lined boulevard is wide and shady and the city's favourite place for an evening stroll ❸

Groppi's café
(see p72)

CENTRAL CAIRO

ISLAMIC CAIRO

RHODA ISLAND & OLD CAIRO

LOCATOR MAP
See Street Finder Map 5

Sharia Qasr el-Nil

The shops along Qasr el-Nil are filled with glitzy paraphernalia. The street is situated in the heart of the financial district where some fine architecture can still be seen **5**

Felfela restaurant
(see p292)

Sharia Talaat Harb

Central Cairo's main street is a bustling, thoroughfare filled with colourful hoardings, shops and cafés **4**

Midan Tahrir

The cafés located on the south and east sides of Midan Tahrir are ideal spots to break during sightseeing or to simply sit and people-watch **2**

Mogamma Building

Omar Makram Mosque

Semiramis Intercontinental Hotel *(see p271)*

The Arab League Building, meeting place for Arab world leaders.

American University in Cairo

The Neo-Islamic-style building that currently houses the American University will be opened to visitors as an Islamic museum when the university relocates in 2008 **3**

Two Cairenes, dressed in traditional garments called *galabiyyas*, in Midan Tahrir

Egyptian Museum ❶

See pp74–7.

Midan Tahrir ❷

Map 5 B4. Ⓜ *Sadat.*

Midan Tahrir was not always the dauntingly urban square that it is today. Until the 19th century, the area was a swampy plain, flooded each summer by the Nile. When Khedive Ismail (1863–79) came to power, however, he had the land drained as part of his grand scheme to transform Cairo by building a European-style city of tree-lined boulevards and grand public squares.

The Qasr el-Nil (Palace of the Nile) was built beside the river, fronted by an extensive plaza named Midan Ismailia (Ismail's Square). However, Ismail's glory was short-lived: his ambitious scheme drained not only the swamps, but also the state coffers, as Egyptian debt to European lenders spiralled out of control.

In 1882, the British stepped in to take control *(see p59)*, requisitioning Qasr el-Nil as their headquarters, and later as the barracks for their army of occupation. Overcrowded with Allied soldiers during World War II, the building gained a reputation for the remarkable tenacity of its bedbugs. The barracks were evacuated at the end of the war and the palace was demolished. In 1959, the Nile Hilton Hotel was built on the site – the first modern international hotel to be built in Egypt. The

1952 revolution saw all traces of the old regime wiped away, including the name of Ismail, and the largest square in the city was reincarnated as Midan Tahrir (Liberation Square).

Midan Tahrir is the closest Cairo gets to having a centre, and several major airlines have their offices here, along with tourist agencies, the Omar Makram Mosque which serves as a venue for state funerals, and the enormous monolithic structure of the Mogamma Building. Housing around 18,000 civil servants, this is where foreign tourists have to go if they need to extend their visas.

American University in Cairo ❸

Qasr al-Aini, Midan Tahrir. **Map** 5 B4. Ⓜ *Sadat.* ◯ *8:30am–5pm Sun–Thur, 10:30am–5pm Sat.*

Although overshadowed by an ugly concrete wing, the core building of what is now the American University in Cairo (AUC) is built in an attractive Neo-Islamic style. Attending the private AUC is Egypt's equivalent of an Ivy-League education and beyond the means of most Egyptians. Visitors are admitted, on proof of identity, to the excellent bookstore and art exhibitions in the Sony Gallery.

Flags fly above the Neo-Islamic façade of the American University

The AUC, which has over 5,000 full-time students, is due to move to a larger, purpose-built site in New Cairo by 2008. This building will then become an Islamic museum.

Shar Hashamaim Synagogue, near Sharia Talaat Harb

Sharia Talaat Harb ❹

Map 5 C3. Ⓜ *Sadat.*

Running from Midan Tahrir to Midan Orabi, Sharia Talaat Harb is quintessential modern Cairo. Its pavements are permanently crowded and the road is jammed with horn-honking traffic. As you walk along, music blares from cars on one side and shops on the other, while the air is heavy with car fumes mingled with the smells of cooking and incense. Rising above this pandemonium is some grand architecture, especially around Midan Talaat Harb, where Parisian-style buildings dwarf the statue of Talaat Harb, founder of the National Bank.

On the square is **Groppi's**, a tearoom that once supplied confectionery to the royalty of Great Britain; the only clues to its more glamorous past are the delightful, spangly mosaics around the entrance. More memories of a golden era now past are evoked by the Art Deco lines of the

PARIS BY THE NILE

Inspired by Baron Haussmann's plans for the modernization of Paris in the mid-19th century, Khedive Ismail turned to foreign architects to realize his dream of a modern Cairo. Drawing on Renaissance, Baroque and even Gothic styles, their buildings were adorned with wrought-iron grilles, plaster mouldings, carved foliage, cherubs and angels, plus some local flavouring in the form of scarabs and sphinxes. Later buildings began to take more account of Egypt's heritage, incorporating Islamic motifs such as striped stonework and crenellations. Downtown streets, including Qasr el-Nil and the intersecting Mohammed Farid and Emad ad-Din, still contain a wealth of these beautiful buildings.

Kubri Qasr el-Nil (Qasr el-Nil Bridge), part of the European-style Cairo planned by Khedive Ismail

---

Metro Cinema, which opened in 1939 with *Gone With the Wind*. It now screens low-budget action movies – fun to attend for the experience of Egyptian cinema-going, where the bad guys are dispatched to a round of applause.

Little mention is made, in the current climate of Arab-Israeli tension, of Egypt's own Jewish community. However, in Sharia Adly (which joins Sharia Talaat Harb beside the Metro Cinema) the Babylonian-style Shar Hashamaim Synagogue is evidence of their historical presence. It can only be viewed from the outside.

Talaat Harb terminates in another elegant square, named after the nationalist politician Ahmed Orabi who sought political reform in 1881. Off to the east is pedestrianized Sharia Alfy, full of small bars and restaurants, including the excellent Alfi Bey *(see p290).*

Sharia Qasr el-Nil ❺

Map 5.C3. **M** *Sadat.*

A frenetically busy shopping street running in front of the Nile Hilton Hotel in Midan Tahrir to Midan Opera, Qasr el-Nil is taken up almost exclusively with shop windows that display the bright-est and gaudiest of goods. The streets on either side of Sharia Qasr el-Nil traditionally constituted Cairo's financial district. At the junction with Sharia ash-Sharif is the National Bank of Egypt building. Here, too, is the Bourse, or stock exchange, which is enjoying a new lease of life since the government undertook a programme of privatization in the late 1990s.

Statue of Mustafa Kamel overlooking his square

The boom in trading was reflected in a renovation programme that covered a huge 60,000 sq m (645,000 sq ft) section of downtown Cairo. The area around the Bourse has been pedestrianized and many of the roads are now paved. These walkways are also furnished with 19th-century-style lamp posts, along with flower beds, greenery and palm trees. Some of the buildings in this area have also been renovated, including the lovely Trieste Insurance Building on the corner with Sharia Sherif. This was designed by the Italian architect Antonio Lascaic (1856–1946), who was responsible for many of central Cairo's most beautiful Belle Epoque buildings.

Sharia Qasr el-Nil crosses over Midan Mustafa Kamel, named after the founder of the Egyptian Nationalist Party, formed in 1907. Kamel was an early opponent of British occupation and his statue looks out over the square.

Sharia Qasr el-Nil continues past some jewellers' shops and a few outlets selling street signs (you can have your name put on one) to emerge on Sharia al-Gumhuriyya. This leads into Midan Opera *(see p78),* which was once one of Cairo's grandest squares, but is now occupied by a vast car park and the derelict Continental-Savoy hotel.

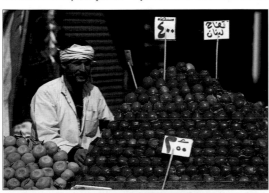

Small fruit stall set up in an alleyway off Sharia Talaat Harb

Egyptian Museum ●

Gold bracelet from Tanis

Founded by a Frenchman, Auguste Mariette (1821–81), Egypt's first national museum of Pharaonic antiquities opened in 1863. It quickly outgrew two homes before settling in these premises in 1902. A bigger museum, due to open in 2011, is being built in Giza. More than 120,000 items are on display here, with another 150,000 reputedly stored in the basement. Pride of the collection are the artifacts from Tutankhamun's tomb, but there are great pieces from every period of ancient Egyptian history, from the Narmer Palette, dating from around 3100 BC, through to the Graeco-Roman Fayoum Portraits of the 2nd century AD.

GALLERY GUIDE

The museum has two floors. Artifacts on the ground floor are organized in a roughly chronological order, running clockwise from the entrance and atrium, while the first-floor collection is arranged by themes. The central hall houses large monumental statuary.

Royal Tombs of Tanis

Middle Kingdom Models

Yuya and Thuyu collection

Animal mummies

★ **Royal Mummy Room**
In respectful silence, the mummies lie in state, arranged chronologically around the room in an anti-clockwise order.

First floor

Ground floor

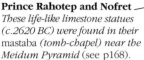

Prince Rahotep and Nofret
These life-like limestone statues (c.2620 BC) were found in their mastaba *(tomb-chapel) near the Meidum Pyramid (see p168).*

STAR EXHIBITS

- ★ Tutankhamun Galleries
- ★ Royal Mummy Room
- ★ Amarna Room
- ★ Statue of Ka-Aper

Triad of Menkaure

Entrance

★ **Statue of Ka-Aper**
This skilfully carved statue's eyes have rims made of copper, whites of opaque quartz and corneas of clear rock crystal, drilled and filled with black paste.

★ **Tutankhamun Galleries**
This life-sized gold mask is just one in a collection of 1,700 items from the tomb of the boy king.

VISITORS' CHECKLIST

Midan Tahrir, Cairo.
Map 5 B3. M Sadat. 🚌 🚌 to Midan Tahrir. **Tel** (02) 578 2448, (02) 578 2452. ◯ 9am–6:30pm daily (last admission 6pm); 9am–3pm during Ramadan. 💳 📷 ♿ Ø 🖥 📷 Left luggage facilities available.
Royal Mummy Room ◯ same hours as main museum. 📷

Ancient Egyptian Jewellery
Made with beads of gold and lapis lazuli, this c.11th-century BC neck-lace is one of several examples of the royal jewellers' exquisite skill.

The Fayoum Portaits
are remarkably lifelike studies of Egyptians from the Graeco-Roman period.

Tutankhamun's Throne
On the back of the lavishly decorated throne is this portrayal of Tutan-khamun and his wife under the rays of Aten, the sun.

★ **Amarna Room**
During Akhenaten's 15-year rule, not only was the old religion abandoned (see p175) but also its art. A new style developed which depicted figures with elongated heads (as in this bust of the king) and protruding bellies.

Colossus of Amenhotep III and Queen Tiye

KEY

☐ Old Kingdom	☐ Tutankhamun Galleries
☐ Middle Kingdom	☐ Royal Mummy Room
☐ New Kingdom	☐ Middle Kingdom Models
☐ Late Period	☐ Miscellaneous exhibits
☐ Coffins and Sarcophagi	☐ Non-exhibition space

Exploring the Egyptian Museum

Tuya's golden funeral mask

While not particularly large, the museum is densely packed with artifacts and anybody with more than a passing interest in ancient Egypt will need more than one visit to take everything in. When the museum is busy, long queues can form outside the room holding Tutankhamun's funeral mask. To view the mask at some leisure, it is best to visit the museum just as it opens or late in the afternoon and make straight for the Tutankhamun Galleries, visiting the rest of the museum afterwards. Independent guides tout for business at the entrance to the museum and, as the labelling inside is sparse, it may be worthwhile hiring one.

Khufu, builder of the Great Pyramid. The room also contains an alabaster canopic chest that was used to store the internal organs of the deceased. The chest was found in Hetepheres's tomb at Giza, with the remains of its contents still visible.

NEW KINGDOM

Ancient Egypt's New Kingdom represented an artistic golden age, but many of the best pieces are housed at the Luxor Museum (see p187). However, Room 3 contains fine artifacts from Amarna, the short-lived capital of the 'heretic king' Akhenaten (see p175). Here, the sleek muscular forms of traditional Pharaonic art are replaced by swollen bellies, heavy thighs and almost cartoon-like elongated faces. This is particularly evident on a set of reliefs showing the king and his young family worshipping the sun god, Aten, whose solar rays end in strange hook-like hands. One of the notable exceptions to this style is an unfinished, sculpted head of Nefertiti, Akhenaten's wife, which displays a stunning and wholly human beauty.

Head of Queen Nefertiti (c.1340 BC)

Wall frieze, known as the Meidum Geese, painted on plaster (c.2620 BC)

OLD KINGDOM

All the museum's great pieces of monumental statuary are housed on the ground floor. These start in the museum's atrium with King Djoser's empty-eyed statue carved in limestone nearly 5,000 years ago. It was discovered at Saqqara (see pp162–4) in his *serdab*, a small sealed room beside his Step Pyramid. Other Old Kingdom highlights on the ground floor include a statue of Khafre, builder of the middle pyramid at Giza, in Room 42. He is seated on his throne with the wings of the falcon god Horus wrapped protectively around his head, symbolizing the divine sanction of the king's rule (the term *pharaoh* was rarely used before 1500 BC). Also in Room 42, the figure of Ka-Aper, a 5th-Dynasty official, puts his left foot forward in a stylized pose that suggests movement and, along with his gleaming eyes, brings the statue to life. Further examples of the vitality of the ancient artists are exhibited in Room 32 in the lifelike, seated

statues of Prince Rahotep and Princess Nofret, whose real hairline can be seen poking out from under her wig, and in the carefully observed Meidum Geese panels, which were discovered at Fayoum (see p162). Room 37 contains a touchingly personal collection of alabaster ornaments and bedroom furniture, including a golden four-poster bed, an armchair and a jewellery box all of which belonged to Hetepheres, the mother of

18th-Dynasty relief of Amenhotep III riding over bound Nubian captives

Tutankhamun's carved throne inlaid with gold and ebony

TUTANKHAMUN GALLERIES

Commencing with the two life-size statues of the young king that stood guard at the entrance to his tomb, the Tutankhamun Galleries fill the upper floor's east and north wings. There are some 1,700 items on display, ranging from board games and hunting implements to couches and beds and, of course, the fabulous death mask. A great glass cabinet is filled with some of Tutankhamun's *shabtis*. These were small effigies of the deceased that were buried with the body to carry out any tasks that the deceased might be asked to do in the afterlife. In all, 413 *shabtis* were found in the tomb; one for each day of the year, plus foremen. Nearby is the dazzling royal "lion" throne, named after the golden lion heads and legs on each side. Aside from the craftsmanship, this throne is of great interest in that it reveals influences of the "Amarna period" when the Aten cult still thrived *(see p175)*. The Aten sun-disk and rays resemble reliefs from Amarna, and the pharaoh's name from this period, Tutankhaten, is inscribed on the back of the throne.

One of Tutankhamun's gilded fans

In the north wing is the alabaster canopic chest holding four jars with Tutankhamun-head stoppers. This stands in front of Room 3, which holds Tutankhamun's solid gold death mask and the two inner coffins, one of gilded wood set with semi-precious gems, the other cast of solid gold. The young king's body lies in its tomb in the Valley of the Kings on the west bank of the Nile.

MIDDLE KINGDOM MODELS

The daily life of the less-exalted ancient Egyptian is well illustrated in several rooms in the west wing, which hold finely detailed 11th-Dynasty models of domestic scenes. These include a weaver's workshop, a house with a garden and pool and a set of seated scribes recording their master's cattle. The models provide a wealth of detailed information about Egyptian life, as well as reflecting an interest in factual artistic representation. These models were found in a tomb at Deir al-Bahri on the west bank at Thebes *(see pp196–7)*.

Model servant girl (c.2010 BC)

ROYAL MUMMY ROOM

There is a separate fee to see the mummies, which is payable at the ticket desk at the top of the southeast stairs. This allows the experience of coming face to face with some legendary kings such as Tuthmosis II, Seti I and the mighty Ramses II. The good condition of the bodies belies the fact that they all died more than 3,000 years ago. The beak-nosed face of Ramses II barely resembles his sleek bust downstairs in the New Kingdom galleries.

MISCELLANEOUS EXHIBITS

In addition to the human mummies, the museum holds a fascinating collection of neatly parcelled animals in Rooms 53 and 54. The ancient Egyptians revered certain animals, for example the ibis and baboon were sacred to the god Thoth, the crocodile sacred to Sobek, and cats sacred to Bastet. In the regions where these cults thrived, great numbers of these mummified creatures have been unearthed at sanctuaries associated with such gods. Most recently, tombs full of thousands of mummified birds were discovered at Saqqara.

Across the hall, in Room 43, are 18th-Dynasty funerary artifacts from the tomb of Yuya and Tuya, the great grandparents of Tutankhamun who were buried on the west bank at Thebes. Discovered in 1905, the tomb is overshadowed by Tutankhamun and his treasures, the beautiful sarcophagi and other lustrous items here undeservedly ignored by most visitors.

Better known are the Graeco-Roman funerary paintings known as Fayoum Portraits, after the oasis where many of them were discovered *(see pp168–9)*; Room 14 contains a collection of these haunting faces, along with some of the mummies to which they were attached.

Two relatively new galleries devoted to the Royal Tombs of Tanis and Ancient Egyptian Jewellery contain some of the museum's finest small pieces. Tanis was a major city in the Delta during the 21st and 22nd Dynasties *(see p237)*. In 1939 archaeologists found a series of intact royal tombs that contained a marvellous haul of death masks, coffins and intricate jewellery. One of the items, the coffin of Psusennes I is interesting not just for its striking hawk's head but also for the fact that it is made of solid silver. Rare in Egypt, silver had to be imported, making it a highly prized commodity.

Midan Ramses ⑥

Map 2 D3. Ⓜ *Mubarak.*

Marking the northernmost extent of central Cairo, Midan Ramses is the gateway to the city. In ancient times, when the river followed a different course, a port here served the Pharaonic city of Heliopolis. When Salah ad-Din (Saladin), ruler of Egypt, refortified Cairo in the 12th century, he built a great gate here, the Bab al-Hadid, or Iron Gate, which remained standing until 1847, when it was demolished to make way for the new railway station.

Mahattat Ramses (Ramses Station) is still Cairo's main rail terminus and the place to catch trains for all destinations, such as Alexandria, Aswan and Luxor. The **Egyptian National Railway Museum**, housed at the eastern end of the station, has a fascinating collection of engines, ornate carriages and numerous models and plans.

The 9m- (30ft-) high colossus of Ramses II found at Memphis in the 1950s used to stand in the centre of the square. In the late 1990s, the authorities finally acknowledged the damaging effects of pollution on the statue, and the colossus was returned to Memphis, for display in a new open-air museum. It was replaced by a

Former Tiring department store designed by Oscar Horowitz in 1911, Midan Ataba

replica, but that has also been moved now, to the Egyptian Museum in Medan Al-Remaya. The square is currently undergoing reconstruction.

🏛 Egyptian National Railway Museum
Midan Ramses. **Map** 2 D3.
Ⓜ *Mubarak.* **Tel** (02) 576 3793.
◯ 8am–2pm Tue–Sun. 📷

Midan Opera and Midan Ataba ⑦

Map 6 D2 & E2. Ⓜ *Ataba.*

In just five months in 1868, labour gangs constructed a completely new opera house for the inaugural celebrations marking the opening of the Suez Canal. To mark the occasion, the Italian composer Giuseppe Verdi had been commissioned to write a new opera, *Aida,* but he was unable to finish it in time, so the new Cairo Opera House opened instead with a performance of Verdi's *Rigoletto.*

Modelled on Milan's La Scala and built entirely of wood, the Opera House was the loveliest landmark in central Cairo – until it was burnt to the ground in 1971. A less lovely multistorey car park was built on the site, but the square is still known as Midan Opera. In the middle of the paved plaza is a statue of Ibrahim Pasha (1789–1848), general and viceroy of Egypt, who successfully campaigned in Syria in 1832–3.

Just beyond Midan Opera is Midan Ataba, which forms a dividing point between so-called "European" Cairo to the west and the old medieval city, known as Islamic Cairo, to the east. From this point, the streets get narrower, the buildings smaller and more decrepit. The square itself is a knot of snarled traffic, but

Clothes stall in front of mosque in Midan Ataba

in the surrounding streets are various markets. To the north-west is an extensive area of secondhand bookstalls; there is a clothing market to the northeast, electronics to the southeast and, in the southwest, a few stalls sell cards and stationery. The latter run, appropriately enough, in front of the central post office, an old building with an attractive courtyard and an annexe where the **National Postal Museum** is housed. Egypt was one of the first countries in the world to issue stamps (1866). The museum is small, but there is a lot crammed into the space, including models of carriages and delivery bikes, old mail boxes and a vast collection of stamps.

Also on Midan Ataba is the **Cairo Puppet Theatre**, which puts on regular colourful puppet shows for children and adults.

Ibrahim Pasha's statue, Midan Opera

🏛 National Postal Museum
Midan Ataba. Ⓜ *Ataba.*
◯ 9am–1pm Sat–Thu.

🎭 Cairo Puppet Theatre
Midan Ataba. Ⓜ *Ataba.* **Tel** (02) 591 0954. ◯ Oct–May: show at 11am Tue–Sun, also 6:30pm Thu & Fri.

Museum of Islamic Art ⑧

Sharia Port Said. **Map** 6 E3. Ⓜ *Mohammed Naguib.* **Tel** (02) 390 9930.
◯ 8:30am–4pm daily (9am–3pm Ramadan). ● 11:30am–1pm Fri. 📷

Often overlooked by the crowds that throng the Egyptian Museum, this little-visited place was renovated in 2004 and contains some beautiful pieces of medieval decorative art salvaged from the houses, mosques and palaces of Islamic Cairo at the instigation of Khedive Tawfiq. Most striking of all are the large *mashrabiyya* screens, which are constructed of thousands of individual pieces of wood. Still seen today in many old buildings, such screens shaded rooms from the sun, at the same time admitting cooling breezes. They were also important as they allowed the women of the house to look out without themselves being seen.

The museum houses other examples of creative woodworking taken from mosques around the city, including huge ivory-inlaid doors, carved friezes and a fine 14th-century *minbar* (pulpit).

Three ornamental fountains provide the best examples of another speciality of Egyptian craftsmen – inlaid stone and marblework. These pieces, dating from the Mamluk and Ottoman periods, would have decorated the reception halls of rich merchants' houses. Look out, also, for enamelled glass lamps; these beautiful objects, many of

them decorated with stylized Arabic lettering, would have been suspended by chains from the ceilings of mosques. Other exhibits include Persian and Turkish ceramics, illuminated manuscripts and books, and carpets and rugs.

Cannon yard of the Abdeen Palace Museum

A manuscript in the Museum of Islamic Art

Abdeen Palace Museum 9

Sharia al-Gamaa. **Map** 6 D4. M *Mohammed Naguib.* **Tel** *(02) 391 0042.* 10am–2pm Sat–Thu *(10am–1pm Ramadan).*

Abdeen is a former royal palace, part of which is now open to the public as a museum that embraces several collections. These include displays of weaponry, presidential gifts, royal acquisitions and silver plate.

From the time of Salah ad-Din in the 12th century, Egypt was ruled from the safety of the Citadel *(see pp104–7)*, but tradition was broken 700 years later by Khedive Ismail, who

ordered a new European-style residence to be built on the edge of his new city. Designed by the French architect Rousseau, the 500-roomed palace was begun in 1863 and took over ten years to complete. Over the years, it was constantly remodelled and expanded, with the addition, in the 1930s, of a Byzantine throne room.

Following the overthrow of King Farouk in 1952, the Abdeen Palace was vacated, but later put to its present use as a venue for receiving visiting heads of state.

In the late 1980s, President Mubarak ordered that the palace be restored. The work took longer than anticipated because the palace was hit by the 1992 earthquake. The museum was inaugurated by the president in 1998.

Entered via neat gardens at the rear of the palace, the museum occupies a complex of unadorned halls; the more extravagantly decorated state rooms remain off-limits to the public. A lot of space is given over to the collection of guns, swords and daggers, many of which were gifts to Egypt's various khedives, kings and presidents. There are also displays of medals and other decorations, as well as a room of awards and gifts presented to President Mubarak. A silver-ware section contains a display of silver, crystal and *objets d'art* belonging to the family of Pasha Mohammed Ali.

Centrally located in the museum is the fountain court-yard, where the fountain is surrounded by the busts of Mohammed Ali, Khedive Ismail and King Fuad I.

Entrance to Abdeen Palace, museum and gardens

Beit as-Sennari ⑩

Harat Monge, off Sharia Khayrat.
Map 4 D2. **Tel** (02) 391 5565. **M** Saad
Zaghloul. ○ 9:30am–3pm Sat–Wed.

Napoleon invaded Egypt in
1798, bringing with him an
army of scientists, scholars
and artists to establish a French
cultural base in the country.
Over the next few years, they
carried out the first European
study of Egypt and published
their findings in the *Description
de l'Egypte (see p20)*.

This *beit* (house), which
was built in 1794 for Ibrahim
Katkhuda as-Sennari, an
occultist from Sudan, was
requisitioned by Napoleon
and housed many of his
artists during the occupation.
It has some fine wooden
mashrabiyya
screens, an
attractive court-
yard and a
well-preserved
complex of
rooms. After
extensive renov-
ation, the house
has reopened as
the Institute for
Applied Arts, with
displays of glass-
ware, textiles, and
pottery and other
work by local artists.

**Side view of *mashrabiyya* bay on
first floor of Beit as-Sennari**

Mausoleum of Saad Zaghloul ⑪

Sharia Mansour. **Map** 5 B5.
M Saad Zaghloul.

Saad Zaghloul (1853–1927)
spent most of his life trying to
get the British out of Egypt.
He became a national spokes-
man for self-rule and held the
post of prime minister for a
time. Zaghloul was highly
respected, even by the foreign
governors he opposed, and
shortly after his death this vast
mausoleum was erected in his
honour. Built of granite, the
mausoleum's design echoes
that of a Pharaonic temple,
with an outward-curving
cornice and entrance flanked
by two great lotus pillars.

**Elegant, curving façade of a building in Garden
City flanked by tree-lined pavements**

It is also possible to visit
Zaghloul's house, **Beit al-
Umma** (House of the Nation),
which is just a short distance
west. Most of the rooms have
been preserved with Zaghloul's
original furnishings and
belongings still in place.

🏛 **Beit al-Umma**
Sharia Darih Zaghloul. **M** Sadat.
○ daily. 🖼

Garden City ⑫

Map 5 A5. **M** Sadat.

Garden City, one of the most
attractive and tranquil of
Cairo's quarters, was created
by the British in the early
years of the 20th century as
a leafy green suburb, where
officers and administrators
could pretend they were still
living in rural England, far
from the dusty, dry streets
of Cairo. The roads
were designed to
curve and wind like
country lanes but,
instead of England's
oaks and beeches,
leafy coverage was
provided by native
palms, rubber and
mango trees.

As well as housing
the British, the villas
of this exclusive
suburb were home
to Egypt's most
prominent doctors,
lawyers, bankers
and politicians.

Today, Garden
City suffers from an
onslaught of concrete high-
rise buildings, but it remains
a very desirable address: the
British, American and several
other embassies are located
here. Garden City still offers
a welcome respite from the
hustle of Cairo, and a walk
through the area reveals a
wonderfully eclectic array
of architecture, including the
building known as **Grey
Pillars** – the British Army's
headquarters in Egypt during
World War II. This can still be
seen on Sharia as-Suraya.

Corniche el-Nil ⑬

Map 5 A4. **M** Sadat.

Although it is one of the
city's busiest highways, the
Corniche el-Nil is also where
Cairo comes to relax. In a city
chronically short of public
green spaces, this is as close

View across the Nile from the Corniche north of Rhoda Island

◁ Sharia Ramses and Kubri 6 October winding their way into the heart of Downtown Cairo as it gets to a park. Each evening, the wide pavements of the Corniche are packed with promenading families, roaming college kids, and young lovers, all enjoying the pleasant water-borne breezes and the sense of open space that the river provides.

An even better way to enjoy the river is on a *felucca*, one of the small triangular-sailed boats used on the Nile since antiquity. The boats (which can be hired by the hour) and their captains gather at various landing stages, including one opposite the Semiramis Hotel and another at Dokdok, opposite the northern tip of Rhoda Island. Lazily scudding about the river while the sun drops towards the skyline makes for a calming end to a hectic day of sightseeing.

Façade of Cairo's Mahmoud Khalil Museum

Regnault's painting of a fleeing Mamluk, in the Manial Palace

Manial Palace ⑭

Sharia al-Saray, Rhoda. **Map** 3 B2.
Tel (02) 531 5587. Ⓜ *Sayyida Zeinab.* ◯ 8:30am–4pm daily. 🖼

Located on the northern tip of the island of Rhoda, the Manial Palace is a former royal residence, now open to the public. It was built for Prince Mohammed Ali Tawfiq, a descendant of Egypt's famed ruler Mohammed Ali, and the uncle of King Farouk. The palace was constructed between 1899 and 1929 and is a curious ensemble of five separate buildings, executed in a variety of Islamic styles.

Beside the mock-Medieval gateway is a Moorish tower attached to the Turkish-tiled Mosque of Mohammed Ali. Nearby, the building called the Hunting Museum has a somewhat grim display of over 300 mounted gazelle heads strung along its narrow gallery.

The eccentrically contrived design extends to the interiors. The Main Residence is a series of rooms decorated in a mixture of styles. The Syrian room has an elaborately painted wooden ceiling, an Ottoman room is furnished with turquoise ceramics from Anatolia, while the Egyptian corner has windows featuring *mashrabiyya* screens. Also included among the valuable displays is a painting of a Mamluk and his mount leaping over the Citadel walls. The painting, by Henri Regnault (1843–71), hangs in the Blue Salon, and depicts an alleged incident that took place during Mohammed Ali's suppression of the Mamluks' 1826 revolt.

Behind the residence, through the banyans, palms and Indian rubber trees, is the Throne Hall, complete with red carpet, sunburst ceiling and portraits of the prince's illustrious forebears. While Prince Mohammed Ali Tawfiq never attained the throne of Egypt, he was able to hold his own court of aristocratic friends here at Manial Palace.

Detail of Mohammed Ali Mosque, Manial Palace

Mahmoud Khalil Museum ⑮

1 Sharia Kafour, off Sharia Giza.
Map 1 A4. **Tel** (02) 336 2358, (02) 336 2359. Ⓜ *Doqqi.*
◯ 10am–5:30pm Tue–Sun 🖼

It may come as a surprise to learn that Cairo has a fine collection of Impressionist paintings. They were amassed by Mohammed Mahmoud Khalil (1876–1953), a devout Francophile and patron of the arts, and an important figure on the political scene during the 1930s and 40s. Khalil bequeathed his art collection to the state, along with the house – a beautiful late-19th-century Parisian-style mansion overlooking the Nile.

Khalil's paintings were removed when the house was taken over as the official residence during Sadat's term as Egyptian president (1970–81). In the early 1990s, after the assassination of Sadat, however, the house was refurbished and returned to the public domain. The paintings are now on show in cool, temperature-controlled rooms and include three floors of works by Corot, Degas, Ingres, Millet, Monet, Pissarro, Renoir, Sisley and Toulouse-Lautrec. Pride of place goes to Gauguin's *La Vie et la Mort* and Van Gogh's *Genêts et Coquelicots.*

Sculpture in the grounds of the Opera House Complex

Opera House Complex ⑯

Sharia at-Tahrir, Gezira. **Map** 1 A5.
Ⓜ Gezira. **Tel** (02) 739 8144.

A gift to Egypt from Japan, the Opera House Complex was opened in 1988, replacing the original Opera House, which burned down in 1971 (see p78). At the heart of the complex is the **New Cairo Opera House**, where a busy programme of classical music and dance, including visits from international performers such as the Bolshoi Ballet, is staged (see pp310–13).

Situated across the lawn, the **Museum of Egyptian Modern Art** displays the work of Egyptian artists since 1908. One who deserves far greater recognition than he is currently given is Mahmoud Said (1897–1964) (see p244), whose use of warm, glowing colours and subject matter of dignified, proud fellaheen (peasants) is reminiscent of the Mexican artist Diego Rivera (1886–1957). Several of Said's paintings are displayed in the

museum. There are two more art galleries within the grounds: the Nile Gallery and the Hanager Gallery, which both host changing exhibitions of contemporary work.

🏛 Museum of Egyptian Modern Art
Opera House Complex, Gezira.
Ⓜ Gezira. **Tel** (02) 736 6665.
◯ 10am–1pm, 5–9pm daily. ▨

Cairo Tower ⑰

Sharia Hadayek el Zuhreya. **Map** 1 B5. Ⓜ Gezira. **Tel** (02) 735 7187.
◯ 8am–midnight daily. ▨

The southern half of Gezira (the Arabic word for "island") is almost completely flat, making it the ideal site for the 185-m (610-ft) Cairo Tower, which affords excellent views of the city. Built in the late 1950s, the tower takes the form of a latticework tube that fans out slightly at the top, supposedly in imitation of the lotus blossom. From the top, it is possible to make out the easternmost extent of Cairo, where the dark grey buildings run up against the cliff face of the Muqattam Hills. Looking to the west, the Pyramids mark the limits of the city and the start of the desert while, directly below, the Nile flows serenely north to the Mediterranean, slicing Cairo in two.

The best time to come up here is at sunset, when millions of lights twinkle into life, accompanied by the haunting evening call to prayer.

Horse-drawn carriage (hantour) for hire on the River Promenade

River Promenade ⑱

Gezira. **Map** 1 B5. Ⓜ Gezira.

Newly created in the late 1990s, Gezira's river promenade is a wide paved avenue down by the Nile, with fine views of the central city skyline opposite. The promenade starts at the foot of the elegant Qasr el-Nil Bridge, which was designed and built by Dorman Long & Co., the British architects responsible for Australia's Sydney Harbour Bridge. The promenade will eventually extend to Zamalek, in the northern part of the island.

Between the promenade and the main road is the small, neat **Andalusian Garden**, with lawns, benches and an obelisk from Heliopolis. A small admission charge keeps out the crowds. On the street beside the garden, hantours (also called caleches) wait for hire. A quick spin in one of these horse-drawn black carriages is a fine way to see the island – but expect to pay inflated prices for the pleasure.

Moored off the promenade is a string of former Nile cruisers, most of which have now been converted into upmarket floating restaurants and bars (see pp290–95).

Zamalek ⑲

Gezira. **Map** 1 A3. 🚗

Occupying the northern half of Gezira, Zamalek is a well-to-do residential district. The main thoroughfare Sharia 26 July, which runs diagonally through the area, is the best place to come for European-style comforts. Simonds makes the only decent cappuccino in town and Maison Thomas does the best pizza in Egypt. European newspapers and magazines are sold at local news stands.

View from Rhoda Island of New Cairo Opera House and Cairo Tower

For hotels and restaurants in this region see pp268–71 and pp290–95

Entrance to Cairo Marriott Hotel, formerly the Gezira Palace

Zamalek's most prominent landmark is the twin orange towers of the Cairo Marriott. This modern and luxurious hotel *(see p270)* was built around the palace created for Empress Eugénie of France when she attended the opening of the Suez Canal in 1869. It has an attractive garden terrace, open to non residents, which is an excellent spot for lunch or a beer.

Tucked away behind the Cairo Marriott is a small 19th-century, Islamic-style villa, now home to the **Gezira Arts Centre**. It houses a collection of decorated ceramic jugs, plates, lamps, bowls and tiles. Nearby, the **Akhenaten Centre of Arts** is housed in a larger, luxurious, European-style villa. This state-run gallery complex organizes regularly changing exhibitions of the work of contemporary local artists. To the north of

the island, the quiet, orderly streets are a treasure trove of splendid villas and mansion blocks in a variety of styles, from Gothic to Baroque to Arts and Crafts. Many of the finest properties here are embassies, but the **Greater Cairo Library** is open to visitors. This is now Egypt's main resource for information about its capital and contains many interesting books, maps, documents and surveys relating to the history of the city.

⛫ Gezira Arts Centre
1 Sharia Sheikh al-Marsafi. *Tel* (02) 737 3298. ⏲ 10am–1:30pm & 6–10pm (5–9pm winter) Sat–Thu. 🖼

⛫ Akhenaten Centre of Arts
1 Sharia Mahaad al-Swissri. *Tel* (02) 735 8211. ⏲ 10am–1:30pm & 6–10pm (5:30–9pm winter) Sat–Thu.

⛫ Greater Cairo Library
15 Sharia Mohammed Mazhar. *Tel* (02) 736 2280. ⏲ 9am–5pm Sat–Thu.

HOUSEBOATS

On the narrow stretch of water separating Zamalek from the Nile's western bank sits a small flotilla of tatty, two-storey wooden houseboats. They are all that remains of the floating neighbourhood that once lined the river from the city's southern edge to the north. The community flourished in the early 20th century when, supplied with gas, electricity, fresh water and telephones, the boats provided homes or served as cafés, casinos and nightclubs. In 1943, on a houseboat owned by belly-dancer Hekmat Fahmy, a German spy, John Eppler, was arrested. The episode formed the basis of Ken Follett's thriller *The Key to Rebecca*. All the boats are now private residences and are not open to visitors.

One of the houseboats moored near 15th May Bridge

Looking south from 15th May Bridge towards high-rise buildings lining the waterfront in west Zamalek

ISLAMIC CAIRO

Following their conquest of Egypt in 641 AD, the Muslims built their city, Al-Fustat, on what is now the southern border of modern Cairo. Successive dynasties established their own capital, each one further to the northeast of the old, until Salah ad-Din built the impressive Citadel (*Al-Qalaa*) on a rocky spur and settled the capital's location. During the Mamluk era which lasted from 1250 to 1517, a wealth of mosques, mausoleums and Islamic buildings were added. Today, Islamic Cairo's maze of narrow, congested streets teems with life, challenging the senses with its unique blend of sights, sounds and smells, and vivid glimpses of the past. Most of the mosques are open to non-Muslims, and charge a small entrance fee.

Sacks of spices in Khan al-Khalili

SIGHTS AT A GLANCE

Mosques and Historic Buildings

Al-Ghouri Complex **7**
Bein al-Qasreen **8**
Beit as Suhaymi **12**
Beit Zeinab Khatoun and Beit al-Harawi **5**
The Citadel pp104–7 **21**
Dervish Theatre **24**
Mosque of al-Aqmar **11**
Mosque of al Azhar **4**
Mosque of al-Hakim **14**
Mosque of ar-Rifai **23**
Mosque of as-Salih Talai **19**
Mosque of Ibn Tulun pp110–11 **26**
Mosque of Sayyidna al-Hussein **3**
Mosque of Sultan Hassan **22**
Northern Cemetery **16**
Qasr Beshtak **9**
Sabil-Kuttab of Abdel Katkhuda **10**
Sabil-Kuttab of Qaitbey **25**
Sharia al-Muizz li-Din Allah **13**
Wikala of al-Ghouri **6**

Bazaars and Markets

Carpet Bazaar **17**
Khan al-Khalili **1**
Sharia Muski **2**
Tentmakers' Market **20**

Walls and Gates

Bab Zuweila **18**
Northern Walls and Gates **15**

KEY

Street-by-Street map
See pp88–9

Street-by-Street map
See pp94–5

0 metres   800

0 yards   800

GETTING AROUND

The best way to explore this area is on foot, spending at least a couple of days wandering the densely packed, historic streets and buildings. Start at a point easily accessible from Downtown Cairo, such as Khan al-Khalili or the Citadel, and explore the sights at a comfortable pace.

◁ Dominating the skyline of Islamic Cairo, the silver domes of the Mosque of Mohammed Ali in the Citadel

Street-by-Street: Around Khan al-Khalili

Stall on Al-Muizz li-Din Allah

Any exploration of Islamic Cairo begins at the medieval bazaar of Khan al-Khalili, the commercial heart of the quarter. The original Khan area lay between Al-Muizz li-Din Allah and Midan Hussein but today it encompasses a wider area made up of several markets selling everything from souvenirs to spices. Traders line the streets all the way to the old city gates, a mile to the north and south, but the bazaar's narrow alleyways are at their densest and most beguiling in the original Khan area. The quarter's many old mosques, houses and palaces offer an escape from the incessant sales pitches.

Mosque of al-Ashraf Barsbey
Built in 1423, this mosque boasts a beautifully-carved wooden pulpit, inlaid with ivory.

Al-Muizz li-Din Allah
This congested thoroughfare was for centuries the main route through the medieval city of Cairo.

SHARIA AL-MUIZZ LI-DIN ALLAH

SHARIA AL-MUSKI

SHARIA AL-AZHAR

Al-Ghouri Complex
The mausoleum and madrassa complex of Al-Ghouri is housed in twin striped buildings and boasts a unique, red-chequered minaret **7**

Egyptian Pancake House
(see p291)

Mosque of Abu Dahab

KEY

- - - - Suggested route

★ **Wikala of al-Ghouri**
This wikala *or caravanserai is Cairo's best preserved example of a medieval merchants' hostel. It is now an arts and crafts centre, its courtyard occasionally serving as a theatre* **6**

STAR SIGHTS

- ★ Mosque of al-Azhar
- ★ Khan al-Khalili
- ★ Wikala of al-Ghouri

★ Khan al-Khalili
Filled with glittering paraphernalia, this bazaar is Cairo at its most magical. The lanes of the original Khan area are lined with shops selling everything from waterpipes and handicrafts to silks and spices ❶

Medieval gates

LOCATOR MAP
See Street Finder Map 2

0 metres   50

0 yards   50

Mosque of Sayyidna al-Hussein
The holiest site in Cairo, this mosque is said to contain the head of Hussein, grandson of the Prophet Mohammed. Built in 1870 on the site of a 12th-century mosque, it is off-limits to non-Muslims ❸

SIKKET AL-BADESTAN

MIDAN HUSSEIN

Gates

Fishawi's coffee house
(see p90)

Sharia Muski
This busy market street is where Cairenes come for serious bargains on everything from wedding dresses to plastic furniture and children's toys ❷

SHARIA AL-AZHAR

★ Mosque of al-Azhar
Founded in AD 970, this mosque and centre for Islamic study is one of the oldest in the city. It displays a mix of architectural styles including this 18th-century Gate of the Barbers ❹

One of two medieval, carved stone gates in Khan al-Khalili

Khan al-Khalili ❶

Map 2 F5. 🚌 *or taxi to Midan al-Hussein.* ☐ *daily (most shops closed Sundays).*

Built in 1382 by Garkas al-Khalili, Master of Horses to Sultan Barquq, Khan al-Khalili is one of the biggest bazaars in the Middle East. This is the oriental bazaar of fable, where gold, silver, brass and copper goods glitter enticingly in the cave-like interiors, and sacks overflowing with exotic spices fill the air with their pungent scents. Its maze of narrow, canvas-covered alleyways is crammed with shops selling a huge variety of goods. Here, too, traditional Egyptian crafts, such as dyeing, carving and sewing, are practised as they have been for centuries.

Khan al-Khalili is, of course, also a major tourist attraction. Hordes of tourists arrive here, by the coachload, to haggle and stock up on the kitsch trinkets and souvenirs that are sold in nearly every shop in the main part of the bazaar.

The bazaar grew up around several *khans* (also known as *wikalas*), which served as both warehouses and lodgings for travelling merchant caravans. Most have been swallowed up by later structures, but a few remain. On a side street off Sharia Muski, stairs lead to the upper level of the **Wikala of Silahdar** (1837), where the

former living quarters can be made out, ranged around the central courtyard. Two carved stone gates in the Badestan area, added during the reign of Sultan al-Ghouri (1501–16), are the oldest surviving part of Khan al-Khalili.

Apart from exploring and haggling, the bazaar's other great attraction is **Fishawi's**, located in an alley one block in from Midan al-Hussein. Open day and night for the past 200 years, it is possibly Cairo's oldest coffee house and is crammed with small copper-topped tables, while huge antique mirrors line the walls. Here, patrons puff on *sheeshas* (waterpipes) and sip mint tea round the clock.

For further information on shopping in Egypt and Cairo, see Shopping in Cairo (*pp150–51*) and What to Buy (*pp306–7*).

Apple vendor in the bustling street market of Sharia Muski

Sharia Muski ❷

Runs between Midan Ataba and Midan al-Hussein. **Map** 6 F3.

In a city that is bursting at the seams, Sharia Muski is possibly the single most crowded street of all. Before

Sharia al-Azhar was bulldozed through the area in the mid-20th century, Muski was the main route between Khan al-Khalili and downtown Cairo. The street is crammed with budget-end clothing emporia and bargain-basement market stalls that are piled high with synthetic goods: clothing that is guaranteed to bobble and fade; wedding outfits, plastic toys and garden furniture. At the Khan al-Khalili end of the street, clothing gives way to perfume and "antiques" but, just before Midan al-Hussein, there is one last glorious burst of glitzy glamour in the form of outfitters selling lavishly decorated belly-dancing outfits.

The sounds that fill Sharia Muski are as much part of the experience as the goods on display. The sales patter of the stall-keepers, the warning cries of barrow-men as they push through the crowds, drink vendors selling liquorice water, all contribute to the lively character of the street.

Mosque of Sayyidna al-Hussein ❸

Midan al-Hussein. **Map** 2 F5. 🚫 *to non-Muslims.*

This is the most important mosque in all Egypt, so sacred that only Muslims are allowed to enter. Hundreds come here to pray each day, and as many as 10,000 on Fridays. Replacing an earlier 12th-century mosque, it was built in 1870 and is reputed to shelter one of the holiest relics of Islam – the head of

Brass and leather goods for sale in Khan al-Khalili

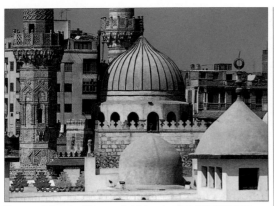

Domes and minarets of Mosque of al-Azhar seen from Zeinab Khatoun

to sit in the peace and shade of its arcades to memorize their Quranic texts, much as they have done for centuries.

Before entering the mosque, women must cover their heads; no admission will be granted to anyone with bare legs.

Al-Hussein, grandson of the Prophet Mohammed. After the Prophet's death in AD 632, control of the caliphate was assumed by the Umayyad clan. The Prophet's son-in-law Ali, claiming to be the natural successor, took up arms and was killed. His son, Al-Hussein, led a revolt but died in AD 680 at the battle of Kerbala, Iraq, where the rest of his body is said to lie. Islam is still divided into followers of Al-Hussein (Shiites) and Sunnis, who hold the Umayyads to be the true successors to Mohammed.

During the annual ten-day Moulid of Al-Hussein and other feast days, thousands throng Midan al-Hussein to enjoy the fair and join in the festivities.

Mosque of al-Azhar ❹

Sharia al-Azhar. **Map** 2 F5. ☐ daily.
🕌 for noon prayers Fri. 🖼

Just southwest of Midan al-Hussein is one of Cairo's most venerable institutions. Al-Azhar was founded in AD 970 as the main mosque and centre of learning for the city that had just been built by the new Fatimid rulers from North Africa. Though the Fatimids were swept from power some 200 years later, their mosque and university remained central to religious and political life in Egypt.

Today, the Sheikh of al-Azhar is the highest religious authority in the land and the university the most revered

centre of learning in the Sunni Islamic world. Although now housed in several modern campuses around the country, including a separate faculty for women, the university continues to provide free education and board for Muslim students from all over the world. They come to study the Quran and Islamic law along with other traditional subjects such as grammar, logic and rhetoric.

Since a reorganization of Al-Azhar in 1961, new faculties have been formed for the study of medicine, agriculture, engineering and commerce.

Little remains of the original structure of the mosque, which now exhibits a mix of styles from different periods. The double-arched **Gate of the Barbers**, where students traditionally had their heads shaved, dates from the mid-18th century. Visitors now enter through this gate, which leads into an enclosure flanked by two *madrassas* (places of study). Both *madrassas* date to the early part of the 14th century; the one on the left is usually open and is worth visiting to see the beautifully ornate *mihrab* (niche indicating the direction of Mecca).

In the centre of the mosque is the main *sahn* (courtyard), which dates as far back as Fatimid times. Although classes are no longer held here, small circles of students still come

Beit Zeinab Khatoun and Beit al-Harawi ❺

Harat al-Azhar. **Map** 2 F5. ☐ daily. 🖼

Running between the south wall of Al-Azhar Mosque and a long, low, medieval *wikala*, a narrow alley leads to a small garden square. Projecting into the square on its northern side is Beit Zeinab Khatoun, an Ottoman-era house (*beit*) originally built in 1486 and restored in the 1990s. On the southern side of the square is Beit al-Harawi, built in 1731 as the home of a rich Cairo merchant and also recently restored.

Both houses are beautiful examples of the sophisticated domestic architecture that once filled the city. Beit al-Harawi, in particular, contains some fine *mashrabiyya* (carved wooden screens) and elegant painted ceilings. Built around central courtyards, both houses are designed to stay as cool as possible with their airy rooms, shaded stone floors and interior fountains.

The houses are open to visitors during the day and, since being restored, also operate as cultural centres, where regular performances of music and theatre are staged (*see pp308–11*).

Wooden *mashrabiyya* screen covering the window of Beit Zeinab Khatoun

Tapestry of women carrying water, an example of the craft items on sale in the Wikala of al-Ghouri

Wikala of al-Ghouri ❻

Sharia al-Azhar. **Map** 2 F5. *Tel (02) 511 0472.* ⬚ 9am–3pm daily. 🈺

Also known as *khans* or caravanserais, *wikalas* were hostels used by merchants arriving in caravans from North Africa, Arabia and the east. As well as accommodation, they provided stables, storage space and a place where merchants could trade. *Wikalas* were typically rectangular in shape with a central courtyard and a main gate that could be locked at night. On the ground floor were the storage rooms and stables while the merchants slept in private rooms on the upper floor. During the Mamluk era, Cairo's golden age, some of the city's *wikalas* were up to four or five storeys high. Unfortunately, none of these have survived. The finest remaining example is the Wikala of al-Ghouri,

which dates from the early 17th century and is three storeys high. It boasts beautiful *mashrabiyya* (carved wooden screens) on the upper floors and a once graceful fountain in the courtyard. Although parts of the building are closed for restoration, it now serves as an arts and crafts centre. Its rooms have been converted into artists' studios, a shop and a small exhibition of Bedouin crafts, while its courtyard is used as a concert hall and theatre.

Carpenter at work in the Wikala of al-Ghouri

Al-Ghouri Complex ❼

Sharia al-Muizz li-Din Allah. **Map** 2 F5. *Tel (02) 511 0472.* ⬚ 9am–midnight daily. ◼ 11:30am–1:30pm Fri.

One of the finest buildings in Cairo, the Al-Ghouri Complex is made up of twin, boldly

striped black-and-white buildings situated opposite each other across a narrow market street. Dating from 1505, the structure was built by Qansuh al-Ghouri, the last of the powerful Mamluk sultans, who ruled between 1501–16 and died at the hands of the Ottoman Turks. The sultan's body was never recovered from the battlefield and his mausoleum, the building on the east side of the complex, was used for his short-lived successor, Tumanbey. Several attempts to construct a dome over the tomb chamber failed, hence the tomb's unusual flat, wooden roof. Part of the mausoleum now serves as a cultural centre and theatre where Whirling Dervishes perform every Wednesday and Saturday evening. Opposite the mausoleum, on the west side of the complex, is the Al-Ghouri Mosque and Madrassa offering fine views from its rooftop. Of note is the mosque's unique square minaret which is topped by five bulbs. In the 18th century these twin buildings were linked by a wooden roof, creating a covered area that housed the city's silk market.

WHIRLING DERVISHES

Cairo's Whirling Dervishes are members of the Mawlaiyya sect of Sufis, followers of a semi-mystical branch of Islam. Sufis were originally associated with poverty and self-denial and wore rough woollen clothes next to their skin – the name Sufi originates from *suf*, the Arabic for wool. Sufis aspire, through meditation, recitation, dance and music, to attain union with God. The Whirling Dervishes, so called because of their ritual spinning dance, offer a rare glimpse of this otherwise underground phenomenon. The group performs twice-weekly at the Al-Ghouri Complex. Questions of authenticity aside, the show is a marvellous spectacle. Dancers in brightly coloured outfits turn like spinning tops while a line of musicians create a hypnotic pulse, tossing their heads jerkily from side to side. Performances are popular so it is necessary to arrive well before the 8pm start time to be sure of a seat. See p308 for more details.

Whirling Dervishes performing their mesmerising dance ritual

Central courtyard of the three-storey Wikala of al-Ghouri

Minarets and Domes

One of the greatest achievements of Cairo's medieval artisans was the decorative carving of stone surfaces, seen at its best on the city's myriad minarets and domes. The craft flourished under the Mamluk dynasty (1250–1517) during which time minarets evolved from short, stubby towers, with little decorative detail, to slender, elegant spires boasting carved balustrades and stalactites. The stone domes of the city's mausoleums are also a

Crescent moon symbol

characteristic of Mamluk architecture, beginning their development in the early 14th century and reaching their zenith in the latter part of the 15th century. Originally small and plain, domes rapidly progressed to vast structures adorned, in the first instance, with a simple rib pattern followed by zigzags and finally explosions of star patterns and floral arabesques. The flourishing of this art form was brought to an abrupt end by the Ottoman invasion.

MINARETS

These elegant towers, attached to Cairo's mosques, fall broadly into three categories: the square-based towers of the Fatimid period, the lavish three-tiered spires of the late-Mamluk era and the pencil minarets of the Ottoman Turks.

Brass crescent

Pear-shaped bulb

A pavilion of eight columns supports a crown of stalactites.

Stalactites or *muqarnas* decorate the transitional area between sections.

This three-tiered *spire, adorning the Mosque of Qaitbey (see p102), displays the elaborate decorative stonework typical of late Mamluk minarets.*

Pepperpot caps adorn these early, square-based minarets.

This external staircase is a unique feature of the Mosque of Ibn Tulun.

The minaret of *the AD 879 Mosque of Ibn Tulun (see pp110–11) was inspired by the great Mosque of Samarra in Mesopotamia.*

Simple wooden railings and modest stalactite decoration were favoured by the Ottomans.

This simple minaret of the *1528 Mosque of Suleiman Pasha (see p107) has typical Ottoman styling such as a pointed cap and little decorative detail.*

STONE DOMES

Developed by the Mamluks, decorating domes became an increasingly sophisticated art form.

The dome *of Madrassa Sultaniya (c.1370) in the City of the Dead (see p103) has a rib design.*

This cupola, *in the City of the Dead, illustrates the progression to a more elaborate zigzag pattern.*

The dome *of the Mosque of Qaitbey (1474) combines geometric and floral designs in its decoration.*

Street-by-Street: Fatimid Cairo

Founded by the conquering Fatimid dynasty in AD 969 as "Al-Qahira" (the Victorious), Islamic Cairo became the imperial capital of Egypt. Although they created an extensive royal quarter of grand palaces and mosques hidden by towering walls, little remains of the Fatimids' architectural achievements. Later dynasties recycled the earlier monuments, constructing their own displays of grandeur, such as the Mamluk complexes on al-Muizz li-Din Allah and fine Ottoman residences. Today, the narrow streets of this small quarter serve as a living museum of medieval architecture.

A horse-drawn cart

Sabil-Kuttab of Abdel Katkhuda
In the centre of what was once Cairo's main street is one of many sabil-kuttabs (structures with fountains) in Islamic Cairo **10**

Madrassa of Sultan Barquq
(see p97)

★ Bein al-Qasreen
Once the site of two Fatimid palaces, Bein al-Qasreen is now dominated by the minarets of three grand Mamluk complexes **8**

Madrassa and Mausoleum of Sultan an-Nasr Mohammed
(see p96)

The Madrassa and Mausoleum of Sultan Qalawun is an example of the ambition of Mamluk architecture. As well as the madrassa and mausoleum it also houses an ancient hospital *(see p96)*.

BEIN AL-QASREEN

Khan al-Khalili

SHARIA BEIT AL-QADI

MIDAN BEIT AL-QADI

Glass Goods
Locally made "Muski" glassware can be found in the alleys off Sharia al-Muizz li-Din Allah.

Qasr Beshtak
This 14th-century palace affords fine views over Islamic Cairo from its upper storeys **9**

★ **Beit as-Suhaymi**
This 16th- and 17th-century Ottoman house is an example of the luxury residences enjoyed by wealthy merchants in medieval Cairo **⑫**

Mosque of Suleiman Silahdar

LOCATOR MAP
See Street Finder Map 2

Sharia al-Muizz li-Din Allah
Once a main thorough-fare, this street is now home to garlic and onion stalls as well as a coppersmiths' market **⑬**

Several derelict *wikalas*, hostels offering lodgings to travelling merchants, can be found in this area. Some of them are still in use.

Northern Walls

| 0 metres | 30 |
| 0 yards | ·30 |

KEY

– – – Suggested route

Mosque of al-Aqmar
The carved sea-shell design on this 12th-century mosque is an early example of deco-rative stonework on mosque façades **⑪**

Midan al-Hussein

STAR SIGHTS

★ Beit as-Suhaymi

★ Bein al-Qasreen

Detail of inscription and motifs in the Mausoleum of Sultan Qalawun

Bein al-Qasreen 8

Sharia al-Muizz li-Din Allah. **Map** 2 F4.

Bein al-Qasreen, which translates as "between the two palaces," is the local name for the stretch of Sharia al-Muizz li-Din Allah that runs immediately to the north of Khan al-Khalili. The name is a testament to the tenacity of history in Cairo, because the two palaces to which it refers ceased to exist more than 600 years ago. Facing each other across a busy public square, the two palaces formed the splendid centrepiece of Al-Qahira (the Victorious), the original Fatimid city, which was founded in AD 969.

Subsequent dynasties replaced them with buildings of their own, but the area was always reserved for only the grandest of building projects.

Today, Bein al-Qasreen is lined on the western side by a sequence of spectacular façades, belonging primarily to three early Mamluk religious complexes. The most southerly is the **Madrassa and Mausoleum of Sultan Qalawun**, which also happens to be the oldest of the three, having been completed in 1279. Three hundred Crusader prisoners took part in its construction, which was completed in

only 13 months. The Christian involvement may account for its almost Gothic façade. Inside, a long, dark corridor separates the *madrassa*, on the left, from the mausoleum, on the right. The latter is one of the most spectacular and stunning interiors in Cairo. Inspired by Jerusalem's Dome of the Rock, it has an octagonal arrangement of columns, two pairs of which are massive granite pillars that originated in some Pharaonic structure. The walls are covered in vivid geometric mosaics tracing the name "Mohammed" in florid strokes. Lavish amounts of gold gleam as they are picked out by the coloured rays of sunlight filtering through countless stained-glass windows.

View across the rooftops to the balconies on the minaret of the Madrassa of Sultan Barquq

Despite the sumptuous interior decor, the complex as a whole still has a slightly decrepit air, which nevertheless adds to its charm. Built as part of the complex, set back from the street, is a *maristan* or hospital which treated the sick for free and amazingly, over 700 years later, still operates as a clinic.

Continuing north, adjoining the Qalawun complex is the lower, less expansive façade of the **Madrassa and Mausoleum of Sultan an-Nasr Mohammed**. It was erected between 1299 and 1304 by a sultan who, despite being deposed twice, fought back to regain the throne on both occasions and reigned for a total of 42 years. During this time, he endowed Cairo with over 200 buildings, the best known of which is his mosque at the Citadel (*see pp104–7*).

NAGUIB MAHFOUZ

The West was introduced to the work of writer Naguib Mahfouz (1911–2006) in 1988, when he won the Nobel Prize for Literature. Mahfouz grew up in the back streets of Islamic Cairo, and his work was greatly influenced by the neighbourhoods and people of his youth. His best-known work is *The Cairo Trilogy*, a vast work spanning the generations of one family. Each title in the trilogy takes its name from a particular locale: the first, *Bein al-Qasreen*, was translated as *Palace Walk*. The award of the Nobel Prize rekindled opposition to Mahfouz's earlier novel *Children of the Alley*, which caused uproar when serialized in *Al-Ahram* in 1959. In 1994 the author was attacked near his home, receiving injuries that affected his physical ability to write.

1966 novel by Naguib Mahfouz

Dome and minaret in Bein al-Qasreen

Sultan an-Nasr's monument in Bein al-Qasreen is in a bad state of repair and may not be open to the public. It is possible, however, to admire from the outside the detailed North African-style stucco-work covering the minaret and the Gothic black and white doorway. The latter was removed from a church in Acre (now Akko, Israel) and re-erected in Cairo to mark the final defeat of the Crusaders by the Mamluks in the Holy Land in 1291.

The northernmost building in Bein al-Qasreen is the **Madrassa of Sultan Barquq**, built around 1384–6. While a *madrassa* does not appear to be noticeably different to a mosque on the outside, it is actually a school for teaching Islamic law. Barquq's complex, has four doors, each intricately decorated with bronze, leading off the main courtyard to four separate sets of classrooms and student cells – one for each of the schools of Islamic law. The mausoleum, just off the prayer hall, resembles an ornate jewellery box, with marbled walls under a lovely gilded dome. It is not Barquq but rather his daughter who lies here: the sultan is buried in the Northern Cemetery *(see pp102–3)*. Sometimes visitors are permitted to go up the minaret and on to the roof for a splendid panoramic view across Cairo.

C Madrassa and Mausoleum of Sultan Qalawun
Map 2 F4. ⬜ *daily.* ⬤ *11:30am–1:30pm Fri.* 🖼

C Madrassa and Mausoleum of Sultan an-Nasr Mohammed
Map 2 F4. ⬜ *daily.* ⬤ *11:30am–1:30pm Fri.* 🖼

C Madrassa of Sultan Barquq
Map 2 F4. ⬜ *daily.* ⬤ *11:30am–1:30pm Fri.* 🖼

Qasr Beshtak ⑨

Sharia al-Muizz li-Din Allah.
Map 2 F4. ⬜ *daily.* ⬤ *11:30am–1:30pm Fri.* 🖼

Qasr Beshtak or Beshtak Palace is easy to miss: from the outside it presents just a plain, two-storey façade, decorated with a few small *mashrabiyya* windows. However, a narrow alleyway on the left leads to a court-yard with steps leading up to an impressive reception hall, complete with a marble floor and inlaid panelling.

Beshtak was a powerful emir in the 14th century, a notorious rake who married the sultan's daughter and accrued great wealth and influence. His palace, which was built in 1334, was the sumptuous venue for fabulous balls.

During the Mamluk era, however, great wealth and influence was a dangerously double-edged sword, and so it was almost inevitable that a jealous rival succeeded in having Emir Beshtak arrested and executed, at the same time seizing all his possessions.

From what is now the roof of the palace (but which used to be just the second storey of five), there is an excellent panoramic view of Islamic Cairo, looking down Sharia

Mashrabiyya screens on the façade of Qasr Beshtak

al-Muizz li-Din Allah and over the rooftops to the impressive collection of minarets and domes around the Citadel.

The second-floor chamber *(qaa)*, with its *mashrabiyya*-screened galleries, stained-glass windows and gilt and painted wood panelling is a fine example of a private chamber of the period.

The entrance ticket for the Qasr Beshtak also includes admission to the Sabil-Kuttab of Abdel Katkhuda *(see p98)*.

RECYCLING HISTORY

Since Pharaonic times, the rocky Muqattam Hills to the east of Cairo have been quarried for stone. However, it was often found to be more convenient to use materials from closer to hand – in particular, from other buildings. Throughout history, Cairo has been shaken by earthquakes that have reduced great swathes of the city to rubble. Just as frequently, succeeding dynasties have not been above dismantling the existing monuments and reusing the materials for new ones. The Mausoleum of Qalawun, for example, is supported on red granite pillars of Pharaonic origin, while the Mosque of an-Nasr Mohammed at the Citadel *(see pp104–7)* has a

Pharaonic carving on Cairo's Northern Walls

courtyard arcade that is made up of oddments of Roman and Coptic columns and capitals. Most striking of all, though, are the blocks embedded in the interior corridors and rooms of the Northern Walls, which are carved with ancient Egyptian gazelles, hippos and figures – clear evidence of the fact that the stone for these fortifications was scavenged from the ruins of the ancient city of Memphis.

Sabil-Kuttab of Abdel Katkhuda ⑩

Sharia al-Muizz li-Din Allah.
Map 2 F4. ◯ *daily.* ● *11:30am– 1:30pm Fri.* 🏛

Islamic Cairo is dotted with odd-shaped buildings with large windows covered by lacy grilles and what looks like a water trough where the windowsill should be. The *sabil*, or fountain, was kept full of fresh water and copper cups were attached to the grille so that thirsty passers-by could help themselves to a drink. Wealthy warlords and nobles would often build a *sabil* to curry favour with both the city populace and their god above.

On an upper floor above the *sabil* was often a small terrace open to the breezes on three sides, which was set aside for the teaching of the Quran and known as a *kuttab*. Thus a *sabil-kuttab* provided two things commended by the Prophet Mohammed – water for the thirsty and spiritual enlightenment for the ignorant.

Built in 1744, this structure has been carefully renovated. Faïence tiles depicting Mecca adorn the lower floor, while the upper floor is decorated with carved wooden pillars and beams. The exterior of the building has some fine "joggling" – panels of different coloured blocks of marble fitted together like a jigsaw. The entrance fee should be included in that of the Qasr Beshtak, whose guardian also holds the key.

Carved stone stalactites between ribbed arches on Mosque al-Aqmar

Mosque of al-Aqmar ⑪

Sharia al-Muizz li-Din Allah.
Map 2 F4. ◯ *daily.* ● *for noon prayers Fri.*

The name of the Mosque of al-Aqmar (the Moonlit Mosque) was supposedly inspired by the luminous quality of its grey stone. These days, coated in centuries of Cairo grime, the mosque does anything but shine. Nevertheless it is considered to be an architectural gem.

The mosque was built in 1125 by one of the last Fatimid caliphs, and is the oldest stone-built mosque in Egypt (earlier buildings were made of brick faced with plaster). The layout of the mosque is interesting as it uses an outer wall of varying thickness to realign the interior, reconciling the conflicting geometry imposed by the street plan and the direction of Mecca. The façade also displays the earliest use of decorative features that were later to become popular under the Mamluks, such as the sculpted stone "stalactites" (*muqarnas*) and carved ribbing in the hooded arch.

Beit as-Suhaymi ⑫

19 Darb al-Asfar, off Sharia al-Muizz li-Din Allah. **Map** 2 F4. ◯ *daily.* ● *for noon prayers Fri.* 🏛

The most elegant remaining residence in Islamic Cairo, Beit as-Suhaymi is really two houses, one built in 1648 and the other in 1796, joined to create a structure of almost palatial proportions. Its traditional design means entry is gained through a right-angled passage (which ensured complete privacy) into a central courtyard. Originally this would have had been filled with copious greenery ranged around a central fountain.

The rooms on the ground floor comprise the *salamlek*, an area reserved for men; those on the upper floor form part of the *haramlek*, for women and the family. Here, the effect of the stained glass and wonderful painted ceilings combined with the dappled light from the *mashrabiyya*-covered windows is entrancing. These large wooden screens overlook the courtyard, filtering sunlight and cool breezes into the rooms, as well as allowing the women to observe the goings-on below without themselves being seen.

Some of the newly restored decoration is sumptuous, particularly in the ground floor *qaa* or reception room, which features intricate paintwork and a polychrome marble fountain set into the floor.

Sharia al-Muizz li-Din Allah ⑬

Map 2 F5.

Al-Muizz li-Din Allah was the Fatimid caliph who conquered Cairo in AD 969. This street was the former main thoroughfare of medieval times, entering the city through the southern gate of Bab Zuweila and exiting out of Bab al-Futuh to the north. Over the centuries, buildings have encroached on its width and it is no longer very grand, but it is still vital and busy. Lined with stalls, at

"Joggling" on southern facing arch of Sabil-Kuttab of Abdel Katkhuda

For hotels and restaurants in this region see pp268–71 and pp290–95

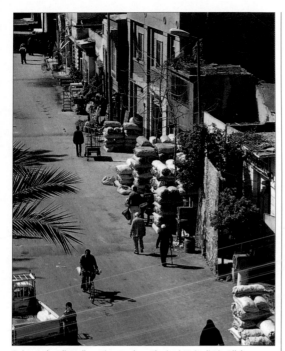

Onion and garlic stalls setting up along Sharia al-Muizz li-Din Allah

of the mosque. They are unique in style, with stubby little pepper-pot tops supported on massive bases, reminiscent of the pylons of Pharaonic temples.

Northern Walls and Gates ⓯

Sharia al-Galal. **Map** 2 F4. ◯ *daily.* ◉ *11:30am–1:30pm Fri.* 🎦

The medieval city of Cairo was completely walled around with at least ten huge gateways, but only a short northern section of the ramparts and two gates now remains, as well as one other gate to the south, Bab Zuweila *(see p103)*. The two northern gates, the square-towered Bab an-Nasr (Gate of Victory) and the rounded Bab al-Futuh (Gate of Conquests), were built in 1087 and later strengthened by Salah ad-Din. It is possible to explore the interiors of the gates and walk along the top of the walls by climbing the stairs just inside the neighbouring Mosque of al-Hakim and crossing the roof.

Steps in the gate towers lead into a vaulted corridor running the whole length of the wall, through which mounted guards could ride. The passage is lit by daylight filtering through arrow slits. These were widened to accommodate cannons in 1789 when, a year after his failed conquest of Egypt, Napoleon garrisoned troops within the walls. Evidence of their stay remains in the names the French gave to the towers, which they painted over the doorways.

Immediately north of the walls is Bab an-Nasr cemetery containing the tomb of Jean-Louis Burckhardt (1784–1817). He was the first European in modern times to visit ancient Petra and also to rediscover the two amazing temples at Abu Simbel *(see pp214–15).*

Khan al-Khalili it is home to the coppersmiths' market and an assortment of workshops. Further along are shops selling a miscellany of coffee-house equipment such as tin-topped tables and *sheeshas*, before finishing with the garlic and onion stalls near Bab al-Futuh.

Sheesha pipe manufacturer on Sharia al-Muizz li-Din Allah

Mosque of al-Hakim ⓮

Sharia al-Muizz li-Din Allah. **Map** 2 F4. ◯ *daily.* ◉ *for noon prayers Fri.* 🎦

Al-Hakim, the third Fatimid caliph (997–1021), was one of the most notorious rulers in Egyptian history. He ruled from the age of eleven and had his tutor murdered when he was fifteen. Infamous for his bizarre laws and arbitrary acts of violence, he proceeded to burn areas of Cairo, when people objected to the substitution of his name for Allah at Friday prayers. He was also a virulent misogynist and banned the manufacture of women's shoes in order to keep them indoors.

The mosque that bears his name was actually started by his father, but completed by Hakim in 1013. Since that time it has been variously used as a prison for captured Crusaders, as a stable by Salah ad-Din, a warehouse by Napoleon and a boys' school. After existing for centuries in a ruined state, the mosque underwent a somewhat heavy-handed restoration during the 1980s. Now it gleams with polished marble and glitzy golden chandeliers. The minarets are the only original features

Unique style of minaret at the Mosque of al-Hakim

Intricate Mamluk designs on the Mosque of Qaitbey's minaret, Northern Cemetery

Northern Cemetery ⑯

East of Sharia Salah Salem.
🚌 🚐 102, 103 from Midan Tahrir.

On the edge of the city, across the six-lane Salah Salem highway, the Northern Cemetery (al-Qarafah) is not just a place of burial, it is home to the living too. While several magnificent funerary complexes dominate the area, a lot of the more modest, low-rise tombs double as family homes.

By the end of the 14th century, Cairo's population may have numbered 500,000, making it the largest urban centre in the world. Land was at a premium, so the Mamluk sultans looked beyond the city walls for the building space to match their egos. The great mausoleums they built here rank as some of their finest achievements. Best of these is the **Mosque of Qaitbey**, completed in 1474. A beautifully proportioned structure, with a simple but dazzling sunlight-infused interior, it is topped by the most elegant of minarets and intricate carved stone domes. The Qaitbey mosque features on the Egyptian one pound note.

Further south, down the sandy main street, a stone wall encloses the **Complex of Sultan Ashraf Barsbey**. Much of this has been lost over the centuries but the central mosque remains, topped by a beautiful dome carved with interlocking stars. If the door is unlocked, it is worth

looking at the fine marble floor and the ivory-inlaid *minbar*.

Further north lies the fortress-like bulk of the **Mausoleum of Ibn Barquq**. This was built by the son of the Barquq whose complex sits on Bein al-Qasreen *(see p96)*. The building is quite unique in being perfectly symmetrical with two domes and two minarets. It served as a *khanqah*, a monastery for Islamic mystics called Sufis *(see p92)*, and has rows of small cells ranged around the courtyard. Beneath the twin domes are tomb chambers, one for the women, one for the men, with bright, painted ceilings. It is possible to get up onto the roof and climb the minarets.

The best route to the cemetery is to walk east for ten minutes along Sharia al-Azhar from the Khan al-Khalili area.

🇨 **Mosque of Qaitbey**
Sharia Sultan Qaitbey.
⬜ *daily.* ⬛ *for noon prayers Fri.*

🇨 **Complex of Sultan Ashraf Barsbey**
Sharia Sultan Qaitbey. **Map:** 4 D2.
⬜ *daily.* ⬛ *for noon prayers Fri.*

🇨 **Mausoleum of Ibn Barquq**
Sharia Sultan Qaitbey. **Map:** 4 D2.
⬜ *daily.* ⬛ *for noon prayers Fri.* 🖼

Carpet Bazaar ⑰

Sharia al-Muizz li-Din Allah. **Map** 6 F3.

Khan al-Khalili's markets continue south of Sharia al-Azhar, where tourist trinkets give way to items that the locals might want to buy. The alleyways east of the Al-Ghouri Complex *(see p92)* are home to the Carpet Bazaar. Here, rugs of coarse wool or camel hair are sold, either striped in varying shades of beige and brown, or featuring colourful, stylized images of birds, camels and country scenes.

Back on Sharia al-Muizz li-Din Allah, just south of the Al-Ghouri Complex, are two *tarboush* workshops, making the hat better known in the

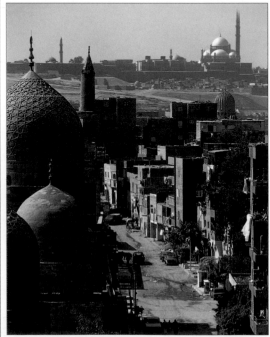

Northern Cemetery, including dome of Sultan Ashraf Barsbey Mosque

◁ **View through the morning mist over Islamic Cairo**

West as a fez. Once common street wear, they are now a parody of their former elegant self, sported only by a few waiters and restaurant staff.

Courtyard of Mosque of Sultan al-Muayyad, by Bab Zuweila

Bab Zuweila ⑱

Sharia Ahmed Mahir. **Map:** 6 F4.
🕐 daily. 🕐 11:30am–1:30pm Fri. 📷

Bab Zuweila is the sole remaining southern gate of the city walls of Fatimid Cairo. It was built in the late 11th century. In Mamluk times, it was from the platform of Bab Zuweila that the sultan would watch the start of the annual pilgrimage to Mecca. This was also the site of executions, and the heads of criminals were displayed on top of the walls. This bloody habit persisted until the 1800s: after the 1811 Citadel massacre (see p59), the heads of the slain Mamluks were mounted on spikes here.

The towering minarets that soar over the gate were added when the adjacent **Mosque of Sultan al-Muayyad** was built in 1415. It is possible to climb the minarets for one of the best views of the city.

Across the entrance to Bab Zuweila is the Sabil-Kuttab Nafisa al-Bayda, a splendid building that combines a water dispensary with a school for orphans.

🅲 Mosque of Sultan al-Muayyad
Sharia Ahmed Mahir. **Map:** 6 F4.
🕐 daily. 🕐 for noon prayers Fri.

Mosque of as-Salih Talai ⑲

Sharia Ahmed Mahir. **Map:** 6 F4.
🕐 daily. 🕐 for noon prayers Fri.

The last of the Fatimid mosques of Cairo, the Mosque of as-Salih Talai was built in 1160. It was the first mosque to be built on an upper storey, resting on top of a layer of shop units. However, over the centuries, through the gradual accumulation of rubbish and dirt, the street level has risen by some 3 m (10 ft), so the mosque is now at ground level and the shops are in the basement.

The façade has five pointed arches, while the interior reveals columns with florid capitals taken from pre-

Appliqué motif from the Tentmakers' Market

Islamic sites. The prayer hall walls are decorated with superb stained-glass windows. The mosque also features a splendid *minbar* (pulpit), which was donated in 1300 by amir Baktimur al-Jugandar.

Tentmakers' Market ⑳

Sharia al-Khaimiyya. **Map:** 6 F4.

Leaving the Fatimid city via Bab Zuweila, the old main street runs south, passing through a venerable covered market known in Arabic as Sharia al-Khaimiyya, or the Street of the Tentmakers. Cairo's only remaining covered market, it was built in 1650 by Radwan Bey, who was in charge of the annual pilgrimage to Mecca. It is here that at one time a huddle of small workshops produced the brightly coloured printed fabrics that adorned the caravans bound for Mecca. Similar decorative material is now used in the large pavilions, frequently seen around Cairo, that are erected for weddings and funerals and the opening of new businesses. Huge rolls of the mainly blue or orange cloth are sold at the small, open-fronted kiosks that line the dimly lit street. These places also stitch brightly coloured appliqué work more suited to the tourist.

LIVING WITH THE DEAD

Death has always been a significant part of Egyptian life. Even when the country abandoned Pharaonic beliefs, becoming first Coptic and then Islamic, practices such as visiting the dead were maintained. Most family tombs included a room where visitors could eat and rest and even stay overnight. Inevitably, the city's homeless took to occupying these tombs, some as early as the 14th century. Today, the Northern (and Southern) Cemeteries contain a mixture of tombs and homes; as well as tombs that are homes, where the living and the dead coexist side by side.

Children playing amongst the tombs in the Northern Cemetery, sometimes known as the "City of the Dead"

For hotels and restaurants in this region see pp268–71 and pp290–95

The Citadel ㉑

Home to Egypt's rulers for almost 700 years, the Citadel (Al-Qalaa) is today one of the most popular tourist sites in Cairo. Originally founded in 1176 by the famed Muslim commander Salah ad-Din (also known as Saladin), its mosques, museums and battlements reflect a diverse heritage. Divided into three sections, the Citadel's main tourist area is in the Southern Enclosure, where the Mosque of an-Nasr Mohammed (the Citadel's only surviving Mamluk structure) is dwarfed by the 19th-century Mosque of Mohammed Ali. The upper terraces of the Citadel offer spectacular views over the city.

Mosque of an-Nasr Mohammed
The Persian-style tiling on the minarets is unique in Egypt.

Police Museum
Entered via a mock-Gothic gateway, the museum traces the gory history of Egyptian crime and punishment.

Bab al-Azab (1754) was built in the Ottoman period as the new main gate.

Lower Enclosure

★ **Mohammed Ali Mosque**
Built in a wholly Turkish style between 1830 and 1848, this mosque has nevertheless become a symbol of Cairo.

★ **Views over Cairo**
Superb views of the city's minarets and domes are afforded from the Citadel's fortifications. In the foreground here is the Mosque of Sultan Hassan.

Qasr al-Gawhara, also called the Jewel Palace, is now a museum depicting the court life of Mohammed Ali.

Southern Enclosure

THE HIPPODROME

Now a large roundabout known as Midan Salah ad-Din, the area to the west of the Citadel walls was once the Hippodrome, an important site in medieval Cairo. Created by An-Nasr Mohammed as a cavalry training ground, this was where the Mamluks – renowned for their feats of horsemanship – practised complex military manoeuvres. Equestrian games were also frequently held here, including horse-racing and polo.

19th-century engraving of Bab al-Azab and the Hippodrome area

VISITORS' CHECKLIST

Sharia Salah Salem. **Map** 4 F2.
🚌 🚐 ⬜ summer: 8am–6pm daily; winter: 8am–5pm daily (museums close at 4:30pm). ⬤ religious holidays. 🎟 (additional charge for Northern Enclosure).

The upper ramparts, entered at ground level, can be explored, offering views across the Citadel.

The statue of Ibrahim Pasha is a replica of the one in Midan Opera (see p78).

Bab al-Gadid (entrance)

★ **Mosque of Suleiman Pasha**
Dating from 1528, this beautiful mosque has a cluster of domes and brightly painted interior woodwork, which has recently been restored.

Northern Enclosure

Sand Tower

Garden Museum

The Carriage Museum contains a small collection of 19th-century horse-drawn carriages.

Bab al-Gebel (entrance)

Military Museum
Once the Harem Palace of Mohammed Ali, the museum has displays of weapons, uniforms and decorations, and a scale model of the Citadel.

STAR FEATURES

★ Mohammed Ali Mosque

★ Mosque of Suleiman Pasha

★ Views over Cairo

Exploring the Citadel

Although its main attraction is the Mohammed Ali Mosque, the Citadel has a great many other features worthy of attention. This fortified complex serves as a museum of Islamic architecture, with numerous fine examples of Mamluk and Ottoman-era mosques and fortifications from the time of Salah ad-Din (1171–91). With four separate museums also enclosed within its walls, a visit to the Citadel can occupy the best part of a day. Visitors should be aware that certain parts of the complex are out of bounds, notably the lower enclosure leading down to the Bab al-Azab gate.

Arcaded courtyard of the Mosque of an-Nasr Mohammed

Detail of a water fountain in the Mosque of Mohammed Ali

on delivery and has yet to be repaired. Mohammed Ali's body lies in a marble tomb to the right on entering the vast space of the prayer hall.

◖ Mosque of an-Nasr Mohammed

When Mohammed Ali came to power, the greatest threat to his authority came from the Mamluks, former overlords of Egypt and still a force to be reckoned with. In addition to his infamous massacre of 500 Mamluks at the Citadel in 1811 (see p59), Mohammed Ali ordered all the Mamluk structures in the Citadel to be destroyed. This one mosque survived because it had been put to use as a stable.

Situated just behind the Mosque of Mohammed Ali, this simple structure is all that remains of a massive building programme undertaken by Sultan an-Nasr Mohammed (1294–1340), whose *madrassa* and mausoleum stand on Bein al-Qasreen (see p96).

◖ Mosque of Mohammed Ali

Dominating the eastern Cairo skyline, the Mohammed Ali Mosque is a relative newcomer, having been constructed as recently as the mid-19th century. It was erected on the orders of the reformist ruler Mohammed Ali, who is regarded as the founder of modern Egypt. When he came to power in 1805, Egypt was a backwater province of the Ottoman empire. By the time of his death in 1849, however, the country was once again a regional superpower.

Mohammed Ali's imposing mosque was a grand gesture that was meant to echo the great imperial mosques of the Ottoman capital. It is modelled along classic Turkish lines, with a great central dome and two towering, yet slender, minarets. The ornate clock in the courtyard near the entrance to the mosque was a gift from King Louis-Philippe of France, in exchange for the obelisk in the Place de la Concorde in Paris. The clock was damaged

Built between 1318 and 1335 as a congregational mosque, where everyone gathered to pray, the building has two unique, corkscrew minarets with bulbous finials, covered with faïence tiles in a fashion more Persian than Egyptian.

There are two entrances to the mosque: one is in the form of a three-lobed arch and was used by soldiers, while the other arch was used exclusively by the Sultan.

Although many of the columns within the arcaded courtyard were salvaged from Pharaonic, Roman and Byzantine buildings, they nevertheless all blend together surprisingly well.

The marble panelling that once graced the mosque's courtyard was removed by Sultan Selim I in 1517 and sent to Constantinople.

A view of the Mosque of Mohammed Ali, within the Citadel walls

⌂ Police Museum

Built on top of the former Mamluk-era Lion's Tower – so-called because of the statues of big cats at the base of the building – this small museum illustrates the history of Egyptian policing through the ages. Exhibits include uniforms and weapons, a small display on political assassinations and accounts of infamous Egyptian criminals, including Raya and Sakina. Included in the museum is the small row of cells that were in use as recently as 1983. Among their last inhabitants were President Sadat's assassins, held here while awaiting trial in 1981. The museum terrace offers some of the best views over the city.

Statue of a lion at the entrance of the Police Museum

⌂ Military Museum

Built by Mohammed Ali in 1827, this was the residence of the Egyptian royal family until 1874, when Khedive Ismail moved into the newly built Abdeen Palace (see p79).

The building served as a military hospital during British occupation in World War II but it became a military museum when control of the Citadel reverted to Egypt in 1946.

Displays include uniforms, weaponry and dioramas of battles. Some of the palatial interiors are impressive, especially the superb trompe l'oeil in the main salon.

⌂ Mosque of Suleiman Pasha

This mosque was built in 1528 by Suleiman Pasha, who ruled Cairo after the Turks defeated the Mamluks in 1517. It was the first of many Ottoman mosques to be built in Egypt and, though modest in scale, it is one of the most charming. On the underside of the domes is some exquisitely painted decoration inspired by Turkish tiling. There are also some fine examples of traditional

Mihrab (prayer niche) and minbar (pulpit) in Mosque of Suleiman Pasha

inlaid marblework. In the mosque is a small mausoleum with tombs marked by turban-like headstones. These mark the burial places of Ottoman military officers, who were known as Janissaries.

⌂ Towers, Gates and Walls

Punctuated by towers and gates, the Citadel walls extend for over 3 km (2 miles). The former main gate, the Bab al-Azab, has been closed for decades and entrance is now through the Bab al-Gebel (Mountain Gate), created in 1786, or the Bab al-Gadid (New Gate). This enormous vaulted portal was built in 1826 by Mohammed Ali.

The oldest parts of the walls are those around the northern enclosure. Fortifications here date back to the Ayyubid era. Salah ad-Din built the original walls and all the small half-

round towers (1171–93). These were strengthened in the early 13th century by his successors, who also added most of the larger towers. It is possible to visit the interior of Salah ud-Din's two eastern-most towers, Burg al-Haddad and Burg al-Ramla.

⌂ Other Museums

Al-Gawhara Palace was built by Mohammed Ali in 1814 to house his administration and as a place to receive guests. The former Audience Hall now serves as a museum and is crammed with furniture, portraits and life-sized models of Mohammed Ali and other monarchs and their courtiers. Numerous royal carriages, mainly from the reign of Ismail (1863–79), are on display in the **Carriage Museum**. They include one used at the Suez Canal opening in 1869.

RAYA AND SAKINA – SISTERS IN NOTORIETY

Egypt's most infamous criminals, sisters Raya and Sakina, were tried and hanged in 1921 for the murders of 17 young women. The sisters lived in the poorest quarter of Alexandria where, with the connivance of their husbands, they ran a string of brothels. Their victims were picked up in the market place, lured back to one of their houses and strangled. The motive was money: only girls wearing expensive-looking jewellery were selected. The eventual arrest of Raya and Sakina occurred after a policeman became suspicious of the strong smell of incense emanating from Raya's home. He ordered a search that led to the discovery of the corpses. Since then, the grisly murders have provided lasting inspiration for writers, dramatists and film-makers, and Raya and Sakina have become part of popular Egyptian mythology.

Raya

Sakina

Mosque of Sultan Hassan (*left*) and Mosque of ar-Rifai (*right*) seen from the Citadel

Mosque of Sultan Hassan ㉒

Midan Salah ad-Din. **Map** 4 E2.
◯ *daily.* ● *for noon prayers Fri.* 🈂

One of the most interesting of the capital's mosques, this is also Cairo's finest example of early Mamluk architecture. The mosque overlooks what were the fields of the Hippodrome (now Midan Salah ad-Din), across from the precipitous walls of the Citadel. The dimensions of this massive structure are truly staggering: 150 m (492 ft) long, with walls 36 m (118 ft) high, the tallest minaret rising to 68 m (223 ft).

The construction of the mosque was funded with money from the estates of people who had died in the Black Death (which struck Cairo in 1348). This policy increased the unpopularity of the sultan, An-Nasr Hassan, who was already renowned for his greed. Building work began in 1356 and five years later, in 1361, one of the minarets collapsed, killing hundreds of people. This turned out to be a bad omen: it was only a matter of time before the downfall of the sultan himself. By the end of 1361, two years before his mosque was completed, Hassan had been murdered. Despite the unhappy history of Hassan's grand monument,

the interior of the mosque is overwhelming. Through a magnificent portal, a dimly lit corridor leads to a high-walled central courtyard. On the four sides of the courtyard are great, recessed arches, known as *iwans*, which were formerly used for teaching. Each *iwan* was devoted to one of the main schools of Sunni Islam.

At the rear of the eastern *iwan*, situated to the right of a particularly beautiful *mihrab* or niche, a bronze door leads to the mausoleum. The largest in Cairo, it was never occupied by the sultan, whose murdered body was not recovered. However, the mausoleum was used for the burial of two of his sons.

Detail of wall and steps from the Mosque of Sultan Hassan

Tickets for the mosque are sold at a kiosk to the right of the main entrance, in a small, unkempt garden that also contains an open-air café.

Mosque of ar-Rifai ㉓

Midan Salah ad-Din. **Map** 4 E2.
◯ *daily.* ● *for noon prayers Fri.* 🈂

Separated from the Mosque of Sultan Hassan by a canyon-like pedestrian street, the similar scale and symmetry of the Mosque of ar-Rifai suggests that it was erected at the same time as its neighbour. In fact, 450 years separate them.

Founded in 1819, the Mosque of ar-Rifai was not completed until 1912. Its patron was Princess Khushyar, mother of the Europhile Khedive Ismail, who intended the mosque as a tomb for her family. It was deliberately built in a pseudo-Mamluk style, with decoration copied from existing period mosques. The result is rather clumsy compared with the Mosque of Sultan Hassan. The over-wrought interior is filled with glitzy tombs of members of the royal family, including the Khedive Ismail and Farouk, the last king of Egypt. Also buried here is the last shah of Iran, who found refuge in Egypt after fleeing Khomeini's Islamic revolution in 1979.

Directly in front of the Mosque of ar-Rifai, facing the Citadel, is the **Mosque of Amir Akhur**. Dating from the late Mamluk period, the building is distinguished by its *ablaq* banding of red and white stone, its imposing dome and double minaret finial. The lower end of its sloping site incorporates a *kuttab* or Quranic school century.

C **Mosque of Amir Akhur**
Midan Salah ad-Din. **Map** 4 F2.
◯ *daily.* ◉ *for noon prayers Fri.* 🖼

Dervish Theatre ㉔

Sharia as-Suyufiya. **Map** 4 E2.
◯ *daily.* 🖼

In the gardens behind the Mosque of Hassan Sadaqa (also known as Sunqur Sadi) is a restored 19th-century theatre. Entrance to the theatre is from a small court-yard garden, which is reached via a door on the right of the façade of the mosque, in Sharia as-Suyufiya. Its circular, polished-wood stage is surrounded by a two-storey gallery. The theatre was built by an order of Mevlevi Dervishes, who extended the religious complex on this site to include a hostel (*khanqah*) and a theatre. The Dervishes (*see p92*) are Sufis, who follow a spiritual offshoot of Islam, and who believe that their whirling dance leads to

A view of the interior of the Mosque of Sultan Hassan

oneness with Allah. From the floor of the theatre, you can see down into the tomb of Hassan Sadaqa, for whom the mosque was built.

Part of a complex dating from 1321, the Mosque of Hassan Sadaqa is in poor condition, its foundations threatened by rising ground water. It is, however, distinguished by the fine stuccowork on its minaret and dome, visible from the street. The complex originally included a monastery (*ribat*), which was replaced by the theatre, and a place of study (*madrassa*), which no longer exists.

C **Mosque of Hassan Sadaqa**
Sharia as-Suyufiya. **Map** 4 E2.
◯ *daily.* ◉ *for noon prayers Fri*

Sabil-Kuttab of Qaitbey ㉕

Sharia as-Saliba. **Map** 4 E2.

Just 200 m (650 ft) west of Midan Salah ad-Din, at the western end of Sharia as-Saliba, is the huge, block-like structure of the 15th-century Sabil-Kuttab of Qaitbey. Although in poor condition, this Quranic school is notable for the fine marble-inlay decoration on its western façade. The building itself is closed to the public.

Qaitbey was a ruthless sultan who started life as a slave-boy to the previous sultan. He built some of Cairo's most beautiful monuments, including his spectacular mosque in the Northern Cemetery (*see p102*).

Further west, Sharia as-Saliba passes between the **Mosque of Sheikhu** on the right and the **Khanqah of Sheikhu** on the left. These buildings were built around the middle of the 14th century and are still in use. A *khanqah* is a Sufi hostel, where the sheikh resides, teaching his disciples.

Beyond another small mosque, a dusty street leads up on the left to the entrance to the Mosque of Ibn Tulun (*see pp110–11*). Back on Sharia as-Saliba, a short walk straight ahead takes you to Midan Sayyida Zeinab – a good place to get a taxi back to the centre.

C **Mosque and Khanqah of Sheikhu**
Sharia as-Saliba. **Map** 4 E2.
◯ *daily.* ◉ *for noon prayers Fri.*

DECORATIVE MAMLUK MOTIFS

The buildings created between 1250 and 1517, in the time of the Mamluk sultans, represent the pinnacle of Islamic art in Egypt. A fusion of the building traditions of the Near East, they blend Armenian stonework with North African stucco, Byzantine golden mosaics, and Syrian polychrome marble inlays. It is the latter that provide the most striking element. Created by painstakingly cutting small pieces of different coloured stone and fitting them together like a jigsaw puzzle, the intricate orna-mentation forms incredibly complex geometric patterns that are completely abstract in character. Repetitive and hypnotic, it has been suggested that the complex decoration aided prayer by heightening the viewers' sensory experience.

Detail of the marble inlay on the Sabil-Kuttab of Qaitbey

Mosque of Ibn Tulun ㉖

Decorative motif on arch

One of the largest and oldest mosques in the country, Ibn Tulun was built between AD 876 and AD 879 by an Abbasid governor sent from Baghdad to rule Egypt. Called a "Friday Mosque", its open-air courtyard is large enough to hold the whole male congregation of the district for prayers on the holiest day of the week. Built entirely of mudbrick, the mosque is surrounded by an outer courtyard, which was meant to act like a moat and keep the secular city at bay. This, and its curious spiral minaret, make it unique in Egypt. Contrasting with the geometric simplicity of the mosque, the maze of rooms in the nearby Gayer-Anderson Museum is filled with a diverting collection of artifacts.

★ Mihrab
A niche indicating the direction of Mecca, this mihrab *dates back to the 13th century. Next to it is the* minbar, *or pulpit, one of the finest in Egypt.*

Gayer-Anderson Museum

Lectern
Called a dikka *in Arabic, the wooden platform, in line with the* mihrab, *is used for Quranic recitations and calls to prayer inside the mosque.*

Entrance

Arcades
Running around the courtyard, the arcades (riwaq) *provide shade for worshippers. The largest, on the southeast side, is five columns deep and serves as the mosque's prayer hall. Quranic verses are inscribed along the whole length of the ceiling in the arcade.*

Outer Courtyard

STAR FEATURES

★ Mihrab

★ Spiral Minaret

★ Fountain

GAYER-ANDERSON MUSEUM

This charming museum is the legacy of John Gayer-Anderson, a British officer serving in Cairo. In the 1930s, he lovingly restored two adjacent 16th- or 17th-century houses. Lavishly decorated with *mashrabiyya* screens and marble inlays, they were further ornamented by a vast amount of interesting and often intriguing orientalia. He also added a room, decorated in lacquer and gold, taken from a 17th-century house in Damascus. The cumulative effect of all these items makes the museum one of the most magical places to visit in Cairo.

Reproduction bust of Nefertiti

Inner courtyard or *sahn*

★ **Fountain**
The original had a beautiful gilded dome but this collapsed in AD 968. The current dome is a 13th-century replacement.

Pointed arches are inscribed with geometric designs.

The windows have ornately decorated stucco grills, no two of which are the same.

Outside staircase

★ **Spiral Minaret**
Inspired by the tower at the Great Mosque of Samarra in Iraq, Ibn Tulun's minaret is an easy climb, rewarded by excellent views of the city.

Crenellations
The design of these brick-built crenellations is supposed to have been inspired by ranks of standing soldiers.

RHODA ISLAND AND OLD CAIRO

For several centuries following the decline of the old Pharaonic religions and before the arrival of Islam, Egypt was a predominantly Christian country. Alexandria was then the country's capital, while Cairo had yet to be founded. Around the 6th century AD the site of the city consisted of little more than a Roman fortress beside the Nile, guarding a crossing point on the route between the ancient Egyptian cities of Heliopolis and Memphis. When Arab general

Virgin icon in Hanging Church

Amr Ibn al-Aas set up camp in its shadow and built a capital nearby, he was placing the marker for the future foundation of Cairo. Known today as Old Cairo (Misr al-Qadima), this ancient part of the city contains a bastion of Egyptian Christianity, known as Coptic Cairo, and many historic churches. The area also takes in the southern tip of the island of Rhoda, site of the Nilometer which has been used to measure the height of the river Nile since Pharaonic times.

SIGHTS AT A GLANCE

Holy Places
Ben Ezra Synagogue ❸
Church of St George ❶
Church of St Sergius ❺
Church of St Barbara ❹
Convent of St George ❻
Hanging Church ❼
Monastery of St Mercurius ❿

Mosque of Amr Ibn al-Aas ❾
Tomb of Suleiman al-Faransawi ⓫

Archaeological Sites
Fustat ❽

Museums & Historic Buildings
Coptic Museum ❷
Nilometer ⓬

| 0 metres | 500 |
| 0 yards | 500 |

GETTING AROUND

Old Cairo is most easily reached by Metro; Mar Girgis station is just four stops south of Midan Tahrir (Sadat Metro). River buses to Old Cairo depart from a point below the Corniche in front of the Radio and TV Union Building. From the landing stage, it is only a short walk to Coptic Cairo, the oldest part of modern-day Cairo.

KEY

▩	Street-by-Street *See pp114–15*
Ⓜ	Metro station
🚏	Bus station
🚢	Riverbus terminal

◁ **A haven of peace and tranquillity among the high-walled cobbled alleyways of Coptic Cairo**

Street by Street: Coptic Cairo

Coptic Museum window panel

Coptic Cairo is the modern name for the oldest part of the city. The compound lies within the walls of the 3rd-century AD Roman fortress of Babylon and is a haven of quiet, narrow lanes and ancient holy places. The main entrance, leading to the interesting Coptic Museum and the beautiful Hanging Church, is between two round Roman towers, against which the waters of the Nile once lapped before the river shifted course to the west some centuries ago. A second, stepped entrance to the north leads along a sunken alley to the rest of the churches, the synagogue and the cemeteries.

Convent of St George
While not allowed inside, visitors can re-enact the persecution of Palestinian St George, famed for his dragon slaying, and be wrapped in chains ❻

Church of St George
Although Coptic Cairo is a prime destination for tourists, its churches are still frequented by members of the local Christian community who regularly come here to light candles and say prayers ❶

★ Coptic Museum
Artifacts here trace the origins of Christian art in the Near East. The building itself is beautiful, especially the older, southern wing. There is also a garden and a café (currently under restoration) ❷

★ Hanging Church
This most beautiful of Cairo's churches has an ornately decorated interior consisting of three barrel-vaulted, wooden-roofed aisles, ivory inlaid screens and a finely carved marble pulpit ❼

Subterranean entrance to compound

SHARIA MAR GIRGIS

Convent of St George

Entrance

Church of St George

Mari Girgis Station **M**

Church of St Sergius

Entrance to Hanging Church

ROMAN TOWER

Coptic Museum

Hanging Church

KEY

- Built-up area
- Roman wall
- Railway line
- **M** Metro station

Church of St Barbara

Dedicated to the saint who was beaten to death by her father for trying to convert him to Christianity, St Barbara's is one of Egypt's largest and finest churches. There is a domed apse behind the altar with seven steps decorated in bands of black, white and red marble **4**

Amr Ibn al-Aas Mosque

LOCATOR MAP
See Street Finder Map 4

| 0 metres | 50 |
| 0 yards | 50 |

The Nuptial Hall was part of a church first founded in AD 681.

Ben Ezra Synagogue

This is Egypt's oldest synagogue and it has been heavily restored in recent times. Ben Ezra is a testament to the ancient and significant presence of Jews in this region **3**

Church of St Barbara

Ben Ezra Synagogue

GREEK ORTHODOX CEMETERY

Church of St Sergius

Since this, the oldest church in Coptic Cairo, was built, ground levels have risen. It is now entered down some steps. Legend says that the Holy Family sheltered in a cave below the altar **5**

GREEK CATHOLIC CEMETERY

Cemeteries

The cemeteries around the compound belong to the Coptic, Greek Orthodox and Greek Catholic communities. They are filled with impressive statues and elaborate mausoleums, such as this one.

STAR SIGHTS

★ Coptic Museum

★ Hanging Church

A 7th-century painting in the Coptic Museum depicting the Virgin Mary and the infant Jesus flanked by saints

Church of St George ❶

Coptic Cairo compound. **Map** 3 B5.
Ⓜ *Mar Girgis.* ⬡ *8am–12:45pm &
2:30–3:15pm daily.*

Long before the Crusaders
carried tales of his legendary
exploits back to Europe, St
George was venerated
throughout the Christian
Middle East as Mar Girgis.
He is said to have been a
Roman legionary who defied
a decree by the Emperor
Diocletian outlawing the
worship of Christ and was
martyred for his beliefs some
time in the 3rd century.

There has been a church
dedicated to St George on
or near the present site since
at least the 10th century,
but today's striking round

**Worshippers at the entrance to the
Church of St George in Old Cairo**

structure dates only to the
beginning of the 20th century.
The circular form of the church
echoes the shape of the 1st
century AD Roman gate tower
on top of which it was built.
The remains of the tower are
still visible beneath the church
on the north side and previous
floodwater has been drained.

Coptic Museum ❷

Coptic Cairo compound. **Map** 3 B5.
Ⓜ *Mar Girgis.* **Tel** *(02) 363 9742.*
⬡ *9am–5pm daily (9am–3pm
Ramadan).* 📷

Largely built in 1947, this
charming museum houses
the finest collection of Coptic
art in the world. The building
itself has undergone extensive
renovation since suffering
earthquake damage in 1992,
and boasts elaborately painted
wooden ceilings, elegant
mashrabiyya windows, and a
garden courtyard.

The exhibits date back to
Egypt's Christian era and both
Pharaonic and Islamic influences are evident in the
artifacts on display. Early
exhibits carry motifs and
symbols, such as *ankhs* and
Horus-like falcons, that are
recognizably ancient
Egyptian. Elsewhere, carved
capitals from an early Coptic
cathedral in Alexandria display
a mastery of stone carving that
would later come to fruition
during the era of the Mamluks.
A 6th-century Coptic stone

pulpit resembles the stairs and
shrine of the pyramid complex
at Saqqara *(see pp162–3)*, and
also prefigures the *minbars*
found in all Cairo mosques.
Still more fascinating are the
crudely painted depictions
of Mary suckling Jesus, which
directly echo images found
all over Egypt of Isis nursing
Horus. Many of the pieces are
also Classical in inspiration, a
legacy of
Alexander's
Ptolemaic
dynasty and
Roman rule.

On the upper
floor are the
finely woven
textiles for
which the
Copts were
once famous. There are also
lavishly embroidered silk garments, icons, and what is
claimed by some to be the
oldest book in the world, the
1,600-year-old Coptic book of
the Psalms of David.

**Carved stone
capital, Coptic
Museum**

Ben Ezra Synagogue ❸

Coptic Cairo compound. **Map** 3 B5.
Ⓜ *Mar Girgis.* ⬡ *8am–4pm daily.*

Jewish history in Egypt dates
back to the era of the Old
Testament and the stories of
Moses and the persecution by
the pharaohs. After the Roman
expulsion of Jews from Jerusalem in the first century AD,
Alexandria became the

world's most important centre of Judaism. As recently as the early 20th century the Jewish community in Egypt remained significant and prominent. This changed dramatically with the creation of Israel in 1948. Those Jews that had not already left by choice were forced out of Egypt when the country went to war against the newly formed Jewish state. Monuments to the long history of the Jews in Egypt are few and, of these, Ben Ezra is the oldest. Legends link it with Moses but in fact the synagogue was formerly a church, built in the 8th century. Around 300 years later the church was destroyed and the site and its ruins given to Abraham ben Ezra, a 12th-century rabbi of Jerusalem.

Repairs in the 19th century unearthed hundreds of Hebrew manuscripts from the synagogue's intact *geniza*, or treasury. In Egypt any paper bearing the name of God had to be preserved and this has resulted in a legacy of thousands of documents dating largely from the 11th and 12th centuries. Together, they amount to a minutely detailed chronicle of life in medieval Cairo.

The synagogue underwent extensive renovation in the 1980s and although it is no longer used for worship it is in a pristine state.

Church of St Barbara ❹

Coptic Cairo compound. **Map** 3 B5.
Ⓜ *Mar Girgis.* ◯ *8am–4pm daily.*

This church was named after an early Christian martyr who lived in the 3rd century AD. Daughter of a merchant, she was killed by her father for trying to convert him to Christianity. Occupying the site of an earlier church dedicated to St Cyrus and St John, the church of St Barbara was built in the 11th century and is one of the largest and finest in Egypt. It boasts a beautiful 13th-century iconostasis, or sanctuary screen, of wood inlaid with finely carved

Carved 13th-century iconostasis in the Church of St Barbara

ivory. There is also a series of striking icons, dating to around 1750, depicting Jesus, Mary, two archangels and various saints and apostles.

Church of St Sergius ❺

Coptic Cairo compound. **Map** 3 B5.
Ⓜ *Mar Girgis.* ◯ *8am–4pm daily.*

Perhaps the most famous church in all Egypt, St Sergius owes its reputation to the widely held belief that the Holy Family took shelter in a cave on this spot during their "Flight into Egypt" (see p123).

The cave is preserved in the form of a crypt, currently in the process of being cleared of underground water.

Whatever the truth of the Holy stopover, the church is likely to be the oldest existing structure within the fortress, with foundations dating back to the 5th century AD. Rebuilt and reconstructed many times, most of the fabric of the building dates to between the 10th and 12th centuries.

Convent of St George ❻

Coptic Cairo compound. **Map** 3 B5.
Ⓜ *Mar Girgis.* ◯ *8am–4pm daily.*

This convent dates back at least as far as the 15th century when it was written about by the Arab chronicler Al-Maqrizi. The convent is still inhabited by nuns but visitors are permitted to enter the high-ceilinged Great Hall where there is a shrine containing a famed icon of St George.

The convent is also known for its unusual chain-wrapping ritual still practised by the nuns. The chains symbolize the persecution of St George.

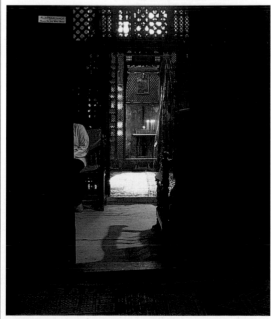

The shrine dedicated to St George in the Convent of St George

Hanging Church ⓿

Icon of St George

Dedicated to the Virgin Mary, this church is popularly called the "Hanging" or "Suspended" Church (Al-Muallaqa in Arabic) because it was built on top of the Water Gate of the old Roman fortress of Babylon. The original structure was built possibly as early as the 4th century AD, but it was destroyed and rebuilt in the 11th century. Expansion and reconstruction has gone on ever since, making it difficult to date precisely any specific part of the church. A marble pulpit and the inlaid ivory screens that hide the three altar areas date from between the 10th and 13th centuries. Despite its venerable nature, the church is still used for regular public services, which are held every Friday and Sunday morning.

Outer Porch
Decorated with glazed tiles in geometrical designs, the porch dates from the 11th century.

Inner courtyard

Carved Frieze
The church incorporates some fine old decoration, such as this frieze of Christ flanked by angels, but the earliest pieces are now housed in the nearby Coptic Museum (see p116).

On the porch at the top of the staircase are stalls selling cassettes of Coptic liturgies and videos of papal sermons.

Priests' quarters

★ Façade
Surmounted by its distinctive twin bell towers, the whole front section is a relatively recent addition, dating only from the 19th century.

STAR FEATURES

★ Façade

★ Sanctuary Screen

◁ Detail from the interior of the dome in the Coptic Museum

★ Sanctuary Screen
Carved from cedarwood and delicately inlaid with ivory, the central screen that shields the main altar is the finest of its kind in Egypt.

VISITORS' CHECKLIST

Coptic Cairo compound, Sharia Mar Girgis. **Map** 3 B5. M *Mar Girgis.* from Midan Tahrir. from Maspero terminal. *Tel* (02) 363 9742. 9am–4pm daily. 8–11am Fri, 7–10am Sun. (Restoration of the church interior is currently taking place.)

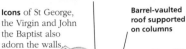

Icons of St George, the Virgin and John the Baptist also adorn the walls.

Barrel-vaulted roof supported on columns

Top of the screen adorned with icons

Pulpit
Made of marble and dating from the 11th century, the pulpit rests on 13 columns representing Christ and his disciples.

The Chapel of Takla Haymanot was part of the original 4th-century church. Built in one of the bastions of the Water Gate, it honours the patron saint of Ethiopia.

Roman Towers
The towers belonged to the southwestern bastion of the original Roman fortress and date from around the 1st century AD.

Interior of Church
Three barrel-vaulted roofs are supported on columns with Corinthian capitals, indicating that they were recycled from earlier buildings.

The foundations of the Church can be seen from the courtyard of the Coptic Museum.

Coptic Christianity

The word "Copt" is a corruption of the Arabic *Qibti*, which is derived from the Greek word *Aegyptios*, meaning "Egyptian". According to tradition, St Mark, one of the 12 Apostles, introduced Christianity into Egypt in the first century AD. Alexandria was one of the first five patriarchates – branches of the Christian church headed by patriarchs claiming descent from the Apostles – and by the 4th century, Christianity was the official religion of Egypt. Egyptian Christians split from the orthodox church after the Council of Chalcedon proclaimed, in AD 451, the dual human and divine nature of Christ. Dioscurus, patriarch of Alexandria, refused to accept this definition, believing only in Christ's divinity.

The ankh, *symbol of eternal life in ancient Egypt, is transformed into a Christian cross.*

Dating from *c.1400 BC, this sculpture of Isis with the infant Horus is an image akin to later depictions of the Virgin Mary and the Infant Christ. This, along with the ankh and the belief in the afterlife, are some of the more obvious parallels between the ancient Egyptian religion and Christianity, and may explain the ease of Egypt's conversion to the new religion.*

POPE SHENOUDA III

The 117th patriarch of the Coptic church, Pope Shenouda III, and several Coptic priests attend midnight mass at St Mark's Cathedral in Cairo. The Pope was once a monk at Wadi Natrun (*see p169*), from where the Coptic pope is traditionally chosen.

The Coptic language, *shown here on an early engraving, has its origins in ancient Greek and Egyptian hieroglyphics. Copts claim to be direct descendants of ancient Egyptians. The Coptic language is still used today in religious ceremonies.*

Boutros Boutros-Ghali
(*see p63*), *the former UN Secretary-General, is an internationally renowned Copt. Always an economically powerful minority, Copts have long provided an educated elite in Egypt, filling many of the country's important posts.*

THE HOLY FAMILY IN EGYPT

According to biblical tradition, the Holy Family fled to Egypt to escape Herod's "massacre of the innocents". Coptic tradition links their visit to several sites around the country. At Matariyya, a northeastern suburb of Cairo, is the Virgin's Tree, a gnarled sycamore under which Mary is said to have rested. In Coptic Cairo *(see pp116–17)*, part of the Church of St Sergius is a cave in which the family dwelt, while the town of Asyut *(see p176)* is the southernmost point associated with the route the family took.

The Flight into Egypt by Jean-Léon Gérôme (1824–1904)

Monks, *like this one from the Monastery of St Anthony in the Eastern Desert, still wear traditional black robes and a hood with distinctive gold embroidery. Today, monasticism is experiencing a renaissance and attracting many new recruits.*

St Anthony's Monastery (see p232) *represents the beginning of the Christian monastic tradition. It was later followed by Coptic monasteries like Wadi Natrun (see p169) and St Catherine's in Sinai (see pp222–5).*

This is a typical *Egyptian town in Middle Egypt, dominated by a Coptic church and surrounded by fertile fields. There are approximately 6 million Copts – 10 per cent of Egypt's population – and most live in Middle Egypt. Despite the odd claim and counter-claim, Copts and Muslims live harmoniously side by side.*

Fustat ⑧

Sharia Ain as-Sirah. **Map** 3 C5.
Ⓜ *Mar Girgis.*

There is little for the visitor
to see at Fustat except hard,
sun-baked earth but it
represents nevertheless almost
1,400 years of Egyptian history.

When the armies of Islam,
led by their general Amr ibn
al-Aas, conquered Egypt in
AD 640 they chose not to
occupy any of the existing
cities of Alexandria, Memphis
or Karnak. Instead they set
up camp immediately north
of the Roman fortress of
Babylon beside the Nile.

In time the canvas city was
replaced by one of mudbrick
and stone but was still known
as Fustat, meaning "tent". It
flourished and became Egypt's
first Islamic capital. Under the
Fatimid dynasty (969–1171),
however, the new rulers built
their own city further to the
north *(see pp94–5)* and in 1168
put Fustat to the flame rather
than risk its capture by the
Crusaders. From the 13th to
the 16th century, the Mamluks
used the area as a rubbish
dump and today it is a vast
wasteland. Once inhabited
by thousands of people who
earned a living as potters and
rubbish-collectors, now only a
few remain on the outskirts. To
archaeologists it is a treasure
chest waiting to be opened –
an ancient city preserved under
the garbage of hundreds of
years. To date, only the foundations and remnants of the city
walls have been revealed.

A pottery on the edge of Fustat,
Egypt's first Islamic city

Mosque of Amr ibn al-Aas ⑨

Midan Amr ibn al-Aas. **Map** 3 B4.
Ⓜ *Mar Girgis.* ◯ *daily.* ◯ *to non-
Muslims at prayer times.* 📷

Named after the general
who conquered Egypt for
Islam in AD 640, the original
Mosque of Amr ibn al-Aas
was the first place of Islamic
worship in Egypt and therefore the first mosque on the
continent of Africa.

According to contemporary
accounts, the mosque was a
basic building of mudbrick
walls, unpaved floor and a
palm-thatch roof supported
on palm columns. It had no
mibrab, courtyard or minaret,
but it was large enough to
hold Amr's army at prayer.
Apart from the site, however,
nothing of the original remains
in the present mosque, which

is a patchwork of countless
rebuildings and restorations.
It is said that no two of its 200
or so columns are the same.
The earliest existing parts date
to the 9th century, when the
original mosque was rebuilt,
almost doubling in size. However, other areas, such as the
entrance, were reconstructed
as recently as the 1980s.

The mosque has retained
an air of simplicity, in keeping
with its humble origins and it
still fills each day for prayers
with a devout congregation.
Visitors to the mosque are
welcome at other times.

Monastery of St Mercurius ⑩

Sharia Abu Seifan. **Map** 3 B4.
Ⓜ *Mar Girgis.* ◯ *9am–5pm daily.* 📷

To the northwest of the
Mosque of Amr ibn al-Aas is
a complex consisting of three
churches and a convent. Surrounded by a high wall, the
compound is entered via
a small doorway off the
main street. This leads
to a narrow, sunken
alleyway that con-
nects the various
buildings. The
monastery
complex was
reputedly named   **Relief painting,**
after a martyred   **Church of**
Roman legionary   **St Mercurius**
and dates from the
early 6th century, but it has
been destroyed and rebuilt
on at least four occasions.

The main building in the
complex is the
**Church of St
Mercurius**, which in
its current form dates
back to 1176. It was
destroyed in the blaze
when the Fatimid
overlord Vizier
Shawar ordered
Fustat to be razed
to the ground.

The church is
now a repository of
fine early Coptic art
with unique wall
paintings, an extra-
ordinary collection
of icons and a fine
wooden altar canopy.
A flight of stairs in

Façade and entrance to the Mosque of Amr ibn al-Aas

For hotels and restaurants in this region see pp268–71 and pp290–95

Ornate ironwork exterior of the Tomb of Suleiman al-Faransawi

the north aisle of the church leads down to a small crypt where, in the 4th century, the ascetic St Barsum the Naked is said to have spent the last 20 years of his life with only a snake for company.

The **Church of the Holy Virgin** and the **Church of St Shenouda** are both open to visitors but the **Convent of St Mercurius**, also part of the complex, is still inhabited by nuns and is off limits.

Tomb of Suleiman al-Faransawi ⓫

Sharia Mohammed al-Saghir. **Map** 3 B5. Ⓜ *Mar Girgis.*

A small cast-iron tomb in a residential square, this is one of the most unusual monuments in Cairo, built in the 19th century in honour of an extremely unusual man.

Suleiman "the Frenchman" (originally a soldier named Joseph Sèves) was a veteran of Napoleon's campaigns who came to Egypt to train the armies of the viceroy Mohammed Ali *(see p59)*. It is said that the Frenchman, who died in 1860, was so despised by his conscripts that they would shoot at him during target practice. Sèves later converted to Islam, taking the name Suleiman, and was rewarded with the honorary title "Pasha" following Egypt's successful campaigns against Greece and Syria. A statue of Suleiman mounted on his horse used to stand in Downtown Cairo on what was Sharia Suleiman Pasha. During the 1952 Revolution

the statue was consigned to the Citadel and the street renamed in honour of the Egyptian nationalist and banker, Talaat Harb.

Nilometer ⓬

Sharia al-Malik Salih. **Map** 3 B5. Ⓜ *Mar Girgis.* ⓞ *daily.* 🖼

Until the construction of the dams at Aswan, Egyptian life was governed by the annual flooding of the Nile. Most years, its waters rose to swamp the river valley, then retreated, leaving behind richly fertile deposits of alluvial soil. Occasionally, however, the floods failed to cover the whole agricultural area and this resulted in low crop yields and sometimes famine. In order to forecast what kind of harvest a particular year might bring,

Nilometer on Rhoda Island showing the simple calibration used to predict the floods

the ancient Egyptians constructed a series of Nilometers, one of which is cut into the bedrock of the island of Rhoda. It takes the form of a deep, square pit containing an octagonal column, marked off with graduations. Water was let in through three channels – these are now blocked up but are still visible. At the annual meter-reading ceremony, a sufficiently high level of water would be greeted by festivities, while a shortfall would trigger anxious prayers.

Although there is evidence that a Nilometer has been here since Pharaonic times, in its existing form it dates from the 9th century – hence the elaborate Islamic inscriptions adorning the walls. Set over the Nilometer is a small Ottoman kiosk with a distinctive conical cap, dating from the 19th century. Decorating its wooden ceiling are some impressive painted arabesques.

Adjacent to the Nilometer is the Rococo **Munasterli Palace**, built in the 1850s. In spring 2002 an arts centre with a museum dedicated to the revered Egyptian singer Umm Kolthum opened here. Classical concerts are held during the winter.

UMM KOLTHUM: THE VOICE OF EGYPT

For much of the 20th century Umm Kolthum was the greatest living cultural icon not just in Egypt, but in the whole of the Arab world. She began singing with her father at weddings in the villages of the eastern Delta around 1910. Astonished by the strength of her voice, friends and family encouraged her to move to Cairo and establish her career. From the 1930s onwards for almost the next 40 years the whole of the country came to a standstill on one Thursday night each month when her concert would be broadcast live on national radio to audiences of millions. During this time she also recorded over 300 songs and appeared in countless films. When she died in 1975 her funeral was the biggest ever witnessed in Cairo. She remains inescapable today; her music is played constantly in coffeehouses and taxis, her voice providing a powerful soundtrack to any visit to Egypt.

Umm Kolthum, Egypt's favourite singer

GIZA AND HELIOPOLIS

Giza and Heliopolis are two Cairo suburbs that are not only geographically opposed, they also epitomize two extremes of Egypt's history. Giza, in the southwest, is famed for its ancient monuments. The Sphinx, usually dated to around 2500 BC and the earliest known monumental sculpture, stands guard over the Pyramids at Giza, and their attendant Queens' pyramids, temples, and tombs. The Pyramids are the only one of the Seven Wonders of the Ancient World to survive. Even the accompanying circus of camel and horse rides, souvenir

Moorish detail from a façade in Heliopolis

and soft drinks vendors, persistent beggars and the nightly Sound and Light show do not diminish their splendour. In the diagonally opposite suburb of Heliopolis, history moves on to the late 19th century and Baron Edouard Empain, the entrepreneur whose vision inspired this garden city in the desert. Built in a mixture of European and Moorish styles, Heliopolis attracted wealthy Egyptians to its leafy grandeur. Although it is no longer separate from Cairo, visitors still come to enjoy its stylish architecture, restaurants and nightlife.

A Queen's Pyramid with a small chapel attached, Giza

GETTING THERE

Bus No.355 picks up by the Egyptian Museum and goes out to the Pyramids, as do the minibuses Nos.82 and 83. From the new bus station behind the Egyptian Museum, bus No.356 departs every 20 minutes for Cairo airport going via Heliopolis. However, it may be easier to take a taxi for both areas.

Giza ❶

Heliopolis ❷

Cairo International Airport

0 kilometres 5

0 miles 3

KEY

▦ Central Cairo

▢ Greater Cairo

— Major roads

— Minor roads

Contrasting European and Moorish architecture in the suburb of Heliopolis

◁ The Sphinx, carved from an outcrop of soft limestone, in front of the Pyramid of Khafre at Giza

The Giza Plateau ❶

Nearly 5,000 years ago, Giza became the royal burial ground (necropolis) for Memphis, capital of Egypt. In less than 100 years, the ancient Egyptians built the three pyramid complexes to serve as the tombs for their dead kings. After the king's death, his body was brought by boat to the valley temple for preparation before being taken up the causeway and buried under, and in some cases within, the pyramid. The mortuary temples were maintained for many years afterwards with priests making daily offerings to the dead god-king. The king's close family and the royal court were buried in satellite pyramids and stone tombs called *mastaba* nearby, seeking to share in the king's power in death, as they had in life.

Pyramids of Giza
Three successive generations built these monumental structures during the 4th Dynasty of the Old Kingdom (2686–2181 BC).

Pyramid of Khafre

Pyramid of Menkaure

Khafre's Mortuary Temple

Queens' Pyramids

GIZA PLATEAU RECONSTRUCTION

The funerary complex included the main pyramid, covered in white limestone, various satellite pyramids and a mortuary temple joined by a causeway to a valley temple.

Pyramids of Menkaure and Khafre
While Khafre's Pyramid is nearly as grand as that of his father, Khufu, the Pyramid of Menkaure, Khafre's successor, is much smaller, hinting perhaps at a decline in power and commitment or simply a change in priorities.

Causeway

Tomb of Khentkawes
This was the last major tomb built at Giza. Queen Khentkawes, daughter of Menkaure, probably gave birth to a new dynasty that moved its necropolis to Abu Sir.

STAR SIGHTS

★ The Great Pyramid

★ The Sphinx

MEANING OF THE GIZA PYRAMIDS

Archaeologists agree that pyramids served as monumental structures for the burial of kings. They were topped with gold-covered pyramidions (pyramid-shaped capstones) which caught the first rays of the sun and their shape perhaps symbolized the mythical, primeval mound of creation *(see p26)*. However, because the exact purpose of some of the rooms and shafts of the Giza Pyramids is unknown, the fact that some air shafts point towards important constellations, that the southeast corners lie on a near perfect diagonal and that their sides align with true north inspires many to look hard for fanciful explanations. However, such alignments are simply consistent with ancient Egyptian funerary beliefs that the king's soul would rise up to join the "eternal stars".

Mastaba tombs were built in the 4th and 5th Dynasty.

Boat pit

★ **The Great Pyramid**
The oldest and largest of the pyramids was built by the 4th-Dynasty king, Khufu (2589–66 BC)

Queens' Pyramids were constructed for the wives, and important relatives of the kings.

Mastaba tombs

Khafre's Valley Temple held the king's body prior to burial.

VISITORS' CHECKLIST

Sharia al-Ahram (Pyramids Road), Giza, 12 km (8 miles) SW of Cairo.
📋 *(02) 383 8823.* 🚌 *82, 83 from Midan Tahrir.* 🚗
Giza Plateau ○ *8am–5pm daily.*
📷 **The Giza Pyramids** ○ *8am–4pm daily (5pm in summer).*
📷 *for each pyramid (one or more pyramids may be closed for restoration).* **Solar Boat Museum** ○ *9am–4pm daily (5pm in summer).* 📷 **Sound & Light Show** *6:30pm, 7:30pm, 8:30pm in winter (1 hour later in summer).*

★ **The Sphinx**
Guardian of the Giza Plateau, the leonine Sphinx is known to the Arabs as Abu al-Hol, *the "father of terror".*

The Giza Plateau: The Great Pyramid

The facts of Khufu's Pyramid, commonly referred to as the Great Pyramid, are staggering. It is estimated to contain over two million blocks of stone weighing on average around 2.5 tonnes, with some stones at the base weighing as much as 15 tonnes. Until the 19th century it was the tallest building in the world. Yet for such a vast structure the precision is amazing – the greatest difference in length between the four 230-m (756-ft) sides is only 4 cm (2 inches). The construction methods and exact purpose of some of the chambers and shafts are unknown, but the fantastic architectural achievement is clear.

Statue of Khufu (Cheops)
Khufu's only surviving statue is this 7.5-cm (3-inch) high ivory figure from Abydos, now kept in the Egyptian Museum.

The Queen's Chamber probably held a statue representing the *ka* or life-force of the king.

The **"air shafts"** may have been symbolic paths for the king's soul to ascend to the stars.

Queens' Pyramids
These three small pyramids were built for members of the king's family, although the actual identity of the occupants is unknown.

Underlying bedrock

★ **King's Chamber**
Probably emptied 600 years after being built, the chamber, despite holding only a lidless sarcophagus, was often broken into by treasure seekers.

Unfinished underground chamber

STAR FEATURES

★ King's Chamber

★ Great Gallery

★ **Great Gallery**
Soaring nearly 9 m (30 ft) high, this is thought to have been used as a slipway for the huge blocks that sealed the passageway.

◁ The Pyramids at Giza set in a timeless desert landscape

RECONSTRUCTION OF THE KING'S CHAMBER

Built to protect the chamber, the stress-relieving rooms also hold the only reference to Khufu in the pyramid – graffiti, from the time of construction, stating the names of the gangs who built the pyramid - one such name being "How powerful is the great White Crown of Khufu".

The cantilevered roof helps distribute the enormous weight of the stones above.

Workers' graffiti

Stress-relieving chambers were built out of huge blocks of granite weighing up to 80 tonnes.

Counter-balanced slabs of granite were lowered to seal the tomb.

King's Chamber

The "air shaft" would have been closed off by the outer casing.

This vertical shaft probably served as an escape route for the workers.

Entrance
The original entrance is now blocked and visitors use a lower opening made by the Caliph Maamun in AD 820.

THE DEVELOPMENT OF PYRAMIDS

It took the ancient Egyptians around 400 years to progress from mudbrick mastaba to smooth-sided pyramid. The last stage, from stepped to "true" or smooth-sided pyramid took only 65 years. In this time each pyramid was a brave venture into the unknown. Rarely in the history of mankind has technology developed at such a rate.

The Red or North Pyramid, at Dahshur (c.2600 BC)

Mastaba
Around 3000 BC the sandy mounds of the graves of the upper echelons of society were formalized into low, box-like mastabas.

Stepped pyramid (c.2665 BC)
A more impressive memorial was made by putting six stone mastabas on top of each other (see King Djoser's Pyramid pp162–3).

Prototype pyramid (c.2605 BC)
The first smooth-sided pyramid was achieved by filling in the steps of a stepped pyramid (see Meidum Pyramid p168). This was followed by purpose-built, smooth-sided pyramids.

Exploring the Giza Plateau

For preservation purposes, each of the pyramids is closed for a spell on a rotating basis and the number of visitors allowed inside is limited. Early morning is therefore the best time to visit, before the heat and crowds become unbearable; it is also worth a trip in the evening for the kitsch but spectacular Sound and Light Show. It can get hot and airless inside the pyramids so clambering inside is not recommended for claustrophobics or the unfit. Horse and camel owners tout expensive rides between the monuments but the area is compact enough to get around on foot.

Egyptian offering camel rides or simply a photo opportunity

The space-age shape of the Solar Boat Museum

🏛 Solar Boat Museum

On the south side of the Great Pyramid sits the pod-shaped, Solar Boat Museum. This holds a full-size ancient Egyptian boat discovered in pieces in 1954, lying in a pit beside the pyramid. Experts spent 14 years putting its 1200 pieces together again using only ancient Egyptian materials of wooden pegs and grass rope.

It is called a solar boat by archaeologists because it resembles the vessels seen in tomb paintings in which the sun-god makes his daily trip across the heavens. It is not clear whether the boat was buried for the sun-god or for the pharaoh's own journey across the heavens. Marks on the wood suggest that the boat had been sailed before being buried. It could be that it served as a funerary barque, carrying the body of Khufu from

Memphis to his tomb at Giza. A second similar boat was located in a nearby pit but remains unexcavated.

🜂 Pyramid of Khafre

The base of the Pyramid of Khafre (also called Khephren), is just 15 m (50 ft) shorter than the Great Pyramid, while in height there is a difference of only 3 m (10 ft). Today, however, Khafre's pyramid appears the larger by virtue of being built on higher ground, and because its summit remains intact. This summit is the only area that retains the limestone casing that originally covered all three pyramids. The rest was taken by the medieval rulers of Cairo who used it for their own monuments.

The interior is simpler than that of the Great Pyramid. It has two descending passageways converging and leading to a single tomb chamber. Whereas Khufu's tomb chamber sits high up inside the structure, Khafre's is dug deep into the bedrock beneath his pyramid. There

Idu, guardian of the burial complexes

is little to see except the king's granite sarcophagus. Khafre's mortuary temple still has parts of a small sanctuary and a courtyard, and sections of the 500-m (550-yard) granite-lined causeway are still visible.

🜂 Pyramid of Menkaure

The last pyramid built on the Giza Plateau, the pyramid of Menkaure (also known as Mycerinus) has a base area less than a quarter of that of its two neighbours. Some attribute this to a reduction in the power of the king. However, others point to a change in priorities; the size of the pyramid has been reduced but its valley and mortuary temples are larger and more elaborate. This can perhaps be viewed as the start of a process that eventually saw pyramids abandoned, in favour of secret, rock-cut tombs with separate large funerary temples.

In the 12th century one of Cairo's sultans attempted to dismantle this pyramid. After eight months the project was abandoned, merely having achieved the vertical scar visible on the north face.

Inside, a passageway descends from the entrance to an antechamber decorated with a stylized false-door motif. Beyond that is another antechamber, from where a passage leads down to the tomb chamber carved from

The Sphinx and Pyramid of Khafre viewed from the edge of the plateau

For hotels and restaurants in this region see pp268–71 and pp290–95

the bedrock. Its barrel-ceiling is carved from a giant granite roof slab. A beautifully decorated sarcophagus was discovered here in the early 19th century but it was lost at sea while being shipped to the British Museum in London.

The Sphinx

Standing guard at the approach to the Pyramid of Khafre, the Sphinx is the earliest known monumental sculpture of ancient Egypt. Archaeologists date it to around 2500 BC, crediting Khafre as the inspiration. It stands 20 m (66 ft) high with an elongated body, outstretched paws and a royal headdress framing a fleshy face, possibly that of the king himself. It is carved from an outcrop of natural rock, augmented by shaped blocks around the base, added during repeated renovations from the 18th Dynasty onwards.

Although it is often written that the Sphinx's nose was shot off by the Mamluks, Ottomans or Napoleon's French army, it was in fact lost some time before the 15th century. Originally the Sphinx also had a stylized false beard, symbol of royalty, but that too fell off. A piece taken from where it lay on the sand is now held by the British Museum in London.

Directly in front of the statue are the remains of the Sphinx Temple, closed to the public. Access to the area around the Sphinx is gained via the adjacent Valley Temple of Khafre, one of the oldest surviving temples in Egypt. At the time the pyramids were built, during the annual Nile flood, the waters came up to the edge of the Giza Plateau. Khafre's Valley Temple stood on a quay and served as a gateway to the pyramid, connected by a long, mostly covered, causeway. Buried in the sand, this was discovered by Auguste Mariette in 1852 and traces of it can still be seen today. The other two pyramids had similar complexes but their temples are not so well preserved.

The historic Mena House Hotel, at the edge of the Giza Plateau

Around the Giza Plateau

There are also several tombs worth a visit. The mastaba tombs near Khufu's Queens' Pyramids include the 6th-Dynasty **Tombs of Qar and Idu**. Qar was a high ranking official in charge of maintaining the pyramids and their associated ceremonies and his son, Idu, was the royal scribe. These have reliefs and statues of the deceased. The nearby tomb of Khufu's son **Khufukhaf** has some perfectly preserved reliefs, while the tomb of Khafre's wife **Meresankh III** is intriguing. Its painted reliefs show Meresankh, a priestess dressed in the leopardskin usually associated with male priests, while her mother, the blonde-haired Hetepheres III, wears a dress with pointed shoulder pads.

After the dusty heat of the plateau, it makes a nice end to the day to have a drink at the luxurious **Mena House Hotel** and to contemplate the Pyramids as they take on the colour of the setting sun.

CLIMBING THE GREAT PYRAMID

At one time, a complete visit to the Great Pyramid entailed not only an exploration of the passages within, but a clamber to the top as well. A 1902 guidebook to Egypt describes how it was done: "Assisted by two Bedouins, one holding each hand, and, if desired, by a third (no extra payment) who pushes behind, the traveller begins the ascent of the steps". Once up there, many commemorated their climb by carving their names in stone. A recent archaeological project has been cataloguing each block of the pyramid. The graffiti noted includes the will of someone who climbed to the top and committed suicide and the names of two lovers carved together for all eternity. As early as 1840 writers complained about the excessive amount of graffiti. This is no longer an issue as since the 1980s, climbing the pyramids has been forbidden, although some people still try. This has been done as much to protect the monuments as to prevent injury and even death to climbers.

19th-century photograph of tourists climbing the Great Pyramid

A Walk Through Heliopolis ❷

A product of the visionary ambitions of a wealthy Belgian entrepreneur, Baron Edouard Empain (1852–1929), Heliopolis was built in the first decade of the 20th century. It was designed by a team of European and Egyptian architects as a self-contained garden city in the desert to the northeast of Cairo, linked to the centre by a tram system. Known in Egypt as Masr al-Gedida (New Cairo), Heliopolis has since been swallowed up by the expanding capital, but still retains some of its extraordinary original architecture. A magnet for wealth, this elegant, leafy suburb has good shops, restaurants and nightlife.

Hindu motif from Baron's Palace

On the terrace of the Amphitrion cafeteria, Heliopolis

Around Uruba Palace

The walk begins where the bus from Cairo swings left beside the high walls of the Uruba Palace ①. Formerly the Heliopolis Palace Hotel, one of the grandest hotels in the African continent, this is now the official residence of the Egyptian president. The palace's distinctive, drum-shaped wing once housed a magnificent ballroom.

Diagonally opposite the palace, at the junction of Sharia al-Ahram and Sharia Ibrahim Laqqany, is the venerable Amphitrion ②, a bar/restaurant that is as old as Heliopolis itself. The food is basic, but it is one of the few places in Egypt where it is possible to drink beer while sitting on the pavement terrace, in full view of passers-by on the street.

SIGHTS ON WALK

Amphitrion ②
Baron's Palace ⑦
Basilica ⑥
Le Chantilly ⑨
Normandy Cinema ④
Palmyra ⑤
Sharia Baghdad ⑧
Sharia Ibrahim Laqqany ③
Uruba Palace ①

Colonnaded façades and teardrop turrets in Sharia Ibrahim Laqqany

Turn left from Sharia al-Ahram into Sharia Ibrahim Laqqany ③, which is the most complete remaining example of the original city planning. Baron Empain's architects designed elaborate façades that owe more to Western fantasies inspired by *The 1001 Nights* than to any authentic Islamic architectural traditions. This particular street has a wonderful sweep of arcades with Moorish arches and balconies, punctuated by pretty little towers and turrets.

The Baron, a train enthusiast, was also responsible for what was then a state-of-the-art electric tramway connecting his satellite city to central

TIPS FOR WALKERS

Sarting point: Sharia al-Ahram.
Length: 4 km (2.5 miles).
Duration: 1.5 hours.
Getting there: Airport bus No. 356 from new bus station behind the Egyptian Museum or taxi.

Cairo. Trams still rattle up the middle of Sharia al-Ahram, but now they are robust Eastern European models rather than the quaint double-deckers of old.

Turning right from Sharia Ibrahim Laqqany into Sharia Sayyid Abdel Wahid and right again, return to Sharia al-Ahram where, a little further along, on the left, is the Normandy cinema ④. Operating as an

Baron Empain's Byzantine-style Basilica, modelled on Istanbul's Aya Sofya

open-air auditorium during the summer, the cinema regularly screens English-language films.

At the junction of Sharia al-Ahram and Sharia Ibrahim Sawra, almost opposite the Normandy, is the Palmyra ⑤, another of Heliopolis's original terrace cafeterias (in Egypt the term "cafeteria" nearly always denotes a bar rather than a place to eat).

Basilica to Sharia Baghdad

Continuing up Sharia al-Ahram, the distinctive central arch of Empain's Basilica ⑥ can be seen straight ahead, serving as a reminder that Heliopolis was built by and for (Christian) Europeans. Empain and his family are buried in a crypt within the

Basilica, which is designed in a highly stylized Byzantine manner. Unfortunately the church is usually kept locked.

Turning right at Shahid Tayyar Nazih Khalila, a ten-minute walk leads to the most magnificent of follies, known as the Baron's Palace (Qasr al-Baron) ⑦. Built in 1910, this was Baron Empain's Cairo residence and, for reasons unknown, he had it designed to resemble a Hindu temple. The French architect, Alexander Marcel, based his design on a temple at Angkor Wat in Cambodia. Its sandstone exterior is covered with carved animals, Hindu symbols and gods. The building originally had a revolving tower, which allowed the owner to follow the sun throughout the day. Sadly, the palace has been empty for decades and its ornate architecture is now home to a variety of birdlife and a colony of bats.

Return to central Heliopolis along Sharia Abd al-Salaam Zaky, turning left onto Sharia Baghdad ⑧, which, like Sharia Ibrahim Laqqany earlier, contains a wealth of fantasy Oriental architecture. About halfway along, on the left, is Le Chantilly *(see p295)* ⑨, an excellent place to stop for a meal or a beer in the garden.

KEY

• • • Walk route

[symbol] Tram stop

═ Tram route

0 metres   250

0 yards   250

Carved sandstone façade of the Baron's Palace

CAIRO STREET FINDER

The map below shows the areas of the city covered by the *Street Finder*. The maps include the major sightseeing attractions and railway, bus and Metro stations. Map references are given for Cairo's restaurants *(see pp290–95)*, hotels *(see pp268–71)*, entertainment venues *(see pp152–3)* and shopping venues *(see pp 150–51)*. Some of Cairo's small streets and alleyways may not be named on the maps.

Some monuments have two names: one in Arabic and often a commonly used English-language form. What we call the Citadel, taxi drivers sometimes know only as *Al-Qalaa*. Refer to the Survival Guide for guidance on taxis *(see p344)*. In this guide and on the following maps, where there is a well-recognized English name, we have used it; otherwise we have used the local Arabic names.

Sightseeing in Cairo

KEY TO CAIRO STREET FINDER

■ Major sight	ℹ Tourist information
□ Place of interest	✚ Hospital
□ Other important building	🚓 Police station
🚆 Railway station	⊠ Post office
🚌 Bus station	C Mosque
M Metro station	✝ Church
🚕 Taxi rank	✡ Synagogue
⛴ River taxi	
⚓ Felucca boarding point	

SCALE OF MAP ABOVE

0 metres 1000
0 yards 1000

SCALE OF MAPS 1-4

0 metres 200
0 yards 200

SCALE OF MAPS 5–6

0 metres 200
0 yards 200

◁ **Cairo at night – view from the Cairo Tower looking south down the Nile over the Opera House Complex**

Street Finder Index

Because of different preferences in the transliteration of Arabic into English, our spellings of street and place names may differ from those on street signs – which, of course, also carry Arabic script.

Note that the word "Sharia", pronounced *shareh*, denotes a street. Other Arabic words used here include "Midan" (a square), "Bab" (a gate), "Beit" (a house), "Kubri" (a bridge) and "Qasr" (a palace).

D   ASH-SHEIKH RIHAN   *Fire Service*   **C**   **E**   **2**   **F**   **4**

SHARIA MOHAMMED FARID

SHARIA

SHARIA

SHARIA

MAGLIS

SHARIA SUWEQAT AS-SIBAYA

AS-SHAAB

SHARIA SUQ MAKKA

SHARIA RATIB BASHA

SHARIA AD-DAWUDIYA

SHARIA AL-MUGHARABLIN

Mosque of al-Maridani

Tentmakers' Market

6

1

L-NASIRIYA

SAMI

-HARIA

SHARIA AS-SINNARI

SHARIA AS-SINNARI

SHARIA AHMED OMER

HIGAZI

SHARIA SALAMA

AS-SAYYIDA ZEINAB

AL-QALAA

AL-MASRI

AL-KHALIG

SHARIA

SHARIA

SHARIA AL-DARB AL-AHMAR

Blue Mosque

C

SEE PAGES 5–6 FOR ENLARGEMENT OF THIS AREA

6

Sennari House

MIDAN YYIDA ZEINAB

SHARIA SUWEQAT AS-SIBAYA

SHARIA

SHARIA AL-JIOD

Dervish Theatre

Mosque of ar-Rifai

C

Mosque of Amir Akbur

C

SHARIA QARAFET BAB AL-WAZIR

SALEM

SHARIA SALAH

1

QUEEN

SHARIA MUH. ABU AD DHAHAB

QADRI

SHARIA NAGM AD-DIN

SHARIA

Mosque of Sultan Hassan

C

AS-SALIBA

MIDAN SALAH AD-DIN

The Citadel

TARIQ AN-NASR

2

Mosque of Qaitbey

C

Mosque of Ibn Tulun

C

SHARIA TULUN

Gayer-Anderson Museum

Sabil of Qaitbey

SHARIA DARB AL-HUSR

SHARIA AL-BAZLI

SHAR A SALAH AD-DIN

SHARIA AL-ARMIDAN

SHARIA SALAH AN-NASR

2

AS-SAYYIDA

SHARIA

SHARIA AS-SAYYIDA NAFISA

SHARIA

SHARIA ARD YAQUB

MIDAN AS-SAYYIDA NAFISA

SHARIA AS-SAYYIDA AISHA

SHARIA SALAH SALEM

SHARIA SIKKET HADID HELWAN

SHARIA AL-QARAFA AL-KUBRA

3

T-TONSI

AL-UYUN

SHARIA AL-IMAM AL-SHAFII

3

MIDAN MAGRA AL-UYUN

SHARIA SALAH SALEM

SHARIA SIKKET HADID HELWAN

4

SALEM

Ain as-Sira

CITY OF THE DEAD

SHARIA AL-IMAM ASH-SHAFII

5

AL-KURDI

SHARIA AL-MADARIS

SHARIA MISR AL-QADIMA

D   **E**   **F**

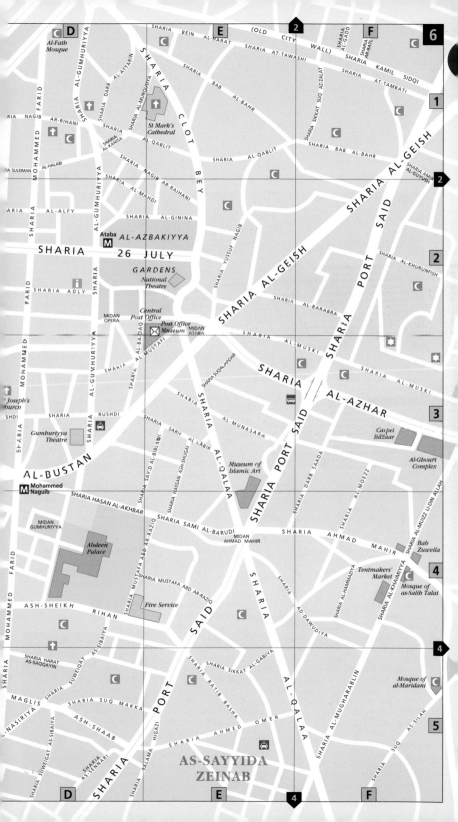

SHOPPING IN CAIRO

The hardest thing about shopping in Cairo is knowing when to stop. Souqs, or markets, sell all manner of goods. Khan al-Khalili is the best known: here you will be able to buy jewellery, statues, papyrus and many other items. Artisans such as coppersmiths and glass-makers tend to be gathered together, which helps keep prices low. Alternatively, shop in a modern mall. Here you will find many Western-style shops with recognizable brand names, but prices will be higher. Haggling, usually acceptable in the big shops, is vital in the souqs. Start at below half the asking price and go up in small amounts.

One of the many stalls in the Khan al-Khalili market

SOUQS AND MARKETS

Khan al-Khalili (see p90) is a large area of souqs and work-shops. Bordering it on its west side is **Sharia al-Muizz li-Din Allah** (see pp98–9), where you will find coppersmiths, goldsmiths, perfumes, spices and carpets. Sections of this wide alley are unofficially named according to the goods on offer: Souq al-Nahhasin (Coppersmiths' Market), Souq al-Sagha (Goldsmiths' and Jewellers' Market) or Souq al-Attarin (Spices Market). Al-Muizz li-Din Allah becomes Sharia al-Khaimiyya, site of **Souq al-Khaimiyya** (Tentmakers' Market) (see p103). The **New Khan al-Khalili** is a market within a market, in the form of a miniature shopping mall in the heart of the souq.

Wikalit al-Balah (Dates Market) is close to the Nile, between Kubri 26 July and the Conrad International Hotel. Everything is sold here – from fruit to car parts – and prices for textiles, curtains and lace are the lowest in Cairo.

Sheesha pipe

MALLS

Beymen has the main designer brands, while the **Arkadia Mall** offers Toys 'R' Us, Timberland and Adidas. Other malls include the **Ramses Hilton Annexe**, **Citystars**, **First Mall** and the **Talaat Harb Centre**.

SOUVENIRS

Most "papyrus" souvenirs are actually machine-printed banana stalk. For the genuine article, head to one of the reputable stores around the Egyptian Museum or to **Al-Ghouri Papyrus Art. Dr Ragab's Papyrus Institute** gives you an insight into papyrus's history and manufacture. You can purchase *sheesha* pipes from **Al Tarbiaa** or, much cheaper, from work-shops in Khan al-Khalili. The **Old Shop Gallery** in Khan al-Khalili sells antiques.

HANDICRAFTS

You will always get a good deal at hard-to-find work-shop **El-Eraki**. Workshops

are also the best places to buy mother-of-pearl boxes, since the artisans will be keen to show you their best work. Muski glass can be found at **Afnan**, in New Khan al-Khalili and other malls; for the rarer red Muski glass, head to **Saed Abd El-Raouf**. Good-quality *mashrabiyya* ornamental woodwork can be found at the workshop of **El Osta Hussein**. For quality leather goods, head downtown to **Vero Chic** and **Silver Eagle**.

MUSICAL INSTRUMENTS

Most music shops are on and around Sharia Mohammed Ali (al-Qalaa), south of Midan Ataba. Instruments for sale include the *rababa*, a sort of fiddle, and the *oud*, a round-bodied stringed instrument. Good shops to visit are **Al Aoud** and **Gawharet El Fan**.

JEWELLERY

The Souq al-Sagha in Khan al-Khalili is thick with jewellers. Try **Mohamed Amin**, **Atlas Jewellery** or **Galal Belal**. Gold and silver are sold by weight: the shopkeeper will weigh the item and quote a price. This is only a starting price to haggle around.

A dazzling array of silver jewellery on display in a market

TEXTILES

For belly-dancing costumes, try **Saad Hassan Bazaar**, in Khan al-Khalili. Colourful *galabiyyas* for special occasions are also on sale at **Fatima**. If you are in search of appliqué, head to the Souq al-Khaimiyya (Tentmakers' Market), and to the **Fattoh Sons** and **El Khiamiah Star** stores in particular.

One of the oldest and largest conventional places to purchase carpets and rugs in Khan al-Khalili is **El Kahhal**. Here you can spend hours taking tea with the owner while every carpet in the shop is displayed for you.

SPICES AND PERFUMES

Spices and herbs make excellent gifts to bring back home from Egypt. Head to Khan al-Khalili for the widest selection at the best prices.

Perfume shops such as **Al-Haroun Bazaar** sell quality perfumes and aromatic oils and you will get a good deal if you haggle hard.

The colourful range of spices for sale at a market in Cairo

DIRECTORY

MALLS

Arkadia Mall
Corniche el-Nil, Bulaq.
Map 1 B2.

Beymen
Four Seasons Nile Plaza,
Corniche el-Nil,
Garden City
Map 3 B1.

Citystars Mall
Starscentre, Heliopolis.

First Mall
Sharia al-Giza, Giza.

Ramses Hilton Annexe
1115 Corniche el-Nil,
Downtown
Map 1 B4.

Talaat Harb Centre
Sharia Talaat Harb,
Downtown.
Map 5 C2.

SOUVENIRS

Al-Ghouri Papyrus Art
(upstairs, beside Wikala al-Ghouri), Sharia al-Azhar.
Map 2 F5.
Tel (02) 512 5859.

Al Tarbiaa
51 Ramses Hilton Annexe.
Map 1 B4.
Tel (02) 575 2399.

Dr Ragab's Papyrus Institute
Orman, Giza
Map 3 A2.
Tel (02) 336 7212
or (02) 348 9035.
www.papyrus
institute.com

Old Shop Gallery
7 Khan al-Khalili.
Map 2 F5.
Tel (02) 787 0378.

HANDICRAFTS

Afnan
25A El Batal Ahmed Abdel Aziz, Mohandiseen.
Tel (02) 304 2563.
Other branches:
The Arkadia,
New Khan al-Khalili,
Ramses Hilton Annexe.

El-Eraki
35 Souq Om al-Golam al-Togary (upstairs, behind Al-Hussein Mosque).
Tel (02) 786 9358.

El Osta Hussein
22 Tabozada (off Sharia Mohammed Ali/Al-Qalaa).
Map 6 E4.
Tel (02) 291 9858
or (02) 731 2730.

Saed Abd El-Raouf
8 Khan al-Khalili.
Map 2 F5.
Tel (02) 593 3463.

Silver Eagle
18 Sharia Adly,
Downtown. **Map** 5 D2.
Tel (02) 393 6704.

Vero Chic
19 Sharia Talaat Harb,
Downtown. **Map** 5 C3.
Tel (02) 393 1895.

MUSICAL INSTRUMENTS

El Aoud
64 Sharia Mohammed Ali (Al-Qalaa), Al-Ataba.
Map 6 E4.
Tel (02) 390 1016.

Gawharet El Fan
160–168 Sharia Mohammed Ali (Al-Qalaa), Al-Ataba. **Map** 6 E4.
Tel (02) 391 3990
or (02) 391 5243.

JEWELLERY

Atlas Jewellery
(opposite the entrance to New Khan al-Khalili).
Tel (02) 590 6139.

Galal Belal Jewellers
12 Ahmed Pasha (north of Fishawi's Coffeehouse), Khan al-Khalili.
Tel (02) 592 7591.

Mohamed Amin
70 Al-Sagha, Khan al-Khalili. **Map** 2 F5.
Tel (02) 592 1214.

TEXTILES

El Kahhal Carpets
Khan al-Khalili.
Map 2 F5.
Tel (02) 590 9128.

El Khiamiah Star
18 Al-Khaimiyya, Al-Darb al-Ahmr. **Map** 6 F4.
Tel (02) 510 6388.

Fatima
157 Sharia 26th July,
Zamalek. **Map** 1 A3.
Tel (02) 736 9951.

Fattoh Sons
29 Al-Khaimiyya, Al-Darb al-Ahmr. **Map** 6 F4.
Tel (02) 512 8853.

Saad Hassan Bazaar
Sharia Gouhar al-Kaad (off Midan al-Hussein), Khan al-Khalili.
Tel (02) 588 0834.

SPICES AND PERFUMES

Al-Haroun Bazaar
Garden City House Hotel,
1101–1103 Corniche el-Nil, Garden City.
Map 5 A4.
Tel (02) 794 7534.

ENTERTAINMENT IN CAIRO

Cairo is a big, bustling city, with plenty to keep you occupied. Be aware that Cairenes are night owls, often not dining until 11pm and then partying on until morning. For a predominantly Muslim city, there is a surprising number of bars, particularly in upmarket districts such as Zamalek, catering mainly to the young and the expat community. The Cairo Opera House is the venue for Arabic music, classical opera and ballet. The Al-Ghouri complex puts on regular shows of whirling-dervish dancing, and you can find displays of belly dancing in many places, though the standard varies.

A colourful performance of whirling-dervish dancing

INFORMATION AND LISTINGS

Your hotel concierge should be able to suggest a range of entertainment options. The listings in local publications will help with any specialized interests, such as classical or jazz music, art exhibitions, theatre or cinema. Get a copy of *Al-Ahram Weekly*, the local newspaper, or the glossy monthly *Egypt Today* for detailed listings. Last-minute changes of programme or venue are not unknown, so call before you set off.

BELLY DANCING

Belly-dancing shows are sometimes held in big hotels – for example, the **Aladin Club** at the Cairo Sheraton, the **Haroun al-Rashid** at the Semiramis Intercontinental or the **Windows on the World** at the Ramses Hilton. Alternatively, embark on a dinner-and-belly-dancing cruise. The **Nile Maxim** is the best, and you have a choice of two sessions: 8–10pm or 10pm–midnight. Less touristy and more exuberant are the **Cave des Rois** and many clubs along the Pyramids Road in Giza.

WHIRLING DERVISHES

Whirling-dervish dancing developed from a religious rite connected with Sufism. Sufis claim that the centuries-old dizzying dance produces a state of trance that brings protagonists closer to God. Wonderfully intense, colourful displays can be seen at the **Wikala al-Ghouri**, just south of the Al-Azhar mosque, on Monday, Wednesday and Saturday nights at around 7pm. There is no charge for entry, so be sure to arrive early to secure a good view.

CLASSICAL AND ARABIC MUSIC

The huge, domed **Cairo Opera House** complex in Gezira is the home to most classical

A classical quintet performing at the Cairo Opera House

music, in the form of the Cairo Symphony Orchestra and the Cairo Opera. There are regular performances in the Main Hall, the Small Hall and the Open-Air Theatre. Look also for performances at **Beit al-Harawi**, the **Goethe Institute Gardens** at Midan al-Missaha in Doqqi and the **Gumhuriyya Theatre**, just south of Al-Ataba.

JAZZ AND ROCK MUSIC

The **Cairo Jazz Club** is the main venue for jazz, electronic, funk and Oriental music. It also offers good food and drink, not to mention a hip ambience that makes it popular with young bar-hoppers. Jazz events are also held at the various venues at the Cairo Opera House. Most of the big hotels have live music in their bars and cafés. The Nile Hilton's **Jazz Up**, for example, offers salsa and Latin dance evenings and live jazz music, while the **51 Bar** at Le Méridien Heliopolis also has jazz nights.

BARS AND NIGHTCLUBS

There is no real centre to the Cairo nightlife, so a night out on the town usually involves taxi-hopping from bar to restaurant to nightclub. Wednesdays and Thursdays tend to be the busiest nights.

The **Sherlock Holmes** in the Ramses Hilton is a quiet English-style pub, and the **Abou Ali Terrace** at the Nile Hilton is a good place to have a beer and a *sheesha*. On the top floor of the same hotel, the **Pyramid Bar and Terrace** affords a great view of the city, though less well-heeled Cairenes prefer the terrace bar of the **Odeon Palace Hotel**, where the beer is much cheaper. **Le Tabasco** is also popular with locals. Two small restaurants in Zamalek, **La Bodega** and **L'Aubergine**, have trendy bars that are open late.

Some of the best nightclubs are at the big hotels – for example, **Latex** at the Nile Hilton and **The Bar** at the Four Seasons Nile Plaza, which is open until 3am. For dancing under the stars, try the floating restaurants at Zamalek: **Le Pacha 1901** and the **Moon Deck on the Blue Nile**. Younger clubbers gather at **Bliss** on the Imperial floating restaurant moored near the Marriott.

OTHER ENTERTAINMENT

Although some find it a little overblown, there is no denying that the **Sound and** **Light Show** held against the stunning backdrop of the Giza Pyramids is impressive. Travellers with children may enjoy a visit to **Cairo Zoo**, while the **Pharaonic Village**, also at Giza, involves a boat trip and a wide choice of museums, historic reconstructions and activities. The **Railway Museum**, near Ramses Station, is a must-see for train enthusiasts.

DIRECTORY

BELLY DANCING

Aladin Club
Sheraton Cairo Hotel Towers and Casino, Midan el-Gala, Doqqi.
Map 3 A1
Tel (02) 336 9700 or (02) 336 9800
www.starwoodhotels.com/sheraton

Cave des Rois
10 Muhammad Ibn Thaqeb (off Sharia Ismail Mohammed), Zamalek.
Map 1 A2.
Tel (02) 736 8980.

Haroun al-Rashid
Semiramis Intercontinental, Corniche el-Nil, Downtown.
Map 3 B1.
Tel (02) 795 7171.
www.ichotelsgroup.com

Nile Maxim
Sharia Saray al-Gezira (opposite Marriott Hotel), Zamalek. **Map** 1 B4.
Tel (02) 632 5917 or (02) 639 3987.

Windows on the World
Ramses Hilton, 1115 Corniche el-Nil, Downtown. **Map** 1 B4.
Tel (02) 577 7444.
www.hilton.com

WHIRLING DERVISHES

Wikala al-Ghouri
off Sharia al-Azhar, Islamic Cairo. **Map** 2 F5.
Tel (02) 510 0823.

CLASSICAL AND ARABIC MUSIC

Beit al-Harawi
Harat al-Azhar, Islamic Cairo.
Map 2 F5.
Tel (02) 735 7001.

Cairo Opera House
Sharia at-Tahrir, Gezira.
Map 1 A5.
Tel (02) 739 8114.

Goethe Institute
5 Sharia al-Bustan, Downtown.
Map 3 A1.
Tel (02) 575 9877 or (02) 574 8261.

Gumhuriyya Theatre
12 Sharia al-Gumhuriyya, Downtown. **Map** 6 D3.
Tel (02) 390 7707.

JAZZ AND ROCK MUSIC

Cairo Jazz Club
197 Sharia 26th July, Mohandiseen.
Tel (02) 345 9939.

51 Bar
Le Méridien Heliopolis, 51 El Oruba St.
Tel (02) 290 5055 or (02) 290 1819.
www.starwoodhotels.com/lemeridien

Jazz Up
Nile Hilton, 1113 Corniche el-Nil, Downtown.
Map 5 A3.
Tel (02) 578 0444 or (02) 578 0666.
www.hilton.com

BARS AND NIGHTCLUBS

Abou Ali Terrace/ Pyramid Bar and Terrace
Nile Hilton, 1113 Corniche el-Nil, Downtown.
Map 5 A3.
Tel (02) 578 0444 or (02) 578 0666.
www.hilton.com

L'Aubergine
5 Al-Sayyid al-Bakri, Zamalek. **Map** 1 A3.
Tel (02) 738 0080.

The Bar
Four Seasons Hotel Cairo at Nile Plaza, 1089 Corniche el-Nil, Garden City.
Map 3 B1.
Tel (02) 791 6878.
www.fourseasons.com/caironp

Bliss
Imperial Restaurant (boat), Saray al-Gezira, Zamalek.
Map 1 B4.
Tel (02) 736 5796/7.

La Bodega
157 Sharia 26th July, Zamalek. **Map** 1 A3.
Tel (02) 735 6761 or (02) 735 0543.
www.delicious-inc.com

Latex
Nile Hilton, 1113 Corniche el-Nil, Downtown.
Map 5 A3.
Tel (02) 578 0444 or (02) 578 0666.
www.hilton.com

Moon Deck
Khan al-Khalili, Blue Nile (boat), 9A Saray al-Gezira, Zamalek. **Map** 5 A3.
Tel (02) 735 3104.

Odeon Palace Hotel Bar
6 Abdel Hamid Said (off Sharia Talaat Harb), Downtown. **Map** 5 C2.
Tel (02) 576 7971.

Le Pacha 1901
Saray al-Gezira, Zamalek.
Map 5 A3.
Tel (02) 735 6730.

Sherlock Holmes
Ramses Hilton, 1115 Corniche el-Nil, Downtown. **Map** 5 A2
Tel (02) 577 7444
www.hilton.com

Le Tabasco
8 Amman St, Doqqi.
Tel (02) 336 5583.

OTHER ENTERTAINMENT

Cairo Zoo
Giza.
Tel (02) 570 8895 or (02) 572 6314.

Dr Ragab's Pharaonic Village
3 Sharia el-Bahr el-Aazam, Giza.
Tel (02) 571 8675/6/7.
www.interoz.com/egypt/village

Railway Museum
Midan Ramses. **Map** 2 D3.
Tel (02) 576 3793.

Sound and Light Show
The Pyramids, Giza.
Tel (02) 386 3469.

EGYPT
AREA BY AREA

Egypt at a Glance

Most of Egypt's great Pharaonic monuments
lie along the Nile Valley, but visitors should not
ignore the variety of sights and activities on
offer elsewhere. From the vast desert expanses
to the biblical scenery of the rocky Sinai interior,
Egypt fully engages the senses. For those who
need to be near the sea, the north coast is lined
with Mediterranean-influenced cities
and beaches, while the
resorts and dive centres
on the Red Sea coast
allow access to the
stunning coral reefs.

The Bent pyramid at Dahshur *(see p165)*
in the pyramid fields around Cairo

**THE DELTA AND THE
NORTH COAST**
(pp234–51)

**AROUND
CAIRO**
(pp158–69)

Statue in the Graeco-Roman
Museum gardens in
Alexandria *(see pp240–47)*

**THE WESTERN
DESERT**
(pp252–61)

Siwa *(see p260)*, the most isolated of Egypt's oases and a
living antiquity in the midst of the Western Desert

Farmer working in the well-watered fields
around Dakhla Oasis *(see p256)*

| 0 kilometres | 150 |
| 0 miles | 100 |

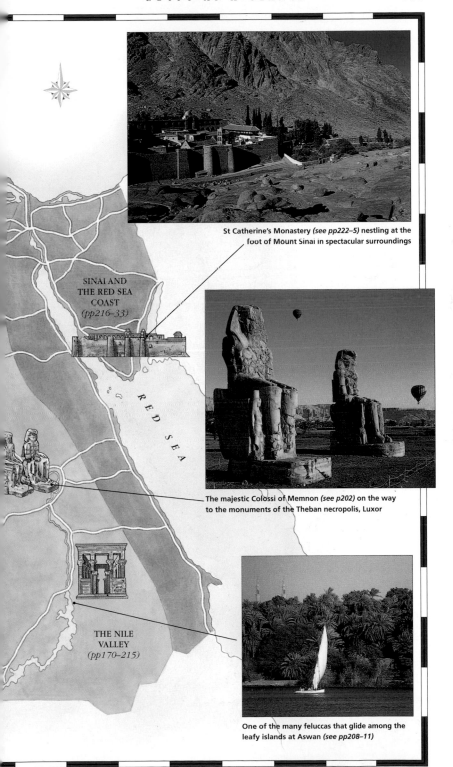

St Catherine's Monastery *(see pp222–5)* nestling at the foot of Mount Sinai in spectacular surroundings

SINAI AND
THE RED SEA
COAST
(pp216–33)

RED SEA

The majestic Colossi of Memnon *(see p202)* on the way to the monuments of the Theban necropolis, Luxor

THE NILE
VALLEY
(pp170–215)

One of the many feluccas that glide among the leafy islands at Aswan *(see pp208–11)*

For additional map symbols *see back flap*

AROUND CAIRO

Desert expanses around the modern capital offer escapism in many forms. Cairenes flock to the greenery of Fayoum and Qanater, while visitors can explore millennia of human ingenuity and achievement in the glorious monuments of Egypt's Old Kingdom burial sites and the monastic retreats of early Christians.

The ruins of Memphis, a religious and commercial centre of vast importance nearly 4,000 years before the birth of Egypt's present capital, are situated on the left bank of the Nile about 30 km (19 miles) south of Cairo. One of the main necropolises of Memphis, Saqqara is rich in fascinating sites: prototype pyramids; tombs with the earliest known examples of Pharaonic decorative writing; the mysterious Serapeum, an underground tomb dedicated to the sacred Apis bulls, and some of the deepest burial chambers in Egypt. Other ancient burial sites nearby include Abusir, where a cluster of pyramids built for the principal 5th Dynasty pharaohs is located on the edge of the desert, and remote Dahshur, home to several stone and mudbrick pyramids including the intriguing Bent Pyramid. West of the Delta region, between Alexandria and Cairo, are the monasteries of Wadi Natrun. Valued by the ancient Egyptians as a source of *natron*, the salt used during mummification, Wadi Natrun became, in the Roman era, a bolt hole for persecuted Christians, and later a centre of monasticism. Of several monasteries here, Deir as-Suriani, Deir Abu Makar and Deir Anba Bishoi are the most beautiful.

Fayoum is famed for its abundant fruits and vegetables, fragrant flowers and orange blossom. Its vast salt lake hosts a rich population of waterfowl. The area is renowned for its prehistoric remains and has numerous Ptolemaic and Roman archaeological sites. To sail along the Nile from Cairo to the gardens of Qanater is another favourite excursion of city residents.

Boating on the lake at Wadi Rayyan, a popular leisure activity for modern Cairenes

◁ The Step Pyramid and vast funeral complex of Djoser, a 3rd-Dynasty king, in the desert at Saqqara

Exploring Around Cairo

When the hustle of Cairo gets too much, it is easy to slow down the pace a little by visiting one of the many interesting sights outside the capital. Saqqara attracts far fewer visitors and covers a larger area than the Pyramids at Giza and so rarely feels crowded, while the pyramid fields of Abusir and Dahshur are often practically deserted. Pharaonic remains are also dotted throughout Fayoum Oasis, although most make the trip for the lush vegetation. The other option for grassy spaces and trees is to sail down the Nile to Qanater, but this is so popular at the weekends that it is often just as congested as the city everyone is looking to escape. For real peace and quiet the best option, as the early Christians discovered, is to head out into the desert. Wadi Natrun is one of the founding sites of monasticism and the monks, although on holy retreat, are gracious when receiving visitors.

View of the mortuary temple and pyramid of Sahure at Abusir

Egyptian farmers tending their sheep near Memphis, the first capital of ancient Egypt

GETTING AROUND

Abusir, Saqqara, Memphis and Dahshur all lie on the same road; unfortunately, it is not served by public transport and the only option is to hire your own. Most hotels in Cairo can arrange a taxi or, even better, a car and driver for the day. Birqash camel market is only really accessible by car or taxi, too. Buses for Wadi Natrun go from Cairo's Turgoman bus station, while those for Fayoum depart from beside the Maryutia Canal, east of Midan Giza.

0 kilometres   25

0 miles   15

Date palms at Fayoum Oasis, inspiration for Pharaonic columns

SIGHTS AT A GLANCE

Abusir ❶
Birqash ❻
Dahshur ❹
Fayoum ❺
Memphis ❸
Nile Barrages (Qanater) ❼
Saqqara pp162–4 ❷
Wadi Natrun ❽

KEY

▬▬▬	Motorway
▬▬▬	Major road
▭▭▭	Minor road
– – –	Track
┄┄┄	Main railway
┈┈┈	Minor railway

SEE ALSO

• *Where to Stay* p272

• *Where to Eat* p296

The Red Pyramid at Dahshur, so called because of ancient red graffiti found inside

Abusir ❶

Off Hwy 27, 27 km (17 miles) S of Cairo. 🚗 🚌 333 from Giza. ☐ 8am–sunset daily. 📷

The cluster of four 5th-Dynasty pyramids at Abusir has not aged as well as the Giza complex *(see pp28–9)*. Instead, the site's appeal comes from its location at the edge of the desert and the fact that few tourists ever venture here.

Only the northernmost and best-preserved **Pyramid of Sahure** can be entered, though this is not recommended for claustrophobics. The pyramid is fronted by a mortuary temple, which has partially reconstructed walls with reliefs of sea voyages and scenes of the king hunting. To the left, the **Pyramid of Nyuserre** is badly dilapidated but has the most complete causeway linking its valley and mortuary temples. Further south is the **Pyramid of Neferirkare.** The brother and successor of Sahure, Neferirkare died while his pyramid was still being constructed, so it was hastily completed with a facing of perishable mudbrick. This has since crumbled away to reveal a six-stepped stone inner core, similar to Djoser's pyramid at Saqqara. Finally, to the southwest lies the unfinished **Pyramid of Neferefre**, still being excavated by Czech archaeologists.

Abusir has also been the site of two major archaeological finds. In the 19th century, a famed set of Old Kingdom papyri, describing schedules of ceremonies and festivals, was discovered. Then, in 1998, a team of Czech archaeologists found the undisturbed tomb of a 6th-century BC Egyptian priest, Iufaa, containing Iufaa's mummy and hundreds of artifacts such as amulets and *shabtis (see p29).*

The pyramids of Abusir on the edge of the desert

Saqqara ❷

A mounted policeman

Saqqara is one of the richest archaeological sites in Egypt. Its monuments span 3,000 years, from the earliest ancient Egyptian funerary structures to Coptic monasteries. Saqqara developed as the royal necropolis for the Old Kingdom capital of Memphis, just to the west. As Memphis grew, so did this city of the dead until it covered an area of 7 km (4 miles), north to south. While Saqqara continued to be used as a burial site for officials for a time, it was eventually abandoned and, apart from Djoser's pyramid, lay buried under sand for centuries. Then, in 1851, Auguste Mariette discovered the Serapeum, since when regular finds have been made at Saqqara.

Step Pyramid of Djoser at Saqqara, built by the architect Imhotep

⋔ Step Pyramid of Djoser
The centrepiece of the Saqqara necropolis is the Step Pyramid of Djoser, the proto-type for the pyramids of Giza and all other pyramids that followed. This remarkable structure was built for 3rd-Dynasty King Djoser by his architect, the high priest Imhotep, in the 27th century BC. It marks an unprecedented leap forward in the history of world architecture. Until then, Egyptian royal tombs had been underground rooms covered with low, flat, mud-brick *mastabas (see pp130–1)*. The great innovator Imhotep chose to use stone rather than mudbrick, and to build not just one *mastaba* but six, one on top of the other, with each additional layer smaller than the one beneath it. The vast enclosure sur-rounding the step pyramid marked yet another major achievement, as it provided the template for subsequent Egyptian art and architecture. Bounded by a finely cut lime-stone wall originally 10.5 m (34 ft) high, this complex included vast open courts, pavilions, shrines and chapels.

A part of the ancient wall, complete with bastions and recesses, has been restored in the south-east corner, and this provides the entrance to the enclosure. A colonnaded corridor of 40 pillars, ribbed in imitation of palm stems, leads into the Great South Court, where things to look out for include a restored section of wall bearing a frieze of cobras. Some of the oldest known examples of tourist graffiti, dating from the 12th century BC, can be seen preserved under perspex in buildings east of the pyramid.

Frieze of cobras, Saqqara

On the north side of the pyramid, there is a life-size painted statue of Djoser installed within a *serdab*, a stone box designed to allow the dead king's *ka* (spirit) to interact with the living world. The statue is a replica – the original is in Cairo's Egyptian Museum *(see p76)*.

⋔ Pyramid of Unas

Just south of the enclosure walls is the crumbled Pyramid of Unas, the tomb of the last king of the 5th Dynasty. Its chambers are covered with vertical columns of hieroglyphic text, recording hymns, prayers and magical spells, designed to protect the king in the afterlife. These so-called Pyramid Texts are the earliest known examples of decorative writing in a Pharaonic tomb chamber. They later formed the basis

Pyramid Texts in the chambers of the Pyramid of Unas, Saqqara

of the New Kingdom Book of the Dead *(see pp28–9)*. Unfortunately, deterioration caused by too many visitors means that the pyramid is now closed to the public.

More than 200 *mastabas* and tombs line the causeway running east of the pyramid. Many of them are beautifully decorated and open to visitors.

⋔ Persian Tombs

Some of the deepest underground burial chambers in Egypt, the Persian Tombs, are situated immediately south of the Pyramid of Unas. A winding spiral staircase leads down from a wooden hut to the final resting places of three Persian noblemen. Psamtik, Djenhebu and Pediese were all officials of the 27th Dynasty, which was founded by the Persians in 525 BC. Colourful inscriptions on the walls of the tombs reveal that Psamtik was chief physician of the pharaoh's court and Djenhebu was a famous Persian admiral.

MAP OF SAQQARA

↑ Giza and Cairo

Mastaba of Ti

Serapeum

Tomb of Mereruka

Philosopher's Circle

Tomb of Ankhma-Hor

Pyramid of Teti

Tomb of Akhti-Hotep and Ptah-Hotep

Step Pyramid of Djoser

Pyramid of Unas

Persian Tombs

Monastery of St Jeremiah

Pyramid of Sekhemket

South Saqqara ↓

0 metres 300
0 yards 300

Pyramid of Teti

From the outside, the pyramid of Teti, first king of the 6th Dynasty, looks like nothing more than a mound of rubble. However, it is worth visiting for its burial chamber, which contains the king's well-preserved giant basalt sarcophagus. The ceiling of the chamber is decorated with stars, and the walls are inscribed with sections of Pyramid Texts. Though found in several pyramids on the Saqqara site, this is currently the only place where these ancient funerary writings are accessible to the public.

Statue of Mereruka emerging from a false door in his tomb at Saqqara

Tomb of Mereruka

An extensive complex of 33 chambers, the tomb of Mereruka, Teti's son-in-law, is one of the highlights of Saqqara. The tomb has some magnificent wall paintings, including a marsh scene with Mereruka hunting among birds, fish and hippos, and in another chamber a scene showing tax evaders being punished. The largest hall, which has a stone ring at its centre for tethering sacrificial animals, contains a life-size statue of Mereruka striding forward from a false door.

Tomb of Ankhma-Hor

A short walk from Mereruka's tomb is the tomb of Ankhma-Hor, also referred to as the "Physician's Tomb" because of its fascinating wall reliefs depicting surgical operations.

These include surgery being performed on a man's toe and, apparently, a circumcision, as practised in the 6th Dynasty.

Serapeum

Saqqara's strangest monument is the eerie underground burial chamber of the sacred Apis bulls. The Serapeum consists of a series of long, dark passageways lined with side chambers, which house 25 giant granite sarcophagi. Weighing up to 70 tons each, the sarcophagi once contained the mummified corpses of the Apis bulls. Seen as an incarnation of Ptah, god of Memphis, the Apis bulls were looked after by priests. When they died they were buried with great ceremony in the rock-cut, subterranean galleries of the Serapeum. The catacombs were begun by Amenhotep III (1390–52 BC) and remained in use until 30 BC.

When Auguste Mariette discovered the site in 1851, he found that all the tombs had been broken into and pillaged except for one, which was remarkably still intact. Inside was a sarcophagus containing a mummified bull, now in the Agricultural Museum in Cairo.

Mastaba of Ti

East of the Serapeum, the Mastaba of Ti is the tomb of a court official who served three kings during the 5th Dynasty. Its wall paintings are unrivalled for the wealth of information they provide about everyday life in Old Kingdom Egypt. The far chamber has the best reliefs and also three slits in the wall revealing Ti's statue in its *serdab*. This was a room for the deceased's statue in which his spirit or *ka* resided.

Philosopher's Circle

This grouping of statues, near the Serapeum, was set in place by the Ptolemaic Greeks. The circle of figures includes such illustrious Greek scholars as Plato and Homer. The circle was originally designed as an adjunct to a temple built by the last truly Egyptian pharaoh, Nectanebo, in the 4th century BC. The temple has long since disappeared, leaving the philosophers sitting alone.

Statue in the Philosopher's Circle, built by the Ptolemies at Saqqara

Environs

Beginning 2 km (1 mile) south of the main complex, **South Saqqara** is a field of smaller, dilapidated pyramids built by pharaohs Pepi I, Pepi II, Djedkare and Merenre. Pepi II's pyramid contains some fine examples of hieroglyphic text. Nearby, the Mastabat al-Faraun, or "Pharaoh's Bench", is a large monolithic mortuary complex of a 4th-Dynasty king. Hiring a horse, donkey or camel from near the Serapeum is the best way to reach these secluded southern sites.

An agricultural scene from the Mastaba of Ti, Saqqara

Palm groves at Memphis, covering the site of the ancient city

Memphis ❸

Off Hwy 27, 47 km (29 miles) S of Cairo. 🚌 from Cairo.

The ancient city of Memphis was the capital of Egypt during the Old Kingdom and most of the Pharaonic period. It is thought it was founded in about 3100 BC by King Menes, the ruler responsible for uniting Upper and Lower Egypt. Situated at the head of the Nile Delta, this majestic city controlled important overland and river routes. While Thebes (the site of modern-day Luxor) became the ceremonial centre of Egypt during the New Kingdom, Memphis was still an important administrative and commercial centre until well into the Ptolemaic era. There are countless descriptions of the city in Classical texts from Greek writers and historians such as Plutarch and Strabo. In the 5th century AD, the historian Herodotus described Memphis as a "prosperous city and cosmopolitan centre". The extent and grandeur of the city's necropolis, centred on Saqqara, give some indication of how large and prosperous Memphis must once have been. Sadly, there is little remaining evidence of this former glory. The city has almost completely vanished. Its magnificent temples and palaces were torn down and pillaged by foreign invaders from the Romans onwards, and the ruins were then buried under the alluvial mud deposited by the annual flooding of the Nile. Palm groves, cultivated fields and villages now cover the site of this once impressive city.

What little has been discovered at Memphis is gathered together in a small open-air **Museum** in the village of Mit Rahina. The showpiece is a colossal limestone statue of Ramses II, which lies, truncated at the knees, in a viewing pavilion. The statue is similar to the colossus of Ramses II found in Memphis and replicated in Midan Ramses (see p78). In the garden there are more statues of Ramses II and an 18th-Dynasty sphinx, at 80 tons the largest calcite statue ever found. The garden also contains several calcite slabs, on which the sacred Apis bulls were mummified before being buried in nearby Saqqara.

Giant calcite sphinx at Memphis

Museum
⬜ daily. 🎫

Dahshur ❹

Off Hwy 27, 64 km (40 miles) S of Cairo. 🚌 from Cairo. ⬜ daily. 🎫

Dahshur is a remote desert pyramid field of great significance in the history of pyramid building. The two Old Kingdom pyramids at the site were constructed by 4th-Dynasty king Sneferu (2613–2589 BC), father of Khufu, the builder of the Great Pyramid (see pp130–31). Chronologically they come after Saqqara and Meidum and before Giza and Abusir. The **Bent Pyramid** is considered to be Egypt's first proper pyramid because until this time pyramids were stepped, like Djoser's at Saqqara. The prevailing theory is that the pyramid is bent because once it began to rise the whole structure became unstable and so it had to be completed at a shallower slope. Unusually for pyramids dating from this period, much of its outer limestone casing is still intact, giving a good impression of what a visually stunning sight it must once have been.

Not happy with his Bent Pyramid, in the thirtieth year of his reign Sneferu began construction of the northern **Red Pyramid**, so called because of its ancient red graffiti. Second in size only to the Great Pyramid, it can be entered via a passage on the north face. At the foot of a long shaft are three chambers, two of which have corbelled ceilings – where the arch is formed by a series of steps.

The two smaller pyramids at Dahshur date from the Middle Kingdom, when there was a revival in pyramid building. They are badly dilapidated and of less interest.

Sneferu's Bent Pyramid at Dahshur with much of its outer limestone casing still visible

Fishermen mending their nets on the shores of Lake Qarun, Fayoum

Fayoum ❺

Off Hwy 27, 100 km (62 miles) SW of Cairo. 🏛 *2 million.* 🚌 *from Cairo.* ℹ️ *Governorate Building, Medinat al-Fayoum (084) 342 313.*

Just an hour-and-a-half's drive from Cairo, Fayoum is Egypt's largest oasis and a popular escape for the smog-choked inhabitants of the big city. They avoid the ugly, modern town of Medinat al-Fayoum (Fayoum City), the oasis's administrative centre, and head instead for the heart of the area, **Lake Qarun**.

This tranquil lake, which existed in antiquity, was linked to the Nile by a series of canals built by the 12th-Dynasty pharaoh Amenemhat III. The area later became a favoured Pharaonic vacation spot.

The Greeks knew the area as Crocodilopolis, named after the reptiles in the lake, which they worshipped. Remains of crocodile temples can be seen at **Kom Aushim**, once the 3rd-century BC city of Karanis, north of Medinat al-Fayoum on the road to Cairo. Some of the objects found on the site are exhibited at the nearby museum. Although the crocodiles are long gone, Lake Qarun is home to an amazing variety of birds. As well as the indigenous species, there are also many migrants and winter visitors.

The ancient Egyptians were aware of bird life throughout the country, which they recorded here in friezes on tomb walls – most famously the Meidum Geese, now in Cairo's Egyptian Museum (*see pp76–7*).

Birding opportunities also exist at **Wadi Rayyan**, a stunning bit of land reclamation, in which excess water from the oasis has been channelled into the desert to create new lakes amongst the dunes. These lakes are well stocked with fish and are a major nesting ground for birds, as well as a big draw for picnicking daytrippers.

Of the pyramid sites around the Fayoum oasis, two are worth visits – but only by keen pyramidologists. Dating from the 12th Dynasty, the **Pyramid of Hawara** was once part of a vast complex: now, only a pile of rubble remains. On the margins of the oasis, the **Pyramid of Meidum** sits alone in the desert. Marking

The inner core of the Meidum Pyramid at Fayoum

an important stage in pyramid development, it was originally built as a 4th-Dynasty step pyramid. The steps were later filled in and an outer casing added, but design flaws caused the sides to collapse some time after the alterations were made.

🏛 **Kom Aushim**
30 km (18 miles) N of Medinat al-Fayoum. 🚌 ⬜ *daily.* 📷

🦋 **Wadi Rayyan**
45 km (28 miles) SW of Medinat al-Fayoum. 🚌 ⬜ *daily.* 📷

🏛 **Pyramid of Hawara**
12 k (7 miles) SE of Medinat al-Fayoum. 🚌 ⬜ *daily.* 📷

🏛 **Pyramid of Meidum**
32 km (20 miles) NE of Medinat al-Fayoum. 🚃 *to Al-Wasta, then taxi.* ⬜ *daily.* 📷

Birqash Camel Market ❻

Off Mansuriyya Canal Road, 30 km (18 miles) NW of Cairo. 🚌 *from Cairo.* ⬜ *mornings.* 📷

Contrary to what many might think, the camel is not indigenous to Egypt: it was probably introduced to Egypt by the Persians or the Ptolemies in the 6th century BC. Having since proved themselves indispensable, camels are now brought up to Egypt in their thousands from western Sudan. Most are taken to Birqash, Egypt's largest camel market, which relocated here from its original site in Cairo in 1995. Hundreds of camels are sold every morning, but trade is at its briskest on Fridays. The sound of the animals bawling competes with traders' voices raised in haggling, and the smell is truly appalling.

Camels and traders at the daily Birqash camel market

◁ **Camels, cattle and other livestock on sale at the Birqash camel market**

Nile Barrages (Qanater) 7

16 km (10 miles) N of Cairo. 56,000. *Corniche el-Nil, in front of Arab Television Building.* from Cairo.

The Nile divides into its eastern Damietta and western Rosetta branches at Qanater, where the main attraction is the Nile Barrages, built to control the flow of water to Lower Egypt. Work on the barrages began in 1834, under Mohammed Ali, and was completed in 1863, when it was discovered that they were ineffectual. The barrages were abandoned until 1883 when a group of British engineers, led by Sir Colin Scott-Moncrieff, finally completed the work.

Nile Barrages at Qanater, where the two branches of the river fork

View across Deir Anba Bishoi monastery at Wadi Natrun

Today the Nile Barrages are surrounded by gardens and are popular with picnickers. Although busy at weekends, Qanater is a pleasant destination for day trips from Cairo, the journey by river bus taking approximately two hours.

Wadi Natrun 8

Off Desert Hwy, 100 km (62 miles) NW of Cairo. from Cairo.

Just west of the Delta region, Wadi Natrun was valued by the ancient Egyptians as a source of the salt deposit natron, a vital ingredient in the mummification process (see p28). Later, during the Roman era, the valley's isolation made it an ideal retreat for early Christians escaping Roman persecution. Initially these monks and hermits lived in caves, but over the years they built many monasteries, of which only four remain today.

The monasteries are easily reached from Cairo by bus, which terminates at the small village of Bir Hooker. All four are surrounded by high, mud-brick walls and resemble desert fortresses. Within the fortified keep of **Deir Anba Bishoi** (the Monastery of St Bishoi), are a well, kitchens, church and storerooms large enough to hold provisions for a year. The church is believed to contain the body of St Bishoi, perfectly preserved in a sealed tube on the altar. He is also commemorated at the Monastery of the Syrians, **Deir as-Suriani**, whose main church (dedicated to St Mary) is built over a cave where St Bishoi is believed to have received a vision of Christ. A bigger draw are the icons and wall paintings, some of which date back to the 8th century.

A little to the north is **Deir al-Baramus**, where the bodies of two sons of the Roman emperor Valentinus are reputed to be buried in a crypt below one of its five churches. 20 km (12 miles) to the southeast is **Deir Abu Makar**, the most secluded of the monasteries: permission to visit must be arranged in advance. Each monastery has a full complement of monks, who will show visitors around and may provide a simple meal, for which a small donation should be offered.

THE FAYOUM PORTRAITS

Although Fayoum is visited by few tourists, many know the name because of the Fayoum Portraits. Several of the portraits, which have been exhibited throughout the world in recent years, were discovered here. Some of the earliest ever examples of portraiture, these eerily lifelike faces with their wide staring eyes date back to the Graeco-Roman period. What makes the portraits particularly haunting is that these are funerary artifacts, painted on wooden boards during the subject's lifetime then, at death, laid over the face of the mummified corpse. Many portraits are now on display at the Egyptian Museum (see pp74–5).

Portrait of an Egyptian dating from 3rd century AD, found at Fayoum

THE NILE VALLEY

gypt has been described as the "gift of the Nile" because without the river the whole country would be a barren desert. Instead, a narrow and verdant strip of cultivated land cuts through the arid country. In ancient times, a great civilization flourished along the river's banks and the incredible wealth of temples and tombs left behind makes the Nile Valley the greatest open-air museum in the world.

For Egypt's *fellaheen* (farmers), the Nile is as central to life today as it was to the farmers and fishermen depicted in the Pharaonic tombs dotted along the valley. For thousands of years the annual flooding of the Nile deposited fresh, fertilizing silt on the surrounding land. Once the flood subsided, the peasants built irrigation channels, planted their crops and waited for the harvest. Though the construction of Aswan's High Dam in the 1960s put an end to the annual inundation, many of Egypt's farmers still live in simple, mudbrick villages and cultivate the precious fertile belt using the same age-old methods.

Since the 19th century, visitors have come to the Nile Valley to gaze in awe at the countless treasures that have been excavated along the banks of the river. Most of the ancient monuments here were rediscovered after being buried for centuries under sand and debris. As a result, some have been preserved in amazing condition.

In addition to the magnificent monuments, the Nile itself is part of the region's attraction. The traditional feluccas, with their distinctive white sails, are part of the Nile Valley landscape as they dart between cruise ships gliding up and down the river between Luxor and Aswan.

Tourism remains the region's main industry. Despite the setback caused by a series of attacks on foreign tourists in the 1990s, visitors continue to flock to the Nile Valley to experience the sense of living history found along the banks of this majestic river – the lifeblood of Egypt.

Villager in Luxor *(see pp184–7)*, setting out his vegetable stall with crops grown in the fertile Nile Valley

◁ View of the Aga Khan Mausoleum *(see p210)* from across the other side of the Nile at Aswan

Exploring the Nile Valley

Most visitors to the Nile Valley head for the tourist magnet of Luxor, where the magnificent Luxor and Karnak temples and the Theban necropolis are the major attractions. Further south, the beautiful ancient garrison town of Aswan is a relaxing place to stay and a good base for exploring the temples on the banks of Lake Nasser, including the stunning Abu Simbel. The sheer number of ancient monuments in the Nile Valley can be overwhelming and to enjoy the region fully it is a good idea to combine sightseeing with a felucca trip on the Nile or a visit to the colourful souqs of Luxor and Aswan.

SIGHTS AT A GLANCE

Abu Simbel pp214–15 **20**
Abydos **7**
Aswan pp208–11 **14**
Asyut **5**
Beni Hasan **2**
Daraw **13**
Dendara pp178–9 **8**
Edfu **11**
Esna **10**
Hermopolis **3**

Kom Ombo **12**
Luxor & Thebes pp182–203 **9**
Minya **1**
Qasr Ibrim **19**
Sohag **6**
Tell al-Amarna **4**
Temple of Amada **18**
Temple of Kalabsha **16**
Temple of Philae **15**
Temple of Wadi as-Sebua **17**

Donkey and cart, a traditional mode of transport for Nile farmers

GETTING AROUND

Luxor and Aswan have airports served by regular flights from Cairo. Trains run frequently between Cairo, Luxor and Aswan, stopping at major towns en route. However, the current political situation means that care should be exercised if visiting sites between Cairo and Luxor *(see p176)*. The road from Cairo to Aswan is good, and buses and service taxis operate between the main cities. Dendara and Abydos are currently best visited on a day trip from Luxor, and Abu Simbel can be reached by air or road from Aswan. There are many cruises on offer between Luxor and Aswan or alternatively, a relaxing two or three-night felucca trip may appeal to the more adventurous *(see pp322–5)*.

The graceful Kiosk of Trajan on the enchanting island of Philae, near Aswan

A selection of exotic spices on sale in Aswan's famous souq, one of the most colourful markets in Egypt

Port Safaga
Qena
8 DENDARA
Qift
Quesir
9 LUXOR & THEBES
El-Rizeiqat
SNA
10
El-Mahamid
El-Kanayis
Marsa Alam
EDFU 11
Nile
2
Silwa Bahari
12 KOM OMBO
13 DARAW
W. el-Kharit
14 ASWAN
15 TEMPLE OF PHILAE
TEMPLE OF KALABSHA
16

Eastern Desert

Lake Nasser

17 TEMPLE OF WADI AS-SEBUA
8 TEMPLE OF AMADA

Wadi Allaqi

KEY

- —— Major road
- ==== Minor road
- —— Scenic route
- —— Main railway
- – – Track
- ▬▬ International border
- ▪▪ Disputed border

SEE ALSO

0 kilometres 100
0 miles 50

Minya ❶

Al-Minya governorate, 245 km (152 miles) S of Cairo. 🏙 200,000.
🚉 🚌 ℹ Governorate Building, Corniche el-Nil (086) 2360 150.

Situated on the west bank of the Nile, the regional capital Minya was a wealthy centre of the cotton industry in the early 20th century. Today it is a semi-industrial city, although it still feels distinctly rural. With its green squares, pretty, tree-lined corniche and run-down Italian villas built by cotton magnates, Minya is a pleasant place to simply wander around. Unfortunately, the surrounding countryside's association with Islamic militants and the relatively high police presence mean that few tourists now venture here. If the security situation improves, Minya is an excellent base for exploring local historical sites such as Beni Hasan. The tourist office is keen to encourage people to come to the town and will help arrange tours to the sites, although the police may insist on escorting visitors.

Beni Hasan ❷

Al-Minya governorate, 20 km (12 miles) S of Minya. 🚌 to Abu Qirkis, then ferry. ◯ daily. 📷

Carved into limestone hills on the east bank of the Nile, the rock tombs of Beni Hasan date from the Middle Kingdom (2055 to 1650 BC).

The necropolis belonged to military and regional rulers who, in a clear assertion of their growing independence, chose to be buried in their own *nome* (province) rather than close to the king at Saqqara (*see p162*). With their deeper shafts and more elaborate layout and decoration than earlier *mastabas*, these tombs mark a transition in style between the Old and New Kingdoms.

Only a handful of the 39 tombs are open to the public but the vivid murals on some of the walls reveal much about life in the Middle Kingdom. Among the most beautiful is the **Tomb of Khnumhotep** (No. 3), which contains colourful scenes of daily life and shows Khnumhotep, a 12th-Dynasty regional governor, hunting with a throwstick and fishing with spears. The **Tomb of Amenemhat** (No. 2) is decorated with desert hunting scenes, while wall paintings in the **Tomb of Kheti** (No.17) depict many aspects of rural life, including wine-making. The wrestling scenes in the **Tomb of Baqet** (No.15) are precursors of the battle reliefs found in New Kingdom tombs.

Tall granite columns, which once supported a Coptic basilica, amid the ruins of Hermopolis

Hermopolis ❸

Al-Minya governorate, 8 km (5 miles) N of Mallawi. 🚌 to Al-Ashmunein. ◯ daily. 📷

Believed by ancient Egyptians to be one of the sites of creation, the city of Khmun was the cult centre of Thoth, god of writing and wisdom. The city was later renamed Hermopolis Magna by the Ptolemies, who associated their own god Hermes with Thoth. During the Ptolemaic era the city was a flourishing centre but it now lies in ruins. Standing out among the rather scant remains are 24 huge **columns** from a Christian basilica and four **sandstone baboons** of Amenhotep III from his original Thoth temple.

Sandstone baboon from Amenhotep III's Thoth temple

Environs
The ancient city's vast necropolis, **Tuna al-Gebel**, lies to the southwest. Thousands of mummified baboons and

The Tomb of Kheti (No.17) in Beni Hasan with detailed scenes of daily life during the Middle Kingdom

ibises, animals sacred to Thoth, once filled the labyrinth of catacombs here. A short walk further south is the "City of the Dead", where streets lined with chapels and tombs lie semi-buried in sand dunes. Most remarkable is the tomb of Petosiris, high priest of Thoth in the 4th century BC, which resembles a small temple and is decorated with detailed reliefs. The Tuna al-Gebel necropolis bordered on Akhetaten (*see below*) and a boundary stele showing Akhenaten and his family is visible north of the tombs.

🏛 **Tuna al-Gebel**
7 km (4 miles) SW of Hermopolis
◻ *daily.* 🈂

Relief showing wine-pressing in the Tomb of Petosiris, Tuna al-Gebel

Tell al-Amarna ❹

Al-Minya governorate, 12 km (7 miles) SW of Mallawi. 🚌 to Deir al-Mawas, then ferry. ◻ *daily.* 🈂

The remains of the city of Akhetaten, built by the rebel pharaoh Akhenaten and his wife Queen Nefertiti, lie at a site known today as Tell al-Amarna. The site, which once stretched an impressive 15 km (9 miles) north to south and boasted magnificent temples and palaces, is now almost desolate but the sense of history and romance remains.

The widely dispersed ruins are spread around a desert plain bounded by the Nile to the west and surrounded by cliffs. South of the landing stage at At-Till, a cemetery covers part of what was once the **Great Temple of Aten**. In contrast to traditional Egyptian temples which had darkened sanctuaries (*see pp24–5*), this temple had a roofless sanctuary, designed to allow the rays of the sun-

god Aten to flood in. To the south, the **Small Temple of Aten** is being restored and the outline of two royal palaces can be made out. Better preserved are the remains of Nefertiti's **Northern Palace**, to the north of At-Till. Here, the remains of some mosaics can still be seen on the floor of summer residence.

The highlights of Tell al-Amarna are the two sets of cliff tombs at either end of the city. Of the **Northern Tombs**, 3 km (2 miles) north of At-Till, one of the finest is the **Tomb of Huya** (No.1), Superintendent of the Royal Harem and Steward to Queen Tiye, Akhenaten's mother. This fascinating tomb is carved with royal banquet scenes, including one that shows the queen wining and dining with her son and his family. In the highly decorated **Tomb of Mery-Re I** (No.4), Akhenaten is shown presenting Mery-Re I with the high priest's golden collar. Reliefs depicting Akhenaten and the Great Temple on the eastern wall of the tomb give an indication of what the city must have looked like during its brief period of glory.

Relief of Nefertiti and her daughter praying to the sun-god Aten, in Cairo's Egyptian Museum

Grouped in clusters, 8 km (5 miles) south of At-Till, the **Southern Tombs** are less accessible but equally rewarding. The **Tomb of Ay** (No.25), Akhenaten's vizier, is considered the finest tomb in Tell al-Amarna. The wall paintings show Ay and his wife receiving ceremonial golden collars from Akhenaten and Nefertiti, watched by a crowd of cheering onlookers. The well-preserved **Tomb of Mahu** (No.9) contains reliefs of Mahu carrying out his duties as Akhenaten's chief of police.

AKHENATEN THE HERETIC

In the 14th century BC, Amenhotep IV turned his back on Thebes and the practice of worshipping several gods to establish a religion based on the worship of just one god, Aten, god of the sun disc. He changed his name from Amenhotep to Akhenaten, meaning servant of Aten, and built a huge city dedicated to Aten at Akhetaten. The city was the capital of Egypt for 14 years but, when Akhenaten died, Thebes was re-established as the capital by Akhenaten's son-in-law and successor Tutankhamun. Akhetaten was destroyed on the order of the priests of Karnak who were determined to eradicate all trace of the heretical pharaoh's new religion.

The rebel pharaoh Akhenaten

Asyut ⑤

Asyut governorate, 110 km (68 miles)
S of Minya. 🏙 280,000. 🚉 🚌
ℹ️ Sharia ath-Thawra (088) 310 010.

Convent of the Holy Virgin, built into the cliffs at Dirunka, near Asyut

In Pharaonic times Asyut was capital of the 13th *nome* (province) and centre of the cult of Wepwawet, the wolf-headed god and avenger of Osiris. At the crossroads of caravan routes to the Western Desert oases and across the Sahara, the city has a long history as a centre of trade. Until the mid-19th century, slaves who had survived the torturous "Forty Days Road" from Darfur in Sudan were sold here alongside camels in Egypt's biggest slave market.

Today Asyut is the largest city in Upper Egypt and has the third largest university in the country. Known for its carpet making, Asyut remains the region's main agricultural trading centre. The area is also associated with the Virgin Mary. In August 2000, the Virgin was reportedly seen above St Mark's Church. For a few months afterwards there were reports of lights around the church towers and many thousands flocked to see them. The apparitions have now ceased.

Icon showing the Holy Family in the Convent of the Holy Virgin

Environs

Coptic Christians believe that Mary, Joseph and the baby Jesus sheltered in caves at Dirunka, 12 km (7 miles) southwest of Asyut. They were escaping from King Herod, who had ordered the killing of all baby boys under the age of two in Bethlehem. A large convent, the **Convent of the Holy Virgin**, was built nearby. During the annual Moulid of the Virgin, held between 7 and 22 August, around 50,000 pilgrims flock here to see icons paraded around the cave-church.

Another place held sacred by Christian Copts is the **Burnt Monastery** (Deir al-Muharraq). This is situated on the edge of the desert, 5 km (3 miles) outside Al-Qusiya, a small town 42 km (26 miles) north of Asyut. The Holy Family is said to have lived in a cave here for a month and it is thought that the church built over it was the first in Egypt. What is now the church's altar stone once blocked the entrance to the cave. The annual moulid, which is held here between 21 and 28 June, attracts many thousands of visitors.

A further 7 km (4 miles) west of the monastery are the **Tombs of Mir**, a burial ground dating from the Old and Middle Kingdoms.

🏛 **Convent of the Holy Virgin**
12 km (7 miles) SW of Asyut. 🚗 from Asyut.

🏛 **Burnt Monastery**
47 km (29 miles) N of Asyut. 🚌 🚗 to Al-Qusiya, then a local taxi.

Sohag ⑥

Sohag governorate, 115 km (71 miles)
S of Asyut. 🏙 133,000. 🚉 🚌 ℹ️
Governorate Bldg (093) 604 453.

An agricultural town and commercial centre, Sohag has a large Coptic Christian community and, like many other cities in Middle Egypt, is a place of sporadic unrest. Although the atmosphere is less tense than in Asyut, Sohag is not recommended as a place to stay. However the Egyptian government wants to encourage tourists, and a new 6-hectare (15-acre) tourist village is being built on Araman island in the Nile, opposite the city. A museum is also planned to house archaeological finds from the area. A large animal market is held in the town each Monday.

SECURITY IN THE REGION

This area has long been associated with religious extremists who want to turn the country into an Islamic state. Asyut University was a hotbed for Islamic fundamentalists in the late 1970s, and the early 1990s saw several attacks on tourists around Qena, Asyut and Dairut. The Egyptian government has tightened security, especially since the 1997 massacre at Luxor, but tension continues and police presence is high. Although tour groups tend to avoid the region, officially it is possible to travel freely in this area and visitors rarely encounter trouble. The most common way to see sites such as the Temple of Hathor at Dendara (see pp178–9) is on a day trip from Luxor, usually with a police escort. The situation is always changing, however, and visitors should contact local tourist authorities and their embassy for the latest advice.

Environs

A short drive west of Sohag, the **White Monastery** (Deir al-Abyad) dates from the early 5th century AD. Named for the colour of its masonry, the monastery was built by the Coptic saint Shenouda using chunks of white limestone taken from local Pharaonic temples. The monastery was once home to 2,000 monks. Today little remains within its high fortress walls apart from a church dedicated to its founder. On 14th July every year thousands of pilgrims attend a moulid at the site.

Four kilometres (2.5 miles) north of the White Monastery lies the **Red Monastery** (Deir al-Ahmar). Built in the 6th century AD by Shenouda's disciple Bishoi – a repentant robber who became a saint – the monastery has two churches within its grounds. The main church contains several interesting, though faded, 10th-century wall paintings. The monastery is hidden within a sprawling village so it may be necessary to ask for directions.

On the eastern bank of the Nile, just across the river from Sohag, is **Akhmim**, which can be reached by microbus. The town is known for its hand-woven hangings and carpets. The town's main attraction, an 11-m (36-ft) high statue of Queen Meret Amun – the daughter of Ramses II – was discovered here in 1982.

Icon of Christ in the White Monastery

White Monastery
10 km (6 miles) W of Sohag.
🚗 🔲 daily. 🎪 14th July.

Red Monastery
14 km (9 miles) NW of Sohag.
🚗 🔲 daily.

The chapel of Osiris in the Cenotaph Temple of Seti I in Abydos

Abydos ❼

Sohag governorate, 46 km (29 miles) SW of Sohag; 10 km (6 miles) W of Al-Balyana. 🚌 *or day trip from Luxor, with convoy.*

Abydos, the cult centre of Osiris, god of the dead, was regarded as the holiest of Egyptian towns in Pharaonic times. All ancient Egyptians tried to make the pilgrimage to the town during their lifetime or hoped to be buried here. Many tombs were painted with scenes of the deceased making the posthumous journey to Abydos. Tradition had it that Osiris – or at least his head – was laid to rest here after he was murdered by his brother Seth and his mutilated body strewn over the country.

Abydos was once a vast walled town with several ancient cemeteries, lakes and temples, including the important Temple of Osiris. Today, almost all that can be seen is the stunning 19th-Dynasty **Cenotaph Temple of Seti I**. Built during Seti I's reign between 1294–1279 BC, it is one of the most intact temples in Egypt. Constructed using white limestone, this secondary mortuary temple possesses some of the finest bas-reliefs of the New Kingdom; many have retained their original colour. After the death of his father, Ramses II (1279–1213 BC) built his own temple to the north of Seti's temple. Although only partially intact, it is noted for its interesting hieroglyphs.

Entrance to the temple is gained via the first hypostyle hall. The temple's highlights include the bas-relief scenes in the second hypostyle hall, which show Seti I with the gods Osiris and Horus. Just beyond, the seven chapels dedicated to a deified Seti I and the gods Ptah, Ra-Harakhty, Amun, Osiris, Isis and Horus are remarkable for their coloured reliefs and delicate decoration. Each chapel contained the statue and barque of the relevant god and would be served daily by the high priests. Behind the temple, Seti had built the Osirieon (the tomb of Osiris) from huge blocks of stone. Today it is partly underwater.

Cenotaph Temple of Seti I
🔲 daily. 📷

The Red Monastery near Sohag, founded by the Coptic saint Bishoi

Dendara ⓐ

Bes, patron god of childbirth

Dendara, where Hathor supposedly gave birth to Horus's child, the god Ihy, was Hathor's cult centre from pre-Dynastic times. Buried under sand until the 19th century, the vast Temple of Hathor remains remarkably intact. The current temple is Graeco-Roman but its design imitates typical Pharaonic temple architecture – a series of large hypostyle halls leading to a dark sanctuary, surrounded by a maze of store rooms, chapels and crypts. Other buildings within the mudbrick walls of the complex include two *mammisi* (birth houses) and a Coptic basilica.

★ Astronomical Ceiling
In this detail from the ceiling, the sun-god Ra is shown sailing his sacred barque across the sky.

Temple Façade
The pylon-shaped façade shows Roman emperors Tiberius and Claudius making offerings to Horus and Hathor.

The roof offers glorious views of the whole Dendara site.

TEMPLE OF HATHOR RECONSTRUCTION

The intricate carved reliefs that adorn the temple were originally painted in vivid colours.

Entrance to temple

★ Hathor-headed Columns
Hathor is shown in her human form with cow's ears at the head of the 18 columns in the hypostyle hall.

CULT OF HATHOR

Hathor was the goddess of pleasure and love, and wet nurse and lover of Horus. Every year she was carried on a barque to Edfu *(see p181)* to be reunited with Horus. The Festival of Drunkenness, celebrating the divine union, followed. On New Year's Day, Hathor's statue was carried up the decorated west staircase of the temple to the open-air kiosk on the roof, where it was revitalized by the sun.

Hathor with the sun disk and cow horns

STAR FEATURES

★ Astronomical Ceiling

★ Hathor-headed Columns

Cleopatra and Caesarion
A huge relief on the southern exterior wall shows Cleopatra making offerings to Hathor. Caesarion, her son by Julius Caesar, stands in front of her burning incense.

VISITORS' CHECKLIST

5 km (3 miles) SW of Qena, the provincial capital; 60 km (37 miles) N of Luxor. 🚌 or tour from Luxor. **Travel restrictions may apply in this area (see p332).** ◻ daily. ▨

The east staircase led back down into the temple.

The open-air kiosk was the focus of the New Year celebrations. It may have had a light wooden cover that was removed to expose the statues to the sun.

The New Year Chapel is where rituals were performed before Hathor's statue was taken up to the roof. The ceiling shows Nut giving birth to the sun.

Roman Mammisi
This small temple celebrated the divine birth of Hathor's son. The southern wall has some exquisite reliefs on its exterior.

Elaborate bas-reliefs depicting offerings to Hathor

DENDARA SITE PLAN

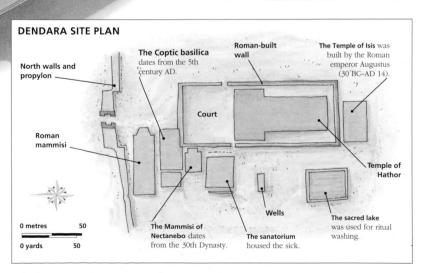

North walls and propylon

The Coptic basilica dates from the 5th century AD.

Roman-built wall

The Temple of Isis was built by the Roman emperor Augustus (30 BC–AD 14).

Court

Roman mammisi

Temple of Hathor

0 metres 50

0 yards 50

The Mammisi of Nectanebo dates from the 30th Dynasty.

Wells

The sanatorium housed the sick.

The sacred lake was used for ritual washing.

Luxor and Thebes ➒

Detail from the Colossi of Memnon

Modern Luxor grew out of the ruins of Thebes, once the capital of ancient Egypt's New Kingdom (1550–1069 BC). The monumental temples at Luxor and Karnak were famed throughout the ancient world and have attracted tourists since Greek and Roman times. Across the Nile, on the West Bank, lies the Theban Necropolis, perhaps the world's richest archaeological site. To foil thieves, the Theban kings hid their tombs deep in the surrounding hills, away from their mortuary temples on the flood plain. Visiting the Luxor monuments is straightforward, but due to the number of sights and the distances involved, some planning is needed to get the most out of a visit to the West Bank.

Medinat Habu ➉
Second only to Karnak in size, the Mortuary Temple of Ramses III was modelled on the Ramesseum.

LUXOR AND THEBES

① Luxor Temple (pp186–7)
② Luxor Museum (p187)
③ Karnak Temple (pp188–90)
④ Valley of the Kings (pp192–4)
⑤ Tombs of the Nobles (p195)
⑥ Hatshepsut Temple (pp196–7)
⑦ Valley of the Queens (pp198–9)
⑧ The Ramesseum (pp200–1)
⑨ Colossi of Memnon (p202)
⑩ Medinat Habu (p202)
⑪ Deir al-Medina (pp202–3)
⑫ Temple of Seti I (p203)
⑬ Howard Carter's house (p203)
⑭ New Gurna (p203)

KEY

🚉 Train station

⬜ Town area

0 kilometres   1

0 miles   0.5

Valley of the Kings ④

Hatshepsut Temple ⑥

Tombs of the Nobles ⑤

Deir al-Medina ⑪

Valley of the Queens ⑦

The Ramesseum ⑧

Ticket kiosk

Colossi of Memnon ⑨

Medinat Habu ⑩

New Gurna ⑭

T H E B E S

Hatshepsut Temple ⑥
Discovered only in the mid-19th century, and still undergoing restoration, the Mortuary Temple of Hatshepsut rises out of the desert in a series of terraces that merge with the sheer limestone cliffs behind.

◁ A flotilla of feluccas heading south up the Nile at Luxor

GETTING AROUND

Luxor Temple is in the centre of town and easily accessible on foot; Karnak Temple can be reached by minibus, bicycle, taxi or caleche. Most Luxor hotels offer tours to the West Bank including the services of a guide, but a private arrangement may be cheaper. Alternatively, to get around Thebes, hire a taxi, donkey or bicycle (bikes hired in Luxor can be taken on the ferry) for the day.

The Ramesseum ⑧
Built to perpetuate the pharaoh's glory, the Mortuary Temple of Ramses II was part of a large complex that included a royal palace and a great many granaries and storerooms. Both pylons are decorated with scenes from the Battle of Qadesh.

⑬ Howard Carter's house

⑫ Temple of Seti I

RIVER NILE

Karnak ③ Temple

② Luxor Museum

L U X O R

Tourist ferry
Local ferry
Local ferry
Tourist ferry
Car ferry

① Luxor Temple

Karnak Temple ③
The Karnak complex was known as "Ipet-Isut" ("the most perfect of places") to the ancient Egyptians.

Luxor Temple ①
Founded by Amenhotep III, Luxor Temple was dedicated to the Theban triad of Amun, Mut and Khonsu, who are celebrated at the annual Festival of Opet (see p190).

Street-by-Street: Luxor

Built on the site of the New Kingdom capital city of Thebes, Luxor has returned to prominence as the tourist mecca of the Nile Valley. The exciting excavations that were led by European archaeologists in the 19th and early 20th centuries, especially the discovery of Tutankhamun's tomb, aroused international interest in the town and visitors have been coming to marvel at the amazing concentration of ruins here ever since. Today the livelihood of Luxor's resident population depends almost entirely on tourism and visitors can expect to be approached by salesmen and touts at every turn. The bustling town is centred around the magnificent Luxor Temple, an enduring symbol of its glorious past.

Stone Ramses II at Luxor Temple

Felucca on the Nile at Luxor

The Corniche
The riverside Corniche, which leads from Luxor to Karnak, is one of the busiest streets. Most visitors stick to the stretch between the Winter Palace and the Luxor Museum.

★ Luxor Museum
Located on the Corniche, halfway between Luxor and Karnak Temples, the museum has a collection of statues and funerary goods, including this fine relief of Tuthmosis III (see pp186–7).

KEY

‑ ‑ ‑ Suggested route

| 0 metres | 100 |
| 0 yards | 100 |

Train station

SHARIA AL KARNAK

Avenue of sphinxes

Brooke Hospital for Animals
(see pp186–7)

Souqs

Luxor Museum and Karnak

Winter Palace Hotel
Founded in 1887, the most famous of Luxor's hotels has played host to celebrities such as Agatha Christie and Noel Coward.

VISITORS' CHECKLIST

Qena Governorate, 674 km (419 miles) S of Cairo. ✈ 150,000. ✈ 🚉 🚌 🚏 *Tourist bazaar, Corniche el-Nil (095) 2372 215.* 🚢 *daily.* 🎭 *Moulid of Abu al-Haggag, two weeks before Ramadan.*

Tourist Bazaar
Luxor's tourist bazaars sell mainly souvenirs. The more traditional souqs, selling everything from hardware to spices, lie north of the temple.

Corniche

★ Luxor Temple
With its grand colonnades, Luxor Temple is one of the most impressive ancient monuments in Egypt. It is situated on the waterfront in the heart of modern Luxor and looks particularly beautiful when illuminated at night (see pp186–7).

The Abu al-Haggag Mosque stands amid the ruins of Luxor Temple.

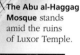

★ Mummification Museum
The ancient Egyptian practice of mummification is explained in detail in this fascinating museum close to the river (see pp186–7).

STAR SIGHTS

★ Luxor Temple

★ Mummification Museum

★ Luxor Museum

Exploring Luxor

Spread out along the east bank of the Nile, Luxor today is a bustling town of some 150,000 inhabitants. The main tourist attractions are concentrated in the heart of town between Sharia al-Karnak and the Corniche. Luxor Museum is a short distance away on the Corniche in the direction of Karnak. Walking around town is a great way to soak up the atmosphere though it can also be fun to ride through the streets in a *caleche* (carriage).

The first pylon, built by Ramses II, forming the façade of Luxor Temple

Luxor Temple

Corniche el-Nil. ☐ *winter: 6am–9pm daily; summer: 6am–10pm daily.* ☒
Dominating the banks of the Nile in the centre of town, Luxor Temple is an elegant example of Pharaonic temple architecture. Dedicated to the Theban triad of Amun, Mut and Khonsu, the temple was largely completed by the 18th-Dynasty pharaoh Amenhotep III and added to during the reign of Ramses II in the 19th Dynasty. Although the temple was further modified by later rulers, including Alexander the Great, its design remained strikingly coherent in contrast to the sprawling complex that developed at nearby Karnak. In the 3rd century AD the temple was occupied by a Roman camp and the site was subsequently abandoned. Over the centuries it was engulfed in sand and silt, and a village grew up within the temple walls. Then in 1881 archaeologist Gaston Maspero rediscovered the temple in remarkably good condition, but before excavation work could begin the village had to be removed. Only the **Abu al-Haggag Mosque**, built by the Arabs in the 13th century, was left intact, standing high on the layers of silt accumulated over the years.

The temple is approached by an avenue of sphinxes, which once stretched all the way from Luxor to Karnak, almost 2 km (1.2 miles) away. Fronting the entrance to the temple, the gigantic first pylon is decorated with scenes of Ramses II's victory over the Hittites in the battle of Qadesh. Two enormous seated colossi of Ramses and a huge 25-m (82-ft) high pink granite obelisk flank the gateway to the temple. The obelisk was originally one of a pair; the other was removed in

The Abu al-Haggag
Mosque in Luxor Temple

the early 19th century and re-erected in the Place de la Concorde in Paris, a gift from the Egyptian ruler Mohammed Ali to the people of France.

Beyond the first pylon lies the Court of Ramses II, with the Abu al-Haggag Mosque towering incongruously over the courtyard to the east. The height of the mosque above the stone floor demonstrates the depth of debris that once buried the entire temple. The western corner of the court incorporates an earlier barque shrine (to house the gods' sacred boats) dedicated to the Theban triad. A double row of papyrus-bud columns encircles the court, interspersed with huge standing colossi of Ramses II.

More giant black granite statues of Ramses guard the entrance to the original part of the temple, which begins with the majestic Colonnade of Amenhotep III, with its avenue of 14 columns. The walls here were embellished during the reign of Tutankhamun and depict the annual Opet festival, when the images of Amun, Mut and Khonsu were taken in procession from Karnak to Luxor *(see p188)*. The western wall shows the outward journey to Luxor and the eastern wall the return journey to Karnak. The colonnade leads to the superb Court of Amenhotep III, which is noted for its double rows of towering papyrus

The avenue of sphinxes leading to the entrance of Luxor Temple

Colonnade of Amenhotep III with its lofty papyrus columns

columns, the best preserved and most elegant in the temple. In 1989, work here on the foundations of the court led to the discovery of 22 New Kingdom statues, now on display in the Luxor Museum.

The hypostyle hall on the southern side of the court served as a vestibule to the main temple. It has 32 papyrus columns in four rows of eight, bearing the later cartouches of Ramses II, Ramses IV, Ramses VI and Seti I. The antechamber beyond was converted into a church by the Romans in the 4th century AD, its Pharaonic reliefs being plastered over and covered with Christian paintings. A second, smaller antechamber, the offerings chapel, leads on to another columned hall with the Sanctuary of the Sacred Barque in the centre. Rebuilt by Alexander the Great, this granite shrine was where Amun's barque ended its journey from Karnak in the Opet festival *(see p188)*. It is decorated with scenes of Alexander making offerings to the Theban triad. The birth room to the east has reliefs depicting the divine birth of Amenhotep III, intended to validate his claim to be the son of Amun. Finally, behind the Sanctuary of the Sacred Barque, another hall leads to a small, damaged sanctuary that once housed a golden statue of Amun.

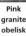

Pink granite obelisk

Mummification Museum

Corniche el-Nil, opposite Mena Palace Hotel. *Tel* (095) 2381 502. ◯ 9am–1pm and 4–9pm daily (5–10pm summer); 9am–3pm Ramadan.

This small museum on the banks of the Nile houses a fascinating display describing the process of mummification performed by the ancient Egyptians *(see pp28–9)*. Instruments for removing internal organs, substances to treat the body and items needed by the mummy on its journey to the afterlife are all displayed here. The intact mummy of Maseharti, a 21st-Dynasty high priest and general, was found at Deir el-Bahri along with Maseharti's painted coffin. A mummified cat, the symbol of the goddess Bastet, and a mummified ram, the symbol of the god Khnum, are among the other exhibits. Among the informative items on display is a cross-section of a mummified skull, stuffed with material where the brain has been removed. There is also a piece of a mummified toe.

Brooke Hospital for Animals

Montazah Sharia, next to Luxor Temple. *Tel* (095) 2381 305. ◯ 8:30am–1:30pm and 5–7pm daily.

In 1934, Dorothy Brooke, the wife of a major-general in the British army, established the Brooke Hospital for Animals in Cairo to care for the many starving and mistreated horses and mules that had been brought to Egypt from Britain during World War I. Further clinics opened throughout Egypt and the rest of the world. The Luxor branch opened in the 1960s and looks after dozens of sick horses. Visitors are welcome.

Luxor Museum

Corniche el-Nil, Luxor. *Tel* (095) 2370 569. ◯ 9am–1pm and 4–9pm daily (5–10pm summer); 9am–3pm Ramadan.

Situated on the Corniche half-way between Luxor Temple and Karnak, this well-designed

museum has an excellent collection of statues and artifacts found in temples and tombs in the Luxor area. Near the entrance is a stunning gilded head of Hathor, the cow-goddess, discovered in the tomb of Tutankhamun in the Valley of the Kings. Also on the ground floor look out for the large pink granite head of Amenhotep III and the beautiful carved figure of a youthful Tuthmosis III.

On the first floor further exhibits from Tutankhamun's tomb include a funerary bed and two model barques. Also exhibited here are two busts of Amenhotep IV (Akhenaten) and a reconstructed wall made up of 283 sandstone blocks from Akhenaten's temple at Karnak. The relief scenes depict daily life during Akhenaten's reign and show the heretical pharaoh and his wife Queen Nefertiti making offerings to the sun-god Aten.

The spectacular new hall near the exit on the ground floor is a highlight. It displays a collection of beautifully preserved New Kingdom statues, discovered at Luxor Temple in 1989. Priests are thought to have buried the stone statues in ancient times to make room for new statuary. Twenty-four pieces can be seen, including a near-perfect 2.5-m (8-ft) high statue of Amenhotep III and a statue of the gods Mut and Amun.

Statue of Tuthmosis III in the Luxor Museum

Painted relief from Akhenaten's Karnak Temple in Luxor Museum

Karnak: Temple of Amun

Statue of a scarab beetle

At the heart of the immense Karnak complex lies the Temple of Amun, dedicated to the king of the gods. With its endless courts, halls and colossi and huge sacred lake, the scale and complexity of this sprawling temple is overwhelming. From its modest 11th-Dynasty beginnings, pharaoh after pharaoh added to and changed the existing buildings, seeking to make their mark on the country's most important temple. No expense was spared and during the 19th Dynasty some 80,000 men worked in the temple as labourers, guards, priests and servants. The temple lay buried under sand for more than 1,000 years before excavation work began in the mid-19th century. Today, the huge task of restoration continues.

★ Great Hypostyle Hall
The glorious highlight of Karnak, this cavernous hall was supported by 134 gigantic columns.

★ Colossus of Ramses II
An imposing granite statue of Ramses II, with one of his daughters at his feet, stands in front of the entrance to the Great Hypostyle Hall.

Tomb of Seti II
dedicated to the Theban Triad.

RECONSTRUCTION OF THE TEMPLE OF AMUN
The temple's brightly coloured exterior is visible in this reconstruction, which shows how the temple would have looked in around 1000 BC.

A row of sphinxes
led to the Nile.

Temple of Ramses III

PLAN OF KARNAK COMPLEX

KEY
☐ Reconstruction

Precinct of Montu
Precinct of Amun
Sacred Lake
Pylons
Temple of Amun
Open-air museum
Temple of Khonsu
Temple of Opet
Precinct of Mut
To Luxor

0 metres 300
0 yards 300

Botanic Gardens
Part of the temple built by Tuthmosis III, this roof-less enclosure lies behind the Great Festival Temple. It is decorated with reliefs of exotic flora and fauna, brought back to Egypt by the pharaoh during his campaign in Syria.

★ Great Festival Temple
The central hall of this temple built by Tuthmosis III was supposedly designed to resemble the tent in which he lived whilst on campaign.

The Ninth Pylon was built by Horemheb using blocks from the demolished Aten temple.

Flagpoles

Eighth Pylon

To Precinct of Mut

Row of Sphinxes

Sacred Lake
Priests purified themselves in the holy water of the Sacred Lake before performing rituals in the temple. North of the lake is a huge stone scarab of Khepri, built by Amenhotep III.

STAR FEATURES

★ Great Hypostyle Hall

★ Colossus of Ramses II

★ Great Festival Temple

Exploring Karnak

After the pyramids of Giza, Karnak is Egypt's most important Pharaonic site. Excavations over the years have gradually uncovered the original structure of the temple complex, which was built over a 1300-year period and covers a vast area just north of Luxor. As well as the colossal Temple of Amun, the 100-acre site comprises a fantastic array of temples, chapels, pylons and obelisks, all testifying to the importance of Thebes.

Statues of the lioness-goddess Sekhmet line up in the Precinct of Mut

⋔ Temples of Khonsu and Opet

Dedicated to the son of Amun and Mut, the well-preserved Temple of Khonsu was built largely during the reigns of Ramses III and IV. The main entrance is via a magnificent gateway, built by Ptolemy III, which is still virtually intact.

Close by is the smaller Temple of Opet (the goddess thought to be the mother of Osiris). It contains some finely decorated reliefs dating from Ptolemaic and Roman times.

⋔ Open-air Museum

Located to the northwest of the Precinct of Amun, the open-air museum contains a fine collection of monuments that were discovered during an excavation of the Third Pylon. Among the museum's main attractions is the lovely, reconstructed, 12th-Dynasty White Chapel of Senusret I. This has delicate carvings of the king making offerings to Amun. The newly restored 18th-Dynasty Red Chapel of Hatshepsut can also be seen here; the chapel served as a shrine for the barque of Amun. Other attractions include the Alabaster Chapel of Amenhotep I and the Shrine of Tuthmosis III.

A separate ticket for the museum must be purchased before entering the complex.

⋔ Precinct of Mut

Built by Amenhotep III, the precinct contains the ruins of a temple dedicated to Amun's consort Mut. Huge, black granite statues of the lioness-goddess Sekhmet line the temple courts. To the west of the sacred lake surrounding the temple is the ruined 20th-Dynasty Temple of Ramses III. Relics of the Temple of Amenhotep III, dedicated to Amun, lie to the northeast.

⋔ Precinct of Montu

The Precinct of Montu is just north of the Temple of Amun. Montu, the warrior god, was the original deity of Thebes and was still worshipped after Amun rose to pre-eminence. The precinct contains Amenhotep III's Temple of Montu and the Temple of Amun, which was added during the 20th Dynasty. Both are closed to the public at present.

THE FESTIVAL OF OPET AT KARNAK

Amun was the principal god of Thebes who, along with his consort Mut and their son Khonsu, was worshipped as part of the Theban Triad. Once a year, during the flood season, the Festival of Opet celebrated the king's rebirth as the son of Amun. Accompanied by priests and revellers in a riotous festival, the images of Amun, Mut and Khonsu were carried on decorated barques to the Nile and then to Luxor Temple. Even today, elements of the Opet festival live on in the Islamic Moulid of Abu al-Haggag, a five-day event preceding Ramadan. Luxor stages a recreation of the festival for tourists on the 4th of November each year, the anniversary of the discovery of Tutankhamun's tomb.

Priests carrying the image of Amun in his barque during the Opet festival

Cruising the Nile

Along with the Grand Tour of Europe, a trip to Egypt was one of the most exciting journeys available to the 19th-century traveller. Having disembarked at Alexandria, wealthy European and American tourists were transported to Cairo – in the early days by boat, later by train. After several days visiting the sights of Cairo, often staying at the world-famous Shepheard's Hotel, passengers would board a *dahabiyya* (large sail boat) or steamer, and set off

Death on the Nile by Agatha Christie

for a trip up the Nile. The pace was languid: a steamer took three weeks to reach Aswan, while a sailing boat could take six to twelve weeks. Slow days on deck alternated with treks through the desert to marvel at the newly found secrets of ancient Egypt. It was not uncommon for tourists to come across or even fall into hitherto undiscovered tombs. Expeditions were led by local guides, while servants carried supplies of food and drink for picnics amid the ruins.

Thomas Cook, *the founder of modern tourism, played a dominant role in the development of Egyptian travel. He once owned all the steamers plying the Nile.*

Florence Nightingale *described her 1848 trip up the Nile in a series of published letters. Other writers inspired by the trip include Agatha Christie, who wrote* Death on the Nile.

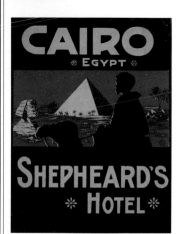

Shepheard's Hotel *was the focus of European life in Egypt from its founding in 1841 until it was burned down in 1952.*

The highlight of a trip *to Egypt for 19th-century travellers was then, as now, a visit to the Great Pyramids and the Sphinx at Giza. As seen in this illustration, these sites had yet to be fully excavated.*

Exciting new *discoveries from Egypt's ancient past provided an added thrill for early visitors to the country. Each year new finds were made.*

Thebes: Valley of the Kings

The most famous tomb in Thebes

The remote, barren Valley of the Kings was the necropolis of the New Kingdom pharaohs. By digging their tombs deep into the Theban Hills, pharaohs from Tuthmosis I (c.1500 BC) on hoped to stop robbers stealing the priceless possessions buried with them. It was an unsuccessful strategy. Despite their hidden locations, every burial chamber was raided except for those of Yuya and Tuya (see p77), and Tutankhamun, discovered by Howard Carter in 1922, its glorious treasures still intact (see pp74–7). But for all that, the structures themselves remain, their dramatic corridors and burial chambers stunningly adorned with symbolic accounts of the journey through the underworld and ritual paintings to assist the pharaohs in the afterlife.

Tomb of Horemheb (No.57)

Horemheb was the final pharaoh of the 18th Dynasty. His tomb departs from the usual style of 18th-Dynasty tombs in that it consists of a single straight corridor with side-chambers. It is decorated with reliefs from the Book of Amduat.

Valley of the Kings, chosen as a burial ground because of its secluded location amid limestone hills

THE VALLEY TOMBS

Sixty-two tombs have been found in the Valley of the Kings and all are numbered on the map in the order of their discovery. The most significant tombs, some of which are described on p194, are marked with a red bullet. Of all the tombs, only a few are open at any one time.

Tomb of Tuthmosis III (No.34)

Dug 30 m (98 ft) above ground in a vain attempt to stop thieves, today the tomb is reached by a metal staircase. The walls are painted with rows of figures portraying the Book of Amduat (see p29), and a red granite sarcophagus is the sole remaining artifact.

Tomb of Seti I (No.17)
Finely carved bas-reliefs and gilded paintings decorate this stunning tomb. The burial chamber is particularly remarkable with its astronomical ceiling and western wall illustrating the Book of Amduat (see p29).

0 metres   75

0 yards   75

Café

Ticket kiosk for Tomb of Tutankhamun

Tomb of Ramses VI (No.9)
Originally built for his predecessor Ramses V, this large tomb was expanded by Ramses VI. Among its most striking features are the vaulted astronomical ceiling and the inner sarcophagus of the pharaoh, which was recently reassembled.

Tomb of Tutankhamun (No.62)
Tutankhamun's tomb is small with parts undecorated. Yet the burial chamber, whose walls depict the "Opening of the Mouth" ceremony (see p29), is unique in that it still contains the king's body inside the gilded coffin.

Tomb of Ramses IV (No.2)

Although Greek and Coptic graffiti mar the walls of this 20th-Dynasty tomb, there are some beautiful, vividly coloured scenes from the Book of the Dead. In the burial chamber, the goddess Nut stretches across the blue ceiling. The enormous pink granite sarcophagus is covered with magical texts and carvings of Isis and Nephthys, designed to protect Ramses's mummy from danger.

Tomb of Ramses IX (No.6)

This typical late Ramesside tomb is long and steep, with interesting scenes on the sloping corridor walls taken from the Litanies of Ra, a religious work celebrating the solar deity's nightly journey. A four-pillared room precedes the burial chamber, which has an impressive astronomical ceiling, featuring the goddess Nut surrounded by sacred barques full of stars. Gods and demons are painted on the dark walls. Only the mark of the sarcophagus remains on the floor.

Tomb of Merneptah (No.8)

The tomb of 19th-Dynasty pharaoh Merneptah, son of Ramses II, was excavated by Howard Carter in 1903. Reliefs of Isis and Nephthys worshipping the solar disc decorate the tomb's entrance. From here the corridor descends steeply to the burial chamber, where the sarcophagus still lies. A false burial chamber did not fool robbers, who escaped with treasures but dropped the heavy sarcophagus lid in one of the corridors.

Tomb of Ramses III (No.11)

Discovered by the Scottish traveller James Bruce in 1768, the tomb of Ramses III is known as the "Tomb of the Harpists" after the bas-relief of two blind musicians in one of the side chambers. It is beautifully preserved and, unusually for a royal tomb, its colourful reliefs include scenes taken from everyday Egyptian life.

Tomb of Queen Tawsert/ Sethnakht (No.14)

Originally built for the wife of Seti II, Queen Tawsert, this tomb was appropriated by 20th-Dynasty pharaoh Sethnakhte after he ran into difficulties building his own tomb. The well-preserved wall paintings include depictions of the "Opening of the Mouth" ceremony and, in the burial chamber, the gods greeting Sethnakhte.

Tomb of Ramses I (No.16)

The tomb of Ramses I, founder of the 19th Dynasty, is small but exquisitely decorated. Discovered in 1817 by the Italian explorer Giovanni Battista Belzoni, the walls are painted with scenes relating to the Book of Gates. A large granite sarcophagus remains in the burial chamber.

Tomb of Amenhotep II (No.35)

This is one of the deepest tombs in the valley, with 90 steps leading down to different levels. Although thieves made off with the treasure, Amenhotep's mummy was still in its decorative sarcophagus when the tomb was discovered by

Victor Loret in 1898. Nine other royal mummies, hidden in the tomb by priests, were also found. The pillared burial chamber is decorated with illustrations and texts from the Book of Amduat.

Colourful wall painting from the well-preserved Tomb of Siptah

Tomb of Siptah (No.47)

The Tomb of Siptah, who reigned briefly at the end of the 19th Dynasty, is one of the longest in the valley, stretching 106 m (350 ft) into the rock. Lightly coloured bas-reliefs decorate the walls and the ceiling is painted with a procession of vultures whose wings spread the width of the corridor.

KV5

In 1994 the American archaeologist Kent Weeks began excavating a tomb that had previously been considered unimportant by Egyptologists. What he found is the largest and most complex tomb in the Valley of the Kings. Known as KV5, the tomb is believed to be the burial site for Ramses II's sons. A 16-pillared entrance hall, several corridors and more than 100 chambers have so far been discovered and although no treasure has been found, thousands of important artifacts have been recovered from the rubble. The tomb is currently still undergoing excavation.

Amenhotep II's burial chamber, containing the pharaoh's sarcophagus

Thebes: Tombs of the Nobles

Extending over a large area to the south of the Valley of the Kings, the Tombs of the Nobles is made up of more than 400 tombs of Theban nobles and high officials, mainly from the New Kingdom. While the royal tombs were hidden away in a secluded valley, these tombs are closer to the surface of the hills overlooking the Nile. Because of the poor quality of the limestone here, the tombs are painted and there are few carved reliefs. Vivid artworks cover the walls, providing an invaluable insight into daily life in the New Kingdom. The Sheikh Abd al-Gurna Tombs are clustered around the village of Old Gurna. Further east, tombs at the necropolises of Khokha, Assasif and Abu al-Naga are now open to the public.

Richly detailed paintings of life in ancient Egypt in the Tomb of Sennefer

VISITORS' CHECKLIST

Thebes/Luxor, West Bank (follow signposts from Old Gurna for Sheikh Abd al-Gurna Tombs). ☐ daily. 🎟 payable at West Bank ticket kiosk; 2–3 tombs per ticket for Sheikh Abd al-Gurna Tombs.

Sheikh Abd al-Gurna Tombs

All the tombs here date from the 18th Dynasty. The **Tomb of Sennefer (No.96)**, mayor of Thebes and overseer of the gardens of Amun under Amenhotep II, is one of the best preserved. The ceiling is covered with brightly-coloured paintings of vines, and Sennefer is shown with his family and making offerings to the gods. The **Tomb of Rekhmire (No.100)**, a vizier during the reigns of Tuthmosis III and Amenhotep II, shows servants at work and Rekhmire collecting taxes and receiving gifts from foreign lands.

The **Tomb of Nakht (No.52)** is decorated with scenes of rural life, such as fishing, harvesting and hunting in the Nile delta. Nakht was the scribe and astronomer of Tuthmosis IV. The well-preserved **Tomb of Menna (No.69)**, an inspector of estates, shows Menna and his

Treading grapes – Tomb of Nakht

wife making offerings to the gods. It contains a detailed harvest scene and paintings of fishing and hunting.

The **Tomb of Ramose (No.55)**, governor of Thebes before and during Akhenaten's reign, has reliefs showing both the old style of worship and the worship of Aten imposed by the heretic pharaoh. The **Tomb of Userhat (No.56)** has detailed scenes of everyday life, including a trip to the barber's. Userhat was one of Amenhotep II's scribes.

The **Tomb of Khonsu (No.31)**, an adviser to Tuthmosis III, is painted with colourful scenes of the Festival of Montu, while the **Tomb of Benia (No.343)** has vignettes of daily life and statues of the deceased and both his parents.

Khokha Tombs

Three tombs, discovered here in 1915, were opened for the first time in 1995. The **Tomb of Djehuty-Mes (No.295)** shows this 18th-Dynasty priest with his wife and family. The **Tomb of Neferronpet (No.178)**, a scribe during the reign of Ramses II, contains a painting of the scribe and his wife before Osiris. The **Tomb of Nefersekheru (No.296)**, another 19th-Dynasty scribe, shows a similar scene.

Assasif Tombs

The **Tomb of Kheruef (No.192)**, steward to Queen Tiy, contains scenes of the queen and 18th-Dynasty pharaoh Amenhotep III watching a dance in their honour. The nearby **Tomb of Anchhor (No.414)**, overseer of the priests of Amun, is an elaborate structure, but the decoration is not well preserved. The recently opened **Tomb of Pabasa (No.279)**, a 26th-Dynasty official, is noted for the pillared first court with its detailed bee-keeping and fruit-picking scenes.

Abu al-Naga Tombs

The first tombs in this area opened in 1999. The **Tomb of Roy**, a steward in the 18th Dynasty, and the **Tomb of Shuroy**, an 18th-Dynasty official, both have colourful tableaux of daily life.

Recording the harvest scene, Tomb of Menna

Thebes: Hatshepsut Temple

Head of Hatshepsut

Against its stark mountainous backdrop, the partly rock-hewn Mortuary Temple of Hatshepsut at Deir al-Bahri is a breathtaking sight. It was designed by Queen Hatshepsut's architect Senenmut in the 18th Dynasty and is an extraordinary monument which rises from the desert plain in a series of imposing terraces. The temple was damaged by Ramses II and his successors, and Christians later turned it into a monastery (hence the name Deir al-Bahri, which means "Northern Monastery"). However, the ongoing excavation of the site continues to reveal much exquisite decoration. Adjacent to the main temple are the ruins of the much older Temple of Montuhotep II, the ruler of the 11th Dynasty who managed to unite Egypt, and the 18th-Dynasty Temple of Tuthmosis III.

Temple of Montuhotep II
The prototype for Hatshepsut's Temple, the older Temple of Montuhotep II now lies in ruins.

Temple of Tuthmosis III

The imposing Hatshepsut Temple, in its stunning setting at the foot of a sheer limestone cliff-face

RECONSTRUCTION OF THE TEMPLES AT DEIR AL-BAHRI

This reconstruction shows the Temples of Montuhotep II, Tuthmosis III and Hatshepsut as they would have looked during the reign of Tuthmosis III in the 18th Dynasty. Partly rock-cut and partly free-standing, the three temples are set into a natural amphitheatre and are given added majesty by the dramatic cliffs behind them.

STAR FEATURES

★ Reliefs of Punt Expedition

★ Chapel of Hathor

★ Statues of Hatshepsut

★ Chapel of Hathor
This chapel is noted for its Hathor-headed columns. The walls have retained much original colouring, including this relief of the ankh and djed *pillar, symbols of life and stability.*

★ Statues of Hatshepsut
*The columns of the portico
around the upper terrace
were decorated with
Osiride statues of
Hatshepsut, character-
istically represented as a
male king with a beard.
Although many statues
were destroyed by later
pharaohs, several have
recently been reconstructed
from their fragments.*

**The Shrine
of Amun**
was dug
into the cliff
behind the
temple.

VISITORS' CHECKLIST

2 km (1 mile) NE of West Bank
ticket kiosk.
🚍 or on foot from other sites.
🕐 6am–5pm daily. 🎫

**Sanctuary
of the Sun**

Chapel of Anubis
*This chapel contains
brightly coloured
murals, including a
relief of Tutmosis III
making offerings
to the sun god
Ra-Harakhty.*

Myrrh trees planted in the
gardens yielded a gum
that was burnt as incense.

Avenue of sphinxes led
off in the direction of
the temple complex at
Karnak.

★ Reliefs of Punt Expedition
*Stunning reliefs relate Hatshepsut's
journey to the Land of Punt
(Somalia). The king of Punt is seen
here with his wife Ati (left), who
is depicted suffering from obesity.*

Birth Colonnade
*Scenes along the Birth
Colonnade portray the
divine birth of Hatshepsut,
designed to legitimize the
queen's claim to the
throne. On the right, the
young queen is shown
in the arms of the
goddess Neith.*

Thebes: Valley of the Queens

Celestial cow in Nefertari's tomb

Named by Champollion, the Valley of the Queens lies to the southwest of the Valley of the Kings and holds the tombs of many royal wives and children. Although it was used as a burial site in the 18th Dynasty, it was only from the reign of the 19th-Dynasty pharaoh Ramses I that royal wives were laid to rest here. Of the nearly 80 tombs populating the valley, the most famous is that of Queen Nefertari and only a handful are open to the public at any one time.

Tomb of Amunherkhepshep (No.55)

The elegant, well-preserved tomb of Prince Amunher-khepshep (Amun), son of Ramses III, was the highlight of the Valley of the Queens until the reopening of Nefertari's tomb. Amun would have succeeded his father as pharaoh but he died when he was a child and was buried in this royal tomb.

From the entrance, steps lead down to the tomb hall, which contains beautiful, brightly-coloured wall paintings of Ramses accompanying his young son on a visit to pay homage to the gods of the underworld. Amun is easily recognizable because he is wearing the character-istic braided hairstyle of a prince. From here, a corridor decorated with the Keepers of the Gates leads to the burial chamber, where the skeleton of a five-month-old foetus is on display in a glass cabinet. Foetuses have been found in other burial chambers and may have been placed there as part of the ritual of rebirth.

Tomb of Queen Titi (No.52)

Queen Titi was married to one of the Ramesside pharaohs of the 20th Dynasty, although it is unclear which one. Her tomb is small and damaged in parts, but certain sections have particularly colourful paintings. Some of the best scenes are in the burial chamber, where Hathor appears in bovine form in a mountainous landscape and again in human form, pouring water from the Nile to revive the queen. The tomb was closed at the time of writing.

Tomb of Prince Khaemweset (No.44)

This is the tomb of another of Ramses III's sons who died in infancy. Its intricate reliefs have preserved much of their colour. Ramses is shown introducing his son to the different deities and making offerings to them. The goddesses Isis, Nephthys, Neith and Selket are also depicted, addressing Osiris on behalf of the child prince.

Valley of the Queens: Tomb of Queen Nefertari

Regarded as the most beautiful tomb in Egypt, the tomb of Queen Nefertari (No.66), favourite wife of Ramses II, was discovered in 1904 by the Italian archaeologist Ernesto Schiaparelli. Recently restored to its former glory, it is exquisitely decorated with scenes evoking the ritual journey of the soul to the underworld.

Nefertari's sarcophagus originally stood between the four pillars.

Ledge used for offerings

The side rooms housed funerary furnishings.

Staircase descending into burial chamber

Second staircase

Entrance

Queen Nefertari, wearing a white gown and jewels, in the vestibule

KEY

- ☐ Antechamber
- ☐ Vestibule
- ☐ Side chamber
- ☐ Second staircase
- ☐ Burial chamber
- ☐ Pillars

Ra as a ram-headed deity between Isis and Nephthys, in the side chamber

ANTECHAMBER

Entrance to the tomb is gained via a steep staircase, hewn out of rock, which descends into the antechamber. Wonderful, brightly-coloured paintings depicting Queen Nefertari in the company of various gods cover the walls while the blue ceiling is scattered with yellow stars representing the heavens. The paintings to the left of the entrance relate to the Book of the Dead and depict Nefertari playing *senet*, an early version of draughts. On the eastern wall of the antechamber, the entrance to the vestibule is flanked by pictures of Osiris, on the left side, and Anubis, on the right.

VESTIBULE

On the left of this small rectangular room, the goddess Isis is shown introducing Nefertari to the scarab-headed god Khepri. On the right, the falcon-headed Harsiesis (a form of Horus), wearing the double crown of Upper and Lower Egypt, presents Nefertari to the seated Ra-Harakhty and

Hathor-Imentit. The vulture goddess Nekhbet spreads out her wings above the narrow doorway to the side chamber.

SIDE CHAMBER

Through the doorway, the side chamber is ablaze with stunning murals. To the left, Nefertari is seen offering cloth to the god Ptah, who is wrapped in a white mummy shroud in his shrine. On the northern wall, Nefertari stands before Thoth, while the large eastern wall, which faces the visitor on entering the room, shows Nefertari making offerings to Osiris and Atum, on the left and right respectively.

Osiris in the side chamber

SECOND STAIRCASE

A highly decorated stairway corridor leads down into the burial chamber. On the left, the god Anubis, the black jackal, welcomes Nefertari

into the kingdom of the dead. On the right, Nefertari is seen holding out ritual pots, containing liquid offerings, to Hathor and Selket. Lower down, the goddess Maat spreads out her wings.

BURIAL CHAMBER

The burial chamber was where the regeneration of Nefertari's soul was designed to take place. The wall paintings draw inspiration from the Book of the Dead, featuring Nefertari with the guardians of the gates of Osiris's kingdom, through which she would have to pass in order to proceed to the underworld. By uttering magic formulas and the names of the guardians, Nefertari is shown surmounting these potential obstacles to rebirth.

PILLARS

The chamber's four pillars are excellently preserved. Facing the visitor on entering the room, the first two pillars are decorated with Horus wearing the priestly leopard skin. Osiris in typical pose adorns the four inner faces of the pillars on the north/south axis. Facing where the coffin would have been are the striped *djed* pillars representing Osiris's spine and a symbol of reincarnation.

REPAIRING NEFERTARI'S TOMB

Nefertari's tomb was carved from poor quality limestone and over the years its reliefs were damaged by water, humidity and crystallized salt. As a result, the tomb was closed in the 1950s. In 1986 the Supreme Council of Antiquities and the Getty Conservation Institute embarked on an ambitious project to restore the tomb. Salt-damaged plaster was removed, cleaned, strengthened and replaced, and a solution of acrylic resin was injected into cracks. The paintwork was carefully cleaned and the colours returned to their original vibrancy. Work was completed in 1992 and the tomb was reopened in 1995. However, to control humidity levels, visitor numbers are restricted.

The interior of Queen Nefertari's Tomb during restoration

Thebes: The Ramesseum

Pharaoh Ramses II, ruler of Egypt for 67 years in the 19th Dynasty, built his mortuary temple, the Ramesseum, as a statement of his eternal greatness and to impress his subjects. The huge complex, which took more than 20 years to complete, now lies largely in ruins. Dedicated to Amun, it once boasted an 18-m (60-ft) high, 1,000-tonne colossus of Ramses, parts of which lie scattered around the site. The complex also included a smaller temple dedicated to Ramses's mother Tuya and his wife Nefertari, as well as a royal palace and storehouses.

Wall relief of Amun in the hypostyle hall

★ **Osiride Columns**
Statues of Ramses as Osiris, god of the underworld, face into the second court. These figures, arms crossed bearing the crook and flail, signal the funerary nature of the temple.

★ **Head of the Colossus of Ramses**
The shattered head and shoulders of the immense colossus of Ramses now lie in the second court. An image of this evocative sight inspired Percy Bysshe Shelley to write his famous poem "Ozymandias".

Royal palace

RECONSTRUCTION OF THE RAMESSEUM

This reconstruction shows how the Ramesseum would have looked when it was completed in around 1250 BC. The flooding of the Nile and earthquakes later took their toll, leaving today's atmospheric ruins.

Landing stage provided mooring for boats from the Nile.

STAR FEATURES

★ Osiride Columns

★ Head of the Colossus of Ramses

First Pylon
The imposing first pylon was decorated with scenes of Ramses in battle. Sadly, an earthquake badly damaged the pylon, and the gateway to the first court is now supported by concrete.

Hypostyle Hall Plant Capital
*The hypostyle hall roof is
supported by tall columns.
The still colourful
patterns of papyrus
and lotus plants
symbolize the union of
Lower and Upper Egypt.*

Vestibules
led to the
sanctuary.

Mudbrick Stores
*Innumerable vaulted
mudbrick magazines
once surrounded the
temple, used as store-
rooms, workshops and
living quarters.*

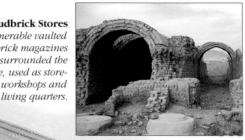

Huge mudbrick
walls protected the
entire temple complex.

**Foundations of the
Temple of Tuya**
*A small temple dedicated
to Ramses's mother Tuya
and his wife Nefertari
stood to the north of
the hypostyle hall.*

BATTLE OF QADESH

Ramses II portrayed himself as a warrior
pharaoh of great bravery and military prowess.
Around 1275 BC, he led the Egyptian army
into battle against the Hittites at Qadesh, an
important trading town in the Orontes Valley
in Syria. Although the battle was really a draw,
Ramses paraded it as a victory on the walls
of several of his great temples,
including the Ramesseum.
Ramses is depicted firing
arrows at the fleeing
Hittites and, in trad-
itional pose, holding
his enemy's head, about
to inflict the fatal blow.

Wall relief on the inner face of the second pylon,
depicting Hittites slain at the Battle of Qadesh

Exploring Other Sites in Thebes

Scattered amid the wadis and hills of the West Bank are several other sites well worth a visit. Often by-passed in favour of the more famous Theban attractions, these additional sites can be visited in relative peace, well away from the tourist hordes. Medinat Habu, in particular, is one of the most underrated monuments on the West Bank, and Deir al-Medina provides a rare insight into the lives of ordinary people in ancient Egypt, as well as containing some exquisite tombs.

The awesome Colossi of Memnon on the flat desert plain of the West Bank

⋔ Colossi of Memnon

1 km (0.6 mile) E of West Bank ticket kiosk.

Soaring 18 m (60 ft) into the sky, the two enthroned statues of Amenhotep III are the first monuments most visitors see on arriving in the West Bank. They originally guarded Amenhotep's mortuary temple – thought to have been the largest ever built in Egypt – which was plundered for build-ing material by later pharaohs and gradually destroyed by the annual floods. All that remains are the two faceless colossi, which, despite the ravages of time, are an impressive sight.

During the Roman period the northernmost statue became a popular tourist attraction as it was heard to "sing" at sunrise.

Prominent visitors to the site to hear this peculiar phenomenon included the Emperor Hadrian, and the colossi are mentioned by classical authors such as Strabo and Pliny. The Greeks had earlier attributed the sound to the legendary figure of Memnon greeting his mother Eos, the goddess of dawn, with a sigh each morning. In fact, the statue had been badly damaged in an earthquake in 27 BC and its musical talent probably had a purely physical cause related to the damage it had sustained. Whatever the reason, once the statue had been repaired in AD 199 by the Roman emperor Septimius Severus, the singing stopped.

⋔ Medinat Habu

W of West Bank ticket kiosk.
☐ daily. 📷

Although second only to Karnak in size and detail, the beautiful temple of Medinat Habu is one of the less-visited sights in Thebes. The complex is dominated by the huge mortuary temple of Ramses III, modelled on Ramses II's mortuary temple at the Ramesseum (see pp200–1). During later invasions of Egypt in the 20th Dynasty, the entire population of Thebes took refuge within the temple's massive enclosure walls.

Ramses III's many military campaigns are recorded in detail on the temple's pylons and walls. In the second court, colourful reliefs depicting religious festivals are well preserved, partly thanks to the early Christians who converted the area into a church and covered the offending images with plaster.

To the west of the first court are the remains of Ramses's royal palace. Also within the enclosure walls is the smaller Temple of Amun, originally built by Hatshepsut but altered by Tuthmosis III and enlarged and modified up to Roman times.

⋔ Deir al-Medina

1 km (0.6 mile) NW of West Bank ticket kiosk. ☐ daily. 📷 (separate ticket needed for Pashedu's tomb).

The craftsmen, servants and labourers who worked on the royal tombs lived in the village of Deir al-Medina,

Painted relief from the Ptolemaic temple at Deir al-Medina

Sennedjem and his wife worshipping the gods of the underworld in his tomb at Deir al-Medina

also known as the Workmen's Village, to the south of the Valley of the Queens. They were buried in the nearby necropolis, in tombs that were intricately decorated and surmounted by a small pyramid. One of the most beautiful is the **Tomb of Sennedjem (No.1)**, a 19th-Dynasty servant. Discovered in 1886, its yellow ochre walls are in perfect condition; they show Sennedjem and his wife, Iyneferti, worshipping different gods and working in the fields of the underworld. The adjacent **Tomb of Inherkhau (No.359)**, the "foreman of the mayor of the Two Lands", is equally beautifully decorated with memorable scenes, including the Cat of Heliopolis killing the serpent Apophis under the holy tree. The small size of these tombs means that only ten people are allowed in them at one time. The recently opened **Tomb of Pashedu (No.3)**, a servant during the Ramesside era, is renowned for its delicate paintings and for a famous scene of Pashedu crouching next to a stream under a palm tree.

To the north of the village is a small Ptolemaic temple, dedicated to the goddesses Hathor and Maat. During the Coptic period it was turned into a monastery, which led to the site being named Deir al-Medina or "City Monastery".

Temple of Seti I
3 km (2 miles) E of West Bank ticket kiosk.
daily.

Away from the popular tourist trail, the 19th-Dynasty mortuary Temple of Seti I, the northernmost of all the temples of Thebes, is dedicated to Amun and to the cult of Seti's father, Ramses I. After Seti's death, his son Ramses II completed the temple. Although the pylons and surrounding buildings are in ruins, the sanctuary, halls and antechambers of the main sandstone temple are well preserved and there are some interesting, high-quality reliefs, including those showing Seti and Ramses II making offerings to Amun. Part of the roof, featuring vultures and the winged sun disc, is still intact. The German Archaeological Institute is currently in the process of restoring the site.

Howard Carter's house
3 km (2 miles) E of West Bank ticket kiosk.

British archaeologist Howard Carter, best known for his discovery of the tomb of Tutankhamun in 1922 *(see pp20–1)*,

lived for many years in this domed house on a barren hillside north of the Temple of Seti I. Plans to turn the house into a museum displaying Carter's personal belongings, pictures of his discoveries and letters to his patron, Lord Carnarvon, have yet to come to fruition.

The Villages of Gurna
Built on and around the Tombs of the Nobles *(see p195)* is Old Gurna. Despite its lack of basic infrastructure the village is alive with bright, mudbrick houses decorated with scenes of pilgrimages to Mecca. Old Gurna has long been considered a threat to the ancient tombs and in the 1940s New Gurna was built to rehouse its residents. Designed by architect Hassan Fathy and completed in 1948, New Gurna was inspired by the traditional domed, mudbrick style of Nubian architecture. Despite the innovative use of local materials it failed to lure the residents of Old Gurna who believe they safeguard both the monuments and tourists. Today, little more than New Gurna's mosque is intact and the government is intent on moving residents northeast to Taref, a purpose-built town.

The domed house of British archaeologist Howard Carter

New Gurna
2 km (1 mile) SE of West Bank ticket kiosk.

Old Gurna
1 km (0.6 mile) NE of West Bank ticket kiosk.

Part of the village of Old Gurna, nestling in the foothills of the Theban hills

Detail of the Temple of Khnum's astronomical ceiling at Esna

Esna ⑩

Qena governorate, 54 km (33 miles) S of Luxor. 🚶 55,000. 🚌 🚗 ⛴ 🚆 from Luxor or Aswan.

The sleepy farming town of Esna lies on the western bank of the Nile, just south of a sandstone dam across the river, built in 1906. Known as Latopolis by the ancient Greeks because the Nile perch (*lates* in Greek) was worshipped here, Esna is today best known for the **Temple of Khnum**. This Graeco-Roman structure was designed to resemble a much earlier temple on the site, built by 18th-Dynasty pharaoh Tuthmosis III (*see p49*). Both temples were dedicated to the ram-headed god Khnum, who, according to one of the Egyptian creation myths, fashioned mankind out of Nile clay using a potter's wheel.

Gradually, repeated flooding by the Nile buried the Graeco-Roman structure under layers of silt and mud, and the modern town of Esna was built on top of it. Excavation work on the site began in the 1860s but this has only cleared one part of the temple, the Roman hypostyle

hall, which was built during the reign of the Roman emperor Claudius (AD 41–54). Today this well-preserved hall stands in a huge excavation ditch 10 m (33 ft) below street level in the centre of town. Its roof, which remarkably is still intact, is on the same level as the foundations of the surrounding houses. The façade of the hall is inscribed with the cartouches of Roman emperors Claudius, Vespasian (AD 69–79) and Titus (AD 79–81). Inside the hall the last emperor mentioned is Decius, who died as late as AD 249. The roof is supported by 24 columns inscribed with hieroglyphs and fascinating texts describing the sacred festivals of Esna and recording hymns to the god Khnum. The bright colours of the astronomical ceiling have faded but it is still possible to make out the zodiac register, remarkable for its subtlety and detail.

🔔 **Temple of Khnum**
🕐 *daily.* 📷

Edfu ⑪

Aswan governorate, 115 km (71 miles) S of Luxor; 104 km (65 miles) N of Aswan. 🚶 56,000. 🚌 🚗 🚆 from Luxor or Aswan.

Edfu stands beside the Nile almost exactly half-way between Luxor and Aswan. It was an important sacred site to the Egyptians because, according to ancient myth,

this was where the falcon god Horus fought a fierce battle with his uncle Seth, who had cruelly murdered Horus's father Osiris (*see p26*).

The **Temple of Horus** at Edfu, which was buried under sand and silt for nearly two thousand years, is the largest and best preserved Ptolemaic temple in Egypt. Construction of the temple began under Ptolemy III Euergetes in 237 BC and the main temple complex took 25 years to complete. However, construction continued up to the time of Ptolemy XII Neos Dionysus (80–51 BC). Despite its relatively recent construction, the temple is of particular interest to Egyptologists because it closely imitates much older Pharaonic designs. The imposing 36-m (118-ft) high first pylon is typically decorated with Pharaonic scenes of Ptolemy XII defeating his enemies in front of Horus and Hathor. Two elegant black granite statues of Horus flank the entrance to the pylon, which leads to a large colonnaded court and the first hypostyle hall. Behind this lies a second, smaller hypostyle hall with chambers off to the side. Gifts for the gods were stored in these rooms before being taken into the hall of offerings beyond. Stairs lead from the hall of offerings to the roof, which has glorious views of the Nile and the surrounding fields. The staircase walls are beautifully decorated with

Granite statue of the falcon god Horus

Pylon of the Temple of Horus in Edfu with reliefs showing pharaoh Ptolemy XII

scenes from the New Year festival, a ritual celebrated in temples all over Egypt. On the first day of the year, in each temple, a procession of priests carried the statue of the temple god up to the roof to be revitalized by the sun. Beyond the hall of offerings is the sanctuary of Horus with its black granite shrine. Several chapels with excellent reliefs surround the sanctuary, one of which contains a model of Horus's sacred barque.

Southwest of the temple lie the remains of Horus's birth house. This was the focus of the annual Coronation Festival, a ritual celebrating the birth of Horus and his incarnation as the reigning pharaoh.

Temple of Horus
Daily.

Postcard of Bedouin and camels – both at home in the desert

SHIPS OF THE DESERT

The *Camelus dromedarius* or one-humped Arabian camel has been an essential part of life in Egypt for thousands of years. Used primarily for transporting goods, the camel also provides milk, wool and meat. Contrary to myth, the camel's hump is not filled with water; it contains fat which allows the camel to survive for up to a week without food. Camels are ideally suited to desert life with their third, transparent eyelid that allows them to see in sand storms, nostrils that close between breaths and their unique body thermostat that minimizes unnecessary water loss through sweating. When they walk, camels move both legs on one side and then both legs on the other. This creates a rolling motion, hence their nickname "ships of the desert".

Relief of Sobek, the crocodile god, in the temple of Kom Ombo

Temple of Kom Ombo ⑫

40 km (25 miles) N of Aswan.
from Aswan or Luxor.
daily.

Surrounded by fields of sugar cane and corn, Kom Ombo is a pleasant agricultural town, home to many Nubians displaced by the creation of Lake Nasser *(see p210)*. The town's ruined yet imposing Graeco-Roman temple is in a particularly beautiful setting overlooking the Nile. The temple building is totally symmetrical with two entrances, two halls and two sanctuaries. This unusual structure is the result of the temple's dedication to two gods – the left side to the falcon god Haroeris (Horus the Elder) and the right side to Sobek, the local crocodile god. The construction of the temple was begun by Ptolemy VI Philometer in the 2nd century BC and mostly completed by Ptolemy XII Neos Dionysus during the 1st century BC. Finally the Roman emperor Augustus added the entrance pylon in around 30 BC. From the largely ruined forecourt, two doors lead to the hypostyle hall, which contains scenes relating to Haroeris on the left wall and Sobek on the right. The many columns are carved with the lotus or lily of Upper Egypt and the papyrus of the Delta. A series of halls and vestibules leads through to the sanctuaries of Haroeris and Sobek.

The Chapel of Hathor, just to the south of the temple, now houses a few crocodile mummies from the nearby crocodile necropolis.

Daraw ⑬

8 km (5 miles) S of Kom Ombo.
31,000. from Kom Ombo.
Tue.

Travellers often combine a trip to Kom Ombo with a visit to the nearby village of Daraw for the famous Tuesday camel market, when hundreds of camels are up for sale. Most of the camels have been brought from Sudan on a month-long journey along "The Forty Days Road", an ancient droving route and former slave trail. The market is chaotic, colourful and very noisy. Traders travel from Cairo to haggle for camels to sell at the famous Birqash camel market, while locals come in search of a bargain.

Camels for sale in the famous Daraw camel market, held every Tuesday

Aswan ⑭

Relief from the Temple of Khnum

Situated downriver from the First Nile Cataract, Aswan is Egypt's southernmost city. From Old Kingdom times, this strategically important garrison town guarded Egypt's southern frontier and was a base for military incursions into Nubia and Sudan. Located at the crossroads of ancient trade routes between Egypt, Africa and India, the town was also a prosperous marketplace, where exotic goods were traded. Aswan stands on the most enchanting part of the Nile, where the desert comes right down to the water's edge and the river is dotted with islands. It is home to a large Nubian community, and the town's laid-back atmosphere makes it one of the most relaxing places in Egypt to visit.

The imposing Sofitel Cataract Hotel overlooking the Nile at Aswan

🏨 Sofitel Cataract Hotel

Corniche el-Nil. **Tel** (097) 2316 000.
The English crime-writer Agatha Christie penned part of her best-selling novel "Death on the Nile" in this impressive Moorish-style hotel, which opened in 1899. Set in beautiful gardens, with superb views over the Nile and Elephantine Island, it is one of the most famous hotels in Egypt. Past guests include the German Field Marshal Rommel, Sir Winston Churchill and King Farouk. It is the perfect place to soak up Aswan's romantic atmosphere while sipping afternoon tea on the verandah or watching the sun set over the Nile.

🏛 Nubian Museum

Off road to Aswan Dam, 1 km (0.6 mile) S of Aswan. **Tel** (097) 2319 111.
⭘ 9am–1pm, 5–9pm daily (6–10pm summer); 9am–3pm Ramadan. 📷
This well laid-out museum traces life in Nubia – the area between Aswan in Egypt and Khartoum in Sudan – from the earliest settlements to the present day. Nubian crafts such as basket making and pottery are featured and there

is a fascinating display about the UNESCO-backed projects to save Nubian monuments from submergence under Lake Nasser (*see p210*). The garden contains a reconstructed cave with prehistoric rock carvings, a Nubian house and a water feature showing the Nile's course and cataracts.

⋔ Unfinished Obelisk

1.5 km (1 mile) S of Aswan, next to Fatimid Cemetery. ⭘ daily. 📷
A gigantic obelisk, dating from the New Kingdom, lies semi-finished in an ancient granite quarry just south of Aswan. Had it been completed, it would have weighed a staggering 1.8 million kg (1,197 tons) and stood 41 m (134 ft) high. Three sides of the shaft were quarried before a flaw was discovered in the stone and the obelisk had to be abandoned, still partly attached to the parent rock. To the west of the quarry, the Fatimid cemetery contains several hundred mudbrick Islamic tombs, built between the 8th and 12th centuries.

🛍 Souq

Sharia as-Souq. ⭘ daily.
From embroidered *galabiyyas* and coloured caps to aromatic spices, live chickens and fresh vegetables, there is a vast array of tempting goods on sale in Aswan's lively and extensive market. The chaotic, tightly packed network of narrow alleyways makes the souq a fascinating place to simply wander around and completes the exotic and colourful atmosphere. The market runs parallel to the Nile and becomes noticeably less tourist-orientated further inland from the busy main street, Sharia as-Souq.

Sharia as-Souq, the main thoroughfare in Aswan's famous market

◁ Detail of a relief showing the journey to the land of Punt – Hatshepsut Temple, Deir al-Bahri

A colourful Nubian village on the banks of Elephantine Island

Elephantine Island

Aswan.

Known as Yebu (meaning "elephant") during the Old Kingdom, Elephantine Island is the oldest inhabited part of Aswan. It is not known whether the island was named after the huge granite boulders at the southern end of the island, which resemble bathing elephants, or because it was a major ivory trading post.

In ancient times, the island was the cult centre of the ram-headed god Khnum, creator of humankind and god of the Nile flood. Among the ruins of the ancient fortress town that once stood on the southern end of the island are the ruins of the **Temple of Khnum**, built by Nectanebo in 4th century BC. An impressive gateway, added in the 1st century BC, showing Ptolemy XI worshipping Khnum, can be seen on the west side of the temple. Immediately to the north is the Graeco-Roman **Necropolis of the Sacred Rams**, and to the east, the **Temple of Satet**, built by Queen Hatshepsut. This area is being excavated by German archaeologists and some areas are out of bounds.

In the middle of the island, three traditional Nubian villages are distinguished by their brightly coloured homes.

Nilometer

Elephantine Island.
☐ daily.

South of the Aswan Museum, the steep Nilometer steps descend into the river. The walls were calibrated to record the height of the annual flood and so indicate the likely crop yield for the next year. Dating from Pharaonic times, the Nilometer was briefly put back into use after its discovery in 1822.

Calibration on walls of Nilometer

Aswan Museum

Elephantine Island. ☐ daily.
The Aswan Museum is set among pleasant, sub-tropical gardens near the southern end of Elephantine Island. It is home to a collection of well labelled artifacts found on digs in and around Aswan and Elephantine Island. Exhibits range from primitive prehistoric weapons to Graeco-Roman mummies and are labelled in chronological order. A new annexe displays recent finds from the island, including jewellery discovered at the island's Temple of Satet and a marriage contract dating from 350 BC.

ASWAN

Aga Khan Mausoleum ⑨
Aswan Museum ⑥
Elephantine Island ⑤
Kitchener's Island ⑧
Monastery of St Simeon ⑩
Nilometer ⑦
Nubian Museum ②
Sofitel Cataract Hotel ①
Souq ④
Tombs of the Nobles ⑪
Unfinished Obelisk ③

Qubbet el-Hawa
⑪ Tombs of the Nobles
River Nile
Train Station
Souq ④
Bus Station
⑩ Monastery of St Simeon
⑧ Kitchener's Island
Elephantine Island ⑤
Aga Khan Mausoleum ⑨
Aswan Museum ⑥
Temple of Khnum
Nilometer ⑦
Ferial Gardens
Coptic Cathedral
Sofitel Cataract Hotel ①
Fatimed Cemetery
Fort
② Nubian Museum
Unfinished Obelisk ③
Airport 25 km (15 miles)
Aswan Dam, High Dam & Lake Nasser

SHARIA ABTAL EL-TAHRIR
SHARIA AL-SOUK
SHARIA ABBAS AL-AKAD
SHARIA SHARO AL-BANDAR
SHARIA ABU ZID
SHARIA SALAH
SHARIA ABBAS FARID
SHARIA QASR EL-HAGGAR
CORNICHE EL-NIL
SHARIA SHARO AL-BANDAR

0 metres   750
0 yards   750

Key to Symbols see back flap

Lush botanical gardens stocked with plants from all parts of the world on Kitchener's Island, Aswan

🔟 Kitchener's Island

Aswan. 🚤 🏞 ⬜ *daily.* 💳
Situated in the Nile, west
of Elephantine Island, the
smaller Kitchener's Island
(also known as the Island of
Plants) is one of the most
delightful places in Aswan.
The lush botanical gardens
that cover the island make it
an ideal place to go for a
peaceful stroll or simply relax
in the shade of the trees.

The British general Horatio
Kitchener was presented
with the island in the 1890s
as a reward for leading the
Egyptian army's successful
campaigns in Sudan. He
made the island his home
and indulged his passion for
beautiful flowers by covering
it with exotic plants imported
from all around the world.

The huge sycamore trees,
coconut palms and date palms
that tower into the sky are
filled with colourful birds

Mausoleum of the Aga Khan on a barren hillside opposite Aswan

and egrets, and as the sun
begins to go down the entire
island rings out with the
sound of their calls.

🏛 Aga Khan Mausoleum

West bank, on the road to the
Monastery of St Simeon.
⬤ *to the public.*
Standing on a barren hillside
on the west bank of the Nile,
opposite Aswan, is the Aga
Khan Mausoleum. Aga Khan
III (1877–1957), the 48th
Imam, or leader, of the Ismaili
sect of Shi'ite Muslims, fell in
love with Aswan, where he
spent the winter every year.
After his death in 1957, his
widow, the Begum, erected a
mausoleum in his honour on
the hillside behind his villa.

The domed and turreted
sandstone construction is
outwardly modelled on
Cairo's Fatimid tombs *(see
p102)*. Inside, there is a
marble shrine and the
Aga Khan's sarcophagus,
inscribed with texts
from the Quran.
Until her

death in 2000, the Begum
spent part of each year in the
villa and would visit the
mausoleum every day to
place a red rose on her
husband's sarcophagus.

Lake Nasser, an enormous blue
expanse in the desert

LAKE NASSER

Stretching south more
than 500 km (310 miles)
from the High Dam and
reaching depths of over
180 m (590 ft), Lake Nasser
is the largest artificial lake
in the world. The lake
was created by the
construction of the High
Dam. It flooded a huge
expanse of land between
Aswan and Abu Simbel,
homeland of the Nubians
since before Pharaonic
times. About 800,000
Nubians were displaced,
many settling in Aswan,
and dozens of ancient
temples had to be carefully
relocated *(see p21)*.

The imposing fortifications of the Monastery of St Simeon, Aswan

⋔ Monastery of St Simeon

West bank. 🚢 🚶 *then by camel or on foot.* ⭘ *daily.* 📷

The desert Monastery of St Simeon, on the west bank of the Nile, was built in the 7th century AD. Once home to a community of around 300 monks, it was abandoned in the late 12th century after an attack by the famous Arab leader Salah ad-Din.

The monastery was built as a fortress and, though the main buildings now lie largely in ruins, the imposing fortification walls remain. The lower levels of the complex, which comprised a church, living areas for the monks, stables and work quarters, are made of stone, while the upper levels are made of brick. In the roofless basilica, frescos of the Apostles are still visible, their faces scratched out by Muslims. In the evening, the monastery offers fantastic views of the sun setting over the desert.

The Tombs of the Nobles in the cliffs on the west bank of the Nile near Aswan

HARNESSING THE POWER OF THE NILE

The Aswan Dam was built to regulate the flow of the Nile and so increase Egypt's cultivable land and provide hydro-electric power. However, it soon proved too small to control the river's unpredictable floods. President Nasser's solution was the construction of the High Dam and the creation of Lake Nasser. The resultant increases in agricultural production and hydroelectricity have arguably saved Egypt from famine, but there have been environmental consequences. The rising water table is destroying ancient monuments and silt, previously deposited in the Delta, is retained in Lake Nasser, forcing Egypt's farmers to use potentially harmful chemicals.

The Aswan Dam, built by the British to regulate the flow of the Nile

⋔ Tombs of the Nobles

Qubbet al-Hawwa, West bank. 🚢 🚶 ⭘ *daily.* 📷

The hills on the west bank of the Nile, north of Kitchener's Island, are pock marked with the rock-hewn Tombs of the Nobles. Dating from the Old and Middle Kingdoms, many of the tombs are decorated with scenes of everyday life. The largest and best preserved tomb is that of Prince Sarenput II (No. 31), governor of southern Egypt during the 12th Dynasty. The burial chamber is decorated with statues of the prince and paintings of him and his son hunting and fishing. The tombs of Mekhu (No. 25), a noble from the 6th Dynasty who was murdered while on a military expedition in Nubia, and his son Sabni (No. 26), are crudely decorated with funeral and family scenes. The tomb of Prince Sarenput I (No. 36), Guardian of the South during the 12th Dynasty, shows him with his family and dogs.

The ancient necropolis is lit up by spotlights at night and looks particularly magical when viewed from across the river in Aswan.

🏛 Aswan Dam

11 km (7 miles) S of Aswan. 🚌 ⌀

Stretching across the Nile, just beyond the First Cataract, the Aswan Dam was built by the British between 1898 and 1902. At the time of its construction it was the largest dam in the world, and its height was twice raised again in an effort to control the river. The roads to Abu Simbel and the airport cross the dam and the views over the river and islands are stunning. Photography around both dams is strictly forbidden.

🏛 High Dam

6 km (4 miles) S of Aswan Dam. 🚌 🚉 📷 ⌀

Built between 1960 and 1971, the immense High Dam is 3,830 m (12,562 ft) across, 111 m (364 ft) high and 980 m (3,214 ft) wide at its base. At the eastern end of the dam there is a visitors' pavilion detailing the construction of the dam and at the western end there is a lotus-shaped tower, built to commemorate the Soviet Union's support in the building of the dam.

The Temple of Kalabsha, dominating the shores of Lake Nasser close to the High Dam

Temple of Philae ⑮

Agilika Island, S of Aswan Dam. 🚌 *from Aswan to Shellal.* 🛥 *from Aswan.* ⏲ *daily.* 🎦 **Sound and Light Show** *6pm, 7:30pm, 9pm in winter; 8:30pm, 10pm, 11pm in summer.*

As the centre of the cult of Isis, the island of Philae was an important place of pilgrimage for worshippers until long into the Christian era. From Philae, Isis was said to watch over the sacred island of Biga, one of the mythical burial sites of her husband Osiris.

After the building of the Aswan Dam (1898–1902), the island's temples were partly sub-merged in water and visitors took to rowing boats to peer at the remains. With the building of the High Dam (1960–71), the monuments were relocated to the nearby island of Agilika. The UNESCO-led project took from 1972 to 1980 to complete, during which time Agilika was land-scaped to look like Philae.

Boats now drop visitors at the southern end of Agilika, near the oldest building on the island, the **Kiosk of Nectanebo II**, which dates from the 4th century BC. From here, a long courtyard, flanked by colonnades, leads to the magnificent **Temple of Isis**, the main building in the Philae temple complex. Built in the late Ptolemaic and early Roman periods, the huge temple combines ancient Egyptian and Graeco-Roman architecture. Ptolemy XII

Neos Dionysos built the first pylon, which has scenes of him massacring his enemies, watched by Isis, Horus and Hathor. The birth house, built by Ptolemy VI and altered by later rulers, is dedicated to Isis's son Horus. To the west of the temple lies the **Gate of Hadrian**, which was inscribed, in 24th August AD 394, with Egypt's last hieroglyphics. On the eastern side of the island, the small **Temple of Hathor** contains reliefs of musicians, among them Bes, the god of singing. Further south, close to the edge of the water, is the classically grace-ful, 14-columned **Kiosk of Trajan**, which has scenes of the Roman emperor burning incense in front of Osiris and Isis. At the northern end of the island, the **Temple of Augustus** and **Gate of Diocletian** lie in ruins.

Lion in the Temple of Isis, Philae

Temple of Kalabsha ⑯

W of High Dam. 🚌 *from Aswan.* ⏲ *daily.* 🎦

The imposing temple of Kalabsha was built under Emperor Augustus in the 1st century AD on the site of earlier buildings by Amenhotep II and Ptolemy IX. Dedicated to the fertility god Marul (known as Mandulis by the Greeks), it was moved 50 km (31 miles) north of its original location in 1970 in a German-funded rescue operation following the flooding of Nubia. The temple now dominates a stretch of Lake Nasser's shore, just west of the High Dam. The land here often forms an island due to the changing water levels.

From the water's edge an imposing causeway leads to the temple's first pylon, beyond which there is a colonnaded court. The roofless hypostyle hall is noted for its ornate

The well-preserved western colonnade leading to Philae's Temple of Isis

For hotels and restaurants in this region see pp272–7 and pp296–8

column capitals and its reliefs, which include Amenhotep offering wine to Marul.

Environs
Moved at the same time as Kalabsha Temple, the battered remains of the Roman **Kiosk of Qertassi** lie to the northwest. Two Hathor-headed columns mark the entrance to this small kiosk, which commands fine views of Lake Nasser. The nearby **Temple of Beit al-Wali**, also relocated from Nubia, was built during the reign of Ramses II. Its walls depict Ramses's great battles, notably against the Nubians.

Avenue of sphinxes leading to the Temple of Wadi as-Sebua

Temple of Wadi as-Sebua **⑰**

140 km (87 miles) S of High Dam. 🚌 🚆 *from Aswan.* ◯ *daily.* 📷

Approached by the remains of an avenue of sphinxes, this temple was built by Ramses II and dedicated to the deified pharaoh, Amun-Ra and Ra-Harakhty. In the early 1960s the temple was moved a short distance west to its current site. Two colossi and statues of Ramses adorn the temple, which is partly carved directly into the rock. The inner sanctuary was converted into a Christian church and faint images of saints can be seen over the ancient reliefs.

Environs
Just to the north, the **Temple of Dakka** was begun by the Ethiopian king Arkamani in the 3rd century BC and added

to in the Ptolemaic and Roman eras. Dedicated to the god Thoth, it was originally 40 km (25 miles) further north. The huge pylon is still in good condition. Also relocated here, the **Temple of Maharraka** dates from Roman times. The best remains can be found in the hypostyle hall.

Finely preserved relief from the tomb of the Nubian viceroy Pennout, near Amada

Temple of Amada **⑱**

185 km (115 miles) S of High Dam. 🚌 🚆 *from Aswan.* ◯ *daily.* 📷

Dedicated to Amun-Ra and Ra-Harakhty, the Temple of Amada was constructed by Tuthmosis III and Amenhotep II, and added to by Tuthmosis IV. Moved just 3 km (2 miles) from its original site, it is the oldest surviving Nubian temple. It also has some of the best preserved Nubian reliefs, including those on the sanctuary's back wall, which depict Amenhotep killing his Syrian prisoners of war.

Environs
A short distance across the desert is the relocated **Temple of Derr**. Built under Ramses II, it was later converted into a church. Although badly damaged, some colourful reliefs remain, particularly in the second pillared hall, where the pharaoh is seen presenting flowers and offering wine to the gods. The nearby rock-cut **Tomb of Pennout**, viceroy of northern Nubia under Ramses VI, was previously 40 km (25 miles) south of Amada in a necropolis of Old and New Kingdom tombs at Aniba. The

tomb is decorated with scenes of Pennout and his family, and the "weighing of the heart" ceremony *(see p29)*.

Qasr Ibrim **⑲**

60 km (37 miles) N of Abu Simbel. 🚌 ◯ *daily.* 📷

The ruined fortress of Qasr Ibrim is on its original site, although the flooding of the region means that whereas it once stood on a high plateau overlooking a valley it is now close to the water's edge. It is believed there was a fort here as far back as 1000 BC. By Roman times, seven temples stood within the fortified walls, including a temple dedicated to Isis and a 7th-century BC temple built by the Nubian king, Taharaqo. One of the last strongholds of paganism, Qasr Ibrim finally submitted to Christianity and a cathedral was built here in the 10th century AD. It resisted Islam until the 16th century, when Bosnians invaded the fort on orders from the Ottoman sultan and the cathedral was turned into a mosque. Still under excavation, the fort can only be visited by cruise boats on the lake.

The ruined fortress of Qasr Ibrim on the shores of Lake Nasser

Abu Simbel ⑳

Carved baboon at Abu Simbel

Hewn out of a solid cliff in the 13th century BC, the Great Temple of Abu Simbel and the smaller Temple of Hathor are a breathtaking sight. Although dedicated to the patron deities of Egypt's great cities – Amun of Thebes, Ptah of Memphis and Ra-Harakhty of Heliopolis – the Great Temple was built to honour Ramses II. Its 33-m (108-ft) high façade, with four colossal enthroned statues of Ramses II wearing the double crown of Upper and Lower Egypt, was intended to impress and frighten, while the interior revealed the union of god and king.

★ Temple Façade
Buried in sand for centuries, the façade was discovered in 1813 by Swiss explorer Jean-Louis Burckhardt.

Store rooms held offerings to the gods and ritual items.

Baboons greeting the rising sun

Statue of Ra-Harakhty

Relocated Temples at Abu Simbel
In the 1960s, as Lake Nasser threatened to engulf the temples, UNESCO cut them from the mountain and moved them to an artificial cliff 210 m (688 ft) back from and 65 m (213 ft) above their original position.

Ramses II Colossi
Accompanied by carved images of captives from the north and south, the four colossi on the temple façade boast of a unified Egypt. Ramses's names adorn the thrones in cartouche form.

The broken colossus lost its head in an earthquake in 27 BC.

STAR SIGHTS

★ Temple Façade

★ Hypostyle Hall

★ Inner Sanctuary

Entrance to temple

The vestibule is adorned with scenes of Ramses and Nefertari making offerings to Amun and Ra-Harakhty.

VISITORS' CHECKLIST

Aswan governorate, 280 km (174 miles) S of Aswan. 🚌 ✈
⬜ 6am–5pm (later when there are evening flights).
Sound and Light Show 7pm, 8pm, 9pm in winter; 8pm, 9pm, 10pm in summer. 📷
www.sound-light-eg.com

★ **Inner Sanctuary**
Ramses II sits with Amun-Ra, Ptah and Ra-Harakhty. On two days of the year the sun's rays reach the once gold-covered statues.

Store rooms

Battle of Qadesh
Reliefs inside the hypostyle hall show Ramses II defeating Egypt's enemies including, on the right hand wall, the defeat of the Hittites in the Battle of Qadesh c.1275 BC.

10-m (33-ft) high statue of Ramses as Osiris

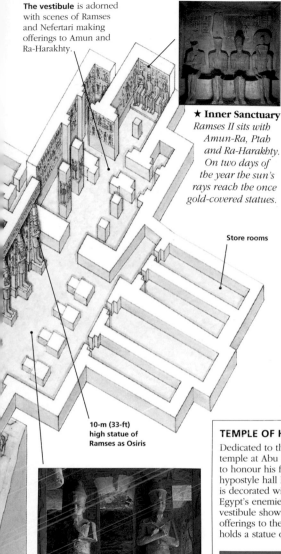

TEMPLE OF HATHOR

Dedicated to the goddess Hathor, the smaller temple at Abu Simbel was built by Ramses II to honour his favourite wife, Nefertari. The hypostyle hall has Hathor-headed pillars and is decorated with scenes of Ramses slaying Egypt's enemies, watched by Nefertari. The vestibule shows the royal couple making offerings to the gods, and the inner sanctuary holds a statue of Hathor in the form of a cow.

★ **Hypostyle Hall**
In Osiride form – carrying crook and flail – the colossi on the southern pillars wear the Upper Egypt crown, while the northern ones wear the double crown of Upper and Lower Egypt. The walls show Ramses II making offerings to his deified self.

Statues of Nefertari as goddess Hathor alternate with Ramses II on the façade of Queen Nefertari's Temple

SINAI AND THE RED SEA COAST

*T*reasured in Pharaonic times for its turquoise, copper and gold quarries, the region today is a magnet for tourists, attracted by the white, sandy beaches and fantastic marine life. Sinai is a region of great religious significance; its rugged interior was the setting for many important events in the Bible and remains a holy place for Jews, Muslims and Christians alike.

Wedged between Africa and Asia, the Sinai peninsula is bordered by the Mediterranean Sea, the Gulfs of Aqaba and Suez, and Egypt's Suez Canal zone. The area has been plagued by conflict, most recently between 1967 and 1982 when it was occupied by Israel before being returned to Egypt in the Camp David peace treaty. However, since the late 1980s tourism has boomed along Sinai's eastern coast with resorts such as Sharm el-Sheikh becoming popular holiday destinations. Besides the dry, sunny climate, the main attraction of the region is the underwater world – the Red Sea coral reefs and teeming marine life make this area one of the world's richest dive sites. Yet despite the rapid growth of tourism, much of

Sinai's stunning mountainous interior, inhabited by the nomadic, tribal Bedouin people, remains unexplored.

Egypt's Red Sea Coast stretches more than 1,250 km (777 miles) from the Suez Canal to the Sudanese border. Separated from the Nile Valley by the hills of the Eastern Desert, the coastline is famed for its brilliant turquoise waters. The area around the diving resort of Hurghada has developed along similar lines to Sinai's eastern coast and many new resorts and hotels are planned here.

The Suez Canal, a phenomenal feat of engineering when it opened in 1869, separates Sinai from mainland Egypt. In the past it was a cause of conflict; today it is one of Egypt's most important sources of revenue.

Shopping for fruit and vegetables in the Red Sea diving resort of Hurghada

◁ Exquisitely coloured coral reef in the warm waters of the Red Sea

Exploring Sinai and the Red Sea Coast

With its combination of mountains and sea, the natural beauty of the Sinai peninsula is awe-inspiring. Most visitors head for the sea, where there is an ever-growing string of tourist resorts from Nuweiba to Sharm el-Sheikh. St Catherine's Monastery in the interior can be visited as a day trip. On the western Red Sea coast, Hurghada is the main resort and from here the monasteries of St Anthony and St Paul make interesting excursions. The Suez Canal to the north is hardly picturesque, but the canal town of Ismailia is pretty and Port Said has good duty-free shopping.

Monastery of St Anthony, inland from the western Red Sea coast

KEY

▬▬	Motorway
▬	Major road
▭▭	Minor road
▬	Scenic route
▬▬	Main railway
▬	Minor railway
--	Track
▬▬	International border
▪ ▪	Disputed border
△	Summit

0 kilometres   100

0 miles   50

Luxury resorts and diving centres around Naama Bay, to the north of Sharm el-Sheikh

SIGHTS AT A GLANCE

Ain Musa ④
Al-Arish ⑭
Al-Quesir ⑲
Dahab ⑩
Hurghada ⑰
Ismailia ②
Marsa Alam ⑳
Monastery of St Anthony ⑮

Monastery of St Paul ⑯
Nuweiba ⑪
Pharaoh's Island ⑫
Port Safaga ⑱
Port Said ③
Ras Mohammed
    National Park ⑨

St Catherine's Monastery
    pp222–5 ⑦
Serabit al-Khadim ⑤
Sharm el-Sheikh ⑧
Suez ①
Taba ⑬
Wadi Feiran ⑥

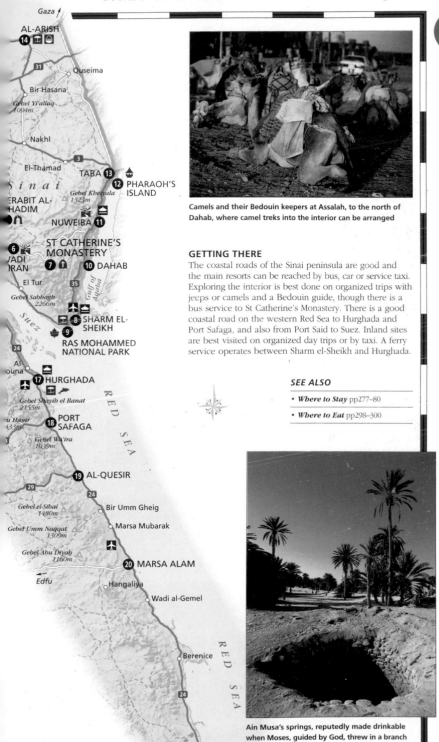

Gaza

AL-ARISH 14

31 Quseima

Bir Hasana

Gebel Yi'allaq
1094m

Nakhl

El-Thamad

3

TABA 13

Gebel Kheyyala
1323m

12 PHARAOH'S
ISLAND

S i n a i

ERABIT AL-
HADIM

NUWEIBA 11

ST CATHERINE'S
MONASTERY

6
ADI
RAN

7

10 DAHAB

El Tur

35

Gebel Sabbagh
2266m

Gulf of
Aqaba

8 SHARM EL-
SHEIKH

9 RAS MOHAMMED
NATIONAL PARK

Suez

24

Al
ouna

17 HURGHADA

Gebel Shayib el Banat
2155m

u Hamr
433m

18 PORT
SAFAGA

Gebel Wa'ira
1039m

3

29

19 AL-QUESIR

24

Gebel el-Sibai
1480m

Bir Umm Gheig

Gebel Umm Naqqat
1309m

Marsa Mubarak

Gebel Abu Diyab
1160m

Edfu

20 MARSA ALAM

Hangaliya

Wadi al-Gemel

Berenice

RED SEA

RED SEA

24

Camels and their Bedouin keepers at Assalah, to the north of
Dahab, where camel treks into the interior can be arranged

GETTING THERE

The coastal roads of the Sinai peninsula are good and
the main resorts can be reached by bus, car or service taxi.
Exploring the interior is best done on organized trips with
jeeps or camels and a Bedouin guide, though there is a
bus service to St Catherine's Monastery. There is a good
coastal road on the western Red Sea to Hurghada and
Port Safaga, and also from Port Said to Suez. Inland sites
are best visited on organized day trips or by taxi. A ferry
service operates between Sharm el-Sheikh and Hurghada.

SEE ALSO

• **Where to Stay** pp277–80

• **Where to Eat** pp298–300

Ain Musa's springs, reputedly made drinkable
when Moses, guided by God, threw in a branch

A fishing boat dwarfed by a cruise ship in the Suez Canal

Suez ❶

134 km (83 miles) E of Cairo.
👥 418,000. ℹ Sharia Suez Canal
(062) 3331 141. 🚌 🚆 🚍

Situated at the southern end of the canal, Suez was a prosperous port in medieval times. In the 18th century, it was used by the British as a staging post on the route to India. Following the opening of the Suez Canal in 1869, it expanded further, but was severely damaged during the 1967 and 1973 wars with Israel. Thanks to money from Gulf states, however, Suez has been rebuilt and it continues to be one of Egypt's most important ports and a major industrial centre. Suez holds little of interest for the tourist but those travelling to or from Sinai will use the Ahmed Hamdi Tunnel, 12 km (7 miles) to the north of town.

Ismailia ❷

120 km (74 miles) NE of Cairo.
👥 255,000. 🚌 🚆 🚍

Named after its founder Ismail Pasha, who ruled Egypt from 1863 to 1879, Ismailia was developed for foreign engineers and labourers working on the Suez Canal in the 1860s.

Ismailia is the prettiest and most populous of the canal towns. South of the railway line, huge European-style villas with lush gardens and large terraces line the wide boulevards. On Mohammed Ali Quay, the house of Ferdinand de Lesseps, director of the Suez Canal Company and French vice-consul to Egypt at the time of its construction, is an impressive example of these grand houses. It now serves as a hotel for guests of the Suez Canal Authority.

The **Ismailia Museum** nearby is home to a large collection of Graeco-Roman artifacts as well as details of the canal's history. To visit the adjacent Garden of Stelae and its Pharaonic remains, permission is needed from the museum.

The Sweetwater Canal, built to bring fresh water from the Nile to the canal workers, leads to Lake Timsah (Crocodile Lake), which has some pleasant beaches. A ferry from Ismailia runs to the east bank of the canal, where Egypt launched its celebrated attack on Israeli forces in 1973.

🏛 **Ismailia Museum**
Sharia Salah Salem. ⭕ daily. 📷

A sphinx outside the Ismailia Museum

Port Said ❸

225 km (139 miles) NE of Cairo.
👥 473,000. ℹ 8 Sharia Palestine
(066) 3235 289. 🚌 🚆 🚍

On the coast where the Suez Canal meets the Mediterranean, Port Said was founded in 1859 by Khedive Said Pasha to house workers on the canal. For years, the city was associated with drugs and smuggling but it has now shaken off its seedy past and is today mostly renowned as a tax-free shopping zone and minor beach resort.

Port Said, which is largely built on land reclaimed from Lake Manzila, is surrounded by water. It was heavily bombed during the 1956 Suez crisis and during the conflicts with Israel in 1967 and 1973, but most of the damage has since been repaired. The distinctive green domes of the Suez Canal Building, built in 1869 on Sharia Palestine, are one of the city's important landmarks.

Nearby, **Port Said National Museum** covers Egyptian history from ancient times; exhibits in the museum include Coptic antiquities and Pharaonic mummies.

A short walk away, the **Military Museum** on Sharia 23rd July presents a vivid account of the various conflicts that have chequered the history of the canal.

A 19th-century colonial-style villa in Ismailia

View across the Suez Canal from Port Said to Port Fuad

🏛 **Port Said National Museum**
Sharia Palestine. ⬜ *daily.* 📷

🏛 **Military Museum**
Sharia 23rd July. ⬜ *daily.* 📷

Ain Musa ❹

25 km (15 miles) SE of Ahmed Hamdi Tunnel. 🚌 *from Cairo or Port Said.*

Also known as the Springs of Moses, Ain Musa lies to the southeast of the Ahmed Hamdi Tunnel, which runs under the Suez Canal near its junction with the Gulf of Suez. According to the Old Testament, it was here that Moses, after leading the Israelites across the Red Sea, turned a bitter spring into sweet drinking water by throwing a branch into it, as instructed by God.

Although Ain Musa was a main source of fresh water for the local town until the 1860s, only one of the 12 springs mentioned in the Book of Exodus remains today. Ain Musa was used as a strategic stronghold by the Israeli army during their occupation of Sinai from 1967, but it was recaptured by Egyptian forces in October 1973. Surrounding palm groves were damaged during the Sinai conflicts.

Just over 3 km (2 miles) north of the springs is the Military Touristic Memorial of Ain Musa, a small museum dedicated to the achievements of the Egyptian army.

Serabit al-Khadim ❺

32 km (20 miles) E of Abu Zneima, Sinai.

Built during the 12th Dynasty, the rock temple of Serabit el-Khadim (Heights of the Slave) is perched on a 755-m (2,500-ft) summit to the east of the petroleum-industry town of Abu Zneima. In Pharaonic times the area was rich in copper and turquoise and thousands worked in the mines. The temple was dedicated to Hathor, goddess of love and "Mistress of the Turquoise". Some jeep safaris

from Naama Bay (near Sinai's southern tip) include Serabit al-Khadim in their tours of this beautiful part of Sinai's rugged interior. Hiring a four-wheel-drive vehicle is an alternative, but it is advisable to take a local guide with you.

Wadi Feiran ❻

60 km (37 miles) W of St Catherine's Monastery, Sinai. 🏛 *650.*

Lying halfway between St Catherine's Monastery and the Red Sea coast, at the foot of the 2,000-m (6,560-ft) high Mount Serbal, Wadi Feiran is the largest oasis in south Sinai. A winding valley, thick with shady palms, tamarisks and orchards, the oasis is believed to be the *Rephidim* mentioned in Exodus – the last place of rest for the weary Israelites before they reached Mount Sinai.

An early Christian community flourished here and, in AD 451, it became the seat of a bishopric that governed St Catherine's Monastery *(see pp222–5).* The bishop's palace and convent were destroyed in the 7th century, but a small convent was rebuilt on the site with stone from the original Byzantine buildings. Today, the oasis belongs to the Tawarah tribes.

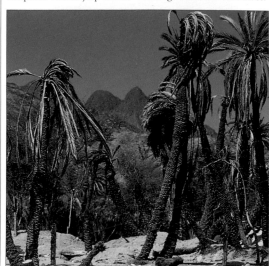

Palms flourishing in the oasis of Wadi Feiran, south Sinai

St Catherine's Monastery ➐

Nestling at the foot of Mount Sinai, the Greek Orthodox monastery of St Catherine is thought to be the oldest continuously inhabited Christian monastery in the world. Founded in AD 527 by Emperor Justinian, it replaced a chapel built by the Empress Helena in AD 337 on the site where it is believed that Moses saw the Burning Bush. The monastery was renamed St Catherine in the 9th or 10th century after monks claimed to have found the intact body of the saint on a nearby mountain.

Library
The collection of priceless early Christian manuscripts is one of the most important in the world.

★ Icon Collection
The monastery holds 2,000 icons, including this of St Peter. A selection is kept on view in the Basilica.

The Walls of Justinian, dating from the 6th century, are part of the complex's original structure.

The Burning Bush
This evergreen is said to be from the same stock as the bush from which God instructed Moses to lead his people out of Egypt to the Promised Land.

The Chapel of the Burning Bush, where the miraculous bush supposedly grew, is the most sacred part of the monastery.

★ Basilica of the Transfiguration
This richly decorated church owes its name to a rare 6th-century Mosaic of the Transfiguration in the apse. The mosaic is located behind the gilded 17th-century iconostas

STAR FEATURES

★ Basilica of the Transfiguration

★ Icon Collection

Bell Tower
Built in 1871, the tower houses nine bells donated by Tsar Alexander II of Russia. They are only rung on religious festivals.

The Mosque was built in 1106 by converting a chapel originally dedicated to St Basil. Its creation was an attempt to placate local Muslim rulers.

Monks' quarters

St Stephen's Well

Dispensary

Guest house

Charnel House

Monastery Gardens
A cemetery is located in the orchard from where monks' bones are periodically exhumed and taken to the Charnel House.

The elevated entrance, reached by a pulley system, used to be the only access.

The underground cistern was dug to store fresh water from the monastery's springs.

Visitors' entrance

Well of Moses
Inside the outer wall lies the monastery's main water source where Moses is said to have met his future wife, Zipporah, Jethro's daughter.

ST CATHERINE OF ALEXANDRIA
St Catherine was one of the most popular early Christian saints. Supposedly born into a wealthy Alexandrian family in the early 4th century, she was tortured for her beliefs, first spun on a spiked wheel (hence Catherine wheel) and then beheaded by the pagan emperor. A marble sarcophagus in the monastery's Church of St Catherine contains two silver caskets said to hold part of her remains, found by monks 600 years after her death.

Detail of St Catherine from clerical vestments

Exploring St Catherine's Monastery

Completely isolated for many years, and surrounded by red granite mountains, the monastery is now on the main tourist trail and busloads of visitors arrive each day. Around 20 or so monks (mostly from Greece) still live in the monastery, and hence its opening times are strictly controlled. The surrounding mountains are incredibly beautiful and most visitors climb the well-worn path to the top of Mount Sinai – where Moses is said to have received the Ten Commandments – to enjoy the spectacular view over this setting of profound biblical significance.

Ornately carved wooden inner door to the 6th-century Basilica

Inside the monastery

Entry is through a small postern or gateway in the north-eastern wall. The elevated entrance above it contains a pulley and used to be the only way into the monastery after the main gate was blocked as a defence against raiders in the Middle Ages. Parts of the huge granite walls date from the 6th century although they have been substantially rebuilt over the years – firstly, after an earth-quake in the 14th century and again in 1800 when Napoleon sent masons from Cairo to restore the stonework.

The monastery's main church, or Basilica, built by Emperor Justinian's architect Stephanos Ailisios in AD 527, is known as the Basilica of the Transfiguration. It is one of the few remaining churches in the region which survive from this period. Massive 11th-century wooden doors open onto the narthex (porch). Beyond is another door, carved with reliefs of animals,

birds and flowers, which is believed to be the original from Justinian's church. The central nave is flanked by six pillars bearing Byzantine icons of saints worshipped in each month of the year. The marble floor and coffered ceiling are 18th century. A gilded iconostasis, painted in the early 17th century, separates the nave from the altar. Behind this, the roof of the apse is decorated with a superb 6th-century mosaic of the Transfiguration. Beyond the altar lies the Chapel of the Burning Bush, the holiest place of the monastery, which is usually closed to the public. The thorny, evergreen bush, reputedly a descendant of the original Burning Bush from which Moses heard the Lord speak, is of a species found nowhere else in Sinai.

The monastery's library, with over 3,000 ancient manuscripts in Greek and other languages, is second in importance only

Monks' skulls inside the Charnel House

to that of the Vatican. One of the highlights is the *Codex Syriacus*, a 5th-century Syriac version of the New Testament. The priceless icons, dating from the early Byzantine period, are among the only survivors from the Iconoclast era (726–843) when such images were held to be heretical. They include a *St Peter* (5th–6th century), and the 7th-century *Christ in Majesty* and *Ladder of Paradise*. Some are on display in the narthex of the church and there are plans for a larger gallery outside.

In the garden, dense with olive and apricot trees, is the monastery cemetery and the Chapel of St Triphonius. The latter's crypt holds the Charnel House, which contains the bones of monks who have died here over the centuries. The robed skeleton is Stephanos, a 6th-century guardian of the path to Mount Sinai.

Environs

Rising to a height of 2,286 m (7,500 ft), **Mount Sinai** is held to be the Biblical Mount Horeb (Exodus 24) where Moses spent 40 days and nights before receiving the Ten Command-ments. There are two paths to the top, both starting behind the monastery. The more gentle "Camel Path", created by Abbas Hilmi I, Pasha of Egypt from 1849–54, is the usual route up. Camels can be hired from the foot of the mountain, though the last 700

Chapel of the Burning Bush, viewable only by special dispensation

For hotels and restaurants in this region see pp277–80 and pp298–300

View of St Catherine's Monastery from path leading to Mount Sinai

steps have to be undertaken on foot. The 3,700 steps of the "Stairs of Repentance" is a steeper route. Along it are several votive sites, including Moses' Spring, which gushes from a small cave, and St Stephen's Gate. Most visitors climb at night to reach the summit in time for sunrise.

Around 700 steps below the summit is **Elijah's Basin**, a sandy plain dotted with cypress trees, one of which is estimated to be 1,000 years old. This is where those who accompanied Moses are said to have waited while he climbed to the summit alone. Camping here, rather than at the summit, is recommended for those wanting to spend the night on the mountain.

At the summit, where God is believed to have spoken to Moses from a fiery cloud, is a 12th-century mosque and the small **Chapel of the Holy Trinity**, built in 1934 on the site of a 6th-century church. Neither of these is currently open to the public.

To the southwest of Mount Sinai, **Mount Catherine**, Egypt's highest mountain at 2,642 m (8,666 ft), offers a steep but picturesque climb. At the summit, which can be busy, there is a small chapel containing many icons, and a truly outstanding view, taking in the gulfs of Aqaba and Suez and the mountains of both Africa and Saudi Arabia.

St Catherine's Protectorate
Formally established in 1996, the Protectorate covers an area of 4,350 sq km (1,672 sq miles) around Mount Sinai. Its aim is to protect the area's plant and animal life and conserve historic and religious sites. A Trekkers' Code urges visitors to avoid leaving litter, removing rocks or plants and writing or carving graffiti.

A series of guides produced by the Protectorate details hikes in the area along **Wadi Arbaein** and **Wadi Shrayj**,

taking in cultural sites and beauty spots. One describes the climb up **Abbas Pasha Mountain**, which leads to an incomplete 19th-century palace at 2,383 m (7,816 ft) – intended as a sanatorium for the sick Pasha. The books can be purchased and guides organized (walkers must be accompanied by a Bedouin guide) from the Visitors' Centre near the monastery and at the Protectorate Management Office in St Catherine's village.

THE BEDOUIN OF THE SINAI PENINSULA

The Bedouin of the Sinai, descendants of tribes from the Arabian peninsula, have lived a nomadic lifestyle in harsh arid regions for centuries, depending on sheep, goats and camels for a livelihood and sleeping in tents made of goatskin. Their name derives from the Arabic word *bedu*, meaning "desert dwellers". The Bedouin are distinctive in their traditional garb: the women don black garments with sequinned veils and the men wear long white robes. Their tightly wrapped figures invariably accompany images of bleak, sandswept landscapes. But life is rapidly changing for these denizens of the desert. With government resettlement programmes and tourism encroaching all over the Sinai, the old ways are under threat. TV aerials protrude from concrete houses and children are increasingly dressed in western-style clothes. While some Bedouin are still nomadic livestock breeders, many now work with jeeps not camels, and make a living from the tourist trade.

Bedouin woman in traditional dress

Naama Bay, Sharm el-Sheikh, showing the coral reefs just off shore

Sharm el-Sheikh 8

300 km (187 miles) SE of Suez. ✈
🚌 🚢 ℹ *Ras Mohammed National Park (069) 3660 559, (069) 3660 668.*

The popular resort of Sharm el-Sheikh, north of Ras Mohammed, stretches over 20 km (12 miles) along the coast and is a renowned diving and snorkelling destination.

Sharm, as it is known to visitors, is divided into two parts – the town and port to the south and **Naama Bay**, the upmarket tourist enclave 7 km (4 miles) to the north.

After it was captured in the 1967 war, the port was developed by the Israelis, who began to build hotels along the coast. The development that began in Naama Bay in the late 1980s is still booming. Europeans, and especially the Italians, favour it as a package holiday destination.

With diving schools and hotels lining the Corniche, Naama is far removed from the traditional Bedouin way of life. Nevertheless the water here is beautiful and there are many accessible dive sites along the coast – both for beginners and more experienced wreck divers. Excursions to St Catherine's Monastery and the Sinai interior are easily arranged from any good hotel.

Environs
Around 10 km (6 miles) north of Naama is **Shark Bay**, a cheaper, quieter and much smaller resort, although the recent building of a five-star hotel has changed the laid-back atmosphere and more

development is likely. The coral gardens and tropical fish here are beautiful – and despite its name, there are no sharks around. North of Shark Bay, where the Red Sea meets the Gulf of Aqaba, lie the Tiran Straits. Diving trips to **Tiran** and **Sanafir Island** leave from Naama, Sharm and Shark Bay. Further up the coast is the **Nabq National Park**. Popular with bird-watchers, the most northerly mangrove forests in the world are home to many birds such as grey and white herons, ospreys and storks. Animals suited to the arid conditions, such as gazelles, rock hyraxes and desert foxes, live inland.

Turtle swimming in the Red Sea

✈ Nabq National Park
29 km (18 miles) N of Sharm el-Sheikh. 🚗 🚌 ◯ *daily.* 🎥 🎦

Ras Mohammed National Park 9

20 km (12 miles) S of Sharm el-Sheikh. 🚶 🚌 to Sharm el-Sheikh, then taxi. ℹ *Visitors' Centre (069) 3660 559, (069) 3660 668.* ◯ *daily.* 🎥 🎦

Covering the southernmost tip of the Sinai peninsula, Ras Mohammed became Egypt's first marine National Park in 1989. The wealth of underwater life and extensive reefs dotted with brilliant corals and sponges make it one of the best places for diving and snorkelling in the world. Over 1,000 species of colourful fish populate the clear waters and barracuda, reef sharks, turtles and manta rays are among the more unusual creatures to look out for. Above water, the park is home to ibexes, gazelles and a wide range of birdlife. The mangrove forests here grow in a shallow channel south of the peninsula and are an important breeding area for birds. A visitors' centre in the park shows videos about the area and also offers a map of the colour-coded tracks which lead to the different beaches. Although thousands of tourists visit the park each year, considerable effort is made to protect the area from serious damage by not allowing any hotels to be built and carefully restricting the number of dive boats.

One of Sharm el-Sheikh's many diving centres

Coral Reefs of the Red Sea

Coral reefs are one of the richest ecosystems on earth. Coral is made up of colonies of tiny animals called polyps that need precise environmental conditions to grow. There are two types of coral: hard corals, which form hard outer skeletons for themselves, and soft corals, that do not. Most reefs are built over thousands of years from the accumulated skeletons of dead hard corals. In places, the Red Sea reefs form sheer walls covered with exotically shaped corals of pastel pink,

Colourful racoon butterfly fish

yellow and red. Scuba diving in the Red Sea is the highlight of many visitors' holidays and the area is well served for dive centres (see pp316–21). However, if using an aqualung does not appeal, the reefs create shallow lagoons, perfect for exploring with a snorkel. These beautiful, calm lagoons serve as nurseries for schools of smaller fish. A word of caution: although the reefs seem robust, they are an extremely fragile environment and swimmers should look but not touch.

Soft corals *require salty, clear water and warm, gentle currents to bring them their food. At night the coral polyps use their fine tentacles to sting and capture plankton as it swims past.*

The jewel grouper *favours shady areas of the reef, for in the dim light this hunter's stunning colouring becomes surprisingly good camouflage as it waits for its smaller prey to swim past.*

Sea anemones *look like colourful plants but they are in fact animal predators. They use their stinging tentacles to stun their prey and feed it to their centrally located mouth.*

Blue-spotted rays *glide across the sea floor scooping up snails, worms and crabs before crushing them with special flattened teeth.*

Reef walls *plunge to depths of 80 m (260 ft) or more and provide a home for over 1,000 species of fishes and more than 150 types of coral.*

Camels and their Bedouin keepers near Dahab

Dahab ⓾

100 km (62 miles) N of Sharm el-Sheikh. 🚌 🚗

The word *dahab* means gold in Arabic, and the name of this popular resort derives from its tawny golden beaches. The resort grew up around the Bedouin village of Assalah, to the north of the town, where the camp-sites, beach huts, cheap hotels, restaurants and market stalls lining the waterfront cater mostly for independent young travellers on tight budgets.

To the south of the town, the scene is distinctly up-market, with luxury holiday villages and dive centres attract-ing a very different clientele. For all tourists, however, the sea is the main attraction, and the coral reef, with its immensely rich marine life, is close to shore. A popular dive site is the Blue Hole, to the north of Dahab. This is almost entirely surrounded by coral reefs and drops to a depth of 80 m (260 ft) just a few metres from the shore. The Blue Hole and the nearby Canyon can be dangerous for inexperienced divers and several lives are lost here every year. A safe alternative is to use snorkelling equipment to admire the reef here.

Jeep and camel safaris into the mountains can be easily arranged from Dahab. These are a great way to explore Sinai's beautiful, rugged interior and to see something of the Bedouin way of life.

Nuweiba ⓫

85 km (53 miles) N of Dahab. 🚌
⛴ from Aqaba (Jordan).

Located midway along the Gulf of Aqaba coast, Nuweiba is divided into three areas, spread over a 10-km (6-mile) stretch. To the north is the Bedouin settlement of Tara-been, where campsites with bamboo huts line the beach. In the village are the ruins of a 16th-century fortress, which was built by the Mamluk sultan Ashraf al-Ghouri. About 1 km (0.6 mile) south of Tarabeen, more luxurious accom-modation can be found in Nuweiba City. If you are planning to catch the ferry to Aqaba, there are several hotels in the unattractive port of Nuweiba, which is 8 km (5 miles) further south.

Windsurfer on the Gulf of Aqaba, Dahab

All along the coast around Nuweiba, hotels and camp sites are being built, offering a choice of 5-star and budget accommodation. The setting is particularly beautiful with

the Sinai mountains providing a hazy backdrop and those of Saudi Arabia clearly visible across the water.

Nuweiba is a quiet resort offering magnificent beaches and a chance to unwind. Watersports, including water skiing and diving, are popular here and snorkelling provides an easy way to explore the magnificent coral reefs and marine life. Dolphins are known to swim with visitors at nearby El Mezinah.

Also popular is a trip to the ancient city of Petra, taking the catamaran from Nuweiba port to Aqaba. This spectacular metropolis, 96 km (60 miles) north of Aqaba, was carved out of desert rock between the 3rd century BC and 1st century AD.

Environs

Nuweiba is a good base for exploring the interior, and jeep and camel trips are easily arranged. The **Coloured Canyon**, about 30 km (19 miles) inland from Nuweiba, is a popular destination. It is reached via the oasis of Ain al-Furtaga, usually by four-wheel-drive vehicle, though it is possible to get there (more slowly) by camel. The narrow gorge gets its name from the pink, brown, green and yellow layers caused by the oxidation of minerals.

South of Nuweiba is the **Abu Galum Nature Reserve**, a prime destination for dive safaris. Inland from its lovely deserted beaches is a maze of wadis teeming with plants and wildlife, including desert foxes, ibexes and hyraxes.

A new resort near Nuweiba, with Saudi Arabia visible across the sea

◁ St Catherine's Monastery, founded in the 6th century AD in a valley at the foot of Mount Sinai

Crusader castle on Pharaoh's Island, south of Taba, in the Gulf of Aqaba

Pharaoh's Island 12

7 km (4 miles) S of Taba. then ferry.

Surrounded by fabulous reefs, Pharaoh's Island (known as Coral Island by Israelis) is very popular with divers. The island is just 250 m (820 ft) from the shore, close to the border with Israel, and boats leave from the Salah ad Din Hotel on the coastal road opposite the island.

Worth exploring are the restored ruins of a 12th-century Crusader castle, strategically placed to ensure the safety of pilgrims to the Holy Land. The castle was captured by Salah ad-Din in 1170 and used as an Arab stronghold against the Crusaders until 1183, when it was eventually abandoned.

Taba 13

70 km (43 miles) N of Nuweiba.

On the border with Israel, Taba was only returned to Egypt in 1989 after international intervention. Egypt was determined to reclaim all its land from Israel and the dispute over this area lasted for seven years after the rest of Sinai had been recovered.

There are a few restaurants, cafés and a hotel at Taba, but most visitors are just crossing between the two countries.

The 70-km (43-mile) stretch between Taba and Nuweiba has been dubbed "The Egyptian Riviera" by the government. It is a priority development area with many hotels and resorts currently under construction.

If you are leaving Egypt at Taba, note that an Israeli stamp in your passport means that entry into some Arab countries, notably Lebanon and Syria, will be denied. Ask to have a separate piece of paper stamped.

Al-Arish 14

48 km (30 miles) SW of Rafah. 40,000. **i** Sharia Fuad Zikry (068) 3363 743. Thu.

Sinai's north coast is largely ignored by tourists, but there are some interesting places to visit, including the coastal town of Al-Arish. The palm-fringed white beaches and warm Mediterranean waters are the major attraction here, but Al-Arish is much more conservative than the laidback resorts along Sinai's Gulf of Aqaba coast.

On Thursdays there is a Bedouin market where women in traditional costume sell embroidered clothing and silver Bedouin jewellery. Outside Al-Arish, on the coastal road to Israel, the **Sinai Heritage Museum** exhibits Bedouin handicrafts and stuffed wildlife.

Popular with birdwatchers, the Zerenike Protectorate extends along the coast from the salt lagoon of Lake Bardawil, about 25 km (15 miles) east of Al-Arish.

Sinai Heritage Museum
Outskirts of Al-Arish, on road to Rafah. **Tel** (068) 3324 105.
8:30am–2pm Sat–Thu.

Palm-lined promenade in the Mediterranean resort of Al-Arish

For hotels and restaurants in this region see pp277–80 and pp298–300

The distinctive façade of the Monastery of St Anthony with the Red Sea Mountains in the background

Monastery of St Anthony ⑮

47 km (29 miles) W of Zafarana.
🚌 from Cairo, Suez or Hurghada.
🔲 daily.

Isolated in the Red Sea Mountains, St Anthony's Monastery (AD 361–3), marked the beginning of the monastic tradition. It is the oldest Coptic monastery in Egypt. Legend has it that Anthony, orphaned at 18, retreated to the mountains to serve God. His disciples built the monastery on the site of his grave.

The monastery complex has retained much of its original appearance, despite attacks from Bedouin tribes in the 8th and 9th centuries, from Muslims in the 11th century and a murderous revolt by Bedouin servants in the 15th century. It is the largest in the country, with several churches and chapels and extensive living quarters, but only 25 resident monks. On the interior walls of the Church of St Anthony are some vivid 13th-century murals. Two kilometres (just over one mile) to the north-east of the monastery is the cave where St Anthony is said to have spent his last years.

Monastery of St Paul ⑯

80 km (50 miles) SE of St Anthony's Monastery. 🚌 from Cairo, Suez or Hurghada. 🔲 daily.

A winding road leads to the Monastery of St Paul, hidden behind lofty walls. St Paul (AD 228–348) was from a wealthy Alexandrian family but became the earliest known hermit when he retreated to the Eastern Desert at the age of 16. The monastery's turreted walls were built around the cave where he lived for decades. The main Church of St Paul is painted with murals representing the Virgin and Child, and the archangels. The chapels contain scores of icons while ostrich eggs, a symbol of the Resurrection, hang from

Two of the monks at the Monastery of St Paul

the ceiling. A five-storey keep behind the church, supplied with water from a hidden canal, was used to protect the monks from Bedouin raids.

Hurghada ⑰

320 km (200 miles) S of Suez.
🏙 36,000. 🚶 🚌 🚗 ⛴ daily catamaran and weekly ferry services from Sharm el-Sheikh. 🛈 Sharia Banque Misr (065) 3444 420.

Hurghada, on the Red Sea coast, has undergone a complete transformation since the early 1990s when it was little more than a fishing village. Now a sprawling tourist town with resorts stretching 25 km (15 miles) along the coast, it is famous for its dive centres which offer scuba and snorkel trips to view the fantastic Red Sea marine life. There is a wide choice of accommodation with cheaper lodgings centred

Windsurfer at Sindbad Beach in Hurghada on the Red Sea coast

For hotels and restaurants in this region see pp277–80 and pp298–300

around Ad-Dahar, at the northern end of town, while Sigala to the south is more upmarket. Some hotels have good private beaches, and a variety of off-shore excursions are on offer, including day trips to **Giftun Island**. For those who wish to enjoy the wonders of the deep without getting wet, submarine tours are available from Sindbad Village or trips in a glass-bottomed boat from the Marine Sports Club. There is an **Aquarium** on the corniche and a **Marine Museum** north of town. In response to environmentalists' fears that the influx of tourists was damaging marine life, the Hurghada Environmental Protection and Conservation Association (HEPCA) was set up in 1992 to raise awareness and preserve the reef.

🦈 **Aquarium**
Al-Corniche. ☐ *daily.* 🏷️

Environs
Just 30 km (19 miles) north of Hurghada, **El-Gouna** is a new, luxurious resort. Set on a beautiful strip of coastline, the dome-roofed hotels and villas have a distinct Nubian theme.
   Soma Bay, 45 km (28 miles) to the south of Hurghada, is another recent tourist development with an 18-hole golf course, a marina, and upmarket hotels and villas.
   Remains of two Roman quarries in the Red Sea Mountains are accessible on day trips from Hurghada and the coast. **Mons Porphyrites**, 60 km (37 miles) north of town, was the site of ancient porphyry quarries. The pinky-purple stone was mined by the Romans for building and sent throughout the Empire. Parts of the Roman mining town are still in evidence. The mines at **Mons Claudianus**, around 50 km (31 miles) southeast of Hurghada, supplied the Romans with black granite columns – some of which still support the Pantheon in Rome today. Ruins of the fort and of the Roman town can also be visited.

🦈 **Marine Museum**
7 km (4 miles) N of Hurghada.
☐ *daily.* 🏷️

Traditional ship-building at Port Safaga

Port Safaga ⑱

58 km (36 miles) S of Hurghada.
🚶 *23,500.* 🚗 🚌

Just to the south of several upmarket resorts, Port Safaga is within easy range of some stunning reefs. Local weather conditions are ideal for windsurfing and in 1993 the World Windsurfing Championships were held here. Apart from tourism, Port Safaga's principal activities are exporting locally mined phosphates and ferrying travellers to Saudi Arabia.

Colourful house in a street of the Red Sea port of Al-Quesir

Al-Quesir ⑲

80 km (50 miles) S of Port Safaga.
🚶 *20,500.* 🚗 🚌

The small town of Al-Quesir has a distinguished history. Queen Hatshepsut left from here on her famous expedition to the Land of Punt (*see p197*). Known in Ptolemaic times as

Leukos Limen (White Harbour), it was the largest Red Sea port until the 10th century, popular with pilgrims travelling to Mecca. After the opening of the Suez Canal in 1869, Al-Quesir declined and today is little more than a quiet fishing village. The 16th-century Ottoman fortress of Sultan Selim still overlooks the town.
   As hotel development along the Red Sea coast continues, a growing number of excursions is available. Regular dive trips are offered to the islands of Big Brother and Little Brother, 67 km (42 miles) northeast of Al-Quesir. For those who prefer to sample more of the local life, however, the town has a traditional *souk*, and a Bedouin community. An ancient caravan trail to Qift in the Nile valley leads from the town through the mountains, passing several Pharaonic and Roman sites on the way.

Marsa Alam ⑳

132 km (82 miles) S of Al-Quesir.
🚶 *1,650.* 🚗 🚌

Currently a small fishing village in phosphate mining country, and with a large army base, Marsa Alam also has good offshore coral reefs. Tourism in the region is expanding and an airport is being built between here and Port Safaga. 40 km (25 miles) to the south, a huge luxury resort is under construction at Wadi al-Gemel. A main road crosses the desert to link the town with Edfu, 230 km (143 miles) away in the Nile Valley.

THE DELTA AND THE NORTH COAST

Fanning out between the two main branches of the Nile, the Delta is a green triangle in a desert landscape. Several Pharaonic dynasties ruled from here but, apart from the ruins of Bubastis and Tanis, most sites have long disappeared. The resorts of the North Coast are popular with Egyptians seeking relief from the summer heat.

The Nile Delta, Egypt's most fertile and densely populated region, produces the bulk of the country's crops, helping to feed the huge and ever-increasing population. To the east of the Delta, beyond the Suez Canal, lies the Sinai peninsula; to the west is the legendary city of Alexandria and a sandy coastline that stretches for over 500 km (310 miles) to the Libyan border.

Although the north coast between Alexandria and Libya enjoys clear seas and beautiful beaches, many stretches are inaccessible because of landmines left over from World War II. However, there are dozens of holiday villages along the route to Marsa Matruh and more are planned.

Most visitors to Lower Egypt, as the north of the country is called, head straight for Alexandria, Egypt's cosmopolitan second city. Its rich history,

links with Cleopatra's reign, moderate climate and pleasant beaches, make Alexandria the region's key attraction.

Although usually ignored by tourists, the Delta itself is worth exploring. This is the rural heart of the country: criss-crossed by irrigation canals, the flat land is rich with cotton, maize, sugar cane and vegetables. Buffalo plough the fields, donkeys pull carts, and mudbrick pigeon huts punctuate the picturesque landscape.

The lakes in the northeast attract an amazing variety of birdlife, especially during the annual winter migration south. Off the tourist trail, Rosetta's rich Ottoman architecture is one of the highlights of the area. Another is the cycle of lively *moulids* (religious festivals) that begin in October and transform the Nile Delta into a joyful place of celebration.

Colourful river taxis at Rosetta where a branch of the Nile flows into the Mediterranean

◁ Typical architectural motifs of stripes, porticos and balconies near Mosque of Abu al-Abbas Mursi, Alexandria

Exploring the Delta and the North Coast

Annual flooding and plundering over the centuries
have ensured that little remains to testify to the
role of the Delta in ancient Egyptian history.
However, the ruins at Tanis and near Zagazig hint at
the area's importance in ancient times. Damietta and
Rosetta have fine examples of Ottoman architecture,
while Alexandria retains the faded grandeur of 19th-
century colonial architecture and offers glimpses of
its greatness as the Graeco-Roman capital of Egypt.
Along the Mediterranean coast are a growing
number of resorts, while the cemeteries at El-
Alamein serve as reminders of the World War II
battles that were fought here.

One of three sphinxes from a tomb
near Pompey's Pillar, Alexandria

0 kilometres	75
0 miles	40

GETTING AROUND

Alexandria has an international
airport, with daily flights to and
from Cairo. Trains run regularly
between the two cities, and the
desert road linking them makes
car and bus travel easy. Other
towns in the Delta are served by
buses, minibuses, service taxis and
trains. A frequent bus service runs
along the north-coast road to the
Libyan border, and a very slow
train runs between Alexandria
and Marsa Matruh. The latter is
also served by a domestic airport.

Street scene in Marsa Matruh, a resort to the west of Alexandria

For additional map symbols see back flap

Fort Qaitbey, dating from the 1480s and occupying the site of the Pharos – Alexandria's legendary lighthouse

SIGHTS AT A GLANCE

SEE ALSO

• *Where to Stay* pp281–2

• *Where to Eat* pp300–301

KEY

Motorway	
Major road	
Road under construction	
Minor road	
Scenic route	
Main railway	
Minor railway	
Track	
International border	

Sidi Abdel Rahman, near the El-Alamein battlefield memorials

Detail of building in Damietta old town, illustrating Delta-style architecture

Damietta ❶

210 km (131 miles) NE of Cairo.
🚶 78,000. 🚌 🚗 🚊

Damietta, an industrial port known for its furniture, textiles, sweets and fishing, lies on Egypt's north coast, next to the eastern branch of the Nile. A wealthy port in the Middle Ages, the town was frequently attacked by the Byzantines, occupied twice by Christian forces then completely destroyed in 1250 by the Mamluks, who held power in Egypt from the 13th century until the Ottoman conquest in 1517. Damietta was rebuilt by the Ottomans, whose pretty 'Delta-style' villas can still be seen today, and its importance as a port was restored. The completion of the Suez Canal in 1869, and the subsequent growth of Port Said, some 70 km (43 miles) to the east, seriously undermined Damietta's prosperity. Since the late

1980s, however, the port of Damietta has once again experienced an economic revival.

There is not a great deal to do in Damietta itself but nearby, to the east, the huge expanse of **Lake Manzila** – a salt-water lagoon that is separated from the sea by a narrow peninsula – is a popular destination for bird-watchers who come to observe the migrating flamingos, herons, pelicans and storks that stop here. Egypt is on one of the major migration routes for many species, and millions of birds pass through this region every autumn and spring.

To the north of Damietta is the popular small beach resort of **Ras al-Bar**, which has numerous restaurants, hotels and tea houses.

Zagazig ❷

80 km (50 miles) NE of Cairo.
🚶 268,000. 🚌 🚗 🚊

Built in the 1830s to house workers on the Nile Barrages *(see p169)*, Zagazig's main claim to fame is as the birthplace of Colonel Ahmed Orabi, the nationalist who led the 1882 revolt against British rule, and whose statue stands outside the railway station. The town has a small museum that displays archaeological finds from the region.

Just to the southeast of Zagazig are the sparse ruins of **Bubastis**, capital of ancient Egypt in the 22nd and 23rd Dynasties and cult centre of

the cat-goddess Bastet. It is believed that huge festivals in her honour were held at Bubastis and attracted thousands of revellers. The events involved dancing, vast quantities of alcohol and sacrifices to the goddess. Work began on the Temple of Bastet at Bubastis during the 6th Dynasty and, for nearly 1500 years, it was regularly added to; now, all that remains to be seen are scattered stones. Nearby, in the underground galleries of a cat cemetery where mummified cats were buried, bronze statues of the sacred animal have been discovered.

Cat worship near Zagazig

MOULIDS

Meaning "birth" in Arabic, a *moulid* commemorates the birthday of a local saint or holy person. Celebrated by Muslims and Christians alike, the moulid probably has its roots in the customs of ancient Egypt when, on festival days, a statue of the local god was paraded in a boat *(see p178)*. Nowadays, big moulids in Cairo, Luxor and Tanta draw millions of people, allowing everyone a release from everyday concerns. After visiting the tomb or church, revellers might attend a *zikr,* a ritual chanting of Allah's name to induce a trance-like state. *Tartours* (cone-shaped hats) and *fawanees* (lanterns) are sold, while traditional entertainment such as puppet shows and stick dancing take place alongside more modern funfair attractions. Usually lasting a week, moulids climax on the Great Night or *Leila al-Kebira* with a lively *zaffa* or procession.

Reeds of Lake Manzila (Damietta) providing cover for migrating birds

For hotels and restaurants in this region see pp281–2 and pp300–301

Tanta ❸

94 km (58 miles) N of Cairo.
🏛 *373,000.* 🚌 🚉

Tanta, Egypt's fifth largest city
and an important university
town, is best known for its
eight-day festival, or moulid,
which is held each year after
the October cotton harvest.
Up to two million people
take part in the event, which
honours Sayyid Ahmed al-
Badawi, the 13th-century
founder of one of the largest
Sufi brotherhoods in Egypt.
Groups of Sufis from throughout Egypt camp in makeshift
lodgings around the city and
hold *zikrs* – lengthy sessions
of chanting and swaying,
intended to achieve unity
with Allah. A procession led
by the current sheikh tours
the city, ending with a mass
zikr outside the mosque
where al-Badawi is buried.

Although fundamentally a
spiritual occasion, this annual
festival is also an important
social event, allowing young
Egyptians to let off steam in
the boisterous atmosphere.

Panelled wall in the Ottoman House of Amasyali in Rosetta

**21st- and 22nd-Dynasty tombs at
the royal necropolis at Tanis**

Tanis ❹

70 km (43 miles) NE of Zagazig. 🚌

Near the modern village of
San el-Hagar, to the northeast
of Zagazig, lie the jumbled
ruins of the ancient Egyptian
city of Djanet, known by the
Greeks as Tanis. For several
centuries, Tanis was one of
the largest cities in the Delta
and became the capital of
Egypt during the 21st
Dynasty. Flooding led to its
decline, however, and by the
14th century the area was
practically deserted. San el-
Hagar grew up on reclaimed
land during the 1820s.

Excavations at Tanis have
revealed ruins dating back
to the 6th Dynasty: huge
blocks and fragments of
statues from the Ramessid
Temple of Amun, as well as
the foundations of many
other temples, are among
the remains on site. Several
intact 21st- and 22nd-Dynasty
tombs, including those of
Psusennes I and Sheshonq III,
were discovered at the royal
necropolis, which lies to the
south of the temple. The
breathtaking treasures can
be seen at the Egyptian
Museum in Cairo (*see pp74–5*).

Rosetta (Rashid) ❺

65 km (40 miles) E of Alexandria.
🏛 *58,000.* 🚌 🚢

Founded in the 9th century
by Ibn Tulun, the Muslim
governor of Egypt, Rosetta
(also known by the modern
name of Rashid) became one
of Egypt's most important
ports, reaching its heyday
during the 17th and 18th
centuries. With Alexandria's
revival in the 19th century,
however, Rosetta fell into
decline and today it is little
more than an attractive
fishing village surrounded
by palm and orange groves.

Many beautiful Ottoman
houses and mosques –
reminders of Rosetta's more
glorious past – can still be
seen around the town and
several are open to visitors.
Among the most beautiful
are the House of Amasyali on

Sharia Amasyali and Ramadan
House on Sharia Port Said.
The ornate 18th-century
Azouz *hammam* (public
baths) to the south of the
town is almost entirely intact.

Rosetta is best known for
the famous Rosetta stone
(*see pp20–21*), which was
discovered here by French
soldiers in 1799. Part of a
black basalt stele dating from
the 2nd century BC, the stone
was carved with a decree by
Ptolemy V, written in ancient
hieroglyphics, Greek and
demotic Egyptian. From these
inscriptions, French professor
Jean-François Champollion
was able, in 1822, to formulate
a system for deciphering
hieroglyphics – a feat that
was to unlock much of
ancient Egyptian history.

Conceded to the British
in 1801, the Rosetta stone is
now on display at the British
Museum in London.

**Palm trees bordering the Rosetta
branch of the Nile Delta**

Alexandria ⑥

Stretching 20 km (12 miles) along the coast, Alexandria is Egypt's second largest city. Founded in 332 BC by Alexander the Great, the city grew to rival Rome before falling into decline in the 4th century AD. In the 19th century, the Pasha Mohammed Ali revived Alexandria's fortunes as a port by linking it to the Nile. This prosperity drew thousands of Europeans, who fostered the decadent atmosphere chronicled by writers such as Lawrence Durrell, E M Forster and Constantine Cavafy. This era ended in the 1950s as the foreigners fled Nasser's revolution. Little remains of Alexandria's ancient magnificence, but a few faded clues to its cosmopolitan heyday linger on.

Colourful fishing boats in Alexandria Harbour

🏯 Midan Saad Zaghloul
Situated on the seafront, Midan Saad Zaghloul is at the heart of modern Alexandria. From this square, a statue of Egyptian nationalist leader Zaghloul (1860–1927) (see p62) watches over the eastern harbour and the busy tram and bus stations in the adjacent Midan Ramla.

Sadly, nothing remains of the Caesareum, a magnificent temple built on the site more than 2,000 years ago. Begun by Cleopatra VII for Mark Antony and finished by Octavian after their deaths in 30 BC (see pp54–5), only two obelisks survived its destruction in 912. Known as Cleopatra's Needles, they were relocated to London and New York in the 1800s.

Today the square consists of shops, hotels and three 1920s Art Deco cafés, Athineos, Délices and Trianon. South is Sharia Nabi Daniel, believed to be the ancient Street of Soma – a marble road lined with columns. It is

16th-century woodcut showing the Library of Alexandria on fire

now lined with street vendors, and its glory has faded.

🏯 Bibliotheca Alexandrina
Shatbi. *Tel (03) 483 9999, (03) 483 0334/0336/0342/0346.* ⬜ 10am–7pm Wed–Thu & Sun–Mon, 3–7pm Fri–Sat (11am–2pm during Ramadan).
Founded in the 3rd century BC, the Bibliotheca Alexandrina was the greatest library in the ancient world, attracting the best international scholars. The library and cultural centre was re-inaugurated in October 2002, more than two millennia after the original building was destroyed by fire.

The new Bibliotheca Alexandrina is striking in its architecture and also contains a Planetarium and Science Museum. The main library is encased in a giant cylindrical building at the far northern end of the corniche. The circular outer wall is made of Aswan granite engraved with letters from world alpha-

bets. The partly-glazed roof which tilts towards the sea is designed to angle sunlight on to the desks of the seven-tier 2,000-seat reading rooms. Eventually, the library will contain 8 million volumes.

🏨 Sofitel Alex Cecil Hotel
16 Midan Saad Zaghloul.
Tel (03) 487 7173.
One of the more obvious landmarks of Midan Saad Zaghloul is the Moorish-style Sofitel Alex Cecil Hotel, which featured in Lawrence Durrell's *Alexandria Quartet*. Opened in 1929, it is reputed to be built on the site where Cleopatra VII committed suicide after her Egyptian fleet was defeated by Octavian in the Battle of Actium in 31 BC.

During World War II the hotel was used by the British Secret Service and later played host to politicians and writers such as Winston Churchill, Somerset Maugham and Noel Coward. Though restoration has not quite captured its past grandeur, the roof garden or sea-front terrace are pleasant places to enjoy a drink.

Façade of Sofitel Alex Cecil Hotel

🏛 Cavafy Museum
4 Sharia Sharm el-Sheikh, off Sharia Nabi Daniel. ⬜ Wed–Mon.
The poet Constantine Cavafy (1863–1933) was born to Greek parents but spent most of his life in Alexandria. This small museum is housed in the flat where he spent the last 25 years of his life. Some of the rooms are arranged as they would have been when he lived here – the display of possessions includes his bed,

Marble benches capable of seating up to 800 Romans in the Amphitheatre at Kom al-Dikka

desk, death mask, rare editions of his books as well as some of his letters. Cavafy is buried in the Greek Cemetery nearby.

Another room in the small museum is devoted to one of Cavafy's students, the Greek writer Stratis Tsirkas (1911–81).

🎭 Roman Amphitheatre at Kom al-Dikka

Sharia Yousef. ☐ daily. 📷
In 1965, a semi-circular Roman amphitheatre was discovered under what was known as

Kom al-Dikka (Mound of Rubble) after the remains of a Napoleonic fort were levelled for a housing project. The 13 tiered rows of marble seats, excavated by Polish archaeologists aided by the Graeco-Roman Museum, date from the 2nd century AD. Originally a small theatre, the building was altered over time and served as an assembly hall, possibly for the city council. A couple of sections of the original mosaic floor are on view in front of the amphitheatre.

Other excavations are still under way on the site. To the north lie the brick ruins of a Roman bathing complex. A series of basins and channels reveal how water would have

Roman mosaic at Kom al-Dikka

VISITORS' CHECKLIST

Alexandria governorate. 🏛 3.4 million. ✈ 5 km (3 miles) SE of the city. 🚊 Masr Station, Midan al-Gumhuriyya; Sidi Gaber Station. 🚌 15th May Bus Station, Sidi Gaber. 🛈 Midan Saad Zaghloul (03) 485 1556; Masr Station (03) 392 5985.

passed through the heating system to the marble covered baths. To the east lie the ruins of a residential area dating from the 1st century AD, but this site and the Roman baths are closed for excavation work.

Some items found at an underwater excavation near Fort Qaitbey, including part of an obelisk from the era of Seti I and a weather-beaten sphinx, are on show in the amphitheatre grounds.

ALEXANDRIA CITY CENTRE

Attarine Mosque ⑧
Bibliotheca Alexandrina ②
Catacombs of Kom ash-Shuqqafa ⑮
Cavafy Museum ④
Fine Arts Museum ⑯
Fort Qaitbey ⑪
Graeco-Roman Museum ⑥
Hotel Cecil ③

Jewellery Museum ⑱
Mahmoud Said Museum ⑰
Midan Saad Zaghloul ①
Midan Tahrir ⑨
National Museum ⑲
Necropolis of Anfushi ⑫

Ottoman District (Anfushi) ⑩
Pastroudis ⑦
Pompey's Pillar ⑬
Ras el-Tin Palace ⑭
Roman Amphitheatre at Kom al-Dikka ⑤

Alexandria: Graeco-Roman Museum

Situated in the heart of modern Alexandria, the Graeco-Roman Museum contains around 40,000 artifacts, mostly covering around 1,000 years of history from the founding of the city in 331 BC to the Arab conquest in AD 640. The museum was established in 1892 by Khedive Abbas II. Its 25 rooms and central gardens are crammed with items found in Alexandria and the surrounding areas, including a large mosaic from the 3rd century BC portraying a stag hunt. The vast collection of artifacts from ancient Egyptian, Classical and Christian cultures testifies to the complex history of Alexandria.

Terracotta Pharos lantern

Museum Gardens
In the museum's central gardens, amongst a wealth of tombs, statues and other artifacts, sits the head of a once huge statue of Mark Anthony.

Statue of Aphrodite (2nd-century AD)

Tomb Painting
Two oxen driving a waterwheel (an invention of Alexandrian scientists) are depicted in this tomb fresco dating from the 2nd century AD.

White Marble Sarcophagus
A bas-relief from the 2nd century AD depicts Dionysus and his retinue as they find Ariadne asleep on the island of Naxos before she was abandoned by her lover, Theseus.

Sacred Crocodile
This mummified crocodile was carried in procession honouring Sob the crocodile-

Terracotta models of town monuments are displayed in Hall 18.

★ Tanagra Figures
This intriguing collection of Graeco-Roman terracotta figures, found in the city's many necropolises, provides an insight into social life and the costume of the era.

VISITORS' CHECKLIST

5 Sharia al-Mathaf ar-Romani.
Tel (03) 486 5820. 🚌 🚐 🚖
🕙 9am–5pm daily; 9am–3pm during Ramadan. 🕙 11am–1pm Fri. 📷 Extra charge for cameras and videos.

Emperor Hadrian
This 2nd-century AD bronze head has eyes of ivory and glass. Found at Qena, it was once part of a larger sculpture.

GALLERY GUIDE
The museum is organized in chronological order running clockwise from the entrance. This order is interrupted only by two large themed areas: the first contains handicrafts from all eras and the other a vast collection of coins. Also worth visiting is the garden, with some fine statues and a reconstructed temple of the crocodile-god from Fayoum.

Coptic artifacts from the 4th–7th centuries AD are displayed here.

KEY

☐	Coptic
☐	Ptolemaic
☐	Pharaonic
☐	Graeco-Roman
☐	Handicrafts (all periods)
☐	Coins
☐	Non-exhibition space

Entrance

★ Antique Coins
The magnificent collection of coins includes some bearing Cleopatra's profile (above right).

Alexander the Great (356–323 BC)
Sculpted from marble, this head of Alexander the Great is one of several portraits of the leader in the museum. He became the object of a cult worship that spread throughout the ancient world.

STAR EXHIBITS

★ Antique Coins

★ Tanagra Figures

Pastroudis, once a favourite with the Alexandrian literary crowd

Pastroudis
39 Sharia Horreya. **Tel** *(03) 392 9609.*
The wood-panelled Pastroudis is an old-fashioned café from the early 20th century. Written about in Durrell's Alexandria Quartet, Pastroudis used to be a popular haunt of the poet Cavafy and the bohemian crowd. Although the café is no longer fashionable, its street-side tables still provide a good spot to watch the world go by and overlook the Roman amphitheatre and baths.

Sharia Horreya is believed to have been the colonnaded Canopic Way which ran from the Gate of the Sun in the eastern walls to the Gate of the Moon to the west. It is also thought that the inter-section with Sharia Nabi Daniel was once the crossroads of the ancient city where the Great Library of Alexandria and Mouseion once stood.

Attarine Mosque
Sharia Attarine.
Topped by a pretty minaret, the Attarine Mosque lies just south of Midan Tahrir. It was built on the site of the fabled Mosque of a Thousand Columns, which itself stood on the site of a church dedicated to St Athanasius in AD 370.

Napoleon's men removed a seven-ton sarcophagus from the mosque, believing it to be Alexander's. Handed over to the British it was found to be the sarcophagus of Nectanebo II, the last Egyptian pharaoh.

Around the Attarine Mosque, the sprawling antiques district begins. Antique shops, piled high with European furniture, and trinkets dating back to Napoleonic times, fill the backstreets. Here also, the intriguing belongings of many Europeans who fled the 1952 revolution are up for sale. However, the area is well known by international antiques dealers and genuine bargains can be hard to find.

Midan Tahrir
Originally known as Place des Consuls, the square was intended as the centrepiece of Pasha Mohammed Ali's new Alexandria in the 1830s. In 1873 his French-designed equestrian statue was set in its place on a high plinth and the square was thereafter known as Midan Mohammed Ali. After the destruction brought about by the British bombardment in 1882 *(see p59)*, the area was rebuilt as Midan Mansheiyya, before Nasser's revolution in 1952 renamed the square Midan Tahrir.

It was here that an assassination attempt was made on President Nasser as he gave a speech in 1954. This gave him the opportunity to remove any opposition to his rule. Two years later, in 1956, it was from Midan Tahrir that Nasser shocked the Western world and announced the national-ization of the Suez Canal.

To the north is Midan Orabi, a major transport hub with tram, minibus and bus depots. The grand Neo-Classical Monument to the Unknown Soldier, designed by the Italian architect Verucci and erected in 1937, stands on the corniche, facing out to sea.

Detail of Andalusian-styled Mosque of Abu al-Abbas Mursi in Anfushi

Ottoman District (Anfushi)
The peninsula leading to Fort Qaitbey was home to the inhabitants of Alexandria in Ottoman times (1517–1914). The atmosphere here differs from the rest of the city and it is best experienced on foot. To the south, lively souqs sell medicinal herbs and perfume while Turkish-style houses overhang the narrow streets.

Ottoman mosques are also dotted throughout the area, with the El-Shorbagi Mosque Complex at the heart of the district. Built in the mid-18th century it has a distinctive gallery on the first floor with shops below. The Terbana Mosque on Faransa Street was originally built in 1685 and two antique columns, taken from another site, support the minaret. Further north, in Midan El-Gawamaa is a mosque, dedicated to the

Midan Tahrir at the centre of Alexandria

For hotels and restaurants in this region see pp281–2 and pp300–301

PHAROS LIGHTHOUSE

Built in the 3rd century BC on an island in the eastern harbour, the Pharos Lighthouse stood up to 150 m (492 ft) high and was one of the Seven Wonders of the ancient world. Built mainly of limestone to the design of the Asiatic Greek architect Sostratus, the lighthouse had three differently-shaped storeys. The base was square and used as lodgings for mechanics and for storing fuel. The second storey was octagonal and the third, which contained the lantern mechanism, was circular and topped with a huge bronze statue of Poseidon, god of the sea. Used for nearly 1,000 years, the lighthouse was neglected during the Arab occupation.

The lantern collapsed in AD 700 and the lighthouse was later destroyed by a series of earthquakes in the 12th and 14th centuries. Recently, underwater excavation has discovered blocks of stone believed to be from the Pharos Lighthouse and a temple dedicated to Isis *(see pp26–7)* which stood nearby.

Reconstruction of the Pharos Lighthouse

13th-century Andalusian, Sidi Abu al-Abbas Mursi, the city's patron saint of fishermen. The current structure was designed in 1945 by Italian architect Mario Rossi. The octagonal-shaped building has a 73-m (240-ft) minaret.

Fort Qaitbey

Corniche. 📷 *15.* ⬜ *daily.* 🅿️
Although the turretted Fort Qaitbey situated on the tip of the Eastern Harbour looks like some kind of toy castle from the corniche, up close it is an imposing building. The fort was built in the 1480s by Sultan Qaitbey (1468–96) on the site of the Pharos Lighthouse, using stones from the dilapidated building. Within the keep there is a small mosque – the oldest in Alexandria – and a Naval Museum displaying relics from ships sunk nearby, the result of Roman and Napoleonic sea battles. These include bottles of wine and astronomical instruments retrieved from the French

ship L'Orient. The fort was badly damaged by the British bombardment in 1882 when the mosque's minaret was blown clean off. From its elevated position, set back from the corniche, the fort has fantastic views of Alexandria and out to sea.

⌂ Necropolis of Anfushi

Sharia Ras el-Tin, Anfushi. ⬜ *daily.* 🅿️

The five rock tombs in the Necropolis of Anfushi date from around 250 BC and were discovered in 1901 and 1921. Cut into limestone, the tombs consist of a stairway leading down to a central courtyard with individual burial sites located off to the side. Tomb No. 2 is the most interesting and best preserved. The stairway walls are decorated with paintings of Osiris, Horus and Isis with the deceased as well as scenes of daily life and even an example of ancient Greek graffiti. The wall paintings and decoration are significant as they combine features of Greek and Egyptian art. There are also two vestibules with burial chambers; the one to the northeast is painted with black and white squares to resemble more expensive alabaster and marble tiling. The door to the burial chamber is flanked by two small stone sphinxes on stands, keeping watch over the tomb.

Qaitbey from across the Eastern Harbour, built by recycling the stones from the Pharos Lighthouse

Ras el-Tin Palace

Sharia Ras el-Tin, Bahari.

Overlooking Alexandria's Western Harbour, Ras el-Tin Palace is surrounded by elegant, formal gardens. The palace was built originally by Ottoman Pasha Mohammed Ali (1805–48) so that he could keep watch on his new fleet. Under King Fuad I (1917–36), it was redesigned by Italian architects and served as the government's summer seat.

During the 1952 revolution, the palace was besieged by Nasser's men and King Farouk was forced to abdicate and flee to Italy with his family and retinue. The palace is now Admiralty headquarters and is reserved for state guests; however its pleasant gardens are open to the public.

Pompey's Pillar

Sharia Ahmoud al-Saweiri, Karmous. 16. ◯ daily.

To the southwest of the city, in the impoverished district of Karmous, Pompey's Pillar is a striking sight. Made of red Aswan granite, the 27-m (89-ft) high pillar was erected around AD 297 in tribute to the Roman emperor Diocletian. On its base is written in Greek "To the most just of emperors, the divine protector of Alexandria, Diocletian the invincible: Postumus, prefect of Egypt."

The monument's popular name may have come from medieval travellers who thought that the Roman general Pompey, murdered in Egypt in 48 BC, was buried here; in fact, the pillar came from the Serapeum complex or Temple of Serapis, which was built in the mid-3rd century BC. (Serapis was an Egyptian deity, very popular in the Graeco-Roman period, who combined aspects of the gods Osiris and Apis). The pillar would have been freestanding and is all that remains of the temple which was once an important repository of religious texts and the "daughter library" of that of Alexandria.

Enlarged by the Emperor Hadrian in the 2nd century AD, when it was described as second only to the Capitol in Rome, the temple was destroyed by Christians in AD 391.

Pompey's Pillar, once part of the beautiful Temple of Serapis

Nearby there are some underground galleries, where the sacred Apis bulls (*see p164*) were buried, as well as several statues of the Sphinx that originally stood at Heliopolis.

Catacombs of Kom ash-Shuqqafa

Sharia al-Nasserieh. 16. ◯ 9am–5pm daily (Ramadan: 9am–3pm).

Dating from the 2nd century AD, the catacomb complex of Kom ash-Shuqqafa just south of Pompey's Pillar is the largest Graeco-Roman necropolis in Egypt. Dug into the rock to a depth of about 35 m (115 ft), the tomb complex has three levels. However, flooding has made the lowest level inaccessible.

The catacombs are reached via a spiral staircase encircling a shaft down which bodies of the deceased were lowered. On the first level there is a

central rotunda and a large banquet hall, the Triclinium, where friends and relatives of the deceased gathered to pay their last respects.

To the east of the rotunda is the Caracalla Hall, an older burial complex that became accessible from the main chamber when tomb robbers broke through the wall. This area is dedicated to Nemesis, the goddess of sport.

From the central rotunda, stairs lead down to a second storey with a vestibule and burial chamber. Here the decorated sarcophagi and wall reliefs display a mixture of Egyptian, Roman and Greek styles: by the doorway, Anubis, the god god of the dead, is shown as a Roman legionary with a dragon's tail. On either side of the burial chamber, below heads of Medusa, are carved two giant serpents, wearing the double crown of Egypt.

From the burial chamber, eerie passages lead off in all directions to rooms containing more than 300 loculi – small chambers for bodies.

Fine Arts Museum

18 Sharia Menasce. **Tel** (03) 393 6616. ◯ Sat–Thu.

A short distance to the south-east of Masr station, the Fine Arts Museum is housed in a beautiful villa that was donated in 1954 to the city of Alexandria by the wealthy Jewish Menasce family. The museum is used mainly for frequently changing exhibitions of contemporary foreign and Egyptian artists. The museum is also known for hosting the Alexandrian

Relief of Anubis presiding over a mummification at Kom ash-Shuqqafa

Biennial, a showcase for art from Mediterranean countries.

A statue by Mahmoud Mokhtar (1891–1934), who has been acclaimed as the first sculptor in the modern Egyptian art movement, stands in the gardens outside.

🏛 National Museum of Alexandria

110 Sharia Horreya. *Tel* (03) 483 5519. ○ 9am–5pm daily. 📷

Inaugurated in 2003, the National Museum of Alexandria displays over 1,800 artifacts, many in ingenious hanging diagonal glass showcases. The restored three-storey Italianate building dates from 1929 and is set in a large garden of rare trees and plants.

Most of the museum's treasures were excavated in and around the city itself. The basement spans pre-dynastic and ancient Egyptian artifacts, featuring a replica of a tomb similar to those found in the Valley of the Kings, complete with genuine funerary furniture. The first floor has Graeco-Roman finds, including a red granite statue of Caracalla and several beautifully painted terracotta Tanagra figurines.

A black basalt statue of a high priest of the goddess Isis, excavated from the sea-bed in 1998, is a star exhibit of the Coptic and Islamic collection on the third floor. There is also a section devoted to the jewellery of Egypt's former royal family.

🏛 Mahmoud Said Museum Centre

6 Sharia Said Pasha, Gianaclis. *Tel* (03) 582 1688. 🚗 🚆 2. ○ 10am–6:30pm Tue–Sun; 10am–1:30pm, 7–10:30pm Ramadan. 📷

An Alexandrian aristocrat, Mahmoud Said (1897–1967) is one of Egypt's most important modern artists. The museum that bears his name is housed in what was the family villa.

Said trained originally as a lawyer and worked as a judge, but painting was his passion and in 1947 he gave up law to dedicate himself to art. His work combines western techniques with Egyptian and Pharaonic themes to produce stunning, sensuous paintings. His 1924 self-portrait echoes

a haunting Fayoum mummy portrait (see p169).

The first floor of the museum contains works by the prolific Alexandrian painters, the Wanly brothers, Seif (1906–79) and Adham (1911–59). The eclectic choice of paintings includes portraits, landscapes, and even a few cartoons.

🏛 Royal Jewellery Museum

27 Sharia Ahmed Yehia Pasha, Zizinia. 🚗 🚆 2. *Tel* (03) 582 8348. ○ 9am–4pm daily; 9:30am–2:30pm Ramadan. 📷

This recently restored building was originally constructed for Mohammed Ali's grand-daughter, Princess Fatima el-Zaharaa (1903–83), and later used as a palace by King Farouk. The museum has an extensive collection of jewels dating from Pasha Moham-med Ali's rule in the early 19th century to the end of King Farouk's reign in 1952.

Key pieces include a gold snuff box with Mohammed Ali's name spelled out in diamonds, King Farouk's gold-and diamond-studded chess set, and a fabulous platinum crown glittering with well over 2,000 diamonds.

The palace is lavishly, if not always tastefully, decorated with stained-glass vignettes of life in 18th-century France. The two bathrooms, the ladies' tiled with scenes of nymphs bathing in Alpine surrounds and the men's with pictures of French fishermen and sea-gulls, should not be missed.

Montazah Palace, an eclectic mix of Turkish and Florentine architecture

Montazah Palace ❼

18 km (11 miles) E of Alexandria. 🚗 🚌 *Tel* (03) 547 7152. ○ daily. 📷

Montazah Palace is set in extensive gardens and over-looks a truly beautiful stretch of coast. Built at the beginning of the 20th century by Khedive Abbas II, a relative of King Farouk, the palace mixes Turkish and Florentine architecture: the central tower was inspired by the Palazzo Vecchio in Florence. Although the palace itself is closed to the public, the lush park and the semi-private beach are popular places to relax.

To the east lies the private beach resort of **Mamoura**. It has a more relaxed dress code than public beaches and the sand is relatively clean.

🏖 Mamoura

Sharia Abu Qir. 📷

The elegant gardens and groves of Montazah Palace, Alexandria

Abu Qir ❽

24 km (15 miles) E of Alexandria.
👥 *33,000.* 🚍 🚗

The small fishing town of
Abu Qir, on the coast to
the east of Alexandria, is
renowned for two reasons:
historic battles and excellent
fish restaurants. It was at Abu
Qir Bay that Admiral Nelson
destroyed the French fleet in
the dramatic Battle of the Nile
in 1798. With the loss of his
ships and army, Napoleon's
plans for an eastern empire
were effectively ruined. A year
later the tables were turned
slightly when Napoleon's
troops repulsed a landing
attempt by a British contingent
of 15,000 Turkish soldiers and
many thousands drowned.

Since 1998, underwater
excavation work by teams
of French and Egyptian divers
has uncovered many artifacts
from the sunken warships
including gold coins, cannons,
and plenty of everyday items.
There are plans to build a new
museum to display these finds.

Although the beach at Abu
Qir is not suitable for bathing,
at the weekend the streets are
filled with Alexandrians who
come to savour the delights
of a small seaside town. These
include eating in one of the
many seafront restaurants that
serve delicious seafood.
Sitting right on the beach,
the Zaphyrion *(see p300)* – the
ancient Greek name for Abu
Qir – is reputed to be one of
the best restaurants in Egypt.

Brightly painted fishing boats at Abu Qir

Agami ❾

20 km (12 miles) W of Alexandria. 🚍

Agami was traditionally the
summer resort of the Cairene
and Alexandrian elite during
the 1950s. Known as the
Egyptian St Tropez, it is far
less exclusive these days. The
semi-private beaches are less
conservative and less crowded
than in Alexandria, and the
nightlife is livelier. High-rise
apartment blocks have replaced
most of the original resort
architecture. Exceptions include
the **Beit al-Halawa**, designed in
1975 by Abd el-Wahid el-Wakil
and the extreme angular lines
of **Villa Lashin**, built in 1962
by the architect Ali Azzam.

Environs
Other popular resorts nearby
include the small village of
Hannoville, 1 km (0.6 mile)
to the west, notable for its

inexpensive accommodation,
and the private beach resort
of **Sidi Krear**, which lies 14
km (8.5 miles) further west
along the coast.

Abu Mina ❿

63 km (39 miles) SW of Alexandria. 🚍

To the west of Alexandria,
15 km (9 miles) inland from
Abu Sir on the coast, lies the
Coptic Monastery of Abu
Mina (Deir Mari Mina). St
Mina was an Alexandrian-born
Roman legionary who was
tortured and killed in Phrygia
(Asia Minor) at the end of the
3rd century for his Christian
beliefs. His body is said to
have been buried here after a
camel carrying it home refused
to go any further. Legend has
it that a spring with miraculous
powers immediately started
flowing nearby and a church
and basilica were built around
the tomb. After the Emperor
of Byzantium's daughter was
cured by the waters in the 4th
century its fame spread. The
water was exported throughout
Christendom and Abu Mina
became a busy pilgrim town.
However, after repeated
sackings by the Bedouin,
the town fell into decay as
the water source dried up.

Today a modern monastery
dominates the site and there
are few impressive remains to
see, although there are plans
for a museum and archaeo-
logical park. The area is still
important to pilgrims who visit
the monastery, especially on
11th November, St Mina's day.

Monastery at Abu Mina built in 1959 on the site of a much older basilica

◁ Colourful fishing boats on the seafront at Abu Qir

THE WESTERN DESERT

E gypt's vast Western Desert stretches over nearly 3 million sq km (1.2 million sq miles), from the west bank of the Nile to Libya, and from Sudan towards the Mediterranean Sea. Despite covering over two-thirds of Egypt's total land area, the desert is virtually uninhabited, except for the fertile oases where communities and crops flourish amid barren desert surroundings.

There are five oases in the Western Desert: Siwa, Kharga, Dakhla, Farafra and Bahariyya. Except for Siwa, the oases have been under the control of the rulers of the Nile Valley since Pharaonic times, when they were crucial stopping points on the busy caravan trading routes from Africa. The Ptolemaic temples and Roman forts dotted around the oases bear witness to their past importance and ongoing archaeological work is continually uncovering new finds.

Each of the Western Desert oases has its own unique character. While the main settlements of Bahariyya and Farafra are still villages, those of Dakhla and Kharga are large towns, surrounded by fascinating historical sites. In Siwa, isolated near the Libyan border, the inhabitants retain their own language and distinct culture.

In the late 1950s a plan was made to reclaim part of the desert and relocate thousands of people from the crowded Nile delta and valley. The area, covering Bahariyya, Farafra, Dakhla and Kharga oases, was named the New Valley. Although some building began, few people moved, and financial constraints together with the questionable sustainability of the water supply meant that the project was virtually abandoned.

The Western Desert today remains one of the few places in the world where travellers can experience a feeling of total isolation. Its sheer scale is overwhelming. From huge dunes to fantastical rock formations, the landscape varies dramatically and camping out overnight in such astonishing surroundings can be one of the highlights of a trip to Egypt.

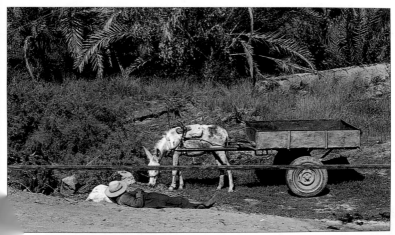

▸ a break during the heat of the day in Dakhla, one of the Western Desert Oases

ndless expanse of the Great Sand Sea, close to Siwa Oasis

Exploring the Western Desert

The Western Desert offers visitors the chance to escape the crowded sites of Cairo and the Nile Valley and sample the peace and tranquillity of the empty desert and its green oases. In the northwest, the remote Siwa is the perfect place to relax. Further east, Bahariyya is a picturesque oasis within easy reach of Cairo. The road leading on to Farafra, the least developed of the oases, passes through the Black Desert and the incredible White Desert, with its mysterious, wind-eroded rock formations. Pockets of fertile land growing fruit, rice and peanuts are dotted among the sand dunes between Farafra and the beautiful Dakhla oasis. For lovers of ancient monuments, Dakhla and the more built-up Kharga have the most to offer.

Statue in the Oasis Heritage Museum, Bahariyya

Dakhla Oasis near Al-Qasr, showing the striking contrast between the fertile soil and the barren, inhospitable desert

GETTING AROUND

Travelling in the Western Desert is much easier than it used to be. Roads now link all the oases and buses run fairly frequently. Siwa Oasis is best reached by bus from Marsa Matruh, on the Mediterranean coast. Bahariyya and Farafra can be visited from Cairo, and Dakhla and Kharga can be reached quite easily from Asyut. There are airports at Dakhla and Kharga with twice weekly flights to and from Cairo. Depending on time pressure and your sense of adventure, the 1,000-km (620-mile) Great Desert Circuit of Bahariyya, Farafra, Dakhla and Kharga is an option. Usually starting at Cairo and ending at Luxor or Asyut, the trip can be taken either with an organized tour or hired transport. Exploring the area around each individual oasis is easy to arrange locally.

Siwa Oasis, with the salt lake Birket Siwa visible in the distance, viewed from the Mountain of the Dead

Marsa
Matruh

Qai

SIWA OASIS
Siwa ⑤ ※ 🏛️ 🏘️

Western
Desert

Great Sand Sea

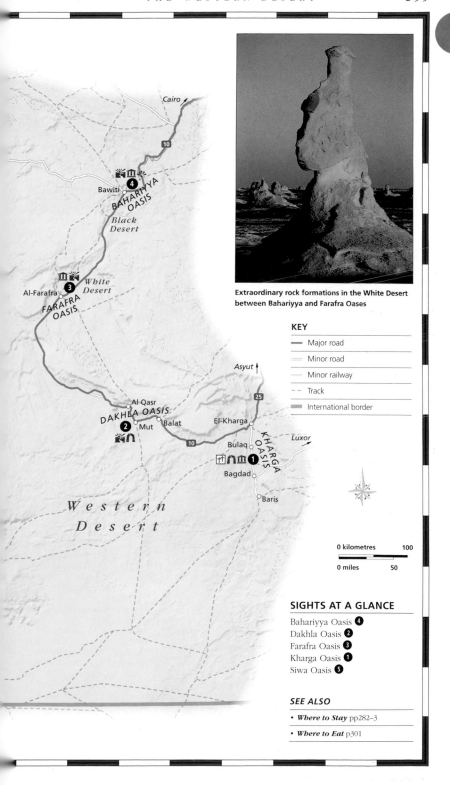

Extraordinary rock formations in the White Desert between Bahariyya and Farafra Oases

KEY

——	Major road
══	Minor road
——	Minor railway
- -	Track
▬▬	International border

0 kilometres 100

0 miles 50

SIGHTS AT A GLANCE

Bahariyya Oasis ❹

Dakhla Oasis ❷

Farafra Oasis ❸

Kharga Oasis ❶

Siwa Oasis ❺

SEE ALSO

- **Where to Stay** pp282–3

- **Where to Eat** p301

Lush date groves surrounding the fertile fields of Dakhla, the prettiest of the Western Desert oases

Kharga Oasis ❶

233 km (144 miles) SW of Asyut. 🏚 65,000. ✈ 5 km (3 miles) N of El-Kharga. 🚌 🛈 Government building, Midan Nasser, El-Kharga (092) 7921 206.

Kharga, the largest of the oases, rose to prominence as the penultimate stop on "The Forty Days Road", the infamous slave-trade route between Sudan and Egypt. Today the modern, sprawling city of El-Kharga is capital of the New Valley governorate, which covers Kharga, Dakhla and Farafra oases. The city lacks charm, but its **Antiquities Museum** displays impressive archaeological finds from Kharga and Dakhla.

Standing in palm groves just north of the city, the **Temple of Hibis**, built by Persian emperor Darius I in the 6th century BC, is the only sizeable Persian temple left in Egypt. Also north of the city is the **Necropolis of al-Bagawat**. This Christian cemetery contains hundreds of domed, mudbrick tombs decorated with Coptic murals, dating from around the 4th to 6th centuries AD. The best-preserved paintings are in the Chapel of the Exodus and portray Moses leading the Jews out of Egypt, away from Pharaoh's pursuing troops.

Environs
Perched on a hill on the road south to Baris are the ruins of the 25th-Dynasty **Temple of al-Ghueita**. Further south, the villages of Nasser and Bulaq are known for their thermal springs, reputed to treat rheumatism.

🏛 **Antiquities Museum**
Sharia Gamal Abdel Nasser.
⬜ daily. 📷

🏛 **Temple of Hibis**
2 km (1 mile) N of El-Kharga.
⬜ daily. 📷

🏛 **Necropolis of al-Bagawat**
3 km (2 miles) N of El-Kharga.
⬜ daily. 📷

🏛 **Temple of al-Ghueita**
18 km (11 miles) S of El-Kharga.
⬜ daily. 📷

Dakhla Oasis ❷

190 km (118 miles) W of Kharga. 🏚 70,000. ✈ 10 km (6 miles) SW of Mut. 🚌 🛈 Sharia as-Sawra al-Khadra, Mut (092) 7821 686.

With hundreds of springs set in a lush, verdant landscape, Dakhla is regarded as the prettiest of the oases.
A long band of pinkish rock sits along the northern horizon, and olives, dates, wheat and rice thrive on the fertile farmland. The capital, Mut, has an **Ethnographic Museum** displaying figures sculpted by a local artist, Mabrouk.

Dakhla's ancient sites are situated in the outlying parts of the oasis. They can easily be reached by hiring a pick-up truck from Mut.

Environs
With its narrow, winding streets and mudbrick houses, **Al-Qasr**, 27 km (17 miles) northwest of Mut, retains a strong medieval feel. The town has a 12th-century mosque and a 10th-century *madrassa* (school) with superb rooftop views. The **Al-Muzawaka tombs** date from Pharaonic times. The two best tombs are those of Petosiris and Sadosiris, which have vivid coloured reliefs. To the west, the remnants of **Deir al-Hagar** temple, built by Emperor Nero in the first century AD, stand isolated in the desert. **Balat** lies 35 km (22 miles) east of Mut on the road to Kharga. A medieval village, it is on the site of an Old Kingdom settlement that traded with Kush (ancient Nubia).

Mudbrick tombs in the Necropolis of al-Bagawat, Kharga Oasis

For hotels and restaurants in this region see pp282–3 and p301

🏛 Ethnographic Museum
Sharia as-Salem. ⬜ *ask at Tourist Office.*

⌂ Al-Muzawaka tombs
5 km (3 miles) W of Al-Qasr. ⬜ *daily.*

⌂ Deir al-Hagar
12 km (7 miles) W of Al-Qasr.
⬜ *daily.* 🖼

Farafra Oasis ❸

310 km (192 miles) NW of Dakhla.
🏛 *2,800.* 🚌

The most isolated and least
populous of the New Valley
oases, Farafra is an extremely
peaceful place to visit. Its
mainly Bedouin inhabitants are
well known for their strong
traditions and religious piety.
The largest settlement, Al-
Farafra, is built like the other
oasis towns around a ruined
fortress, where villagers would
shelter from attacks. Though
the traditional mudbrick,
painted houses remain,

Bizarre rock formations caused by wind erosion in the
White Desert, near Farafra Oasis

concrete developments have
sprung up due to government
efforts to attract outsiders to
the area. Al-Farafra's **Town
Museum** displays sculptures
of oasis life by a well-known
local artist, Badr.

Environs
Farafra is an ideal base for
exploring the **White Desert**,
41 km (25 miles) from Al-
Farafra on the road to
Bahariyya. Named after its
bright-white rock formations,
the White Desert resembles
a haunting lunar landscape.

Bahariyya Oasis ❹

185 km (115 miles) NE of Farafra.
🏛 *33,000.* 🚌 🛈 *Town council
building, Bawiti (02) 847 3035.*

This oasis was a key agricultural centre in Pharaonic times,
exporting large quantities of
wine to the Nile Valley. Today
it is famed for its dates and
olives. Bawiti, the main
village, is very picturesque,
with palm groves surrounding
clusters of mudbrick houses.
The **Oasis Heritage Museum**
has clay figure displays by the

local artist
Mohammed
Eed. Hot and
cold springs
surround the
oasis and just
west of Bawiti
a hot spring,
Ain Bishmu, is
used by the
villagers for
washing and
swimming.
Further afield, a few ruins of
the **Temple of Alexander the
Great**, built in 332 BC, lie just
north of a large discovery of
mummies. The nearby 26th-
Dynasty **Temple of Ain al-
Muftela** is better preserved.
 Bahariyya is surrounded by
hills, and the **Black Mountain**,
7 km (4 miles) northeast of
Bawiti, is worth a visit. Also
called the "English Mountain",
it is crowned with an old
World War I British outpost.
Climbing to the top takes
about an hour, but the view
is very rewarding.

Environs:
The **Black Desert**, created
by wind eroding the dark,
rocky outcrops, begins 20 km
(12 miles) south of Bahariyya.
Further south are the mainly
quartz rock formations of
Crystal Mountain.

🏛 Oasis Heritage Museum
1 km (0.6 mile) N of Bawiti. ⬜ *daily.*

**⌂ Temple of Alexander
the Great**
6 km (4 miles) SW of Bawiti.
⬜ *ask at Tourist Office.* 🖼

⌂ Temple of Ain al-Muftela
5 km (3 miles) W of Bawiti.
⬜ *ask at Tourist Office.* 🖼

GOLDEN MUMMIES

In 1996, more than 100
Graeco-Roman mummies
were unearthed near
Bahariyya, about 3 km
(2 miles) south of the
Temple of Alexander the
Great. The discovery was
made, in the traditional
manner, after a donkey
caught its foot in a hole.
Lavishly gilded and
beautifully decorated,
the mummies are ex-
tremely well preserved.
So far, archaeologists
have unearthed over
100 mummies from the
so-called Valley of the
Mummies but it is said
there may be up to
10,000 mummies buried
in what is the largest
single necropolis in Egypt.
The mummies have not
yet been removed and at
the moment cannot be
visited by the public.

Clay figures in the Oasis Heritage Museum, Bahariyya Oasis

A typical blue-painted mudbrick dwelling in Siwa Oasis

Siwa Oasis ⑤

550 km (341 miles) W of Cairo, 305 km (189 miles) SW of Marsa Matruh. 🏘 30,000. ℹ *Opposite Arous al-Waha, road to Marsa Matruh (046) 460 2883.* 📧

Siwa Oasis seems to spring out of nowhere, its lush, green orchards glistening like a mirage in the surrounding barren and inhospitable desert. More than 300 fresh-water springs and streams sustain this remote desert oasis, feeding 300,000 date palms and 70,000 olive trees. Huge saltwater lakes add to the spectacular scenery. Isolated on the edge of the Great Sand Sea, Siwa remained unchanged and largely unvisited for centuries. Roads now link Siwa to Marsa Matruh on the Mediterranean coast and to Bahariyya Oasis in the southeast, bringing an influx of tourists to the area.

The ruins of the ancient mudbrick town of **Shali** tower above modern Siwa's main square. Built in 1203 to house the 40 survivors of a tribal attack on the nearby settlement of Aghurmi, this walled, hilltop town protected the entire Siwan population for centuries. Though the houses were abandoned in 1926 after heavy rain, the steep maze of streets can still be explored.

Close to Siwa's town centre, the **House of Siwa Museum** displays a collection of typical Siwan clothing, jewellery and handicrafts. The museum was the brainchild of a Canadian ambassador who feared the threat posed by tourism to Siwa's traditional way of life.

A short distance north of the town, the limestone **Mountain of the Dead**, or Jebel al-Mawta, is riddled with tombs from the 26th Dynasty and Ptolemaic era. When fighting spread to Siwa during World War II, the Siwans sheltered in the tombs from bombing attacks. The 3rd-century BC **Tomb of Si-Amun** contains scenes depicting the deceased – a Siwan of Greek origins – with his family and the gods.

Detail from the Tomb of Si-Amun on the Mountain of the Dead, Siwa

About 3 km (2 miles) east of Siwa, the **Temple of the Oracle**, built between 663 and 525 BC, stands on a rock that was once at the heart of the ancient settlement of Aghurmi. The Oracle's fame was widespread and Alexander the Great came here to consult it in 332 BC after liberating Egypt from Persian rule. Though the temple currently lies largely in ruins, the steep climb to the top is worthwhile for the stunning views it affords over the palm trees and lakes below.

Further east, all that remains of the huge 30th-Dynasty **Temple of Amun** is a wall decorated with bas-reliefs and a large pile of rubble. The temple was probably built by Nectanebo II during the 4th century BC. A short distance away is **Cleopatra's Pool**. Despite the name, Cleopatra never bathed here, but many people do venture into the circular pool for a swim, undeterred by algae floating on the surface of the water and onlookers watching from the busy path.

A better place for swimming can be found on **Fatnis Island** (also known as Fantasy Island), on the salt lake Birket Siwa, 6 km (4 miles) west of the town. A narrow causeway leads to the island, which is covered in lush palm trees and has an idyllic, secluded, freshwater pool in the centre. The island can be reached by bike or donkey cart from Siwa.

🏛 **House of Siwa Museum**
Siwa. ⭕ *Sat–Thu.* 📷
⛩ **Tomb of Si-Amun**
1 km (0.6 mile) N of Siwa. ⭕ *daily.*

SIWAN CULTURE

Far removed from the rest of Egypt, Siwans have their own distinct culture and way of life, although these are increasingly threatened by tourism. Siwi, a Berber language, is spoken alongside Arabic, and Siwan women, who are rarely seen in public, dress in costumes decorated with coins. The oasis is renowned for its silver jewellery and handwoven baskets. Siwans are very conservative and visitors should dress modestly.

Traditional handwoven Siwan basket

◁ **Mural on a Siwan house encouraging pilgrims to make the journey to Mecca**

Oasis in the Egyptian Deserts

A welcome sight for tired and weary travellers, oases have sufficient water to allow permanent plant growth and human settlement. The major depressions beneath Egypt's Western Desert give rise to a chain of oases west of the Nile, for here the water table is near the earth's surface. The oasis of Siwa, for example, lies 18 m (59 ft) below sea level. Oases vary considerably in size and can be anything from just a few palms around a spring to large expanses of water capable of sustaining cities. As well as supporting human population, they also offer ideal conditions for many species of wildlife, such as the striped hyena, the Egyptian mongoose and the little green bee-eater. However, the combination of a growing population and increasingly intensive farming is threatening the water supply. The oasis of Fayoum (*see p168*) now has to channel water from the Nile to supplement its inadequate natural resources.

Little green bee-eater

Saltwater lakes *are formed over thousands of years by evaporation. As the water evaporates dissolved minerals are left behind and the salinity of the lake slowly increases.*

Human settlements *have developed around many oases. These isolated, self-sufficient communities are typically surrounded by green patches of cultivation and separated from each other by areas of dry desert.*

Agriculture *thrives on the fertile land of the oases. Rice, wheat, olives, dates, figs, mangoes and apricots are some of the crops grown.*

Date palms *have always been a multi-purpose crop, providing food, timber and leaves for thatching.*

THE FORMATION OF OASES

Rain falling a long way from the oasis seeps into porous rocks, known as aquifers, through which it slowly flows. This water emerges at an oasis, either where the water table is at or near the surface, or where pressure created by the flow of water in the aquifer forces it up through a fault in the rock.

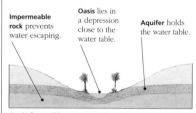

Impermeable rock prevents water escaping.

Oasis lies in a depression close to the water table.

Aquifer holds the water table.

Oasis formed by a natural depression

Fault allows water to escape upwards.

Oasis

Water flows down the porous aquifer, creating pressure.

Oasis resulting from a fault in the rock layers

TRAVELLERS' NEEDS

WHERE TO STAY

In colloquial Egyptian, the word for hotel *(funduq)* derives from a verb meaning "to leave wide open" – as in leaving a door ajar – and this phrase reflects the traditional Egyptian sense of hospitality. Visitors will find "open doors" throughout the country, with hotels offering accommodation at a wide range of prices and an even wider range of quality. At the top end are grand old colonial hotels, along with a growing array of modern, four- and five-star high-rises and resort complexes. Even at such expensive places,

Doorman at Old Cataract Hotel, Aswan

Egyptian hospitality doesn't always translate into good service, but hotel managers and tourism officials are beginning to realize that employees need training to keep guests happy. At the other end of the scale, cheap doesn't have to mean squalid: you can still find simple but clean accommodation in some of the country's most picturesque settings. However, always look closely at what you are getting before handing over your money: demanding customers are more likely to end up as satisfied customers.

WHERE TO LOOK

Tourism has long been a major industry in Egypt and, as a result, you will find hotels just about everywhere. In Cairo, the luxury hotels are clustered in three main areas, catering to the different purposes and needs of visitors to the city. Several are situated to the northeast of the city, around the airport and the suburb of Heliopolis, making them convenient for air travel but rather far away from the city's major tourist attractions. Then there are the downtown luxury hotels, which are found mainly along the banks of the Nile. These

offer great views and are a more convenient base for getting around the city sights, but they leave the traveller right in the thick of downtown Cairo, which can be a daunting prospect. Finally, there are hotels around the pyramids in Giza. For many visitors, staying right next to what they consider to be Egypt's biggest tourist attraction may outweigh the disadvantage of being further away from other sights in central and Islamic Cairo, such as the Egyptian Museum and Khan al-Khalili. Alternatively, you can find smaller and cheaper hotels throughout the city. Many low-budget, back-packer hotels are located in the downtown area near Midan Talaat Harb and Midan Opera, with some truly disreputable premises around the Ramses train station. The leafy island of Zamalek has a few pleasant mid-range hotels and, though the area has few sights of its own, it is handy for the rest of the city.

The same general pattern can be found in most towns in Egypt, with large five-star hotels in the town centre, low-budget places clustered around

Marble-floored foyer of the Old Winter Palace, Luxor

the train station, and mid-range options scattered throughout. Except for the most important tourist destinations, most towns in Upper Egypt and the Delta do not have a five-star hotel.

HOTEL TOUTS

The newly arrived traveller in Cairo may fall prey to hotel touts who attach themselves to the unwary, using every trick in the book to get them to the hotel for which they are hustling. Some taxi-drivers are part of the scam, earning a commission from the hotels to which they take their fares. To avoid being taken in by these tricksters, be alert to their strategies and be very firm about your plans. If possible, book a room in advance and don't be diverted from going there, whatever claims are made. If a taxi-driver says he hasn't heard of your hotel, don't get in his cab. Never let anyone go into the hotel with you.

The Sheraton Hotel on Gezira island, Cairo

◁ Restaurant in Sofitel Old Cataract Hotel, Aswan

BOOKING A ROOM

Higher-category hotels follow standard international procedures for reservations, with customers often being asked to give their credit card number as confirmation of a booking. Hotels lower down the scale may do the same, but with slightly less reliable results. The more popular inexpensive hotels usually operate on a first-come, first-served basis and do not accept reservations.

HOTEL GRADING AND FACILITIES

Egyptian hotels are graded on a star-rating system with up to five stars, which are allocated by the government. Large, internationally run chain hotels generally get into the four- and five-star class, while locally owned premises fill out the middle and lower ranges.

Hotel gradings can appear a little arbitrary at times and, in many cases, seem to owe more to influence than to actual quality and service. Sometimes the only tangible difference between two stars and no stars is price – and five-star hotels are certainly not all equal in the facilities or service offered. A five-star hotel will, however, always include several restaurants, a bar, and some form of night-club or disco. There will also always be a swimming pool and health-club facilities. Five-star hotels at resorts are likely to include facilities such as riding stables, diving centres, tennis courts and similar amenities.

Siwa Safari Paradise Hotel, set in palm groves near the Temple of Amun

A four-star hotel will usually have a coffee shop, restaurant, a bar of sorts, and usually a smaller swimming pool that is good enough for a cooling-off dip.

Hotels at the lower end also usually have some kind of eating establishment, but alcohol will rarely be served in such premises. It is rare to find telephones in the rooms of smaller establishments, but most will have a telephone at the front desk and a fax machine that guests may use.

HIDDEN EXTRAS

Apart from some of the Red Sea resorts, where guests pay a single price to enjoy all the amenities, normal practice is to pay for extras as you use them. Up to 20 per cent tax may be added to your hotel bill, along with charges for phone calls and other services. In smaller, two- and three-star hotels, check exactly what is included in the price: you may find that you are charged extra for breakfast and for having a fridge and TV in your room.

Tipping (baksheesh) is a way of life in Egypt: many hotel workers survive on the tips they get for carrying out minor tasks for guests, such as carrying bags or flagging taxis.

DISCOUNTS

Discounts on hotel rooms are rarely offered and are available only through travel companies. In low season (July–September) in Upper Egypt, however, it may be possible to bargain down room prices, especially in hotels in the lower price categories. Egyptians and foreigners with residence permits, however, qualify for vastly cheaper rates.

CHAIN HOTELS

The familiar international chain hotel names can all be found in Egypt: Hilton and Sheraton are predominant, but Marriott, Sofitel, Meridien, Mövenpick, Swissôtel and Four Seasons are also all present. The big chain hotels are the most luxurious and the most expensive in the market and they generally offer a dependable level of service, despite the occasional variation from international standards.

There is no established chain of cheap or budget hotels in Egypt: the vast number of mid-level and inexpensive hotels in the country are usually family-owned and independently run.

The spectacular entrance hall of a luxury hotel in Alexandria

The Nile Hilton Hotel, Cairo, built in the 1950s on the site of the Qasr el-Nil (Palace of the Nile) *(see p72)*

SMALLER HOTELS

One of Egypt's drawbacks for the independent traveller is that it does not have a strongly developed system of mid-range hotels. With most tourism in Egypt being of the five-star or the budget backpacker variety, there is a great deal of choice at either end of the scale but little in the middle.

Every major destination in Egypt has a wide selection of small, cheap hotels catering for the young traveller. For those willing to forsake private bathrooms and air conditioning, the price can be amazingly low. Many small hotels offer a variety of rooms, including those with or without bathrooms and air conditioning. Some have the option of more than one bed in the room. In Cairo and Alexandria, most small hotels are located on the upper floors of old apartment buildings, which can provide an intimate setting that is full of character. At most places, the price includes a simple continental breakfast.

Two- and three-star hotels, when they can be found, are more likely to take up a whole building. Such establishments often include a coffee-shop and a small restaurant, and their rooms always have bathrooms and air conditioning; they may even have a small swimming pool. Quality varies widely and, while some mid-range hotels are excellent and quite charming, others are not even remotely worth the price. When negotiating for a room in a two- or three-star hotel, check the room to see whether facilities such as hot water and clean bed linen are provided, and confirm with the proprietor whether breakfast is included in the price.

BUSINESS TRAVELLERS

Cairo is rapidly turning into a major business centre and its hotels are adapting to the new market. New, ultra-luxury, five-star hotels are springing up with the

Hotel Metropole, Alexandria

requirements of the travelling business executive in mind, distinguishing themselves by the extra services and facilities that such clients expect. Well-trained concierges and an efficient, well-equipped 24-hour business service are becoming standard in Cairo's new hotels, such as the Four Seasons at the First Residence, on the west bank of the Nile, and the Conrad, on the Nile Corniche. These have rooms furnished with computers, fax, voice mail, and internet connections. Well-equipped meeting rooms and conference facilities are available, as are chauffeur-driven limousines to ferry guests to and from Cairo's international airport.

DISABLED TRAVELLERS

Egypt is not the easiest destination for the disabled visitor. With many cheaper hotels located on the fairly inaccessible upper storeys of tall buildings, wheelchair-bound travellers are usually restricted to the modern five-star hotels. Even many of those still have stairs instead of ramps at vital places, though that is starting to change. What Egypt does have in its favour, however, is friendly people for whom disability carries no stigma and who will be more than ready to assist travellers with extra needs with a minimum of fuss.

CHILDREN

Egyptians love children and consider them a blessing, so bringing them should not present any particular problems. This is not to say that Egyptian hotels make any special provisions in terms of extra activities – the exception being some of the luxury resort hotels, which organize daily programmes for children. Even if you are not staying at a four- or five-star hotel, either in Cairo or at a resort, most of the bigger hotels have swimming pools that they allow non residents to use, often without charge for children, and this can provide an excellent way of soothing frazzled youngsters when the heat and bustle get too much

BUDGET OPTIONS

Egypt can be a paradise for travellers on low budgets, as witnessed by the generations of young backpackers who visit the country, whether seeking Pharaonic ruins, exotic culture, or a bit of sun and surf in the Sinai peninsula.

No matter where you are in Egypt, there will always be hotels offering fairly

The luxury As-Salamlek Hotel in Montazah Palace grounds, Alexandria

decent accommodation at fairly low prices. Youth hostels exist, but comparing their poor quality with the other available options, they are best avoided. why settle for a three-tier bunk bed when a clean room can be found closer to the city centre for only a few pounds more?

In any case, most of Egypt's cheaper hotels, which are not by any means frequented only by young backpackers, offer the camaraderie familiar in youth hostels worldwide.

Camping in Egypt is a little more problematic and is not particularly recommended in most towns. There is a kind of camping

YHA sign at youth hostel in Aswan

area by the Giza pyramids in Cairo and sites can be found in Luxor and some of the other southern cities, but the facilities are rudimentary at best.

Rather better opportunities exist for camping elsewhere in the country, however. There are some beautiful places in the Sinai, including the Ras Mohammed National Park (see p226), near Sharm el-Sheikh, and a night under the stars in the Western Desert is an experience not to be missed.

Safaris, consisting of a guide with a large four-wheel-drive, can be organized out of any of the oasis towns. It should be borne in mind that camping in the Western Desert is mainly a winter activity, and that the nights can be cold. Desert camping is not recommended during high summer and, in fact, few guides will be interested in venturing out during that time. Wherever you camp, follow commonsense rules and keep all your valuables with you, in your tent. Even in well-patrolled national parks, thefts are not unknown.

DIRECTORY

HOTELS OFFERING CENTRAL BOOKING

Hilton Hotels
Tel 0800 856 8000 (UK).
Tel 1-800 445 8667 (US).
www.hilton.com

Inter-Continental Hotels
Tel (020) 8847 2277 (UK).
Tel 1-888 567 8725 (US).
www.interconti.com

Marriott Hotels
Tel 0800 221222 (UK).
Tel 1-888 236 2427 (US).
www.marriott.com

Le Meridien Hotels
Tel 08000 282840.
www.lemeridien-hotels.com

Sheraton Hotels
Tel 353 21 427 9200 (Europe).
Tel 1-888 625 5144 (US).
www.sheraton.com

FINDING A HOTEL

Database of Egyptian Hotels
www.egypthotelsdb.com

Egyptian Tourist Authority (EGAPT)
170 Piccadilly,
London W1V 9DD.
Tel (020) 7493 5283.
www.touregypt.net

MISR Travel
(State-run tourist company)
1 Sharia Talaat Harb, Cairo.
Tel (02) 393 0010.

Tourist Office
Midan Saad Zaghloul,
Alexandria.
Tel (03) 485 1556.
◻ 8am–6pm daily (9am–4pm during Ramadan).

Tourist Office
5 Sharia Adly, Cairo.
Tel (02) 391 3454.
◻ 8:30am–8pm daily (9am–4pm during Ramadan).

ADVICE FOR DISABLED TRAVELLERS

Disability Action Group
Portside Business Park
189 Airport Rd West,
Belfast BT3 9ED.
Tel (028) 9029 7880.

Royal Association for Disability and Rehabilitation
12 City Forum,
250 City Road,
London EC1V 8AF.
Tel (020) 7250 3222.

YOUTH HOSTELS

Egyptian Youth Hostel Association
1 Sharia al-Ibrahimy,
Garden City, Cairo.
Tel (02) 794 0527.

England & Wales Youth Hostels Association
Trevelyan House,
8 St Stephen's Hill,
St Albans, Herts
AL1 2DY.
Tel 0870 870 8808.

Choosing a Hotel

The hotels in this guide have been selected across a wide range of price categories for the excellence of their facilities, location or character. This chart first lists hotels in Cairo, followed by a selection of places to stay in the rest of Egypt. For a listing of recommended restaurants, see pages 290–301.

PRICE CATEGORIES (IN EGYPTIAN POUNDS – EGP)
For a standard double room per night, with breakfast, tax and service charge included.

£ Under 150 EGP
££ 150–250 EGP
£££ 250–550 EGP
££££ 550–1,000 EGP
£££££ Over 1,000 EGP

CAIRO

CAIRO Ismailia Hotel   £
Midan Tahrir, Downtown, Cairo **Tel** *02 7963 122* **Rooms** *27*   **Map** *1 C5, 5 B4*

The Ismailia Hotel is cheap and cheerful, but despite having few amenities, it remains one of the most popular of the hostel-type accommodation in the area. Its location is good for local attractions, shops and restaurants, and there are great views out over the Midan Tahrir. Rooms are simple and bathrooms scarce. **ismahouse@hotmail.com**

CAIRO Mayfair Hotel   £
Sharia Aziz Osman, Zamalek, Cairo **Tel** *02 7357 315 or 02 7359 594* **Fax** *02 7350 424* **Rooms** *45*   **Map** *1 A3*

If luxurious surroundings are a must, then the Mayfair Hotel will probably not fit the bill, but this establishment is clean and attractive. It is also located in one of the upmarket areas of Cairo, at Zamalek, within easy reach of local places of interest. A bustling marketplace is close by. The hotel is popular with backpackers. **www.mayfaircairo.com**

CAIRO Pension Roma   £
169 Sharia Mohammed Farid, Downtown, Cairo **Tel** *02 3911 088* **Fax** *02 5796 243* **Rooms** *32* **Map** *2 D4, 6 D2*

Booking in advance is usually the best policy if you wish to stay at Pension Roma. It is cheap and basic, but it has earned a reputation for being clean and safe. The atmosphere is great – with antique furniture and traditional decor, it is rather like being on an Arabic movie set. Its location is central, too.

CAIRO Bedouin Valley Red Sea   ££
Sharia El Gehad, Cairo **Tel** *02 6352 406* **Fax** *02 6326 665* **Rooms** *20*   **Map** *1 C5, 5 C3*

If watersports such as diving and snorkelling are a passion, combined with the chance to explore Cairo and the desert, then a stay at the Bedouin Valley Red Sea should meet all requirements. Situated right on the beach, it overlooks a reef. Its rooms are fully furnished, and have telephones and private bathrooms.

CAIRO Berlin Hotel   ££
Sharia el-Shawarby, Cairo **Tel** *02 3957 502* **Fax** *02 3957 502* **Rooms** *7*   **Map** *1 C5, 5 C3*

The Berlin Hotel is housed in an unassuming building in one of Cairo's busy thoroughfares, but step inside and the reception area and rooms are presented in a traditional manner and are full of character. The host is generally helpful and will assist with organizing excursions to the Pyramids. **berlinehotelcairo@hotmail.com**

CAIRO Carlton Hotel   ££
Sharia 26th July, Cairo **Tel** *02 5755 022* **Fax** *02 5755 323* **Rooms** *62*   **Map** *1 C4, 5 C2*

The Carlton Hotel is housed in a building constructed in 1935, and although renovated to a high, modern standard that includes air conditioning, it retains many of its original architectural features, which add to its charm. The rooms are attractive, while its restaurant and rooftop bar are full of atmosphere. **www.carltonhotelcairo.com**

CAIRO Fontana Hotel   ££
Midan Ramses, Cairo **Tel** *02 5922 321 or 02 5884 058* **Fax** *02 5922 145* **Rooms** *87*   **Map** *2 D3*

A relatively compact hotel with a huge personality, the Fontana boasts some of the best views imaginable of the frenetic bustle of the Midan Ramses. Just people-watching is a great way to spend some time. This air-conditioned hotel offers pleasingly presented rooms, along with a small rooftop pool and a disco.

CAIRO Horus House Hotel   ££
21 Sharia Ismail Mohammed, Zamalek, Cairo **Tel** *02 7353 634* **Fax** *02 7353 182* **Rooms** *35*   **Map** *1 A3*

The Horus House Hotel is a warm, welcoming little place, full of guests who come back time and again. It may not have many facilities (just a bar and a small restaurant), but everywhere is clean and well presented, especially the rooms. It is located in a smarter area of Cairo, close to many tourist attractions. **www.horushousehotel.4t.com**

CAIRO Lotus Hotel   ££
Sharia Talaat Harb, Cairo **Tel** *02 5915 810* **Fax** *02 5921 621* **Rooms** *50*   **Map** *1 C5, 5 B3*

With an authentic Art Deco interior decor inspired by a local architect's dream of creating a "Paris by the Nile" in the 1900s, the Lotus is a pleasing base in one of Cairo's main downtown thoroughfares. It is popular with both business and leisure travellers, and staying here is like taking a step back in time. **www.lotushotel.com**

Key to Symbols *see back cover flap*

CAIRO New Star Hotel

Sharia Yehia Ibrahim, Zamalek, Cairo **Tel** *02 7351 865* **Fax** *02 7351 321* **Rooms** *28*

Map *1 A3*

A pleasant little hotel that, despite being close to a major intersection of two busy roads, offers a surprisingly quiet and relaxing stay. As well as a cosy restaurant, the hotel boasts an enviable location for the city and the Nile – indeed, most of the large, air-conditioned rooms have panoramic views of one or the other.

CAIRO Windsor House

19 Sharia Alfi Bei, Cairo **Tel** *02 5915 810* **Fax** *02 5921 621* **Rooms** *55*

Map *2 D4, 6 D2*

Built around 1900 as the baths for the Egyptian royal family and used as a British officers' club, Windsor House is one of Cairo's landmark buildings. It retains its colonial atmosphere to this day and has appeared in numerous films. The pleasing rooms are presented in a traditional Egyptian style. **www.windsorcairo.com**

CAIRO Al-Hussein Hotel

Midan Hussein, Hussein, Cairo **Tel** *02 5891 093* **Fax** *02 5918 479* **Rooms** *56*

Map *2 F5*

Located in the Islamic area of Cairo, close to the bustling Khan al-Khalili, this hotel offers good, comfortable accommodation. Not all the rooms have air conditioning or private bathrooms, so it's best to state any specific requirements in advance. Views of the fascinating medieval part of Cairo can be enjoyed from various vantage points.

CAIRO Atlas Zamalek Hotel

20 Gamiat ad-Dowal al-Arabiyya, Cairo **Tel** *02 3466 559* **Fax** *02 3476 958* **Rooms** *75*

Map *1 A2*

A traditional hotel built to a high-rise design, the Atlas Zamalek is well located for getting into the city centre with ease – it is situated right on one of central Cairo's main thoroughfares, at Mohandiseen. Rooms are nicely presented, and the hotel also boasts a characterful restaurant, a pool and a fitness suite.

CAIRO Cairo Airport Hotel

Cairo International Airport **Tel** *02 2267 4568* **Fax** *02 2244 3957* **Rooms** *50*

As its name suggests, the Cairo Airport Hotel is a practical but comfortable stopping-off point for travellers to and from the city. It is, literally, within walking distance of Terminal 1. Registration and checking out procedures are quick, and the rooms have every amenity to help weary guests to unwind, including air conditioning.

CAIRO Cairo Khan Hotel

19 Sharia 26th July, Cairo **Tel** *02 3922 015* **Fax** *02 3906 799* **Rooms** *186*

Map *1 C4, 5 C2*

With its attractive decor, comfortable rooms and a location that could beat all others, the Cairo Khan is one of the most popular mid-priced hotels in Cairo. Close by is a wide range of shopping malls, tourist sites and entertainment venues. Fully air conditioned, the hotel attracts businesspeople as well as tourists. **www.cairokhan.com**

CAIRO Caroline Crillon

49 Sharia Syria, Mohandiseen, Cairo **Tel** *02 3465 101* **Rooms** *35*

Map *2 D4, 6 D2*

A welcoming hotel, the Caroline Crillon is so centrally located for Cairo's tourist attractions, shops and restaurants that you need never venture too far away. This air-conditioned hotel prides itself on providing good Egyptian hospitality and food, not to mention comfortable rooms with a range of high-quality amenities.

CAIRO Cosmopolitan Hotel

Sharia Ibn Tahlab, Cairo **Tel** *02 3923 956* **Fax** *02 3933 531* **Rooms** *84*

Map *1 C3, 5 C3*

A stay at the downtown Cosmopolitan Hotel is sure to enrich your visit to Cairo. It oozes Old World colonial charm and is full of character. Dotted throughout the communal areas are dark lacquered pieces of antique furniture. The rooms are equally charming, and some even have original bathroom fittings.

CAIRO Flamenco Hotel

2 Sharia Gezirat al-Wosta, Zamalek, Cairo **Tel** *02 7350 815* **Fax** *02 7350 819* **Rooms** *162*

Map *1 A2*

This traditionally styled mid-range hotel is popular with businesspeople and tourists alike, thanks to its homely, welcoming feel, despite being quite large in size. Part of the Golden Tulip chain of hotels, the Flamenco sits alongside the Nile and is within walking distance of the city's major attractions. **www.flamencohotels.com**

CAIRO Hotel Beirut

56 Sharia Beirut, Cairo **Tel** *02 4152 347* **Fax** *02 4159 422* **Rooms** *90*

Map *1 A2*

A modern mid-priced hotel located in an upmarket neighbourhood outside the city centre. With air conditioning throughout, well-presented rooms with private bathroom facilities and television, and restaurants offering a mix of international and Egyptian cuisine, the hotel offers excellent value for money.

CAIRO Odeon Palace Hotel

Abdel Hamid Said, Cairo **Tel** *02 5767 971* **Fax** *02 5767 971* **Rooms** *30*

Map *1 C4, 5 C2*

Probably best known for its 24-hour rooftop bar, where guests and locals alike may relax, the Odeon Palace is something of a well-kept secret. It is located in a landmark building in a quiet side street in downtown Cairo and could be easily missed. Its rooms are of a mid-range standard, and its restaurant serves Egyptian fare.

CAIRO The President Hotel

Sharia Taha Hussein, Zamalek, Cairo **Tel** *02 7350 652* **Fax** *02 7361 752* **Rooms** *117*

Map *1 A2*

The President Hotel is one of those establishments that won't fail in its bid to offer a comfortable, pleasant and convenient place to stay. For this reason, it is one of the most popular hotels for businesspeople and visitors in this upmarket area of Cairo, even though it occupies an unassuming high-rise building.

CAIRO Victoria Hotel
🖼️⑪🈁⓪ €€€
Al-Gomhuriyya, Cairo **Tel** *02 5892 290* **Fax** *02 5913 008* **Rooms** *90* **Map** *2 D5, 6 D1*

Oozing colonial charm, this hotel built in the early 1900s is within walking distance of many of Cairo's major tourist attractions. It has its own private gardens, along with restaurants and a coffee shop, while its rooms are nicely presented and have amenities such as satellite television and air conditioning.

CAIRO Cairo Marriott Hotel
🖼️⑪🈔🈂️🈁⓪🈯 €€€€
Zamalek, Cairo **Tel** *02 7394 632* **Fax** *02 7356 667* **Rooms** *1,124* **Map** *1 B3*

Renowned for its lavish Oriental-inspired decor and architecture, this 19th-century hotel was originally built for the opening of the Suez Canal in 1869. It is as popular today as it was then, when visitors first began arriving in Cairo. Facilities include gardens and terraces, as well as spacious rooms full of refinement. **www.cairomarriott.com**

CAIRO Concorde El Salam Hotel
🖼️⑪🈔🈂️🈁⓪🈯 €€€€
65 Sharia Abdel Hamid Badawi, Cairo **Tel** *02 2974 000* **Fax** *02 2976 037* **Rooms** *256* **Map** *1 C4, 5 C2*

A centrally located hotel close to downtown Cairo and the airport, the Concorde El Salam is popular with businesspeople as well as leisure travellers. It has four fine restaurants serving Indian, Chinese, Italian and Oriental cuisine, along with many amenities. The attractive rooms are of a high standard.

CAIRO Hilton Cairo Nile
🖼️⑪🈔🈂️🈁⓪🈯 €€€€
Midan Tahrir, Cairo **Tel** *02 5780 444* **Fax** *02 5780 475* **Rooms** *431* **Map** *1 B5, 5 B3*

One of the first of the large purpose-designed tourist hotels in the Egyptian capital, the Hilton Cairo Nile is set right on the edge of the river. It is close to almost all that the city has to offer in terms of attractions, with the Egyptian Museum literally on the doorstep. Rooms are well presented, and amenities include a rooftop piano bar.

CAIRO Sheraton al-Gezira
🖼️⑪🈔🈂️🈁⓪🈯 €€€€
El Orman, Giza, Cairo **Tel** *02 3411 333* **Fax** *02 3405 056* **Rooms** *436* **Map** *3 A1*

Every room at the 27-storey round Sheraton al-Gezira enjoys a stunning view of the city's landmarks, not to mention top-class facilities such as satellite television and high-speed Internet connections. Restaurants offer multicultural fare. The hotel, which stands on the southern tip of Gezira on the banks of the Nile, is close to Cairo's main attractions.

CAIRO CairoTel Hotel
🖼️⑪🈔🈁⓪🈯 €€€€€
Maadi, Cairo **Tel** *& Fax 02 3506 787* **Rooms** *162*

A modern hotel with a lavish feel, the CairoTel offers rooms with many facilities, including private bathrooms and televisions. The hotel is located within an easy walk of the Nile riverside, and a short drive into downtown Cairo – a combination that makes it popular with both businesspeople and leisure travellers.

CAIRO Conrad International Hotel
🖼️⑪🈔🈂️🈁⓪🈯 €€€€€
1191 Corniche el-Nil, Cairo **Tel** *02 5808 000* **Fax** *02 5808 080* **Rooms** *617* **Map** *3 B5, 1 B5, 5 A5*

Egypt is awash with luxury five-star hotels, and this is certainly among the best. The reception area is designed to capture the essence of Cairo, while the rooms are presented with lavish soft furnishings and every amenity. Most have views of the Nile. The hotel is in a prime spot for quality shops and eateries. **www.conradhotels.com**

CAIRO Europa Hotel
🖼️⑪🈔🈂️🈁⓪🈯 €€€€€
300 Sharia Pyramids, Cairo **Tel** *02 5815 940* **Rooms** *250*

A stay at the Europa Hotel will be memorable for the fact that this beautifully presented establishment stands, literally, a few minutes' walking distance from downtown Cairo. Leisure facilities include a pool and sauna complex, while on-site restaurants serve international cuisine. Rooms are luxuriously appointed.

CAIRO Four Seasons Hotel
🖼️⑪🈔🈂️🈁⓪🈯 €€€€€
35 Sharia al-Giza, Cairo **Tel** *02 5731 212* **Fax** *02 5681 616* **Rooms** *269* **Map** *3 A3*

Located on Cairo's West Bank, at the heart of a prestigious residential and shopping complex, the Four Seasons offers a panoramic view of the Nile and a supremely convenient location. Each room or suite is lavish and comes complete with amenities one would expect from such a luxurious hotel. **www.fourseasons.com**

CAIRO Grand Hyatt Cairo
🖼️⑪🈔🈂️🈁⓪🈯 €€€€€
Midan Tahrir, Cairo **Tel** *02 5780 666* **Fax** *02 5780 475* **Rooms** *714* **Map** *3 B1, 5 A5*

One of the largest of the purpose-designed hotels in Cairo, the Grand Hyatt is located on the northernmost tip of Rhoda Island. It is far enough out to be relaxing, and yet the city centre is within easy reach. Rooms and facilities are as one would expect of a five-star hotel, and the Nile views are breathtaking. **www.cairo.grand.hyatt.com**

CAIRO Hilton Cairo World Trade Centre
🖼️⑪🈔🈂️🈁⓪🈯 €€€€€
1191 Corniche el-Nil, Cairo **Tel** *02 2580 2000* **Fax** *02 2579 0577* **Rooms** *225* **Map** *1 B3*

Part of the World Trade Centre complex on the banks of the Nile, this all-suites hotel attracts both businesspeople and discerning travellers. Its restaurants serve top-quality Mediterranean cuisine, while its rooms have every luxury expected of a top-end hotel, including Internet connection. **www.hilton.com**

CAIRO Hilton Hotel Ramses
🖼️⑪🈔🈂️🈁⓪🈯 €€€€€
1115 Corniche el-Nil, Maspiro, Cairo **Tel** *02 5744 400* **Fax** *02 5757 152* **Rooms** *800* **Map** *1 B3*

A landmark building renowned for the outstanding views of the Nile and the Pyramids from its 36th-floor rooftop restaurant, the Hilton Hotel Ramses is popular with both business and leisure travellers. Rooms exemplify top-end luxury, while the hotel features many leisure facilities, including a spa.

Key to Price Guide *see p268* **Key to Symbols** *see back cover flap*

CAIRO Pyramisa Hotel

60 Sharia Giza, Cairo **Tel** *02 3367 000* **Fax** *02 3605 347* **Rooms** *150*   **Map** *3 A3*

This luxurious hotel is set in the heart of Cairo and overlooks the Nile. It is situated a few minutes' walk from the Cairo Opera House and the Egyptian Museum. Rooms are equipped with a wide range of amenities, such as satellite television and air conditioning, while the hotel offers fine restaurants, a spa, pools and sports facilities.

CAIRO Semiramis Intercontinental

Corniche el-Nil, Garden City, Cairo **Tel** *02 7957 171* **Fax** *02 7963 020* **Rooms** *730*   **Map** *1 B5, 5 A4*

If money is no object, then a stay at the Semiramis Intercontinental will make a trip to Cairo an even more memorable experience. Most of this hotel's rooms, including its collection of luxury suites, which attract the world's wealthiest, look straight out over the Nile. A seemingly endless list of amenities is on offer. **www.interconti.com**

CAIRO Sheraton Cairo Hotel

11 Midan el-Gala, Cairo **Tel** *02 3369 700* **Fax** *02 3364 601* **Rooms** *660*   **Map** *3 A1*

Offering magnificent views of Cairo city or the Nile, the rooms and suites of this five-star hotel are beautifully presented and equipped with the latest technology and facilities. Situated on the West Bank, the Sheraton Cairo is close to most of the major attractions that the city has to offer, including designer shopping centres. **www.sheraton.com**

CAIRO Sofitel Cairo Maadi Towers

29 Corniche el-Nil, Cairo **Tel** *02 5260 601 or 02 5260 602* **Fax** *02 5261 133* **Rooms** *173*   **Map** *3 B5, 1 B5, 5 A5*

Combining luxury with a characterful decor that aims to capture Egyptian architecture and style, this hotel offers attractive, fully equipped rooms, as well as pools, a fitness centre, a casino and facilities for children. It also prides itself on providing for guests with mobility restrictions. Situated 12 km (7.5 miles) from the city centre. **www.sofitel.com**

CAIRO Sofitel Le Sphinx Hotel

1 Alexandria Road, Giza, Cairo **Tel** *02 3838 444* **Fax** *02 3834 930* **Rooms** *274*

If visiting the Pyramids, you couldn't find a hotel that is more conveniently located than the Sofitel Le Sphinx Hotel. It stands in an outstanding park at the very foot of the Pyramids of Giza and the Sphinx. Nearby, you will find many cultural and tourist attractions, superb shopping outlets and a wealth of recreational facilities. **www.sofitel.com**

GIZA AND HELIOPOLIS Novotel Cairo Airport Hotel

Cairo Airport Post, Heliopolis, Cairo **Tel** *02 2918 520* **Fax** *02 2914 794* **Rooms** *204*

At first glance, this establishment seems above all a practical solution for an overnight stay, but in reality it is a surprisingly comfortable hotel with good amenities that include a sauna, tennis courts and restaurants. As its name suggests, it is close to the airport, and as such it is popular with businesspeople.

GIZA AND HELIOPOLIS Baron Hotel Heliopolis

Sharia Maahad El Saharaa, Heliopolis, Cairo **Tel** *02 2912 468* **Fax** *02 2907 077* **Rooms** *126*

A landmark building, the Baron Hotel is located in the Heliopolis district of Cairo. It overlooks the 19th-century Baron Empain's Palace. The hotel has a range of amenities that include a health suite, a nightclub and its own shopping mall. The rooms are attractively presented, and most boast stunning panoramic views.

GIZA AND HELIOPOLIS Le Meridien Heliopolis

Sharia Al Orouba, Al Horreya, Heliopolis, Cairo **Tel** *02 2905 055* **Fax** *02 2908 533* **Rooms** *283*

Whether relaxing at the bar, around the pool or in any one of its elegant restaurants or simply taking it easy in the privacy of your own room, Le Meridien offers a truly chic atmosphere. It is just ten minutes or so from Cairo's airport, and a little longer from the city centre. **www.lemeridien-heliopolis.com**

GIZA AND HELIOPOLIS Mena House Oberoi

Sharia al-Ahram, Giza, Cairo **Tel** *02 3833 444* **Fax** *02 3837 777* **Rooms** *523*

Situated right on the main road to the Pyramids, and overlooking the stunning ancient structures, Mena House Oberoi is always popular with tourists. Golfers, too, are drawn to play its course. The hotel's rooms are attractively presented, while its reception is reminiscent of the 19th-century hunting lodge it once was. **www.oberoi.com.eg**

GIZA AND HELIOPOLIS Mövenpick Jolieville

Cairo-Alexandria Desert Road, Giza, Cairo **Tel** *02 3852 555* **Fax** *02 3835 006* **Rooms** *240*

Location is one of the keys to the success of this exceptionally comfortable hotel. It is ideally situated for the Pyramids and Sharia 26th July, the main thoroughfare into Cairo city centre, for further sightseeing. The hotel offers beautifully presented rooms with many facilities, as well as a large swimming pool and sports amenities. **www.movenpick.com**

GIZA AND HELIOPOLIS Sheraton Heliopolis

Sharia Uruba, Heliopolis, Cairo **Tel** *02 2677 730* **Fax** *02 2677 600* **Rooms** *588*

This five-star hotel is ideal for a short business trip or weekend break, since it is close to the airport and yet within easy reach of Cairo's major tourist attractions and commercial centres. It features every amenity to make your stay memorable, and its restaurants serve international and Egyptian cuisine. **www.sheraton.com**

GIZA AND HELIOPOLIS Sheraton Royal Gardens

Sharia Helmeiat Al-Ahram, Giza, Cairo **Tel** *02 7813 311* **Fax** *02 7811 441* **Rooms** *358*

With the Pyramids less than ten minutes' drive away and Cairo city centre not much further, the Sheraton Royal Gardens is popular with tourists and businesspeople alike. Offering five-star facilities such as a spa, valet service and restaurants serving fine cuisine, it is a good choice in the high-end bracket. **www.sheraton.com**

AROUND CAIRO

FAYOUM Auberge du Lac Hotel

Lake Qarun, Fayoum **Tel** *084 572 001* **Fax** *084 572 003* **Rooms** *76*

It would be difficult to find a hotel that truly offers the chance to get away from it all better than the Auberge du Lac at the Fayoum Oasis. Surrounded by natural fauna and flora, and perched on the edge of Lake Qarun, it was once the hunting lodge of King Farouk, who is said to have spent glorious days here. **www.aubergedulac-fayoum.com**

THE NILE VALLEY

ABU SIMBEL Kariat Abu Simbel

Abu Simbel **Tel** *097 3400 170* **Fax** *097 3400 770* **Rooms** *26*

Built in 2001 in Nubian style, complete with domes and arches, this small and reasonably priced hotel is hugely popular, especially during the winter months. It has its own gardens, which have been neatly laid out and provide the perfect place to relax. Its terrace has a wonderful view out over Lake Nasser.

ABU SIMBEL Seti Abu Simbel Hotel

Abu Simbel **Tel** *097 3400 720 or 097 3400 722* **Fax** *097 3400 829* **Rooms** *138*

The only hotel located right at the foot of the Grand Temple of Ramses, the Seti Abu Simbel enjoys unsurprisingly splendid views over the sights, as well as across the waters of Lake Nasser. The public areas feature striking Nubian-style domes, and there is a pool with waterfalls and a large garden. Live entertainment is arranged most nights.

ABU SIMBEL Nefertari Hotel

Abu Simbel **Tel** *097 3400 508* **Fax** *097 3400 510* **Rooms** *120*

A sizable establishment that stands in its own gardens, the Nefertari is close to the Temple of Ramses II, a must on any traveller's itinerary to Abu Simbel. Its pool is attractive and offers a great view out over Lake Nasser, while its restaurant and rooms are well presented, if a little on the basic side.

ASWAN Hathor Hotel

Corniche el-Nil, Aswan **Tel** *097 2314 580* **Fax** *097 2303 462* **Rooms** *64*

A slightly older-style hotel that holds a few surprises. On the roof, the area centred around the hotel pool has been attractively decorated with pots and shrubs. The views of the Nile are outstanding from here. Most of the rooms have views of the river, too, although these tend to book up quickly.

ASWAN Keylany Hotel

Sharia Keylany, Aswan **Tel** & **Fax** *097 2317 332* **Rooms** *28*

A small and attractive hotel, the Keylany is beautifully clean. Its owners clearly take great pride in it. Although facilities are few (just a small traditional restaurant), the rooms do have bathrooms and fans, and the price tag is small. The hotel's central location to Aswan's attractions is another bonus.

ASWAN New Abu Simbel Hotel

Sharia Abtal el-Tahir, Aswan **Tel** *097 2306 096* **Rooms** *38*

The New Abu Simbel is an unassuming building from the outside, but step inside, and it is a welcoming establishment, its staff friendly and helpful. Rooms are simply decorated but immaculately clean. Location-wise, the hotel is close to the banks of the Nile and within walking distance of the Nubian Museum.

ASWAN Nubian Hotel

234 Sharia Saad Zaghloud, Aswan **Tel** *097 2312 123* **Fax** *097 2312 124* **Rooms** *32*

The Nubian is a cheaper-end hotel. It offers a limited number of frills but is well located in downtown Aswan, and guests can enjoy the many attractions the city has to offer on the doorstep. Rooms are basic but clean, and some offer views of Aswan. Close by are enough shops and restaurants to suit all tastes.

ASWAN Orabi Hotel

Sharia Kaylany, Aswan **Tel** & **Fax** *097 2317 578* **Rooms** *13*

The Orabi is a budget hotel that makes no promises of being luxurious, but it is characterful and clean, and some rooms have air conditioning. Be aware, however, that bathrooms are communal. Location-wise, the hotel stands just off Sharia Souq, making it a great place to stay for seeing the local tourist attractions.

ASWAN El-Amir Hotel

Off Corniche el-Nil, Aswan **Tel** *097 2314 732* **Fax** *097 2304 411* **Rooms** *36*

The El-Amir is small but pleasingly presented; its rooms have a few basic amenities, but they do boast views out over the awesome cityscape of Aswan. The hotel is located conveniently off the Corniche, making sightseeing an easy option. It has a restaurant serving predominantly Egyptian cuisine but no alcohol.

Key to Price Guide *see p268* **Key to Symbols** *see back cover flap*

ASWAN Happi Hotel

Sharia Abtaal El Tahrir, Aswan **Tel** *097 2314 115* **Fax** *097 2307 572* **Rooms** *66*

A good location just off the Corniche el-Nil makes this hotel a good choice for visiting the city, but it is a budget establishment, so don't expect anything too fancy. Rooms are large, and most have views of the river, which is a big plus. A restaurant is located on the sixth floor, from where the view over Aswan to the Nile is truly amazing.

ASWAN Oscar Hotel

Sharia El Barka, Aswan **Tel** *& Fax 097 2326 066* **Rooms** *42*

Despite being a mid- to low-end hotel, the Oscar is a pleasant little place to stay. Its rooms are nicely presented, and some have air conditioning and private bathroom facilities, while the hotel itself has a brightly coloured restaurant where delicious home-made Egyptian cuisine is served.

ASWAN Phiala Hotel

Corniche el-Nil, Aswan **Tel** *097 2312 089* **Fax** *097 2310 572* **Rooms** *66*

The Phiala Hotel must be one of the best bargains in town. Recently redecorated and pleasingly presented, it is competitively priced and yet stands right in the centre of Aswan, at the Corniche. The hotel offers its guests the chance to relax in its restaurant and bar area, in its pretty garden or in one of its spacious rooms.

ASWAN Queen Nourhan Hotel

Sharia Saad Zaghloul, First of Atlas area, Aswan **Tel** *& Fax 097 2326 069* **Rooms** *36*

Set over four floors, the two-star Queen Nourhan offers clean accommodation at very competitive prices. All rooms are air-conditioned, and most of them boast sweeping views of the River Nile. The hotel also incorporates an excellent coffee shop, featuring mostly typical Egyptian and Arabic drinks.

ASWAN Ramses Hotel

Sharia Abtel al-Tahrir, Aswan **Tel** *097 2304 000* **Fax** *097 2315 701* **Rooms** *112*

The staff at the Ramses are friendly and helpful, and always willing to help guests organize their stay, booking trips and excursions on their behalf. Location-wise, the hotel overlooks the river and is within walking distance of bustling Nile Street. Its facilities are good for a budget hotel and include air-conditioned rooms with private bathrooms.

ASWAN Cleopatra Hotel

Sharia Saad Zaghloul, Aswan **Tel** *097 2324 001* **Fax** *097 2314 002* **Rooms** *130*

The rooms in this seven-storey downtown Aswan hotel are well equipped, with air conditioning, telephone, television and balcony as standard. Some rooms even have larger-than-normal beds. Location-wise, the Cleopatra is ideal for shopping and seeing the sights of Aswan. Among its facilities is a rooftop pool.

ASWAN Hotel New Cataract Aswan

Sharia Abtal el Tahir, Aswan **Tel** *097 2316 001* **Fax** *097 2316 011* **Rooms** *144*

Located on the banks of the Nile, opposite Elephantine Island and just metres from the Nubian Museum, this hotel is ideal for sightseeing enthusiasts. Its rooms are well equipped, with facilities such as air conditioning, television and a balcony or terrace, while the hotel itself sits in attractive landscaped gardens.

ASWAN Sara Hotel

Sharia El Fanadek, Aswan **Tel** *097 2327 234* **Fax** *097 2327 236* **Rooms** *131*

A location right above a cliff top, on the edge of a coral island and opposite Salouya Island, ensures that the views from almost every room of the Sara are breathtaking. The hotel has an international flavour, with restaurants serving cuisine from China, Spain, Italy and Holland. Rooms are equipped to a four-star standard.

ASWAN Amon Tourist Village – Ile d'Amoun Hotel

Sahara City, Amon Island, Aswan **Tel** *097 2480 438* **Fax** *097 2480 440* **Rooms** *50*

A lively tourist complex located on its own island, the Amon Tourist Village is run by Club Med and offers good packages for families and groups. It has its own boats to ferry guests to and from the island, and amenities include a disco and restaurants, along with a choice of pools and bars. Rooms are pleasantly furnished.

ASWAN Basma Swiss Inn

Sharia El Fanadek, Aswan **Tel** *097 2310 901* **Fax** *097 2310 907* **Rooms** *180*

Perched on Aswan's highest hill, the Basma Swiss Inn has one of the most panoramic views imaginable, encompassing both the city and the Nile. Its richly planted gardens revolve around a floodlit pool, while inside, the decor is classic and elegant. Rooms are well equipped, with private bathrooms. **www.basmahotel.com**

ASWAN Isis Hotel

Corniche el-Nil, Aswan **Tel** *097 2315 100* **Fax** *097 2315 500* **Rooms** *55*

One of the best things about staying at the Isis is that you can step outside the front entrance and literally be beside the Nile. The hotel has a great location right on the river, in the centre of Aswan, and is a great base for exploring local sights. Rooms are pleasant, with good private bathrooms and air conditioning.

ASWAN Pyramisa Isis Resort

Isis Island, Aswan **Tel** *097 2317 400* **Fax** *097 2317 405* **Rooms** *258*

The Pyramisa Isis Resort stands in what can only be described as an oasis – an island in the middle of the Nile. Its rooms are beautifully presented, most with a view of the river from a private balcony or terrace. The hotel itself features many amenities and facilities, including a health centre, sporting activities and a disco.

ASWAN Sofitel Old Cataract Hotel   €€€€

Sharia Abdal El Iahrir, Aswan **Tel** *097 2316 000* **Fax** *097 2316 011* **Rooms** *131*

A stay at this establishment will feel like taking a step back in time. Providing a backdrop for Agatha Christie's novel *Death on the Nile*, the hotel was built in the late 19th century and retains much of its historic character, albeit with a modern twist. Luxurious and lavish, it has a gourmet restaurant and a pool. **www.sofitel.com**

ASWAN Aswan Oberoi   €€€€€

Elephantine Island, Aswan **Tel** *097 2314 666* **Fax** *097 2313 538* **Rooms** *244*

Situated on the lush, tropical Elephantine Island, with views down the Nile, the Aswan Oberoi is popular with both businesspeople and leisure travellers. It is instantly recognized by its tall tower. Amenities are luxurious and include a spa and solarium complex. Rooms are well presented, most with views of the Nile. **www.oberoi.com.eg**

ASWAN Elephantine Island Resort Aswan   €€€€€

Aswan **Tel** *097 2303 455* **Fax** *097 2313 538* **Rooms** *244*

Refurbished in spring 2007, this waterfront hotel offers the variety of restaurants and sports amenities, such as tennis courts and pools, one would expect of a five-star establishment. Its air-conditioned rooms and suites have a luxury feel, and many have stunning views of the Nile. **www.moevenpick-hotels.com**

ASYUT YMCA   €

Sharia Salah ad-Din al-Ayyubi, Asyut **Tel** *088 323 218* **Fax** *088 313 118* **Rooms** *30*

When checking into a YMCA establishment, one wouldn't generally expect lots of frills, but this air-conditioned youth-style hotel in the very heart of Asyut is surprisingly comfortable and welcoming. Most of its rooms are carpeted and come complete with a private bathroom and television.

ASYUT Assiutel Hotel   €€

Sharia al-Thawra, Asyut **Tel** *088 312 121* **Fax** *088 312 122* **Rooms** *28*

Located right in the centre of Asyut, on the Corniche, this hotel offers excellent views from most of its rooms. The mid-range Assiutel is also a great base from which to explore the surrounding areas. Its amenities include a swimming pool around which pretty gardens have been created.

LUXOR Amon Al-Gezira Hotel   €

Bayarat Al-Gezira, West Bank, Luxor **Tel** *095 2310 912* **Fax** *095 2311 205* **Rooms** *12*

This small budget hotel may not have many facilities, but it certainly makes up for it in personality. Family-run, it is welcoming and clean, and many of the rooms have private bathrooms. It is situated close to the ferry landing in the centre of the village, in its own luxuriant gardens. A roof terrace is ideal for relaxing between sightseeing trips.

LUXOR El Moustafa Hotel   €

Television Street, Luxor **Tel** *095 2374 721* **Rooms** *20*

A traditionally styled hotel over several floors, the single-star El Moustafa offers pleasant rooms at competitive prices. Most have air conditioning and private bathrooms, and afford views over the streets of Luxor. The hotel is located on a quiet side street close to a main thoroughfare leading to the city centre.

LUXOR Happyland Hotel   €

Sharia al-Kamar, Luxor **Tel** *095 2371 828* **Fax** *095 2371 140* **Rooms** *24*

The Happyland doesn't pretend to be luxurious, but it is cheap, cheerful, clean and located within easy distance of Luxor city centre. It features air-conditioned rooms, which is a considerable bonus, especially in summer. The rooms are simply presented, with town views; only a few have private bathrooms. **www.luxorhappyland.com**

LUXOR Marsam Hotel   €

Al-Gurna, Luxor **Tel** *095 2372 403* **Rooms** *23*

Situated on the West Bank and featuring superb views of Luxor, this recently renovated budget hotel offers rooms in its original mud-brick-style building, along with further sleeping quarters in a new modern wing. All are well presented and clean, but only a few have private bathroom facilities. The Marsam is within easy reach of the local sights.

LUXOR St Mina Hotel   €

Sharia Cleopatra, Luxor **Tel** *095 2375 409* **Fax** *095 2376 568* **Rooms** *20*

A good base for a short or long stay in the Luxor area, the St Mina is an attractive little hotel that stands in a traditionally styled building close to the centre of town. It is family-run and the staff are welcoming and friendly, plus they keep the place spotlessly clean. Some rooms have their own bathrooms.

LUXOR Venus Hotel   €

Sharia Yussef Hassan, Luxor **Tel** *095 2372 625 or 095 2361 327* **Rooms** *21*

The Venus is a hotel with few frills but one that impresses money-conscious travellers with its location, close to the city centre. Its rooms are surprisingly comfortable for a budget hotel, and most have their own private bathroom and air conditioning. The hotel also offers a rooftop bar and restaurant with a great atmosphere.

LUXOR Al-Gezira Hotel   €€

Bayrate al-Gezira, Luxor **Tel & Fax** *095 2310 034* **Rooms** *11*

This modernist, two-storey hotel may look unassuming from the outside, but step inside, and a tastefully decorated interior greets you. Rooms are comfortable, with private bathrooms and fans; some even have Nile views. The hotel is situated on the West Bank, and its rooftop restaurant and bar offer views of the river.

Key to Price Guide *see p268* **Key to Symbols** *see back cover flap*

LUXOR Flobater Hotel

Sharia Khaled Edn El Walid, Luxor **Tel** *095 2374 223* **Fax** *095 2370 618* **Rooms** *40*

One of the best things about pre-booking a stay at the three-star Flobater is that you are guaranteed a room with a Nile view, which isn't always the case with some mid-range establishments. The hotel, which is well located for the city centre, doesn't have many amenities, but its pool and international restaurant are pleasant enough.

LUXOR Nur al-Gurna

Gurna Antiquities Inspectorate, Luxor **Tel** *095 2311 430* **Rooms** *9*

The Nur al-Gurna is one of Luxor's newest, and smallest, hotels, and it is distinguished by an intimate and modern feel. Its rooms are of a good standard and nicely decorated for a mid-range establishment; some have views of the Gurna Hills. Close by are Luxor's major West Bank tourist attractions.

LUXOR Pharaoh's Hotel

Bayarat, West Bank, Luxor **Tel** *095 2310 702* **Fax** *095 2311 205* **Rooms** *29*

An unassuming façade belies the fact that this hotel has a classic interior and feels utterly welcoming. Its rooms are simply presented, but clean and air conditioned, while its little restaurant and garden bar offer a mix of international and Egyptian fare. The Gurna Hills can be seen from most viewpoints.

LUXOR Pharaon Hotel

New Karnak, Luxor **Tel** *095 2374 924* **Fax** *095 2376 477* **Rooms** *30*

The Pharaon Hotel is a brand-new establishment set right on the Nile. Traditional in style and offering comfortable rooms with private bathrooms and air conditioning, it provides a quiet place to relax, while being within easy reach of the city centre. Its own restaurant specializes in traditional Egyptian cuisine.

LUXOR Phillippe Hotel

Sharia Dr Labib Habashy, Luxor **Tel** *095 2372 284* **Fax** *095 2380 050* **Rooms** *30*

Visitors looking for a budget hotel that still offers pleasant accommodation combined with a central location close to the main attractions of Luxor could do much worse than the Phillippe Hotel. Rooms at this establishment have air conditioning and bathrooms, while the hotel itself has a restaurant, bar and a swimming pool.

LUXOR Emilio Hotel

Sharia Youssef Hassan, Luxor **Tel** *095 2373 570* **Fax** *095 2370 000* **Rooms** *48*

Popular with tour groups, which is often a good sign, this hotel is modern and clean and offers a range of good amenities, including a rooftop swimming pool, European-style restaurants, a bar and a disco. Rooms are pleasantly decorated and comfortable. The Emilio is also located in the town centre, making it an ideal base for sightseeing.

LUXOR Gaddis Hotel

Sharia Khaled Ibn El Walid, Luxor **Tel** *095 2382 838* **Fax** *095 2382 837* **Rooms** *55*

An international service combined with warm Egyptian hospitality and style is what is promised by the owners of this centrally located Luxor hotel. Offering good four-star amenities at a competitive rate, the Gaddis has attractively presented rooms complete with private bathrooms, satellite television and balconies. **www.gaddishotel.com**

LUXOR Hotel New Winter and Pavilion Palace

Corniche el-Nil, Luxor **Rooms** *237*

With luxuriant gardens and poolside areas lavishly planted with tropical plants, this hotel feels like an oasis in the centre of Luxor. It offers elegant rooms and a touch of luxury at affordable prices. Amenities include pools, a coffee shop, restaurants and a beauty salon. Close to the attractions of Luxor.

LUXOR Sonesta St George Hotel

Corniche el-Nil, Luxor **Tel** *095 2382 575* **Fax** *095 2382 571* **Rooms** *224*

A contemporary seven-storey building located in the centre of Luxor's shopping district. Indeed, the shopaholic will be spoilt for choice, since even the hotel features a lobby shopping arcade specializing in jewellery and local crafts. The hotel and its rooms are all beautifully presented, with top-quality facilities. **www.sonesta.com**

LUXOR St Joseph Hotel

Sharia Khaled Ibn El Walid, Luxor **Tel & Fax** *095 2381 727* **Rooms** *75*

Externally, the St Joseph is less than inspiring, but step inside and a characterful if modern decor will welcome you. This mid-price hotel is situated in one of the newer parts of Luxor, but within easy reach of the city centre. Rooms are well equipped and include private bathrooms, televisions and fridges.

LUXOR Windsor Hotel

Sharia Nefertiti, Luxor **Tel** *095 2375 547* **Fax** *095 2373 447* **Rooms** *120*

The Windsor is a good bet if your budget permits a stay in a mid-range hotel. It is within easy reach of Luxor's major tourist attractions and offers amenities such as a swimming pool, restaurant and fitness suite equipped to European standards. It is popular with tour groups, so be sure to book well in advance.

LUXOR Iberotel Luxor Hotel

Sharia Khaled Ibn El Walid, Luxor **Tel** *095 2380 925* **Fax** *095 2380 972* **Rooms** *185*

Views of the Theban Hills, the West Bank and the Nile can be enjoyed from this hotel's themed restaurants, bars and poolside area, not to mention from some of its contemporary rooms. A pretty hotel centred around its pool, the Iberotel Luxor is within walking distance from the Luxor Temple. **www.iberotel.com**

LUXOR Mercure Inn Luxor Hotel

10 Temple Street, Luxor **Tel** *095 2373 321* **Fax** *095 2370 051* **Rooms** *89*

An attractive hotel that provides leisure amenities, including a nightclub and swimming pool, along with fine food, especially Oriental cuisine, served in its themed restaurants. The Mercure Inn's rooms are presented well and come complete with air conditioning, bathroom and satellite television. Most have views of the Nile. **www.mercure.com**

LUXOR Mövenpick Jolie Ville

Crocodile Island, Luxor **Tel** *095 2374 855* **Fax** *095 2374 936* **Rooms** *332*

Surrounded by tropical fauna and flora, not to mention the River Nile, Crocodile Island is home to this attractive, elegant four-star hotel. Luxor city centre is a short drive away, and the hotel's own free shuttle bus and boat provide the means to make the short hop to the mainland. Rooms are nicely furnished. **www.movenpick-hotels.com**

LUXOR Sol y Mar Tutotel Hotel

Sharia Khaled Ibn El Walid, Luxor **Tel** *095 2377 990* **Fax** *095 2372 671* **Rooms** *256*

Modern-Egyptian in style, the Sol y Mar is built in such a fashion as to provide a different view of Luxor from every vantage point, including a spectacular view out over the West Bank. Rooms are well presented, with amenities that include a private bathroom, satellite television and minibar. **www.solymar-hotels.com**

LUXOR Luxor Hilton

Sharia Karnak, Luxor **Tel** *095 2374 933* **Fax** *095 2376 571* **Rooms** *261*

Deep pockets may be required to stay at the Luxor Hilton, but its amenities and superb location close to the Temple of Karnak, the Temple of Luxor and the Valleys of the Kings and Queens justify the extravagant expense. Luxurious rooms, shops and restaurants are just some of the facilities on offer. **www.hilton.com**

LUXOR M/S Iberotel Crown Emperor

M/S Iberotel Crown Emperor Pier, Luxor **Tel** *02 3738 1125* **Fax** *02 3736 5305* **Rooms** *118*

Sister to the Empress, the M/S Iberotel Crown Emperor takes passengers on a cruise along the Nile. On board, guests will find top-quality restaurants, bars and sleeping quarters. Cabins and suites come complete with a panoramic window to maximize on the river views and private bathroom facilities. **www.iberotel-eg.com**

LUXOR M/S Iberotel Crown Empress

M/S Iberotel Crown Empress Pier, Luxor **Tel** *02 3738 1125* **Fax** *02 3736 5305* **Rooms** *128*

A floating hotel with a difference, the M/S Iberotel Crown Empress offers doubles, single and suites equipped to the highest standard and complete with individually controlled air conditioning. The cruise ship offers the chance to see the Temple of Luxor and Valley of the Kings from the Nile. **www.iberotel-eg.com**

LUXOR Pyramisa Isis Luxor

Sharia Khaled Ibn El Walid, Luxor **Tel** *095 2370 100* **Fax** *095 2372 923* **Rooms** *516*

Located on the banks of the River Nile in around eight acres of landscaped gardens, this five-star hotel is within walking distance of the Luxor Temple and the city centre. Rooms are beautifully presented, with most affording superb views of the West Bank. Amenities include a restaurant serving international cuisine. **luxor@pyramisaegypt.com**

LUXOR Sheraton Luxor

Sharia Khalid Ibn al-Walid, Luxor **Tel** *095 2374 544* **Fax** *095 2374 941* **Rooms** *290*

Situated in one of Luxor's main thoroughfares and close to the city's major tourist attractions, the Sheraton Luxor offers a good location and high-quality amenities. Among them are sports facilities and a range of restaurants serving traditional European fare. Guest rooms are housed in neat chalets dotted among lush gardens.

LUXOR Sheraton Luxor Resort

Sharia Khaled Ben Walid, Awameya, Luxor **Tel** *095 2374 463* **Fax** *095 2374 941* **Rooms** *92*

A complex of 14 chalets totalling 92 rooms is set within an extensive landscaped garden area. Numerous facilities include tennis courts, swimming pools and a range of water sports, a beauty salon and international restaurants. The resort is within walking distance of Luxor city centre.

LUXOR Sofitel Karnak Hotel

Sharia El Zeneya Qebly, Luxor **Tel** *095 2378 020* **Fax** *095 2378 021* **Rooms** *351*

A landmark, five-star hotel located beside the River Nile on the north side of Luxor city centre, the Sofitel Karnak is close to the main attractions, including the Karnak Temple complex. Extensive amenities include tennis courts and a gymnasium. A shuttle bus to the airport is provided. **www.sofitel.com**

LUXOR Sofitel Winter Palace

Corniche el-Nil, Luxor **Tel** *095 2380 422* **Fax** *095 2384 087* **Rooms** *354*

Staying at the Sofitel Winter Palace, a centrally located hotel in a predominantly 19th-century Victorian building, is a somewhat elegant affair. Its rooms, restaurants and facilities are decorated to the high standard expected of a five-star hotel, and they all ooze character and refinement. **www.sofitel.com**

MINYA The Palace Hotel

Midan Tahrir, Minya **Tel** *086 2364 071* **Rooms** *29*

Amenities are few at this colonial-style establishment, but The Palace does offer the chance to stay in a hotel that is full of architectural character. Rooms are simple but offer views out over the landscape of Minya, making a stay here a pleasant, relaxing experience. There are some good restaurants nearby.

Key to Price Guide *see p268* **Key to Symbols** *see back cover flap*

MINYA The Akhenaten 🎳🍽🗐🕆🏊 ⓔⓔ
Corniche el-Nil, Minya **Tel** *086 2365 927* **Fax** *086 2365 917* **Rooms** *48*

The Akhenaten is set right in the centre of the attractive town of Minya and is a good place to stay to absorb the local atmosphere or venture further afield to see the sights. It is a compact hotel housed in a traditional building, but one that offers comfortable rooms, mostly with views of the Nile. **kingakhanaton@hotmail.com**

MINYA Lotus Hotel 🎳🍽🗐 ⓔⓔⓔ
Sharia Port Said, Minya **Tel** *086 2324 500* **Fax** *086 2324 576* **Rooms** *175*

A traditional hotel with simply furnished rooms that have two big advantages: air conditioning and television. The hotel's restaurant is situated on the top floor of this high-rise building, and although its cuisine offers few frills, the views of Minya are outstanding.

MINYA Mercure Nefertiti and Aton Hotel 🎳🍽🏊🎿🗐🕆🏊 ⓔⓔⓔ
Corniche el-Nil, Minya **Tel** *086 2331 515* **Fax** *086 2326 467* **Rooms** *54*

Located on the West Bank of the Nile, close to Beni Hasan, Tel El Amarna and the Coptic ancient monuments, this hotel provides a good sightseeing base. It offers a vast range of facilities for a mid- to high-range hotel, including a fitness suite, swimming pool and tennis courts, and international restaurants. **www.accor.com**

SOHAG Cazalovy 📶🎳🍽🗐 ⓔ
East Bank, Sohag **Tel** *093 4601 185* **Fax** *093 4601 170* **Rooms** *31*

Sohag is a small town that offers the chance to experience what might be referred to as the true Egypt. The area has a handful of hotels, of which the Cazalovy is one of the most popular. A budget-style establishment, it has comfortable rooms and a restaurant that serves some great *koshari*.

SOHAG Merit Amoun Hotel 📶🎳🍽🗐 ⓔⓔ
Madinet Naser, Sohag **Tel** *093 4601 985* **Fax** *093 4603 222* **Rooms** *28*

Located on the East Bank and one of the larger hotels in the Sohag area, the Merit Amoun offers basic but nicely presented and clean air-conditioned rooms. The hotel also features a small restaurant – a good place to relax and eat genuine Egyptian cuisine.

SINAI AND THE RED SEA COAST

DAHAB Bishbishi Camp 🍽 ⓔ
Mashraba, Dahab **Tel** *069 3640 727* **Rooms** *40*

Ideal for young travellers keen for the experience of living close to nature rather than having luxurious surroundings and lots of modern conveniences, Bishbishi Camp comprises a series of beachside bamboo huts equipped with only the bare essentials; some have ceiling fans to help ease the heat of the day. **www.bishbishi.com**

DAHAB Jasmine Pension 🍽 ⓔ
Mashraba, Dahab **Tel** *069 3640 852* **Fax** *069 3640 885* **Rooms** *17*

The Jasmine Pension is an attractive alternative to the many camps that can be found in Dahab, and yet it is as affordable. The rooms are basic but comfortable, and equipped with their own bathrooms and fans. The complex's own restaurant may not be luxurious, but it serves good, hearty food. **www.jasminepension.com**

DAHAB Club Red 🍽🗐 ⓔⓔ
Mashraba, Dahab **Tel & Fax** *069 3640 380* **Rooms** *134*

The Club Red is a no-frills hotel that attracts youngsters because of its close proximity to the sea and to good diving facilities. Discounts are offered to divers. There are rooms available to share to keep costs down, while others come complete with fans and adjoining bathrooms. **www.club-red.com**

DAHAB Blue Beach Club 🍽🏊 ⓔⓔⓔ
Lighthouse, Dahab **Tel** *069 3640 411* **Fax** *069 3640 413* **Rooms** *22*

The attractive rooms that form the Blue Beach Club have great views of the surrounding neighbourhood of Asilah in one direction, and the beach in the other, along with facilities that include fans and fridges. A quiet hotel, it is ideal for couples looking for a relaxing base from which to explore the area. **www.bluebeachclub.com**

DAHAB Nesima Hotel 🍽🏊🎿🗐🕆 ⓔⓔⓔ
Mashraba Asilah, Dahab **Tel** *069 3640 320* **Fax** *069 3640 321* **Rooms** *51*

The Nesima has one of the most popular diving centres in the Asilah area, and it is also known for its good traditional restaurant. Its rooms are well presented, with many featuring domed ceilings and sea views. Its pool overlooks the sea. The hotel is well equipped to accommodate people with disabilities. **www.nesima-resort.com**

DAHAB Hilton Resort 🎳🍽🏊🎿🗐🕆🏊 ⓔⓔⓔⓔ
Dahab Bay, Dahab **Tel** *069 3640 310* **Fax** *069 3640 424* **Rooms** *163*

The Hilton Resort is a landmark building in Dahab Bay. It is beautifully presented, with lush gardens and white-washed rooms that surround a lagoon-style swimming pool. The resort is situated right on the beachside, and offers some superb leisure amenities, including diving and windsurfing centres. **www.hilton.com**

EL-GOUNA Hilton Aim Sukhna Resort

Ain Sukhna Road, Al-Gouna **Tel** *062 3290 500* **Fax** *065 3290 515* **Rooms** *41*

A bustling resort that is popular with families as well as couples and younger travellers, the Hilton Aim Sukhna offers a selection of leisure amenities, such as a gym and pools, and some good eateries all set within luxuriant gardens. The resort is within easy reach of Cairo, making it a good place from which to sightsee.

EL-GOUNA Sheraton Miramar

Al-Gouna Resort **Tel** *065 3545 845* **Fax** *065 3545 885* **Rooms** *338*

The award-winning Al-Gouna Resort, where this hotel is located, is a sprawling collection of villas and hotel apartments, including a few with private butler service. The Sheraton Miramar's leisure amenities are plentiful and include a marina, restaurants, pools, diving and scuba facilities, spas and a golf course. **www.sheraton.com**

HURGHADA Four Seasons Hotel

Ad-Dahar, Hurghada **Tel** & **Fax** *065 3545 456* **Rooms** *14*

A small, attractive hotel, the Four Seasons is within easy walking distance of the beach in the centre of the busy Ad-Dahar area of Hurghada. The beach of a neighbouring resort is available for guests' use. All of the rooms have balconies, some with beach views, although not all have air conditioning.

HURGHADA El-Khan Hotel

Kafr al-Gouna, Hurghada **Tel** *065 3545 060* **Fax** *065 3545 061* **Rooms** *25*

Set in the heart of an extensive resort and benefitting from its leisure amenities, which include spas, a golf course, swimming pools and watersports, this hotel is popular with families. It has an unusual Oriental theme, both inside and out, and the vaulted and domed rooms are attractively decorated.

HURGHADA Empire Hotel

Sharia Sayed Korayem, Hurghada **Tel** *065 3549 200* **Fax** *065 3549 212* **Rooms** *419*

A large hotel built to a traditional style and conveniently located for the centre of Ad-Dahar. The Empire boasts many facilities, including its own swimming pool and gardens, and it is a relatively short walking distance from the beach. Ideal for families, but also for those who are keen to experience local life. **www.empire-hotels.com**

HURGHADA Jasmine Village Hotel

Hurghada **Tel** *065 4464 455* **Fax** *065 3446 441* **Rooms** *446*

The Jasmine Village Hotel is more of a resort than a hotel. Its accommodation is provided in bungalows that are nicely presented and surrounded by leisure amenities. These include a pool, playground and even a zoo. A dive centre and a company running glass-bottomed boats are within the complex. **jasminevillage@hotmail.com**

HURGHADA Dawar al-Umda

Kafr al-Gouna, Hurghada **Tel** *065 3545 060* **Rooms** *64*

If you are after an intimate, chic hotel, then the Dawar al-Umda could fit the bill. Boutique in style, with attractive Arabic-inspired interior design and architecture, it has an elegant feel. It also features its own fitness suite and pool. In addition, since it is located within a large resort, it benefits from numerous leisure facilities. **www.elgouna.com**

HURGHADA Iberotel Arabella

Al-Sakala, Hurghada **Tel** *065 3545 087* **Fax** *065 3545 090* **Rooms** *294*

A lively hotel with bars, a restaurant and one of Hurghada's most popular nightclubs, the Iberotel Arabella is ideal for anyone looking for an activity-packed stay. The town centre is within easy walking distance, and local shops, some good restaurants and tourist attractions are also close by. **www.iberotelarabella.com**

HURGHADA Sheraton Soma Bay Hotel

Soma Bay, Red Sea, Hurghada **Tel** *065 3545 845* **Fax** *065 3545 885* **Rooms** *310*

A beautifully presented hotel right on the beachside south of Hurghada, the Sheraton Soma Bay looks like an Egyptian temple, and indeed its design was inspired by Luxor's Karnak Temple. Extensive leisure facilities include a championship-standard golf course, a dive centre, spa and children's playground. **www.stanwoodhotels.com**

HURGHADA Hilton Hurghada Plaza

Gabal El Hareem, Main Street, Hurghada **Tel** *065 3549 745* **Fax** *065 3547 597* **Rooms** *212*

The Hilton Hurghada Plaza will appeal to those who are after an active experience. Renowned for its scuba diving and watersports, the hotel offers a seemingly endless array of leisure amenities. Whether your fancy is diving, swimming or volleyball, the facilities are there. An on-site restaurant offers international and Egyptian cuisine. **www.hilton.com**

HURGHADA Hurghada InterContinental Resort

Hurghada **Tel** *065 3446 911* **Fax** *065 3446 910* **Rooms** *244*

A large and luxurious low-rise resort, the Hurghada InterContinental is set in extensive landscaped gardens that meander to the beach and the Red Sea. Its amenities include a casino, generally regarded as one of the best in the area, along with shops, a disco, tennis courts, a diving centre and other sporting facilities. **www.interconti.com**

HURGHADA Le Meridien Hotel

Safaga Road, Mikadi Bay, Hurghada **Tel** *065 3590 590* **Fax** *065 3590 595* **Rooms** *236*

Located on a long stretch of sandy beach beside the Red Sea, this hotel offering five-star luxury is a natural choice for discerning travellers. Rooms are spacious, while the resort caters for guests of all ages, with facilities that include what is widely believed to be the largest swimming pool in the Middle East. **www.lemeridien.com**

Key to Price Guide *see p268* **Key to Symbols** *see back cover flap*

ISMAILIA Nefertari Hotel ⚏ ⓘ £

Sharia Sultan Hussein, Ismailia **Tel** *064 3912 822* **Fax** *064 3910 940* **Rooms** *32*

A small and attractively presented hotel, the Nefertari is located in the heart of Ismailia. It is ideal for exploring the surrounding area or as a base for venturing further afield to the Red Sea resorts. Air conditioning in the pleasant rooms offers relief from the heat, as do the refreshingly cool drinks served in the bar.

ISMAILIA Mercure Forsan Island £££££

Gezirat al-Forsan, Ismailia **Tel** *064 3916 316* **Fax** *064 3918 043* **Rooms** *152*

It would be hard to find a hotel that is quite so convenient as the Mercure Forsan Island. Situated in the heart of the city centre, close to attractions and yet enjoying the tranquillity of a private beach, it offers something for everyone. There are swimming pools, a restaurant, tennis court, watersports and garden lakeside walks. **h3006@accor.com**

MARSA ALAM Red Sea Diving Safari ££

Shagra Village, Quseir Kosseir, Marsa Alam **Tel** *065 3380 021* **Rooms** *50*

This environmental village is made up of huts and tents with shared bathrooms, and chalets with private bathrooms. It offers an outstanding diving programme and a range of leisure amenities. The complex is situated alongside the beach and opposite the famous Elphinstone Reef, a magnet for divers. **www.redsea-divingsafari.com**

MARSA ALAM Shams Alam £££

Marsa Alam **Tel & Fax** *02 4170 046* **Rooms** *159*

Shams Alam offers the chance to get away from it all, literally. This coastal resort is surrounded by open countryside, with little commercialism to be seen. On-site facilities include squash courts and table tennis, along with a swimming pool and restaurants. Rooms are housed in traditional vaulted buildings. **www.shamshotel.com**

NUWEIBA Basata £

Ras al-Burqa, Nuweiba **Tel** *069 3500 481* **Rooms** *26*

An extremely popular hotel and camp site, Basata lies around 22 km (14 miles) north of Nuweiba. Guests reside in mud and bamboo huts, an essential part of the owner's policy on eco-friendliness. The huts are located on the beach, a few steps from the sea. The hotel features its own kitchen and bakery. There are also a few chalets.

NUWEIBA La Sirene £££

Beach Road, Nuweiba **Tel** *069 3500 701* **Fax** *069 3500 702* **Rooms** *45*

La Sirene is the centrepiece of a resort set right on the beach at Nuweiba, halfway between the port and the city. It is a compact hotel that is pleasingly presented and well located for local amenities. As such, it is extremely popular. Its facilities are few and far between, but they do include diving.

NUWEIBA Hilton Coral Resort ££££

Nuweiba City **Tel** *069 3520 320* **Fax** *069 3520 327* **Rooms** *200*

This resort is located amid quiet beachside gardens and is famed for its tranquillity and beauty. It has lots of amenities, including diving, and tennis and squash courts. Other activities – such as kayaking, windsurfing and even swimming with dolphins – are all within walking distance. **www.hilton.com**

PORT SAFAGA Holiday Inn Resort Safaga Palace £££

Safaga, Red Sea **Tel** *065 3260 100* **Fax** *065 3260 105* **Rooms** *327*

Situated on a long stretch of beach in a bay known for its excellent windsurfing, and with various water- and ball sports on site, this hotel is an activity enthusiast's delight. In addition, it offers good value for money, has well-presented rooms, live entertainment, restaurants and a fitness suite. **www.ichotelsgroup.com**

PORT SAID Hotel de la Poste £

Sharia al-Gumhuriyya, Port Said **Tel** *066 3224 048* **Fax** *066 3221 473* **Rooms** *44*

Entering the Hotel de la Poste is a little like stepping back in time. Although renovated, this elegant hotel retains much of its 1940s architecture. All rooms have private bathrooms and fans. Apart from a small restaurant, bar and a pâtisserie, it has few amenities, but its location in the heart of the city more than makes up for this.

PORT SAID Sonesta Port Said ££££

Sultan Hussein Street, Port Said **Tel** *066 3325 511* **Fax** *066 3324 825* **Rooms** *110*

The Sonesta is a seemingly sprawling hotel set in lush gardens close to the centre of Port Said. It is popular with businesspeople and provides a good range of leisure amenities, such as a pool that overlooks the Suez Canal, a fitness centre, shopping arcade, bars and restaurants. **www.sonestaportsaid.com**

QUSEIR Quseir-Sirena Beach Mövenpick £££££

El Quadim Bay, Quseir **Tel** *065 3432 100* **Fax** *065 3332 129* **Rooms** *250*

This elegant hotel provides the perfect base for travelling the short distance into Quseir or the 125 km (78 miles) to Hurghada, and yet offers the chance of a relaxing break in a quiet resort beside the Red Sea. The rooms are beautifully presented, while leisure amenities include squash, a gym, tennis and diving. **www.movenpick-quseir.com.eg**

RAS SUDR Moon Beach Resort £££

Ras Sudr, South Sinai **Tel** *062 4015 001* **Rooms** *50*

If a quiet, "get away from it all" break is required, then the Moon Beach Resort is perfect. Some 20 km (12 miles) from the nearest town, surrounded only by sand dunes and the clear blue Red Sea waters, it is wonderfully relaxing and therefore popular, especially with Egyptian families. The rooms are located inside domed huts.

SHARM EL-SHEIKH Shark's Bay Camp

Shark's Bay, Sharm el-Sheikh **Tel** *069 3600 942* **Fax** *069 3600 944* **Rooms** *96*

One of the most frequently visited camps in Sharm el-Sheikh and popular with local families. Shark's Bay Camp sits on the beach in an isolated location, and has its own reef and diving centre, as well as a programme of safari and desert activities. Rooms are either bamboo huts or chalets, only the latter with air conditioning. **www.sharksbay.net**

SHARM EL-SHEIKH Amar Sina

Ras Um Sid, Sharm el-Sheikh **Tel** *062 3662 222* **Fax** *062 3662 233* **Rooms** *91*

The Amar Sina complex is designed and built to resemble a traditional white-washed Egyptian village, with architectural features like domes and arches. It has facilities such as a bar, shops, its own fitness centre and restaurants radiating from a central area. Rooms are pleasant, comfortable and air conditioned.

SHARM EL-SHEIKH Camel Hotel

Naama Bay, Sharm el-Sheikh **Tel** *069 3600 700* **Fax** *069 3600 601* **Rooms** *38*

Pretty and compact, the Camel has gained a reputation for providing not only top-class diving facilities, but also great cuisine in its award-winning restaurants. The hotel, which is located in Naama Bay and minutes from Sharm el-Sheikh, is renowned for its extensive facilities for disabled guests. **www.cameldive.com**

SHARM EL-SHEIKH Sanafir Hotel

Naama Bay, Sharm el-Sheikh **Tel** *069 3600 197* **Fax** *069 3600 196* **Rooms** *50*

The Sanafir is best known for being the venue for one of Naama Bay's most popular nightclubs – the hotel comes alive after dark, and as such, it is ideal for travellers looking for nightly entertainment. It has a good choice of bars and restaurants too. The hotel's air-conditioned rooms are well presented. **www.sanafirhotel.com**

SHARM EL-SHEIKH Ritz-Carlton Resort

Om El Seed Peninsula, Sharm el-Sheikh **Tel** *069 3661 919* **Fax** *069 3661 920* **Rooms** *321*

Oozing luxury, this five-star hotel sits in beautifully landscaped gardens where cascading waterfalls combine with subtly lit pools and shrubbery. Its rooms are equally well presented, while on-site facilities include everything from fine international dining to superb golf, watersports and family activities. **www.ritzcarlton.com**

SHARM EL-SHEIKH Sofitel Sharm el-Sheikh

Naama Bay, Sharm el-Sheikh **Tel** *069 3600 081* **Fax** *069 3600 085* **Rooms** *302*

Perched high on the coastline next to the beach, this hotel offers what has to be the best panoramic view of Naama Bay. Amenities are in abundance and include a Turkish bathhouse complex, archery facilities, an ice-cream parlour and numerous restaurants. Guest rooms are attractive, and most have sea views. **www.sofitel.com**

ST CATHERINE St Catherine Guest House

St Catherine's Monastery, St Catherine City **Tel & Fax** *069 3470 353* **Rooms** *40*

Although a little lacking in luxuries, the Auberge St Catherine more than makes up for it in atmosphere. Set against a stunning countryside backdrop at the foot of Mount Sinai and right next to the St Catherine's Monastery, the hotel remains a firm favourite with travellers looking for a relaxing, "away from it all" establishment.

ST CATHERINE Morgenland Village

Dar Elm Shefa Street, St Catherine City **Tel** *02 7956 856 or 069 3470 700* **Fax** *069 3470 331* **Rooms** *200*

Newly refurbished and upgraded, Morgenland Village offers attractive rooms in the main building and a series of chalets in the grounds. Facilities on site include restaurants and a pool, plus a traditional shopping centre where one of the shops sells a selection of medicinal herbs from Sinai.

SUEZ Red Sea Hotel

El Riad Street, Port Tswfik, Suez **Tel** *062 3334 302* **Fax** *062 3334 301* **Rooms** *75*

To some extent, the Red Sea Hotel has cornered the market in the Suez area – it is certainly one of the best hotels in which to stay. It is also known for its sixth-floor restaurant, which not only serves some fine international and Egyptian dishes and wine, but offers a truly great view over the Suez Canal.

TABA Tobya Boutique Hotel

Km 2, Taba International Road, Taba **Tel** *069 3530 274 or 069 3530 275* **Fax** *069 3530 269* **Rooms** *100*

A boutique hotel in every sense of the word. Tobya features outstanding architecture in a prime location, and it offers highly personalized service, distinctive decor and great value. With its superb collection of attractive lamps, rugs and furniture, the hotel evokes a strong, almost museum-like atmosphere. **www.tobyaboutiquehotel.com**

TABA Marriott Taba Heights Beach Resort

Taba and Nuweiba Highway, Taba **Tel** *069 3580 100* **Fax** *069 3580 109* **Rooms** *394*

This is one of many luxury hotels on the extensive Taba Heights development. The Marriott's amenities are complemented by the resort's marina, an 18-hole golf course, a casino, a safari programme and top-class spas. The hotel restaurants cater for every taste from Japanese sushi and Indian dishes to European. **www.marriott.com**

ZAAFARANA Windsor Zaafarana

Coast Road, Zaafarana **Tel** *02 4145 602* **Fax** *02 4199 999* **Rooms** *160*

This stylish hotel is suitable for both active travellers, who will enjoy the range of watersports available at the beach, and those who prefer sightseeing, with the historical areas and monuments nearby. It is close to the St Paul and St Anthony monasteries, which attract many visitors to this part of Egypt. Rooms are air conditioned.

Key to Price Guide *see p268* **Key to Symbols** *see back cover flap*

THE DELTA AND THE NORTH COAST

ALEXANDRIA Acropole Hotel
Midan Saad Zaghloul, Alexandria **Tel** *03 4805 980* **Rooms** *33*

The modest Acropole has few amenities, but it is housed in a fabulous Art Deco-style building with high ceilings and a touch of elegance – and all within easy reach of the beach and the bustling centre of Alexandria. Most of its rooms have balconies with sea or town views.

ALEXANDRIA Union Hotel
164 Sharia 26th, Alexandria **Tel** *03 4807 312* **Fax** *03 4807 350* **Rooms** *40*

A mere ten-minute walk from Midan Saad Zaghloul, a must on the sightseeing agenda, this popular budget hotel is a good base to explore the city of Alexandria. The Art Deco-style building is full of character, while the rooms are comfortable and clean; most have private bathrooms and a balcony.

ALEXANDRIA Le Crillon Hotel
5 Sharia Adib Ishaq, Alexandria **Tel** *03 4800 330* **Rooms** *36*

Housed in a grand period building, Le Crillon Hotel doesn't pretend to be luxurious, but it is well presented and spotless. As such, it is hugely popular, and booking in advance is recommended. Many of the rooms have private bathroom facilities, and some have French doors and balconies with views out over the harbour.

ALEXANDRIA San Giovanni Hotel
205 Al Gueish Avenue, Stanley, Alexandria **Tel** *03 5467 775 or 03 5467 774* **Fax** *03 5464 408* **Rooms** *32*

The mid-range San Giovanni must have one of the best panoramic views in Alexandria – over the beaches of Stanley. Housed in a beautifully restored and lavish landmark building, the hotel stands in luxuriant gardens. It has air-conditioned rooms, and its amenities include a bar and several restaurants. **www.sangiovanni.com**

ALEXANDRIA Aida Beach Hotel
Alexandria-Matrouh Road, Alexandria **Tel** *03 4102 819* **Fax** *03 4102 818* **Rooms** *62*

A popular resort-style hotel with villas set within extensive grounds. Each villa features a separate dining room and lounge. The hotel is located to the west of Alexandria and beside the Mediterranean sea. On-site amenities include tennis courts, a swimming pool and various watersports, along with a children's club.

ALEXANDRIA Intercontinental Metropole Alexandria Hotel
Sharia Saad Zaghloul, Alexandria **Tel** *03 4861 465* **Fax** *03 4862 040* **Rooms** *66*

If a sea view isn't a necessity, but good, clean accommodation with friendly staff is, then the recently renovated Intercontinental Metropole is ideal. It is situated on a busy thoroughfare that is great for absorbing the local atmosphere. The poet Constantine Cavafy is said to have stayed and worked here. **www.interconti.com**

ALEXANDRIA Mercure Alexandria Romance
303 Tarock El Gueish, Saba Pasha, Alexandria **Tel** *03 5880 911* **Fax** *03 5880 526* **Rooms** *81*

In a modern and tastefully decorated high-rise building, this hotel stands proudly on the ridge of the upmarket Saba Pasha district, between Alexandria city centre and the Montazah Palace. Rooms are air conditioned and equipped with satellite television, while hotel facilities include a swimming pool. **www.accorhotels.com**

ALEXANDRIA Renaissance Alexandria
544 El Geish Avenue, Sidi Bishr, Alexandria **Tel** *03 5490 935* **Rooms** *158*

Popular with business people, the Renaissance has above-average and well-presented amenities. These include fine restaurants, a gym and valet service. The hotel is located in the Corniche at Sidi Bishr, overlooking the Mediterranean, and it is ideal as a base from which to explore and sightsee. **www.renaissance-htl.com.eg**

ALEXANDRIA Sofitel Alex Cecil Hotel
Sharia 26th July, Saad Zaghloul Square, Alexandria **Tel** *03 4837 173* **Fax** *03 4836 401* **Rooms** *86*

Popular with corporate guests and tourists alike, this hotel housed in a colonial-style building is located close to the harbour, in the heart of the business district. The beach is just a few kilometres away. On-site facilities include a gym and sauna, international restaurants and a lively nightclub. **info@sofitel.com**

ALEXANDRIA El-Salamlek Hotel
Montazah Palace, Alexandria **Tel** *03 5477 999* **Fax** *03 5473 585* **Rooms** *20*

Staying at the El-Salamlek will be a memorable experience, not least because the hotel is housed in a former palace. Built by HH Khedive Abbas Helmi II in 1892 as a hunting lodge, and later remodelled to become a refined hotel, it stands on a hill overlooking Montazah Bay and the sea. Luxury is guaranteed. **www.sangiovanni.com**

ALEXANDRIA Helnan Palentine Hotel
Montazah Palace, Alexandria **Tel** *03 5473 500* **Fax** *03 5473 378* **Rooms** *231*

This hotel has royal connections – not only does it overlook Montazah Royal Beach, it is surrounded by the gardens of the Montazah Palace, the summer home of the late King Farouk. A host of sports and leisure facilities is offered, along with luxurious rooms and relaxation areas. **www.helnan.com**

ALEXANDRIA Sheraton Montazah Hotel   ⓔⓔⓔⓔⓔ

Sharia Corniche, Montazah, Alexandria **Tel** *03 5480 550* **Fax** *03 5401 331* **Rooms** *285*

The Sheraton Montazah stands at the end of a long stretch of beach in its own gardens. In addition to the luxurious decor, guests will also enjoy the good location: less than 1 km from the Montazah Palace and gardens; around 7 km (4 miles) from the Royal Jewellery Museum; and close to the airport. **www.sharaton.com**

DAMIETTA El Mina Hotel   ⓔⓔⓔ

38 Sharia 59th, Ras el-Bar, Damietta **Tel** *057 3529 290* **Fax** *057 3526 490* **Rooms** *36*

A small, attractive, traditionally styled hotel located right on the beach at Ras el-Bar, at the mouth of the Nile. Its comfortable rooms have private bathrooms, televisions and balconies with great views to the sea. Amenities include restaurants that serve Egyptian, seafood and European cuisine. **www.geocities.com**

MARSA MATROUH Reem Hotel   ⓔⓔ

Sharia El Corniche, Marsa Matrouh **Tel** *046 4933 605* **Fax** *046 4933 608* **Rooms** *59*

This hotel may not have many frills, but it is welcoming and the staff friendly. It is also situated right on the waterfront and close to the centre of Marsa Matrouh, making it a good base for sightseeing, coastal walks or visiting nearby resorts. Its compact restaurant offers a good choice of local and European fare.

MARSA MATROUH Rommel House Hotel   ⓔⓔⓔ

Sharia Galaa, Marsa Matrouh **Tel** *046 4935 466* **Fax** *046 4933 193* **Rooms** *60*

The Rommel House is a small mid-range hotel in the centre of town. It offers pleasingly presented rooms with private bathroom facilities, televisions and fridges. While there is no restaurant as such, the staff are pleased to include breakfast in the price. They are also available to dispense advice for touring the area.

MARSA MATROUH Santa Monica   ⓔⓔⓔ

Marsa Matrouh **Tel** *046 6748 275* **Fax** *046 6748 276* **Rooms** *252*

With a series of pretty private villas surrounding its swimming pool and a children's pool among the facilities offered, the Santa Monica resort is especially popular with Egyptian families and tour groups. It lies on a sandy beach overlooking the sea, and has its own restaurant and Oriental-style café bar.

MARSA MATROUH Beau Site Hotel   ⓔⓔⓔⓔ

Sharia El Shatee, Marsa Matrouh **Tel** *046 4934 012* **Fax** *046 4933 319* **Rooms** *170*

One of the most popular resort-style hotels in Marsa Matrouh, this modern, purpose-designed establishment nestles around its own private beach. It is a favourite of Egyptian families as well as foreign visitors. Air conditioned, it has pleasingly presented rooms with private bathrooms. **www.beausite.masr.com**

TANTA New Arafa Hotel   ⓔⓔⓔ

Station Square, First Tanta, Tanta **Tel** *040 3405 040* **Fax** *040 3405 041* **Rooms** *62*

A mid-range, white-washed establishment that tends to dominate Station Square, the New Arafa Hotel is well known locally and hugely popular, especially during the great Mouild of Sayed Ahmed al-Badawi festival in October, when it gets booked up quickly. Air conditioned and modern, it has a delightful restaurant.

THE WESTERN DESERT

BAHARIYYA Alpenblick Hotel   ⓔ

Bahariyya Oasis, Bawiti **Tel** *010 4419 934* **Rooms** *22*

The oasis location of this hotel is like a magnet to travellers. The Alpenblick promotes a leisurely way of life, full of long evenings spent enjoying its traditional and hearty food and engaging in conversation with fellow guests. Rooms are simple, but most have good private bathrooms and the luxury of hot water.

BAHARIYYA Safari Camp   ⓔ

Bahariyya Oasis, Bawiti **Tel** *010 8471 414* **Fax** *010 8472 090* **Rooms** *20*

The Safari Camp comes as a bit of a surprise. Many of its rooms are beautifully presented, with domes adding to the character, while others have great views around their oasis setting. Most have private bathrooms. The camp, a favourite with travellers, has its own restaurant serving traditional dishes. **ahmed.safari@hotmail.com**

BAHARIYYA Al-Beshmo Lodge   ⓔⓔ

Bahariyya Oasis, Bawiti **Tel** *02 8472 177* **Rooms** *25*

To really get away from it all, you might want to book a stay at the Al-Beshmo Lodge. It is beautifully located beside the palm-fringed Al-Beshmo Springs at the Bahariyya Oasis, and offers an atmosphere of complete relaxation. Its rooms are comfortable and clean, with most featuring en-suite bathrooms and air conditioning.

DAKHLA Bedouin Camp   ⓔ

Sharia Mut al-Qasr, Dakhla **Tel** *092 7850 480* **Rooms** *21*

Be prepared to relax and unwind in simple but delightful surroundings if staying at the Bedouin Camp. Its rooms are basic but comfortable, while its restaurant is housed in a tent, and diners sit on carpets and cushions on the floor. Hearty food is served. The Bedouin Camp is in an isolated location close to Mut.

Key to Price Guide *see p268* **Key to Symbols** *see back cover flap*

DAKHLA Gardens Hotel

Dakhla Oasis, Mut, Dakhla **Tel** *088 7821 577* **Rooms** *12*

Situated just off the main street through the Dakhla Oasis, the Gardens Hotel is in a small but attractive building of traditional architecture. It stands in pleasant tropical gardens and includes a restaurant serving light meals and a terrace area that provides the perfect place to relax. The rooms are simple, and some have en-suite bathrooms.

DAKHLA Mebarez Hotel

Dakla Oasis, Mut, Dakla **Tel** *088 7821 524* **Rooms** *33*

A relatively new and modern establishment, the Mebarez Hotel is popular with tour groups and individual travellers. It is situated on the main road to Al-Qasr and ideal for exploring the area. Rooms are comfortable, and many have air conditioning and private bathrooms. A restaurant serving Egyptian cuisine adds to its charm.

DAKHLA Mut Talata

Dakla Oasis, Mut, Dakla **Tel** *088 7821 530* **Rooms** *11*

The progressive Mut Talata complex opened only a couple of years ago. It offers a choice of tents, chalets or a room inside the villa around which the complex is based. It has its own swimming pool created from a nearby hot spring, and its own restaurant, too.

EL KHARGA El Kharga Oasis

El Kharga Oasis, El Wadi El Guedid, El Kharga **Tel** *092 7921 500* **Fax** *092 7924 940* **Rooms** *30*

A modern hotel, the El Kharga Oasis is a landmark building rising from the sand dune-surrounded oasis in which it stands. The staff are friendly and pride themselves on the lavishness of the well-kept tropical gardens filled with palm trees and native flowers. Rooms are simple and air conditioned.

EL KHARGA Pioneers Hotel

El Kharga Oasis, El Wadi El Guedid, El Kharga **Tel** *092 7927 982* **Fax** *092 7927 986* **Rooms** *102*

A stay at the Pioneers Hotel will feel a little like being on a film set – it is traditionally decorated in pure Egyptian style and stands surrounded by palm trees amid the sand dunes of the desert. The hotel lies minutes from the Hibis Temple and the Al-Bagawat Necropolis, both of which are must-visit sights on the tourist agenda.

QASR AL-FARAFRA Al-Badawiyya Safari and Hotel

Qasr Al-Farafra **Tel** *092 3458 524* **Rooms** *30*

The Al-Badawiyya Safari and Hotel sounds grand. It is, in fact, a traditional mud brick constructed hotel although you wouldn't guess it from its tasteful interior. Rooms are spacious and comfortable, and some have private bathrooms, while its restaurant is one of the best in this small village and serves good food.

SIWA Alexander Hotel

Main Street, Siwa **Tel** *046 4602 081* **Rooms** *17*

A compact hotel and one of the most recently opened in Siwa, the Alexander has a growing base of returning guests. It offers clean rooms with fans, some with private bathroom facilities. The hotel staff are especially proud of its Alexander the Great restaurant and delight in showing the roof terrace.

SIWA Arous al-Waha Hotel

Siwa Oasis, Siwa **Tel** *046 4602 100* **Rooms** *20*

The picturesque setting in the Siwa Oasis is more inspiring than the architecture of the small Arous al-Waha, but nonetheless this hotel has its own charm as you step inside. The rooms are nicely presented, clean and with private bathrooms – plus there are fans to help with the heat. Its cafeteria-style eatery serves local delicacies.

SIWA Palm Trees Hotel

Siwa Oasis, Siwa **Tel** *046 4602 304* **Rooms** *26*

Situated just off the main street in the Siwa Oasis, this attractive little budget hotel stands in beautifully landscaped and tropical gardens. Its staff are friendly and always on hand to help organize excursions into the desert or further afield, but its amenities are few and in need of an update.

SIWA Shali Lodge

Siwa Oasis, Siwa **Tel** *046 4602 399* **Fax** *046 4601 799* **Rooms** *8*

One of Siwa's hidden treasures. If you are planning a stay here, be aware that booking is essential due to the hotel's small size and popularity. The Shali Lodge has just eight rooms, all beautifully presented. They sit around a palm-fringed pool and are just minutes away from the hotel's own restaurant, where the chef delights in banter.

SIWA Siwa Safari Paradise Hotel

Sharia Ein El Arais, Siwa **Tel** *046 4602 289* **Fax** *046 4602 290* **Rooms** *74*

Set in a delightful garden environment and close to the centre of Siwa and its amenities, the Siwa Safari Paradise is popular with travellers and families alike. It resembles a small resort in style, and its pretty bungalows all feature air conditioning, televisions and en-suite bathrooms.

SIWA Adrere Amellal

Sidi Jaafar, Maraki Village, Siwa **Tel** *046 4601 299* **Fax** *046 4601 223* **Rooms** *35*

One of Egypt's first eco projects, the Adrere Amellal features traditional-style architecture and amenities that include its own spring-water supply. Its swimming pool is created out of the natural rocks that surround the spring. Its small restaurant has a tasty menu produced from organically grown produce.

WHERE TO EAT

According to an Egyptian proverb, "the best food is that which fills the belly". Traditional Egyptian cooking combines Arabic and Turkish with European and African influences. The result is sometimes described as bland, but this is unjust. Hearty main dishes are usually accompanied by a selection of pickles and dips, so you can spice up or cool down your meal as you wish. The cuisine is dominated by *semna* (clarified butter), which ensures a rich taste and a heavy impact on the arteries. Egyptians often say no

Staff at central Cairo's Café Riche

meal is complete without meat, yet *fuul* (mashed fava beans), *taamiyya* (deep-fried patties filled with fava bean paste and green herbs, otherwise known as *falafel*) and *koshari* (a mixture of noodles, rice, lentils and onions) – the meatless staples of the poor – are consumed by all classes. Most large Egyptian towns have a few old-fashioned European restaurants, along with growing numbers of fast-food outlets and restaurants serving a wide range of ethnic cuisines. Even better, restaurants are increasingly serving a variety of traditional local dishes.

RESTAURANTS AND BARS

In much of Egypt, the idea of dining out is quite new. As a result, the wide range of dishes that Egyptians eat at home is simply not available in restaurants. Their delicious meat and vegetable stews, for example, are hard to find in a restaurant, except during the month of Ramadan. There is, however, a distinct Egyptian cuisine that adapts remarkably well to modern demands for fast food. *Fuul* sandwiches or roasted chicken (*firakh*), for example, are likely to be sold in any settlement bigger than a hamlet. Most towns have at least one *kebabgi*, offering a selection of kebabs and a choice of several salads. These are often accompanied by dips such as *hummus* (made from fava beans and herbs),

The interior of L'Aubergine, a vegetarian restaurant in Zamalek

tahina (made from sesame paste) and *babaghanoush* (grilled aubergine and *tahina*). Quality varies, but eating out at a good kebab place is an experience not to be missed.

Pigeon is another popular dish in Egypt. It is stuffed with rice and spices and roasted, or cooked in a stew (*tagine*) with onions and tomatoes.

The culture of dining out is most deeply rooted in the cosmopolitan Mediterranean city of Alexandria, where a number of Greek, Italian and French restaurants and cafés still thrive. Alexandria is also rightly famous for its seafood, which can be eaten at an open-air grill or in one of the town's restaurants. Either way it will be fresh and delicious.

In Cairo, the foreign embassy community alone is enough to keep several old European-style restaurants in

business. Younger expatriates and upper-class Egyptians tend to frequent Cairo's trendier restaurant-bars, with flashy décor, loud music and some variation on *nouvelle* Mediterranean fare. More and more ethnic restaurants are opening, and now it is possible to get a full range of Asian food, from Korean and Chinese to Thai and Indonesian.

Many fashionable restaurants double as bars, so going for an evening meal can easily turn into a full-scale night out. Cairo has the remnants of a colonial café scene and some of these places, such as Café Riche, are enjoying a revival. Cairo also has a few traditional-style pubs, which often provide some form of food. Bars usually display signs stating a minimum drinking age of 21, but this guideline is not applied very strictly.

Sofitel Old Cataract Hotel restaurant, Aswan

OPENING HOURS

Street stalls selling snacks of *fuul* and *taamiyya* open at the crack of dawn for a basic breakfast. Juice bars are usually open from 8am–10pm, serving freshly squeezed juice. *Koshari* restaurants and shops selling *baladi* sandwiches (*baladi* is a flat, round, country bread) open around 10am. Most other restaurants, unless specifically serving breakfast, open at midday. Very few establishments open before 1pm on Fridays, except those that cater specifically for foreign visitors.

Egyptians tend to eat their main meal in the afternoon, and most restaurants close around 11pm to 1am.

PRICES AND PAYING

In Egyptian restaurants, dishes are usually ordered individually rather than as fixed combinations. In many establishments, *mezzes (see pp288–9)* will be brought to your table, whether or not you order them. These will be charged for, so send them back if you do not want them and make sure that they are not included on your bill.

A service charge of 12 per cent is added automatically to every restaurant bill, but customers are expected to pay a small tip as well – usually an additional 10 per cent, but not more than LE 10. So once the sales tax of 5 per cent is added on, diners are paying more than 20 per cent over the price of their food.

BOOKING

Reservations are required only at the most upmarket restaurants. Such places will have a telephone, and most of them will have at least some staff who speak English. Attempts to book a table at less upmarket establishments can prove frustrating, however, and it is likely that there will be no record of your call when you arrive at the restaurant. Nevertheless, the staff will probably be most accommodating and make every effort to find you a table.

Selection of snacks available from an Egyptian fast-food outlet

ETIQUETTE

As is the case generally in Egypt, shorts and short skirts are not appropriate attire for restaurants. Other than that, however, most places are quite relaxed as far as dress code is concerned. Egyptians like to dress smartly when going out – including visits to fast-food outlets, which are considered trendy by young Egyptians. Foreign visitors can usually get away with wearing fairly casual clothing, but in more upmarket establishments a shirt with a collar, and shoes rather than sandals, would be advisable. On the other hand, it is not unusual to see women dressed in cocktail dresses in such restaurants, especially late in the evenings.

In Egypt, smoking is inescapable in bars and pervasive in restaurants. Some of the more expensive restaurants in Cairo have established no-smoking sections, but these areas tend to be small and tucked away in a corner, surrounded by smoking tables. Fast-food places are now smoke-free, thanks to a recent campaign by the environment ministry.

CHILDREN

Children are welcome in most restaurants and cafés before about 11pm, though it would not be appropriate to bring them along to places that are primarily drinking establishments. Some restaurants have gardens with play equipment. The Felfela chain, for example, has several branches, including one on the Corniche and another in the Pyramids area, that are geared to children.

A Cairo juice bar, offering a variety of freshly squeezed fruit juices

Stall in Aswan selling deep-fried fava bean and herb patties, known as *taamiyya*

DISABLED CUSTOMERS

Few Egyptian establishments have facilities for disabled customers, such as wheelchair access, though staff will be willing to help customers overcome any obstacles. Public toilets with wheelchair access are unheard of, but at least the traditional hole-in-the-floor type is almost extinct.

FAST-FOOD OUTLETS

While there has been some form of international fast-food in Egypt since the 1970s, the last few years have seen a proliferation of international brand names. All the big American chains (except for Burger King) are here, as well as some less well-known South African outlets. As in the rest of the world, these places have become favourite haunts of the young.

Apart from these international chains, Egypt has its own indigenous fast-food tradition. As well as the ubiquitous street stalls selling snacks of bread *(aish)* stuffed with *fuul* and *taamiyya*, there are stalls that specialize in other traditional snacks. *Koshari*, a mixture of rice, noodles and crispy fried onions in a spicy tomato sauce, is sold at stand-up stalls, also called *koshari*, while more expensive, café-like establishments known as *fatatri* specialize in *fatir*. A cross between pancakes and pizzas, these are made from flaky filo pastry and come with sweet or savoury fillings.

VEGETARIAN FOOD

Vegetarianism is extremely rare in Egypt and, as a result, vegetarian restaurants are almost unheard of – L'Aubergine in Zamalek *(p293)* is one of the few exceptions.

However, many Egyptian dishes contain no meat, and restaurants in the cheaper range frequently serve only meatless dishes. More expensive restaurants will usually have a few vegetarian dishes on the menu. Strict vegans could have a harder time, but staples such as *fuul, taamiyya* and *koshari* should be acceptable to almost anyone. Obviously, places to avoid are those specializing in kofta and kebab or rotisserie chicken.

A starter of blue-cheese salad with baguette at a Cairo restaurant

HYGIENE

Suffering some degree of gastric ailment in Egypt seems to be fairly inevitable for anyone spending more than a few days there, but experienced travellers have come up with a few rules of thumb. Some suggest you avoid raw vegetables and salads, particularly lettuce, because these are often not properly washed. (Pickled

Cairo's Café Riche – a reminder of Egypt's colonial café scene vegetables that come as an appetizer should be safe, however). Others believe that the real problem is with the meat. Although it might seem that eating only at the more expensive restaurants would minimize the risk, there are stories of people getting sick everywhere. Fast food is usually safer but, once again, there are exceptions and people have got just as sick from the big chains' burgers as from kofta sandwiches.

In major towns and cities, tap water is safe to drink though heavy chlorination does little for the taste. New arrivals should stick to mineral water *(mayya maaduniyya)*, which is readily available. When buying bottles of mineral water, always check that the seal is intact. *(See also Health Precautions, pp334–5)*.

RAMADAN

Ramadan is an interesting (though also potentially frustrating) time to be in Egypt. The ninth month of the Islamic calendar, Ramadan is a period akin to Lent in the Christian church, with a fast that involves abstention from food, drink and smoking during daylight hours. The fast is strictly observed and days revolve around waiting for sunset. Then the sunset call to prayer is made, lamps are lit on the minarets and everyone gets down to eating the first meal of the day and enjoying the night-time celebrations.

During Ramadan, restaurants may be open during the day, but only tourists will be eating

Restaurant housed in what was once a Nile cruise ship on Zamalek

and fewer options will be available. Travellers may prefer to postpone their meal until after sunset, especially since the cooks making the food and the waiters serving it will not have eaten all day. At sunset, most restaurants are packed, and many set up huge tents so they can fit in as many customers

Fish restaurant sign in Abu Qir

as possible. These feasts provide a good opportunity to get to meet a cross-section of Egyptian society. Everyone sits together at long tables and will probably be quite friendly – once they've eaten.

A wider, more interesting range of traditional dishes will be available during Ramadan, and restaurants will be open throughout the night, in order to serve *sohour*, the last meal before sunrise. In addition, certain drinks, such as apricot juice *(amar el din)*, and foods are specific to this time of the Islamic calendar.

ENTERTAINMENT

If you are keen to combine dining out with some form of entertainment, then your best bet is to book a table at one of Cairo's five-star hotels. Most of these have night clubs where a flat charge covers an excellent four-course meal and a floor show featuring some of Egypt's most popular dancers and traditional musicians. Smart dress and reservations are required at these venues.

For a variation on this idea, you might like to try one of Cairo's floating restaurants. Many of these offer cruises on the Nile, during which lunch or dinner is served to the accompaniment of live Egyptian music or a floor show complete with belly dancers and band. At Zamalek there are also luxury Nile Cruisers from a bygone era that remain moored, serving food in opulent surroundings. These restaurants often also have live entertainment.

If five-star hotels are beyond your means, there are less expensive nightclubs, where dinner is served and entertainment is provided – though both food and performances are likely to be of variable standard. Several of these nightclubs are located on Pyramid Road.

Remember that nightlife in Cairo doesn't really begin until after midnight, with the floor shows going on as late as 3 or 4 in the morning.

L'Aubergine restaurant in Zamalek, offering a mainly vegetarian menu

The Flavours of Egypt

Egypt shares many dishes with its Mediterranean and Middle Eastern neighbours. The cuisine leans heavily towards earthy pulses, brightly coloured vegetables, gamey meats and hearty stews, with the use of spices and simmering cooking methods infusing dishes with warmth. Cooking techniques from the time of the Pharaohs are still in existence today and the food in this part of North Africa excels in both freshness and flavour. If you are invited to an Egyptian home then you could expect to enjoy soup, some meat and a vegetable-based stew with bread and salad. Desserts are not as rich as those of many other Arab countries.

Fresh figs

Spices sit alongside coloured dyes on a market stall

MEAT, POULTRY & GAME

Egyptian families view meat as a luxury and it is often served in small amounts or combined with rice and vegetables, such as in stuffed vine leaves, to make it go further. As a result, whenever meat is to be served as a main dish it is prepared with a great deal of care and attention. Poultry is usually roasted, and lamb, mutton and veal are also popular, although beef isn't typically eaten. Meat and poultry may be stuffed with fruit, nuts and rice. Try the traditional delicacy that is pigeon *(hamaam)*. These birds are raised throughout the country and are stuffed with seasoned rice before being grilled. But be warned – some chefs serve the head of the bird, buried in the stuffing.

FISH & SEAFOOD

Ever since ancient times, Egyptians have enjoyed fish fresh from the Nile, salted or dried by being hung out in the strong sun to bake. Today Egyptians serve both freshwater and sea fish under the general term of *samak*. The best sea fish come from shallow coastal waters and the best fresh-water ones are found at Aswan, where they are

Hummus   Babaghanoush   Olives   Egyptian salad   Sabanikhiyat   Falafel   Aish
Fuul   Stuffed vine leaves

Some of the many dishes that make up typical Egyptian *mezzes*

EGYPTIAN DISHES AND SPECIALITIES

Koshari is the rich, hearty dish of pasta, pulses and vegetables that has long been considered part of the Egyptian identity, eaten both at home and at market. Another classic dish is *melokiyah* – the best versions of this herby green soup are found in Aswan and Luxor, although variations are found throughout the land. The waters of the Red Sea teem with some of the country's finest perch and tuna, and *sayyaddia* (fish with rice) features on many an Egyptian menu. A *meze* is an easy way to enjoy a whole range of bite-sized Egyptian delicacies such as *sabanikhiyat* (spinach turn-overs), *kofta* (meatballs), *babaghanoush* (a smoky aubergine/eggplant purée), hummus and *fuul* (a lemony broad/fava bean dip). Bread *(aish)*, in particular the flat *baladi* bread, accompanies dips.

Chickpeas (garbanzos)

Melokiyah *soup is named for the muculaginous green mallow leaves that flavour it. It may be served without meat.*

Goods piled high in palm-leaf baskets at a village grocer's shop

DAIRY PRODUCE

Egyptian cheese, known as *gibna*, comes in two varieties. White, fresh *Gibna beida* has a salty, clean taste similar to Greek feta, while *gibna rumy* is a sharper-tasting cheese with a pale yellow colour. They are most often found in salads and sandwiches. *Bbouzat baleeb*, or ice cream, shares little in common with its rich Western namesake. It has a fresh, light texture that even stretches a little as you scoop it. Egyptian yoghurt *(laban zabadi)* is fresh and unflavoured but is usually served sweetened with such things as honey, jam, preserves, nuts, figs or dates.

caught from Lake Nasser. Common bass and sole feature frequently but so do shrimps, squid, scallops and eel. Eel can be sampled, deep-fried, at markets.

VEGETABLES & FRUIT

Robust root vegetables such as garlic and onion are vital to much of Egypt's cooking and are also cherished for their health benefits. Peas and beans are sometimes eaten on their own with a plain oil and vinegar dressing. Potatoes *(bataatis)* are often fried but can also be boiled or stuffed. Dried vegetables are also used a great deal. Egyptian salads *(salata)* feature lettuce, tomatoes, cucumber, potatoes, olives or eggs and sometimes even beans and yogurt. Fruit is eaten after a meal, with juicy

plums and pomegranates joining dates for a rich choice in sweetness. Figs have been hugely popular since ancient times. Fresh, dried or as a syrup, they appear in savoury dishes and breads as well as in sweets.

Waiter bringing a tray of mint teas at a Cairo café

WHAT TO DRINK

Despite Egypt being a Muslim country, alcohol is widely available in restaurants and bars. The local Stella lager is good and the quality of Egyptian wines has improved greatly in recent years. Hot drinks include *chai* (mint tea) and *ahwa* (Arabic coffee) which is strong and either *ziyada* (sweet), *mazboota* (medium) or *saada* (bitter). *Karkade*, an infusion made from hibiscus leaves, is served hot or cold. Freshly squeezed fruit juices, including delicious and unusual ones such as apricot, are widely available and are very refreshing, as is *asab*, a sweet, light-green drink with a foamy head, made from pressed sugarcane.

Koshari *combines pasta, rice, lentils and pulses with a spicy tomato sauce and crispy onions.*

Sayyaddia *is simply a whole fresh fried fish such as sole, flounder, trout or bass, served with rice and lemon.*

Mahallabiyaa *is a delicately rosewater-flavoured ground rice dessert, topped with toasted nuts and cinnamon.*

Choosing a Restaurant

The restaurants in this guide have been selected across a wide range of price categories for their good value, good food, atmosphere and interesting location. This chart lists the restaurants by region. Within each town or city, entries are listed by price category, from the least expensive to the most expensive.

CAIRO

CAIRO Abou Tarek   📋   €
Sharia Cosmopolitan, Cairo **Tel** *02 5761 911 or 02 5775 935*   **Map** *1 C4, 5 C2*

Serving Egyptian and international cuisine, including a great *koshari*, a dish of pasta, rice, lentils and tomatoes with crispy onions, Abou Tarek is a renowned and well-liked eaterie. It is easily spotted, too, since the lovely old downtown Cairo building is decorated in bright reds and yellows, making it something of a landmark.

CAIRO Alfi Bey   📋   €
3 Sharia Al-Alfi, Sharia Mohammed Alfy, Cairo **Tel** *02 5571 888*   **Map** *2 D4, 5 C2*

Alfi Bey is well located for Cairo city centre and a great place to stop for a light lunch in between sightseeing excursions. It serves Egyptian food cooked to traditional recipes, along with salads and starters; your meal comes complete with a moderately priced bill. No alcohol is served, but there is a good choice of other beverages.

CAIRO Koshari Goha   📋   €
Sharia Emad ad-Din, Cairo   **Map** *2 D4, 6 D2*

Koshari Goha is housed in what was probably the former home of an eminent member of Cairo's society: the building features superb neo-Baroque plasterwork on its high ceilings and exudes a feeling of grandeur. A good and varied vegetarian menu is on offer, along with traditional Egyptian and international meat dishes.

CAIRO Koshari Gomhourya   📋   €
Sharia al-Azhar, Midan Hussein, Cairo   **Map** *2 F5*

Eating at Koshari Gomhourya, in the Islamic area of Cairo, is something of an experience. Traditionally decorated, with few frills and sawdust on the floor, the place is endearingly rustic. The food, however, is fresh and wholesome, with Egyptian specialities such as *koshari*, *taamiyya* and *bamiyya* offered with *aish*, a type of bread.

CAIRO Koshari Hilton   📋   €
Midan Tahrir, Cairo   **Map** *1 C5, 5 B4*

Visitors could be forgiven for thinking that this delightful little *koshari* shop had an affinity with the nearby Nile Hilton Hotel, after which it is named. However, this restaurant is privately owned and run by its friendly host. The food here is excellent and comprises mainly quick, inexpensive Egyptian meat and vegetarian dishes and snacks.

CAIRO Abu Bassem Grill   📋🔲   €€
2 Al-Gahini Alley, Midan Hussein, Cairo **Tel** *02 5937 935*   **Map** *2 F5*

One of Cairo's best-kept secrets and a popular haunt of locals, Abu Bassem Grill serves some of the best kebabs and mezes in the Midan Hussein area. Weather permitting, it is possible to eat alfresco. Diners who decide to stay inside, however, can gaze at the restaurant's medieval surroundings, which are outstanding.

CAIRO Aly Hasan Al-Haty & Aly Abdou   📋   €€
Midan Halim Pasha, Cairo **Tel** *02 5916 055*   **Map** *2 D4, 6 D2*

Housed in an elegant, high-ceilinged colonial-style property in a busy area of the city, this restaurant has a long history of being the natural choice for Cairo's elite – in its heyday, it was the haunt of movie stars and politicians. Nowadays, it is frequented by business people and tourists keen to sample its selection of meat and kebab dishes.

CAIRO Andrea   ♿📋🍴   €€
Sharia Abu al-Fida, Zamalek, Cairo **Tel** *02 7370 523*   **Map** *1 A2*

A tastefully decorated restaurant in one of Cairo's upmarket areas, Andrea is popular with both locals and visitors thanks to its good meat and vegetarian menu. Located on the waterfront, it boasts a terrace that offers panoramic views of the Imbaba and Rod Al Farag districts, as well as the old bridge that connects them.

CAIRO An'Nil Restaurant   📋   €€
Sharia al-Bustan, Cairo **Tel** *02 3540 042*   **Map** *1 C5, 5 B3*

Popular with the residents of this downtown Cairo neighbourhood, around the Bab al-Louq market district, An'Nil is a welcoming, friendly place to dine. Its extensive menu features a range of traditional dishes. The restaurant, however, is mostly famed for its good selection of fresh seafood, which is sold by the weight.

Key to Symbols *see back cover flap*

CAIRO Ar-Rifai

Midan Sayyida Zeinab, Cairo **Map** *4 D2*

Dining on tasty traditional Egyptian dishes, with the odd international-inspired offering thrown in, and watching the world go by is what makes Ar-Rifai a special kind of eaterie. Diners don't sit indoors – rather, a series of tables is laid out in the street outside, in the alleyway just off Midan Sayyida Zeinab, at the top of Sharia al-Barrani.

CAIRO Café Ole

Midan Tahrir, Cairo **Tel** *02 5780 444* **Map** *1 C5, 5 B4*

Located within the Hilton Cairo Nile hotel and overlooking the bustling Midan Tahrir, one of the main tourist areas of the city, Café Ole is usually crowded with breakfast and lunchtime customers. It serves a good selection of international and local light meals and snacks, along with a delicious array of pastries.

CAIRO Café Riche

17 Sharia Talaat Harb, Cairo **Tel** *02 3918 873* **Map** *1 C5, 5 C3*

A lively downtown restaurant and café serving traditional Egyptian and international cuisine, Café Riche is popular with both locals and tourists. With lots of atmosphere, this historic eaterie has portraits of some of its best customers, including a few Egyptian film and stage stars, adorning its richly coloured walls.

CAIRO Didos Al-Dente

Sharia Bahgat Ali, Zamalek, Cairo **Tel** *02 7359 117* **Map** *1 A2*

This modern and bright restaurant offers an extensive and varied menu of international dishes. Didos Al-Dente is especially renowned for its pasta creations, which wouldn't be out of place in a top Italian eaterie. It is situated in one of the main thoroughfares of this upmarket Cairo district, close to tourist attractions and a market.

CAIRO Egyptian Pancake House

Midan Hussein, Cairo **Map** *2 F5*

If you are after pancakes – or *fateers*, the Egyptian equivalent made of pastry and served with chicken, fish or other meats, or fruit and honey as a filling – then the Egyptian Pancake House will satisfy your appetite. Located just off Midan Hussein, this place is easy to find and well worth seeking out.

CAIRO Fatari Pizza Tahir

Sharia at-Tahrir, Cairo **Tel** *02 7953 596* **Map** *1 C5, 5 B4*

Visitors to this 24-hour downtown eaterie could be forgiven for thinking that it serves Italian pizzas. In fact, Fatari Pizza Tahir serves *fateers*, which are more like pancakes and thoroughly enjoyable. Toppings include various cheeses, meats and fish. Sweet versions with honey and fruit are also available.

CAIRO Felfel Restaurant

9 Sharia Mohammed Farid, Cairo **Map** *4 D1, 6 D5*

Felfel is situated at Al-Nasariyya, in the Sayyida Zeinab district of Cairo, and is usually bustling with happy tourists looking for a snack. Although rather unassuming in appearance, the Egyptian and European-style food is fresh, wholesome and quickly served, making Felfel a good stop between sightseeing excursions.

CAIRO The Greek Club

Sharia Qasr el-Nil, Cairo **Tel** *02 5750 759* **Map** *1 C5, 5 C3*

The Greek Club, or Le Club Hellenique, is a great place to dine on traditional European dishes, especially in the summer months, when everyone moves outside on to the terrace area to eat alfresco. Colder evenings are spent in the colonial-style dining hall, which also oozes charm. This eaterie has its own bar and a wide-ranging wine list.

CAIRO Jo Sushi

47 Sharia Mohammed Mazhar, Zamalek, Cairo **Tel** *02 7357 746* **Map** *1 A2*

One of the favourite haunts for the local community. This busy, successful restaurant is a great little place serving authentic Japanese and Chinese dishes at outstandingly good prices. The decor is a little plain, but the atmosphere and free starters more than make up for it.

CAIRO Maison Thomas

157 Sharia 26th July, Zamalek, Cairo **Tel** *02 7357 057* **Map** *1 A2*

Maison Thomas is widely regarded as the place to go for European-style sandwiches, light snacks, takeaways and Italian pizzas. Being located in the heart of the Zamalek district, close to many of Cairo's major tourist attractions, it makes a good stopping-off point for a quick bite between sightseeing tours. It is open round the clock.

CAIRO Sangria

Corniche el-Nil (opposite the World Trade Center), Garden City, Cairo **Tel** *02 5796 511* **Map** *1 B2*

Elegant dining in an intimate atmosphere is available at Sangria, a restaurant that is perfect for special celebrations and romantic evenings. In addition to stunning views of the Nile, Sangria offers diners a wide range of cuisines: Japanese, Chinese, Lebanese, Italian, French and many more. Make sure you leave room for the divine desserts.

CAIRO Angus

Sharia Yehia Ibrahim, Zamalek, Cairo **Tel** *02 7351 865* **Map** *1 A2*

A cosy restaurant situated within the intimate and relaxing New Star Hotel, the Angus is an Argentine-themed steakhouse. As is to be expected, the extensive menu features mainly red-meat dishes served with an assortment of fries and salads, although there are also a few non-steak alternatives.

CAIRO Asia House   ££££

Helnan Shepeard Hotel, Corniche el-Nil, Garden City, Cairo **Tel** *02 3553 800*   **Map** *3 B1, 5 A5*

Asia House could be an ideal choice if you are planning a memorable meal for a special occasion. Housed in a great hall, it serves authentic and high-quality Chinese and Indian cuisine; indeed, a chef from each country oversees the kitchen to ensure that quality and authenticity are maintained. It is open for lunch and dinner.

CAIRO Cinzano   ££££

Sharia Amerika al-Latineya, Garden City, Cairo **Tel** *02 7925 261*   **Map** *3 B1, 5 A5*

Venturing down the steps to a Mediterranean-style cellar and catching your first glimpse of Cinzano is a remarkable experience. This is a thoroughly modern eaterie that works surprisingly well with its rustic surroundings. Young, trendy people eat Italian pasta dishes and drink fine wines at beautifully set tables.

CAIRO Estoril   ££££

Sharia Talaat Harb, Cairo **Tel** *02 5743 102*   **Map** *1 C5, 5 B3*

Located in downtown Cairo, away from the hustle and bustle of the city centre, this much-frequented Franco-Levantine restaurant renowned for its good food is a great place to dine at a relaxed pace. The menu features a good range of vegetarian dishes and mezes, including numerous local delicacies.

CAIRO Felfela   ££££

15 Sharia Hoda Shaarawi, Cairo **Tel** *02 3922 751 or 02 3922 833 (take-away)*   **Map** *1 C5, 5 C3*

A cosy restaurant in downtown Cairo, Felfela has a true European flavour. Its staff speak good English, and its menu of chicken, meat, fish and vegetarian dishes is clearly designed to attract the tourists. However, the place is renowned for serving good-quality food at good prices. Don't miss one of the delicious, if extravagant, desserts.

CAIRO Five Bells   ££££

13 Sharia Ismail Mohammed, Zamalek, Cairo **Tel** *02 7358 980*   **Map** *1 A2*

The menu at Five Bells has a tempting selection of classic French and Mediterranean dishes; none disappoints. Diners can choose to eat in the tastefully designed dining hall or, on warmer days and evenings, outside in the restaurant's own garden. A fine wine list completes the superior experience.

CAIRO Ha Na   ££££

21 Sharia Aziz Abaza, Midan Sidki, Zamalek, Cairo **Tel** *02 7382 972*   **Map** *1 A2*

Ha Na serves authentic Korean cuisine, including some vegetarian and meat dishes cooked over hot coals at your table. The restaurant's wine list includes a range of varieties that perfectly suit the style of food. This lower-level Oriental-themed eaterie is generally softly lit, which gives it an intimate atmosphere.

CAIRO Harry's Pub   ££££

Cairo Marriott Hotel, Sharia Saray al-Gezira, Zamalek **Tel** *02 7358 888*   **Map** *1 A2*

Harry's Pub is a popular restaurant-bar attracting mainly English tourists nostalgic for some familiar dishes. Its extensive menu offers roasts, cottage pie, and steak and kidney puddings, all served with lashings of gravy; there's also a wine list to complete the meal. Sports fans can enjoy matches on the big-screen televisions.

CAIRO Il Piccolo Mondo   ££££

Le Pacha 1901, moored off Sharia Saray al-Gezira, Zamalek, Cairo **Tel** *02 7356 730*   **Map** *1 A2*

An interesting venue because of its location and ambience, Il Piccolo Mondo is part of a complex of restaurants on a boat moored off this central Zamalek thoroughfare. Parking is provided. This elegant eaterie serves traditional and classic Italian cuisine with complementing wines. It also features a great salad buffet.

CAIRO Khan Al-Khalili Restaurant and Café   ££££

5 Al-Badistan, Cairo **Tel** *02 5932 262*   **Map** *2 F5*

Managed by the Oberoi Hotel group, the über-slick Khan Al-Khalili offers traditional Egyptian dishes in dramatic surroundings that have been created to resemble an Eastern salon. It is mostly frequented by tour groups and tourists who have been tipped off by their holiday companies.

CAIRO Kowloon   ££££

Sharia al-Bustan, Cairo **Tel** *02 5759 831*   **Map** *1 C5, 5 B3*

Dining at Kowloon is a memorable experience, not least because of the large illuminated fish tank that dominates the dining area. The food is also wonderful though, and inspired by the best Chinese and Korean standards of cuisine. A well-selected wine list complements the food perfectly. Kowloon is situated within the Cleopatra Hotel.

CAIRO La Babila   ££££

20 Sharia al-Rieadh, Cairo **Tel** *02 3055 832*   **Map** *1 B3*

The lavish fabrics and soft furnishings that decorate this modern Turkish restaurant are so richly coloured, they resemble shining jewels and precious stones. La Babila offers a menu of Turkish and Oriental dishes to tempt its diners. It is located in Al Mohandesn, a district of Cairo just off the Sharia Shihab.

CAIRO La Baguite   ££££

15 Sharia Mohammed Hassanain Hekel, Cairo **Tel** *02 2709 813*   **Map** *2 D4, 5 C2*

An extensive list of Syrian and Oriental dishes is offered at this takeaway restaurant behind Al Gama'a Al Omaleya, in Cairo's Nasr City. Also on the menu is a good selection of Kuwaiti and Gulf desserts. La Baguite is a well-established source of good food to eat out, and its atmosphere, aided by Oriental drawings, is utterly welcoming.

Key to Price Guide *see p290*   **Key to Symbols** *see back cover flap*

CAIRO La Bodega
157 Sharia 26th July, Zamalek, Cairo **Tel** *02 7356 761* **Map** *1 A2*

La Bodega is located in one of Zamalek's landmark buildings, the fabulously historic Art Deco-styled Baehler Mansions. Lively, fun and considered trendy among Cairo's younger, wealthy residents, it also provides a great romantic experience for visiting couples. The menu has an international flavour, and there is a lengthy wine list.

CAIRO L'Aubergine
Sharia Sayed al-Bakry, off Sharia Hassan Sabry, Zamalek, Cairo **Tel** *02 7380 080* **Map** *1 A2*

Serving an extensive range of vegetarian dishes, along with traditional Egyptian and international cuisine (some of it aimed at meat-eaters), L'Aubergine is frequented by discerning locals, arty types, businesspeople and tourists. The food is creatively presented, and its location close to the city centre makes it popular.

CAIRO Le Grillon
8 Sharia Qasr el-Nil, Cairo **Tel** *02 5743 114* **Map** *1 C4, 5 C3*

A delightful Arabic-inspired garden with shrubs and vines surrounds the dining area, making a meal at Le Grillon a special experience. The restaurant serves classic French and European cuisine, along with traditional Egyptian fare. The emphasis is on refined, freshly prepared dishes, which makes it popular with diners in the know.

CAIRO Le Steak
Le Pacha, moored off Sharia Saray al-Gezira, Zamalek, Cairo **Tel** *02 7356 730* **Map** *1 A2*

This floating restaurant moored in an upmarket area of Cairo allows you to experience the delights of sitting on a boat on the Nile, enjoying outstanding panoramic views of the area, fine wines and a menu of steaks and Middle Eastern specialities. Le Steak is always popular, and a smart dress code is in place.

CAIRO Paprika
1129 Corniche el-Nil, Cairo **Tel** *02 5789 447* **Map** *1 B4, 5 A2*

Egyptian and international fare – such as top-quality mezes, *koshari* and stuffed vegetables, steaks, French classics and Italian pasta dishes – is served at this popular restaurant, along with a fine wine list. Paprika is located in the Maspero area of Cairo, close to the Arab Television Building, and therefore easy to find.

CAIRO Roy's Country Kitchen
Sharia Saray al-Gezira, Zamalek, Cairo **Tel** *02 7358 888* **Map** *1 A2*

With no pretence to being luxurious, this fun and lively US-style eaterie serves abundant and hearty portions of Tex-Mex and southwestern American food. Its seemingly endless buffet breakfast will set you up for the day, although lunch and dinner menus are offered, too. Roy's Country Kitchen is located inside the Cairo Marriott Hotel.

CAIRO Sax
3 Midan Orabi, Cairo **Tel** *02 5787 630* **Map** *2 D4, 5 C2*

In the Al-Tawfeqeya area of downtown Cairo, this Oriental-themed restaurant is especially popular with tourists, since it is located close to many hotels. Local residents, however, enjoy Sax's food too, and can often be seen dining here. Sax tends to specialize in fish and seafood options, although a good vegetarian menu is available. Open late.

CAIRO Ciao Italia!
Sheraton al-Gezira, Cairo **Tel** *02 7361 555* **Map** *3 A1*

Located within the Sheraton al-Gezira hotel, on the southern tip of Gezira, beside the Nile, this restaurant comes complete with a red, white and green decor and offers arguably the most authentic Italian cuisine in the city. The chefs all come from Italy, as does the fresh produce. Small and intimate, Ciao Italia! is an elegant, yet fun, eaterie.

CAIRO Elbeet Beetak
3 Sharia Bin Katheer, Corniche el-Nil, Cairo **Tel** *02 3389 993* **Map** *3 B5, 1 B5, 5 A5*

Lebanese and Oriental dishes are served at Elbeet Beetak. The restaurant, situated just behind the Saudi Embassy, is easy to find and well known for hosting special events and parties; it often features singers from the Arab Gulf states to entertain its diners. Food is delicious and served with creative flair.

CAIRO The Fish Market
Sharia Saray al-Gezira, Cairo **Tel** *02 7374 833* **Map** *1 B3*

The Fish Market is a something of a landmark restaurant located on a boat moored in front of the Cairo Marriott Hotel, in the upmarket Zamalek area. It offers international and Egyptian cuisine, along with a wonderful selection of fresh fish. A good wine list and a dessert trolley help complete the superlative experience.

CAIRO Lan Yuan
84 Sharia 9th, Cairo **Tel** *02 3782 702* **Map** *3 B5, 1 B5, 5 A5*

Lan Yuan was built in 1993 and has a clean, modern feel. The attractive Chinese decor and soft background music create the scene for the sumptuous Oriental cuisine on offer. Both the menu and the wine list are extensive. The restaurant is located in the Maadi area of Cairo, within easy reach by taxi if staying in one of the downtown hotels.

CAIRO Maharaja Restaurant
1115 Corniche el-Nil, Maspiro, Cairo **Tel** *02 5744 400*

Located within the Hilton Hotel Ramses, in the centre of Cairo, and open to non-residents, the Maharaja serves exquisite Indian dishes straight from the kitchen's tandoori oven. Known for its curries and tandoori banquets, the restaurant is decorated with brightly coloured fabrics and silks.

CAIRO Romeo and Juliet   £££€
1 Alexandria Road, Giza, Cairo **Tel** *02 3838 444*

Informal yet elegant, Romeo and Juliet is every inch a Mediterranean eaterie, its decor and menu beautifully capturing the essence of southern Europe. The restaurant, located within the Sofitel Le Sphinx Cairo hotel, beside the Pyramids, serves various pasta dishes, buffet-style salads and pizzas, along with a wide selection of desserts.

CAIRO Schatz   ££££
55 Sharia Al Shahid Abdel-Moneim Hafez, Cairo **Tel** *02 2903 170*   **Map** *3 B1, 5 A5*

Located in the Nasr City area of Cairo, and within easy reach of the local attractions, this Italian restaurant is a popular haunt for visitors. It serves dishes straight from the recipe books of Italy, including, of course, pizzas and pastas. There is also a good vegetarian selection, although no wine list.

CAIRO Alexandria Restaurant   £££££
1 Alexandria Road, Giza, Cairo **Tel** *02 3838 444*

Located within the Sofitel Le Sphinx Cairo hotel, the elegant Alexandria is situated in parklands at the foot of the Pyramids of Giza and the Sphinx, providing excellent views of these sights. It serves buffet and à la carte international dishes, along with a selection of Egyptian specialities. The cellar holds a large range of wines from all over the world.

CAIRO Boss   £££££
17 Sharia 257, Cairo **Tel** *02 5164 231*   **Map** *3 B5, 1 B5, 5 A5*

A wide choice of Korean-only food is served at this restaurant, which is in the Maadi area of Cairo, a 15 minutes' taxi ride from the city centre. Boss has an American-style decor, is clean and modern and run by the enthusiastic Mr Choi, who offers wireless Internet connection for diners. It has two bars and regularly hosts karaoke nights.

CAIRO Tropicana Garden   £££££
Midan Tehrir, Cairo **Tel** *02 5780 444*   **Map** *1 C5, 5 B4*

The Tropicana Garden is within the Hilton Cairo Nile hotel, which is set beside the river and close to all the major attractions. This bright and lively eaterie serves traditional Egyptian specialities, such as *koshari* and mezes, along with more international fare, such as steaks, grills and pasta dishes. It offers sumptuous desserts and a good wine list.

CAIRO Windows on the World Restaurant   £££££
1115 Corniche el-Nil, Maspiro, Cairo **Tel** *02 5744 400*

Ask anyone where the Windows on the World Restaurant is, and they will tell you it is on the 36th floor of the Hilton Hotel Ramses in Corniche el-Nil – it is that well known. Affording a great view of the Pyramids and the city, it serves top-quality Mediterranean cuisine accompanied by fine wines – all in an elegant environment.

GIZA AND HELIOPOLIS Abu Haidar   £
15 Sharia Ibrahim al-Laqqani, Heliopolis

If you adore freshly squeezed mango juice and meat burgers straight off the grill, then a lunchtime stop at Abu Haidar could be the order of the day. Located on a busy thoroughfare in the Roxy area of historic Heliopolis, this streetside grill specializes in all manner of steaks, fish and traditional grilled Egyptian cuisine.

GIZA AND HELIOPOLIS Al-Kods   £
52 Sharia Haroun al-Rashid, Heliopolis, Cairo **Tel** *02 6323 467*

This small and characterful eaterie is something of an institution in the Heliopolis area, especially since it has been run in the same manner for well over 40 years. Local residents and tourists alike visit it time and again. Much of the food is homemade, and its hummus, *fuul*, *aish* bread and falafel, along with its desserts, are really tasty and filling.

GIZA AND HELIOPOLIS Koshari Hind   £
Sharia Thawra, Heliopolis, Cairo

Located near the Midan Korba and a few minutes' walk from the Baron's Palace, one of Heliopolis's major landmarks, Koshari Hind is well known for its excellent *koshari* – a mix of pasta, rice, lentils and tomato sauce, all topped off with crispy fried onions and served with *aish* bread. It is open late.

GIZA AND HELIOPOLIS Tut Express   £
1 Sharia al-Saad al-Aali, Doqqi, Cairo **Tel** *02 3350 915*

Tourists the world over frequent fast-food establishments, and no city would be complete without one. The Tut Express is just such a place, and a jolly good one at that. It serves traditional Egyptian take-away foods, such as *shawarma* and *aish* bread, along with a few more international-themed foods. It is well known for its range of juices.

GIZA AND HELIOPOLIS Al-Amoudi   ££
4 Sharia Zamzam, Mohandiseen, Cairo **Tel** *02 7499 694*

If Yemeni food is a passion, or if you don't mind experimenting with flavours that are not often found in western restaurants, then Al-Amoudi should provide a good destination for lunch or dinner. Renowned as one of the best Yemeni restaurants in Cairo, it is styled in a traditional fashion.

GIZA AND HELIOPOLIS Andrea's   ££
4–5 Sharia Saqqara, Al-Maryutiya, Cairo **Tel** *02 3810 205*

One of a small chain of restaurants that is well respected throughout the area, Andrea's serves good Egyptian and European dishes, including a varied range of vegetarian specialities. Its wine list is carefully selected to complement the menu. Diners may choose to eat inside or in the shadows of its garden dining area.

Key to Price Guide *see p290* **Key to Symbols** *see back cover flap*

GIZA AND HELIOPOLIS Ataturk

20 Sharia al-Riyadh, Mohandiseen, Cairo **Tel** *02 3475 135*

A restaurant serving an extensive menu of traditional dishes from Turkey, Ataturk is usually buzzing with diners. Its mezes are especially popular: as a seemingly never-ending succession of dishes arrives at your table, you begin to wonder how long the meal will go on for. Mezes can comprise up to 20 dishes. No alcohol is served. Open late.

GIZA AND HELIOPOLIS At-Tekkia

12 Midan Ibn al-Walid, Doqqi, Cairo **Tel** *02 7496 673*

Conveniently located in the centre of Doqqi, near the shooting club, and specializing in good, home-cooked Egyptian food, this air-conditioned restaurant is a good bet to experience local cuisine. The dishes are well presented, the atmosphere is welcoming, and the staff are helpful and friendly.

GIZA AND HELIOPOLIS Americana Fish Market

26 Sharia El-Nil, Giza, Cairo **Tel** *02 5709 693*

Ideally located for a light lunch or evening meal following a sightseeing trip around the Pyramids, the Americana Fish Market is lively, has a colourful decor and serves a vast array of fish and seafood cooked to traditional Egyptian recipes. Prices won't break the bank, and the restaurant is open until late.

GIZA AND HELIOPOLIS The Cairo Jazz Club

197 Sharia 26th July, Agouza, Cairo **Tel** *02 3459 939*

The Cairo Jazz Club, near the Midan Sphinx, has earned a name for being "the" place to hear good, live jazz. This well-deserved reputation means the place is always buzzing with locals, as well as with tourists looking for a good evening's entertainment. The menu is Egyptian with a modern twist, and there is a good wine selection, too.

GIZA AND HELIOPOLIS Le Chantilly

11 Sharia Baghdad, Heliopolis, Cairo **Tel** *02 2907 303*

The name Chantilly suggests a restaurant oozing French chic. Indeed, although it serves dishes from all around Europe, this restaurant's menu would not look out of place in a Parisian brasserie. Breakfasts are continental, with fresh breads and croissants made in its adjoining bakery. The decor resembles a Swiss chalet. There's outside dining, too.

GIZA AND HELIOPOLIS Chopsticks

23b Sharia Syria, Mohandiseen, Cairo **Tel** *02 3048 568*

Chopsticks, as its name implies, is a lively, colourful restaurant serving some of the finest Chinese and Malaysian dishes in Cairo. Authentic specialities from Singapore are also on the menu. With prices that are competitive and a good wine list, the restaurant is popular with local residents, businesspeople and tourists alike.

GIZA AND HELIOPOLIS Hot Bite

132 Sharia Othman bin Affan, Heliopolis, Cairo **Tel** *02 2907 030*

Built in the early 1990s, this popular fast-food eaterie serves some great sandwiches, which are made fresh on the premises and contain such fillings as seafood, chicken and other meats, along with salads and sauces. The decor is bright and colourful and is true Egyptian style, and there's a large area outside to enjoy eating alfresco in the summer.

GIZA AND HELIOPOLIS Jaitta

120 Sharia al-Thawra, Heliopolis, Cairo **Tel** *02 4152 326*

Jaitta is one of the best Lebanese restaurants in Heliopolis, its speciality being a delicious version of *kofta*, a traditional dish of minced meat fashioned into balls and cooked in juices with herbs and spices. Be sure to try a water pipe, too. The restaurant has a traditional decor and is a good place to meet friends.

GIZA AND HELIOPOLIS Kandahar

Sharia Gamaat al-Dawal al-Arabiyya, Mohandiseen, Cairo **Tel** *02 3030 615*

One of the best-established restaurants in Cairo, located just off the Midan Sphinx, Kandahar has a cosy, traditional ambience, which makes it a popular place. It serves a good selection of Far Eastern food, especially Indian dishes, which can be hot or moderate, according to the diner's request.

GIZA AND HELIOPOLIS Le Tabasco

8 Midan Amman, Mohandiseen, Cairo **Tel** *02 3365 583*

Ask anyone where Le Tabasco is, and chances are they will have been there themselves – if they are of a certain age. Widely regarded as the coolest nightspot in town, it is frequented by Cairo's young and trendy, along with visitors to the city. The menu includes well-prepared Mediterranean dishes such as crêpes and pasta.

GIZA AND HELIOPOLIS Moghul Room

Sharia al-Ahram, Giza, Cairo **Tel** *02 3833 222*

Located within the 19th-century former hunting lodge that is now the Mena House Hotel, this ornately decorated restaurant has been designed to resemble a Moghul house. Its menu comprises good Indian food served in generous portions. Live music adds to the atmosphere and helps to make Moghul Room one of Cairo's most popular places.

GIZA AND HELIOPOLIS Swiss Restaurant

El Nasr Building, Sharia Nile, Giza, Cairo **Tel** *02 7610 165*

The Swiss Restaurant is one of three similar eateries in and around Cairo, each offering a wonderful choice of breakfast, lunch and evening dishes that might have delighted generations of Swiss residents. There's also a vegetarian menu, along with a good wine list. The pretty decor is Swiss-inspired. A good place to relax.

AROUND CAIRO

FAYOUM Queen Hotel

Sharia Lotfaliah Hassan, Fayoum **Tel** *084 346 819*

Located within the Queen Hotel and close to the centre of Fayoum, this restaurant is a good place to enjoy a leisurely dining experience, either at lunchtime or during the evening. The varied menu includes local delicacies, such as the fruits and vegetables for which Fayoum is famed, as well as international dishes such as grilled chicken.

FAYOUM Auberge du Lac-Fayoum

Lake Qarun, Fayoum **Tel** *084 572 001*

Set right on the edge of Lake Qarun and featuring a relaxing atmosphere, the Auberge du Lac-Fayoum is an elegant, sophisticated restaurant serving top-notch food. It is housed in a building that was once King Farouk's hunting lodge, and you can admire the wildfowl species that frequent Fayoum's salt lakes as you enjoy your lunch.

THE NILE VALLEY

ASWAN Hamam

Corniche el-Nil, Aswan

Hamam has no pretences of grandeur, but it does serve some exceptionally good and wholesome meals round the clock. Located in the very heart of Aswan and open 24 hours a day, it's one of those places that always seem to be buzzing with activity. It specializes in roasted meats, and every dish is served with rice.

ASWAN Sayida Nafisa

Sharia al-Souq, Aswan

Amid the hustle and bustle of the marketplace off the Sharia al-Souq, in the centre of town, is this tiny, unassuming restaurant. The fact that this place is always bursting at the seams with locals as well as tourists speaks volumes about its authenticity. Sayida Nafisa serves a menu of pure Egyptian fare and mouth-watering fruit juices.

ASWAN Al-Masry

Sharia al-Matar, Aswan **Tel** *097 302 576*

This air-conditioned restaurant is a veritable breath of fresh air when the sun is at its hottest, offering a welcoming place to linger over a light lunch or an evening meal. Al-Masry serves a wide and varied selection of Egyptian and European cuisine, including grilled chicken and fish. Its dessert trolley is utterly tempting.

ASWAN Aswan Moon

Felucca Quay, Aswan

Located right on the waterfront in a lively area of Aswan that is an easy walk from the centre of town, Aswan Moon provides a glorious setting for a truly memorable meal. Top-quality Egyptian and European cuisine is served here, including a good choice of vegetarian dishes.

ASWAN Aswan Panorama

Corniche el-Nil, Aswan **Tel** *097 306 169*

Aswan Panorama caters for alfresco dining enthusiasts, with a lavishly planted garden and a pretty outside eating area, although the interior is also pleasantly decorated. Situated on the riverside, the restaurant offers hearty meat and fish grills and classic Egyptian delicacies such as *koshari* and tagines, along with vegetarian dishes.

ASWAN Darwish

Sharia Saad Zaghloul, Aswan

Centrally located and within easy reach of Aswan's attractions, this beautifully presented restaurant offers a seemingly endless menu of typically Egyptian starters, mains and desserts. Darwish is renowned for its meat dishes, but significantly more so for the fresh fish that has come straight from the waters of Lake Nasser.

ASWAN Emy

Corniche el-Nil, Aswan

Emy is where the locals head when they have a celebration in the family or just want a special meal. A floating restaurant moored conveniently for the centre of town, it has wonderful views of Lake Nasser and Elephantine Island. Grilled fish is one of its most popular offerings, and the menu boasts a good selection of quality Egyptian cuisine.

ASWAN Medina

Sharia al-Souq, Aswan

A trip to the marketplace is a must during a visit to Aswan, but the hustle and bustle can become tiring in the heat, and the need for refreshment inevitable. Medina, a cosy little restaurant just opposite the landmark Cleopatra Hotel, has a good selection of juices and beverages, along with light Egyptian meals.

Key to Price Guide *see p290* **Key to Symbols** *see back cover flap*

ASWAN Mona Lisa

Corniche el-Nil, Aswan

A classically elegant restaurant along the riverside, Mona Lisa offers a good and varied menu of Italian pasta dishes, as well as Egyptian delicacies such as mezes. It is frequented by locals, businesspeople and travellers, and the mixed clientele gives it a convivial atmosphere. Look out for the view of Elephantine Island, especially at sunset.

ASWAN Nabian Restaurant

Essa Island, Aswan

Hop on the free ferry from the dock opposite the EgyptAir office and take a memorable trip across the water to the tiny Essa Island to eat at the Nabian Restaurant – it will be worth the effort! Serving good international and Egyptian food, and offering live entertainment most nights, Nabian is a popular eaterie that attracts tourists.

ASWAN The Terrace Bar & Restaurant

Sharia Abdul El Tehrir, Aswan **Tel** 097 2316 000

Located within the Sofitel Old Cataract Hotel, a wonderful 19th-century colonial establishment that featured in Agatha Christie's novel *Death on the Nile*, The Terrace Bar & Restaurant is a luxurious venue overlooking the river, and the ideal place for an elegant meal. The cuisine has an international flavour, and there is a good wine list.

ASYUT Akhnaton Restaurant

Akhnaton Hotel, Asyut **Tel** 088 337 723

A varied menu of international dishes (pizzas, steaks and chicken, salads) with prices that won't break the bank is on offer at Akhnaton. Located within the eponymous hotel, this is a popular restaurant, especially in the evenings. Centrally located, it is frequented by travellers en route from the Western Desert across the Sahara.

EDFU New Egypt Restaurant

Midan Maabad, Edfu

Edfu, a small farming town on the West Bank of the Nile, has few eateries, and New Egypt Restaurant is probably the best option for lunch or dinner. Its menu is not necessarily adventurous, with grilled meats, chicken, rice dishes, stews and vegetables being the staples, but the food is cooked well and is remarkably tasty.

KOM OMBO Venus Cafeteria & Restaurant

Close to the Temple of Kom Ombo

The picturesque setting of this restaurant – alongside the Nile, on the main route to the great Temple of Kom Ombo – makes it a popular choice for visitors to this small agricultural town, but then, there are few alternatives. Venus's selection is fairly basic and not dissimilar to fast food, but eveything is home-cooked and plentiful.

LUXOR Abu Hagger

Sharia Abdel Moneim al-Adasi, Luxor **Tel** 095 2376 306

This popular air-conditioned restaurant in the centre of Luxor offers a vast range of beautifully cooked and presented Egyptian and international dishes. Among the favourites are its kebabs, mezes and stuffed vegetables. Housed in an ornate building and oozing atmosphere, Abu Hagger is especially busy in the evenings and into the night.

LUXOR Khased Khear Restaurant

Sharia al-Mahatta, Luxor

If you are after authentic, freshly cooked beef and lamb kebabs, then Khased Khear is the place for you. This eaterie may be small, but the divine smells emanating from the grill make it easier to bear the cramped conditions. Close to the railway station, it is a good stopping-off point if you have just arrived or are about to depart from the city.

LUXOR Mensa

Sharia al-Mahatta, Luxor

Located near the train station, Mensa is a frenetic little place. The simple decor might not inspire you to linger over a meal. However, the food is fresh, piping hot and very tasty. Specialities of the house include roasted chicken, which is a safe bet, and spicy stuffed pigeon if you're feeling a little more adventurous.

LUXOR Sultana Restaurant

Sharia Television, Luxor

Sultana will literally come as a breath of fresh air as you enter – its air conditioning provides a welcome respite from the stifling heat of Luxor. A brightly coloured decor and friendly staff add to the welcoming feel of the place. On the menu you will find snacks, sandwiches and Italian pizzas.

LUXOR Al-Gezira

Bayrate al-Gezira, Luxor **Tel** 095 2310 034

A restaurant located on the rooftop of one of Luxor's most popular small hotels, Al-Gezira offers the chance to enjoy a fine meal while gazing across the waters of the Nile to the heady skyscape of Luxor lit up at night, making it a perfect addition to any holiday in Egypt. The menu is essentially Egyptian, with a few European flavours thrown in.

LUXOR Al-Houda Restaurant

Sharia Television, Luxor

If you are looking for a traditional restaurant serving good, honest Egyptian specialities, then a visit to Al-Houda should prove a winner. This air-conditioned restaurant also serves a good variety of Mediterranean-inspired dishes and lots of fruit juices, all at very reasonable prices.

LUXOR Amoun Restaurant
Sharia Karnak, Luxor

Amoun couldn't be better placed for a quick bite – it is close to the main attractions of Luxor and right in the tourist bazaar. Traditional, if a little uninspiring, in decor, it serves great Mediterranean cuisine, including meat and chicken dishes cooked with herbs, along with kebabs.

LUXOR King's Head Pub
Sharia Khalid Ibn al-Walid, Luxor

English tourists keen to catch up on the latest news from home tend to head for the King's Head Pub. Here they can also top up their intake of traditional British dishes like roast with all the trimmings and steak and kidney pie, along with sandwiches, soups and snacks. It even has its own billiards table and dartboards.

LUXOR Marhaba
Sharia Karnak, Luxor

Dining alfresco at this rooftop restaurant is a truly memorable experience, not least because the views of the Luxor, the temples and the Nile are breathtaking. A good selection of food is offered to vegetarian diners, while meat and fish lovers will be spoilt for choice with a vast range of Egyptian and Mediterranean delicacies.

LUXOR Tutankhamun Restaurant
West Bank, Luxor

This restaurant is lavishly decorated to a classic Egyptian style, but perhaps its most talked-about asset is its location – literally on the river Nile. If you are lucky, you may even be able to sit at a table on the bank. Food is wonderfully prepared and presented, and tailored to suit the regal environment.

LUXOR Anubis
Corniche el-Nil, Luxor

After a visit to the Museum of Mummification, one of the top tourist attractions in Luxor, one could simply step outside, go next door and be sitting at a table in this restaurant in no time at all. Right on the riverside, Anubis offers a tourist-friendly approach to Egyptian cuisine. Mezes are among the most popular dishes.

LUXOR Class
Sharia Khalid Ibn al-Walid, Luxor **Tel** *095 2376 327*

As its name suggests, Class is a relatively upmarket restaurant that offers convivial surroundings, a great location in the centre of Luxor and a friendly welcome. The food is based on pan-European cuisine complemented by a few Egyptian delicacies. A good range of wines is available to accompany your meal.

LUXOR Côte Jardin
Sharia Khalid Ibn al-Walid, Luxor **Tel** *095 2380 925*

This elegant French-inspired restaurant serves good-quality buffet-style pan-European dishes. Côte Jardin is the main restaurant of the Iberotel Luxor Hotel. It has an amazing view out over the Theban Hills and the Nile to the West Bank from both the dining hall and its terrace.

LUXOR The Mandarin
Sharia Khalid Ibn al-Walid, Luxor **Tel** *095 2380 925*

Located within the Iberotel Luxor Hotel and overlooking the Nile and Luxor's West Bank, The Mandarin is an elegant Oriental-themed eaterie – the ideal place for an intimate dinner for two. It serves a good range of Chinese and Japanese dishes from its set and à la carte menus, including soups, sushi and desserts.

LUXOR Summer Night
Corniche el-Nil, Luxor **Tel** *095 2380 422*

Set within the lush garden of the Sofitel Winter Palace Hotel, the Oriental-designed Summer Night comes into view from behind shrubs – like a mirage. Step inside, and the ambience is relaxing and the staff helpful. The menu offers a wide choice of Oriental cuisine, with matching wines.

SINAI AND THE RED SEA COAST

AL-ARISH Maxim
Beachside, Sharia Fouad Zakry, Al-Arish

This restaurant is open only in the summer months, where it can usually be found thronging with discerning diners. It is located right on the beach and serves a wide range of top-class international and Egyptian dishes, including a selection of vegetarian delicacies. Maxim promises a memorable experience of dining amid palm trees.

DAHAB Nirvana Indian Restaurant
Lighthouse, Dahab **Tel** *016 1046 061*

Open for breakfast, lunch and dinner, this restaurant offers a mouth-watering selection of traditional Indian dishes. The food is prepared and cooked using only the finest imported spices and the freshest ingredients. Food and drinks are served on the restaurant patio or on the beach.

Key to Price Guide *see p290* **Key to Symbols** *see back cover flap*

DAHAB INMO Divers Home Restaurant
Al-Mashraba, Dahab **Tel** *069 3640 370*

Located right on the beach at Dahab, this restaurant forms part of the INMO Divers Resort and is built to the same architectural style as the main building – that is, with lots of arches and domes. It serves good Oriental, vegetarian and international cuisine, with its speciality being Egyptian buffets and drinks such as *sahlab*.

DAHAB Nesima Restaurant
Mashraba, Dahab **Tel** *069 3640 320*

Nesima is a cosy and intimate restaurant within the Nesima Hotel, which is renowned for its excellent diving centre. The à la carte menu features a range of international dishes, along with Egyptian specialities such as *koshari*, followed by traditional desserts. A rooftop bar completes the dining experience.

HURGHADA Al Dente
Hurghada Intercontinental Resort, Hurghada **Tel** *065 3446 911*

Located within the Hurghada Intercontinental Resort complex, this stylish restaurant offers the chance to enjoy traditional Italian cuisine using ingredients fresh from Italy. Tuscan delicacies, as well as pasta dishes, are a speciality. The restaurant has a refined, elegant decor.

HURGHADA Portofino Restaurant
Sharia General Hospital, El Dahar, Hurghada **Tel** *065 3546 250*

An award-winning restaurant recommended by the Egyptian Ministry of Tourism and local businesses, Portofino is a slick operation. Its staff, and especially its owner, speak around nine languages and cater for an international clientele. Cuisine is predominantly classic Italian and seafood.

HURGHADA El Sol/The Catch
Holiday Inn Hurghada Resort, Corniche Road, Hurghada **Tel** *065 3445 080*

El Sol and The Catch are two "sister" restaurants located in the Holiday Inn Hurghada Resort complex. They serve a varied selection of dishes. El Sol offers daily changing menus of classic international cuisine, while The Catch specializes in seafood. Both enjoy a great location at the beachside resort.

HURGHADA Red Sea 1
Off Sharia Tariq Nasr, Ad-Dahar, Hurghada **Tel** *065 3547 704*

If seafood is your passion, then the traditionally styled Red Sea 1 is the perfect place for lunch or dinner. It is a popular, lively restaurant that can get crowded at peak times, especially if you decide to venture out on to its rooftop terrace for drinks. Traditional Egyptian dishes are also served.

ISMAILIA King Edward Restaurant
171 Sharia at-Tahir Street, Ismailia **Tel** *064 3369 611*

Specialities at the King Edward include classic Egyptian-style fish, seafood and hearty meat dishes, with the chicken being especially renowned. However, this means that it might be difficult for vegetarians to find a dish to suit their taste here. Pizzas are also served. The restaurant's decor is pleasant and traditional.

NAAMA BAY Kokai
Ghazala Hotel, Naama Bay, Sharm el-Sheikh **Tel** *069 3600 150*

This elegant grill room offers superbly flavoured renditions of the finest dishes in Polynesian and Chinese cuisine. Try the duck, the spring rolls and any of the variations on the rice. If you arrive early (around 6.30pm), you can also enjoy the experience of the *teppan-yaki* grill at your table.

NUWEIBA Blue Blue
Hilton Coral Resort, Nuweiba City **Tel** *062 3520 320*

Blue Blue is a bright, modern restaurant that overlooks the extensive beachside gardens of the Hilton Coral Resort. It is an ideal dining destination, both during the day and in the evening, when lighting shines on the pools and the luxuriant shrubs and palm trees. Cuisine is largely international and served buffet-style.

NUWEIBA Leserena Restaurant
Nuweiba Resort, Nuweiba City **Tel** *069 3500 402*

The Leserena Restaurant has an enviable view out over the Nuweiba Resort's beachside gardens and pool area. The cuisine is largely Egyptian, compounded by a selection of classic international staples such as pizzas and pasta dishes, salads and vegetarian choices. There is also an abundance of desserts and fresh fruit.

PORT SAFAGA Al-Fayrouz
Holiday Inn Safaga Palace, Safaga **Tel** *065 3252 821*

Al-Fayrouz may come as a culture shock if most of your holiday has been spent at dive camps or in small traditional Egyptian eateries. Catering for as many as 600 people, this vast restaurant serves a seemingly endless array of international foods buffet-style. Massive displays of fruit are a speciality.

PORT SAID Hotel de la Poste
La Poste Hotel, Sharia al-Gumhuriyya, Port Said **Tel** *066 3224 048*

With an extensive selection of freshly made sandwiches, pasta dishes, pizzas, salads, hamburgers and light snacks, the Hotel de la Poste's restaurant is more of a lunchtime eatery than a place to enjoy a leisurely dining experience. However, it is bright and welcoming, and you can spend a few hours people-watching from the terrace.

PORT SAID Maxim   🗐📋   ££££
Sharia Palestine, Port Said **Tel** *065 3234 335*

This restaurant in Port Said is one of the most popular and expensive in the area, with a reputation based on both the superb views it affords over the Suez Canal and its excellent fish and pasta dishes. The restaurant is located within the shopping centre that lies next to the Sonesta Hotel.

SHARM EL-SHEIKH Al-Fanar Restaurant   🖼   ££££
Ras Un Sid Beach, Sharm el-Sheikh **Tel** *069 3662 218*

Like many of the restaurants in Sharm el-Sheikh, Al-Fanar caters to the Italian hordes that holiday in this area by serving pizza and pasta dishes. What makes it stand out from the rest, though, is that fresh produce from Italy is regularly used. Its location right on the beach below the lighthouse provides an intimate setting. Good wine list.

SHARM EL-SHEIKH La Luna Restaurant   🗐🖼🎵📋🖼   ££££
Ritz-Carlton Resort, Om El Seed, Sharm el-Sheikh **Tel** *069 3661 919*

With an experienced Italian chef who excels in specialities such as calamari, potato gnocchi and home-made pasta, La Luna provides a memorable dining experience. A list of fine Italian wines and grappa is served. The restaurant has a luxurious feel and is located within the Ritz-Carlton Resort.

SUEZ Fish Restaurant   🗐   ££
Sharia as-Salaam, Suez

The Fish Restaurant is one of the Suez's worst-kept secrets – anyone who is anybody has eaten here. The restaurant has gained a remarkable reputation for serving the freshest of fish, which is charged by the weight and cooked so that it melts in the mouth. It is located right near the White House Hotel, in the centre of town.

THE DELTA AND THE NORTH COAST

ABU QIR Zaphyrion Restaurant   🗐🖼   ££
41 Sharia Khalid Ibn al-Walid, Abu Qir **Tel** *03 5621 319*

The place to visit for a refreshing change from the meat-heavy cuisine that appears on so many menus in Egypt. Although it doesn't shy away from meat dishes, Zaphyrion is mostly renowned for its delicious fish and seafood mezes. It is located right on the shores of the bay where Nelson fought the Battle of the Nile.

ALEXANDRIA City Café   🗐   £
21 Salah Salem, Alexandria **Tel** *03 4847 994*

City Café's modernist look, complete with glass walls, is in stark contrast to the ancient buildings that one typically encounters on a sightseeing trip around Alexandria. It is a relaxing place offering pan-European food, mostly from the Mediterranean basin. Or just stop by to enjoy a pastry and the excellent cappuccino.

ALEXANDRIA Fuul Mohammed Ahmed   🗐   £
17 Sharia Shakour, Alexandria **Tel** *03 4873 576*

This traditional little restaurant has earned itself a reputation for serving excellent *fuul*, the Egyptian staple of fava beans mashed with lemon juice, a selection of herbs and oil. In fact, Fuul Mohammed Ahmed has even created a few variants on the theme, adding new flavours for *fuul* lovers, including a spicy version.

ALEXANDRIA Elite   🗐   ££
43 Sharia Safia, Zaghloud, Alexandria **Tel** *03 4863 592*

A popular and lively restaurant, Elite is decorated with art posters, and it benefits from massive windows that open out on to the street, flooding the place with light. It is a great place for watching the world go by. The menu offers a rich mix of European dishes, as well as many vegetarian Egyptian options.

ALEXANDRIA Gezirat al-Malika   🗐   ££
48 Sharia Safr Basha, Ras el-Tin, Alexandria **Tel** *03 4804 996*

Conveniently located for visiting Alexandria's main tourist attractions, and not far from the water's edge, Gezirat al-Malika serves traditional Egyptian dishes such as *fuul* and mezes, along with *kofta*, kebabs and a great selection of stuffed vegetables. The fun, colourful decor resembles that of a local rural village.

ALEXANDRIA Pastroudis   🗐   ££
39 Sharia al-Huriya, Alexandria **Tel** *03 3929 609*

No trip to Alexandria would be complete without a visit to one of its most famous cafés. Pastroudis opened its doors in 1923 and soon earned a reputation for serving fine pastries in an atmospheric setting. Today it still sells tempting cakes and pastries, in addition to sandwiches, light snacks and pasta dishes.

ALEXANDRIA China Restaurant   🖼📋   £££
Midan Saad Zaghloul, Alexandria **Tel** *03 4877 173*

The China Restaurant is housed within the colonial-style Sofitel Alex Cecil Hotel, in one of Alexandria's busiest commercial areas. As such, it is frequented by businesspeople, as well as tourists and locals. As the name suggests, the restaurant offers Chinese cuisine – indeed, some of the best to be found in the city.

Key to Price Guide *see p290* **Key to Symbols** *see back cover flap*

ALEXANDRIA Taverna

Sharia Saad Zaghloul, Alexandria **Tel** *03 4860 986*

Situated right across the street from the tram terminal and easy to find, Taverna is one of a small chain of restaurants. It serves *fateers*, a sort of pastry pancake filled with chicken, beef and fish combinations, or sweet with honey and fruit. Pizzas are on the menu too.

ALEXANDRIA Trianon Restaurant

Sharia Saad Zaghloul, Alexandria **Tel** *03 4860 985*

The decor alone justifies a visit to the Trianon Restaurant. Recently restored, it is pure Art Deco and a symbol of the city's pre-revolution café scene. The menu is varied, with international and Egyptian dishes, not to mention a good dessert selection that includes Trianon's speciality *Umm Ali*, a pastry with nuts and fruit.

ALEXANDRIA Al-Farouk Restaurant

As-Salamiek Palace Hotel, Montazah Gardens, Alexandria **Tel** *03 5477 999*

Housed within one of King Farouk's former hunting lodges that has recently been renovated, the Al-Farouk Restaurant forms part of a complex of elegant dining halls and bars. Its air of opulence is compounded by the top-quality international cuisine on offer and a cellar stocked with the finest wines from around the world.

THE WESTERN DESERT

BAHARIYYA Popular Restaurant

Bawiti, al-Bahariyya Oasis

Bahariyya Oasis offers little in the way of eating establishments other than those located in the handful of hotels, but this is the exception. The Popular Restaurant is cosy and intimate, serving a good selection of typical Egyptian and European cuisine, such as grilled meats and vegetables.

DAKHLA Ahmed Hamdy's Restaurant

Mut, Dakhla Oasis **Tel** *092 7820 767*

A traditionally styled restaurant in the centre of Mut, Ahmed Hamdy's is well known for offering a good choice of dishes at competitive prices. Chicken, kebabs, mezes and stuffed vegetables all feature heavily on the menu. It is close to the Mebarez Hotel and popular with tourists and tour groups.

DAKHLA Garden's Hotel Restaurant

Mut, Dakhla Oasis **Tel** *092 7821 577*

A pleasant place to enjoy traditional Egyptian dishes, such as *koshari*, *fuul* and rice, plus a few European choices, such as grilled meats, omelettes and salads, Garden's Hotel Restaurant is one of the more popular eateries in Mut. It is located in the old part of town and has an outside area for dining alfresco.

FARAFRA Hussein Restaurant

Qasr al-Farafra, Farafra

There are few places to find a good meal in Farafra Oasis, one of the most isolated areas in the Western Desert, but the Hussein Restaurant is certainly among the forerunners. The restaurant doesn't score high for decor, nor for a wide-ranging menu, but it does offer wholesome Egyptian meals all day at competitive prices.

FARAFRA Al-Badawiyya Safari and Hotel

Bawiti road, Qasr al-Farafra, Farafra **Tel** *092 7510 060*

The Al-Badawiyya Safari and Hotel offers good food, the recipes for which have been handed down through generations of Egyptian families. Enjoying a cold beer here, in the unique setting of a small desert oasis town, is sure to be a magical highlight of a holiday spent in Egypt.

KHARGA Pioneers Hotel

El Kharga Oasis, El Wadi El Guedid, El Kharga **Tel** *092 7927 982*

Surrounded by palm trees and sand dunes, and decorated to an authentic Egyptian style, this restaurant within the Pioneers Hotel makes for a memorable experience. Its air-conditioned dining room also provides a welcome respite from the desert heat. The menu is varied and inspired by international cuisine.

SIWA Alexander the Great

Siwa Oasis, Siwa **Tel** *046 4602 081*

This modern little eatery is housed within the recently opened Alexander Hotel, and offers good, traditional Egyptian food with an international twist. Its oasis setting and friendly staff make it a favourite for locals and, especially, travellers exploring this part of the country.

SIWA Siwa Safari Paradise Hotel

Sharia Ein El Arais, Siwa **Tel** *046 4602 289*

This lively restaurant within the Siwa Safari Paradise Hotel regularly hosts traditional Siwan feasts featuring entertainment and dancing. Along with the international-inspired cuisine, this makes it popular with locals, tour groups and travellers alike. The restaurant nestles in the gardens of a resort-style complex.

SHOPPING IN EGYPT

When it comes to shopping, the souqs and bazaars are undoubtedly Egypt's main attraction. The biggest and most famous is Cairo's Khan al-Khalili (see pp88–90), a 500-year-old maze of commerce at the heart of the old Islamic city. While on first encounter it can seem to cater excessively to tourism, explore deeper and the narrow alleys become a bustling hive of small workshops turning out attractive jewellery, glass-, copper and brassware. Here you can buy direct

Souq trader in Luxor smoking a water pipe

from the artisans and cut out the middleman. Most other towns and cities throughout the country also have souqs, with particularly good ones in Alexandria, Aswan and Port Said. For visitors intending to shop in these places it is essential to become acquainted with the art of bargaining. In contrast to the traditional nature of the souq, larger cities, such as Cairo and Alexandria, also possess modern shopping precincts, as well as shopping centres filled with globally recognized brand names.

OPENING HOURS

There are no strictly defined opening hours in Egypt – it depends on each individual proprietor. Generally, however, except for local grocery stores, which open early, business activity begins at around 9 or 10am. Businesses tend to close for a siesta from around 2 to 5pm, except in Cairo, where shops remain open all day. They then typically stay open until 9pm or later. In summer, in busy commercial areas, and especially Khan al-Khalili, the shutters often do not come down until 10 or 11pm, as people prefer to shop when it is cooler. Other souqs keep shorter hours, with stalls and businesses packing up around sunset. Friday is the official day off, although in Cairo many shops are open seven days a week. Those open on Friday may still close for a couple of hours in the middle of the day for noon prayers. Businesses owned by Christians may close on Sunday. During Ramadan shops close 30 minutes before sunset but reopen a couple of hours later. The whole country shuts down on major feasts, which include Moulid an-Nabi, Eid al-Fitr and Eid al-Adha (see p39).

HOW TO PAY

Although their use as a form of payment is increasing, credit cards are typically still only accepted at larger or tourist-oriented shops, such as those

found in hotel complexes or shopping malls. Likewise, traveller's cheques are hardly accepted anywhere. In most places, it is necessary to pay in cash. Egyptian pounds are the country's only legal currency and purchases cannot usually be made in dollars.

SOUQS AND MARKETS

Besides Khan al-Khalili there are numerous other souqs and markets in Cairo, many worth a visit irrespective of whether you intend buying anything. Fruit and vegetables are sold at the many street markets scattered throughout the city. Every neighbourhood has one. In central Cairo there is the Tawfiqiyya market, one block north of Sharia 26th July, open so late that many stallholders don't bother going home; they simply sleep beside their carts. On the east bank of the Nile, opposite Zamalek, again just north of Sharia 26th July, is Bulaq market selling textiles, second-hand clothing, car parts and military surplus.

Cairo's Downtown bookshops are excellent for books on Egypt

An even stranger mix is presented at the weekly Souq al-Gomaa, or Friday market, held just south of the Citadel, where the trade is in bric-à-brac and animals. It must be one of the few markets where you can buy both a set of 1930s crockery and a squawking cockatoo. Next to Ataba metro station, just north of Midan Opera, is Al-Azbakiyya Gardens. Here, second-hand books and magazines, many of them in English, are sold from a collection of cabins.

In Alexandria, Attarine is not so much a market as a maze of narrow alleyways lined with antique shops that spill their goods out on to the street. Al-Arish in northern Sinai also has a colourful Thursday-morning market frequented by local Bedouin who sell embroidered dresses and distinctive, handcrafted jewellery.

Stacked merchandise in one of Cairo's markets

Examining the brass- and copperware in Khan al-Khalili

SHOPPING CENTRES

Cairo – and Alexandria to a lesser extent – has a rapidly growing number of large shopping centres or malls. These are filled with standard arcade-type outlets that sell everything from greetings cards to electrical goods, most of which are US and European imports. They also usually incorporate fast-food outlets and multi-screen cinemas. Egypt's largest mall, **Arkadia Mall**, is on the Corniche el-Nil in Cairo. It houses more than 500 stores and plenty of snack bars. Many international brands have outlets here, including Timberland, Adidas, Nike and Habitat, as well as their Egyptian counterparts. For a chic shopping destination, head to the **First Residence Mall** in Giza, which overlooks the zoo and forms part of an accommodation complex for the rich. The **Ramses Hilton Mall**, adjacent to the Ramses Hilton hotel in the city centre, is more family friendly and offers value-for-money shoes and clothing. On the top floor is a cinema and a snooker hall. Out in Heliopolis *(see pp136–7)* beside the Basilica is the **Horreyya Mall**, which has become a popular place for local kids to hang out.

BUYING ANTIQUES

Most antiquities offered to visitors are anything but antique. "Old" papyrus may well have been painted just last week and probably not on papyrus (which has all but

vanished) but on dried banana leaves. Similarly, so-called ancient scarabs are often made by carving them from old bone and then feeding them to turkeys – the birds' gastric juices create a realistic ageing effect. However, in some respects this is all just as well because genuine antiquities (in general, anything over 100 years old) can only be exported with a licence from the Department of Antiquities.

HOW TO BARGAIN

Buying and selling in Egypt is traditionally a highly ritualized affair, in which bargaining is far more than just haggling for a cheap price. The aim of the exercise is to establish a fair price that both vendor and buyer are happy with. As part of the process, a shop-owner may well invite you to have a cup of tea or coffee and may literally turn the place upside down to show something. You should not feel obliged to buy because of this, as it is a common sales practice and all part of the ritual.

Bargaining even happens in city-centre shops over goods which appear to have a fixed price. It is in the souq, however, that it becomes a necessity if you want to avoid paying greatly over the odds.

Once you have identified an article that interests you, especially if it is an expensive one, be brave enough to offer half the price quoted by the shop-owner. Don't be put off by feigned indignation or mockery on the shop keeper's part, and only raise your next offer by a small amount. Through a process of offer and counter-offer you should eventually arrive at a mutually agreeable price. If you don't reach a price you think is fair then simply say thank you and leave. Making to walk away can often have the effect of bringing the price tumbling down.

In theory, although you may feel uncomfortable, no one gets cheated. You, the buyer, have set the price yourself, so it follows that you are happy with what you have agreed to pay. The shop-keeper, for his part, will never sell at a loss, so he will certainly have made a profit on the deal.

The Sindbad Shopping Mall at Sindbad Beach Resort, Hurghada

Where to Shop in Egypt

Cairo's Khan al-Khalili *(see pp88–90)* is the first place to look for Egyptian souvenirs, while city-centre shopping focuses on the triangle of Sharia Talaat Harb, 26th July and Qasr el-Nil. The island suburb of Zamalek is a great hunting ground for boutiques specializing in ethnic crafts, designer wear and antiques. Elsewhere in Egypt, only the most determined shopaholics will find much to buy – perhaps colourful textiles and spices in Aswan and pottery and jewellery in the oases.

SOUVENIRS

Khan al-Khalili in Cairo and other tourist bazaars in Upper Egypt are crammed with incredibly kitsch items, such as Nefertiti reading lamps, alabaster pyramids, stuffed leather camels and Tutankhamun baseball caps.

There are more worthwhile items to be found, however: attractive backgammon boards, like those used in Egyptian coffeehouses, at least have a practical purpose. Or you could buy your own *sheesha* (waterpipe), though you will also need to stock up on the special tobacco and the small clay pots that the tobacco is stuffed into. Small boxes inlaid with mother-of-pearl are pretty and very inexpensive. Inlaid chessboards are also popular buys.

Almost everyone visiting Egypt picks up some papyrus – often cheap and poor quality, shoddily painted with scenes copied from pharaonic wall paintings. For better quality work, visit one of the **Dr Ragab Papyrus Institutes**, where you can get the genuine article, which will not crack or have the paint flake off when it is rolled.

Souvenir figure of Anubis

BRASS- AND COPPERWARE

Plates, coffeepots and trays of brass and copper are made in the workshops around Khan al-Khalili. For good examples, have a look at the Copper-smiths Market (Souq an-Nahassin) in Sharia al-Muizz li-Din Allah, south of the great mosques on Bein al-Qasreen.

Stallholder selling leather belts in Midan Ataba

HANDICRAFTS

Different parts of Egypt are associated with their own particular crafts, but much of the best of this work makes its way to Cairo. For example, **Al-Khatoun**, which is based in a restored Ottoman house behind the Mosque of al-Azhar, sells wrought-iron furniture that is made in a village just outside Cairo, as well as soft wall hangings, glassware and locally-made leather goods.

The nearby **Wikala of al-Ghouri**, an early 17th-century merchants' hostel, plays host to a number of artisans, whose work is sold on the premises. Opposite the entrance to the Mosque of Ibn Tulun, also in Islamic Cairo, **Khan Misr Touloun** is a beautiful gallery selling handicrafts from the villages and oases of Egypt. These include wooden chests, bowls and plates, blown glass, clay figurines, scarves and woven clothing. Based in Zamalek, **Egypt Craft** has Bedouin rugs and embroidery from Sinai and the northern Western Desert, hand-made paper from Muqattam and shawls from Upper Egypt. Also in Zamalek, located on the first floor of an apartment block overlooking the Nile, **Nomad** specializes in jewellery and traditional Bedouin craft and costumes.

CARPETS AND RUGS

Unlike Morocco, Turkey or Iran, Egypt is not a big carpet producer. What you will find, however, are hardwearing, brown and beige striped, camel-hair rugs of Bedouin origin. The biggest selection is to be found in the Haret al-Fahhamin, a tight maze of alleys behind the Mosque of Al-Ghouri, across the road from Khan al-Khalili in Islamic Cairo. Many of the places mentioned in the Handicrafts section also stock Bedouin rugs. Connoisseurs might want to visit the weekly markets at Al-Arish, in northern Sinai, and in Dahab. In the area of the Pyramids,

Coppersmith's workshop in Sharia al-Muizz li-Din Allah

Locals gather at one of Cairo's colourful carpet bazaars

just off the road to Saqqara, the **Wissa Wassef Art Centre** specializes in very distinctive woollen rugs and wall hangings depicting rural and folkloric scenes. These can also be bought at **Senouhi**, a fascinating little shop on the fifth floor of an apartment block in Downtown Cairo. Senouhi also sells good quality jewellery, antiques, Bedouin rugs and art.

CLOTH AND TEXTILES

Cotton is Egypt's biggest cash crop, and department and clothing stores in central Cairo and Alexandria carry excellent quality, plain cotton shirts, T-shirts and underwear. Look out, in particular, for branches of **Safari**, found in all the big malls and in some hotel shopping complexes. Down in Middle Egypt, just across the Nile from Sohag, the village of Akhmim is the centre of an ancient weaving tradition. Legend has it that pharaohs were buried in shrouds of Akhmim silk. Still in production, but now in factories rather than the local workshops, the cloth comes in deep, rich colours, with elaborate floral and paisley-style patterns. It is extremely beautiful, but hard to find. The best bet is to go direct to the factories; otherwise some of the hotel shops in Luxor carry a small selection.

BELLYDANCING COSTUMES

Sequinned bras, beaded hip-bands, veils and flimsy skirts are sold in a couple of specialist shops in Khan al-Khalili. One is in the small passageway leading from Muski to Fishawi's coffee house. Serious practitioners should pay a visit to the studio of **Amira al-Khattan** in Mohandiseen, who tailors costumes to order.

JEWELLERY

Egypt's gold and silver shops are concentrated in the centre of Khan al Khalili. Jewellery is sold by weight, with a little extra added for workmanship. The current gold prices are listed each day in the *Egyptian Gazette*. The most popular souvenirs are gold or silver cartouches with a given name engraved in hieroglyphics. Most of the shops in Khan al-Khalili can arrange to have this done.

SPICES AND HERBS

Khan al-Khalili in Cairo and the souk in Aswan are both excellent for spices. Generally these are fresher and of better quality than any of the packaged variety sold in the West. They are also much cheaper, especially saffron. The stalls that sell spices often also have heaps of purplish, dried hibiscus leaves. When boiled up, strained and sugared, these make *karkade*, the excellent deep red, iced drink served in coffee houses. Some of the shop owners in the Spice Bazaar are also herbalists, who prepare traditional remedies for a variety of ailments.

A colourful display of aromatic spices in the Spice Bazaar

What to Buy in Egypt

Box inlaid with mother-of-pearl

Egypt's magical souqs and bazaars offer the visitor an eclectic mix of trinkets and souvenirs. The quality can vary greatly so always inspect the items closely and be prepared to haggle over the price (see p303). Sheesha (waterpipes), backgammon boards, decorative boxes and an array of kitsch paraphernalia fill the market stalls alongside traditional handicrafts often made by local artisans. Egyptian copperware and Muski glass are produced in Cairo's Khan al-Khalili (see pp88–9), while Bedouin jewellery traditionally comes from Sinai. The best hand-woven silk and cotton is made in Akhmim in Middle Egypt, famous for the quality of its weaving.

Sheesha
A fixture in every coffee house, a waterpipe makes an excellent gift. Decorated with stainless steel or brass fittings, the pipes use a special fragrant tobacco loosely packed into a clay pot.

Backgammon Board
Backgammon and chess are popular pastimes in Egypt. Sets of varying quality are readily available with the cheaper boards being crudely made and with little inlay. The better sets are made out of hard woods and inlaid with intricate designs of mother-of-pearl, bone or ivory.

Sandals
Reasonably-priced leather items such as bags, wallets and hand-crafted sandals are sold in most bazaars.

Glass and Pottery
Hand-blown, blue Muski glass is uniquely Egyptian and fashioned into plates, vases, glasses and candle-holders. Good hand-made pots, like this sculpted alabaster vase, are also easily found.

Perfume Bottles
These delicate glass perfume bottles are fashioned into intricate shapes. They come in various sizes and make wonderful gifts.

Bedouin Jewellery
Bedouin jewellery traditionally comes from Sinai and Siwa Oasis, and often features coins in its designs. While truly authentic Bedouin jewellery is hard to find, its styles have been widely imitated. Other popular designs include those based on Pharaonic, Islamic and Nubian motifs.

Copperware
A wide range of copper and brass goods is sold throughout Egypt but the Cairo souqs and workshops offer the widest selection. Typical buys include Arabic coffeepots, trays and hanging lamps as well as decorative pieces such as plates embossed with classic arabesques.

Clothes and Textiles

Cotton is one of Egypt's major crops and cotton clothes are popular. Plain and embroidered cotton shirts, trousers and galabiyyas (loose, all-in-one robes) are usually of high quality and good value. The brightly coloured fabrics are excellent as scarves, cushion covers, wall hangings and throws. Garish belly-dancing outfits are also popular purchases.

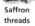

Embroidered cotton shirts   Brightly-coloured woven scarf   Sequined belly-dancing costume

Tourist souvenirs

A myriad of kitsch reproductions of Pharaonic art, alabaster pyramids, stuffed leather camels, busts of Nefertiti and sheets of papyrus painted with scenes from temples or tombs are sold in all tourist areas. These items, along with trinket boxes, ashtrays, chessboards and sheesha make popular and inexpensive gifts.

Stuffed leather camel

Papyrus with Pharaonic scenes

Bust of Nefertiti

Carved figurines of ancient gods

Alabaster ashtray

Egyptian Music

The easiest way to recreate the Egyptian experience is to buy some Egyptian CDs or tapes. The choice ranges from traditional folk music and the mournful sounds of Umm Kolthum (see p125) to modern, bouncy Egyptian pop.

Spices and Flavourings

Colourful and fragrant, Egyptian spices can be located easily in the bazaars. Spices are sold loose by weight and are often far cheaper, fresher and of better quality than the pre-packaged ones sold in the west. One word of caution, however, Egyptian saffron is very cheap but it may not be top quality.

Carob   Cinnamon

Cloves   Chillies   Turmeric

Cayenne Pepper   Cardamon pods   Saffron threads

ENTERTAINMENT IN EGYPT

Most people find that the range of entertainment options in Egypt, especially outside Cairo, is surprisingly limited. Locals tend to fill their free time with visits to friends or family, or, in the case of the menfolk, whiling away the hours in a coffeehouse. A few major, well-attended cultural events punctuate the calendar, notably the Cairo International Book Fair in spring and the Cairo Film Festival in November and December *(see p41)*. Otherwise the annual high spots are tied

Passing time at a street-side coffeehouse in Cairo

into religion – the feast days of Eid al-Adha and Eid al-Fitr *(see p33)*, and the holy month of Ramadan. On these occasions, temporary fairgrounds are often set up in main squares, and there are plenty of performances of traditional music and folk dancing. Recent years have even seen a revival of the age-old art of story-telling, with actors and actresses half-performing, half-narrating tales from the likes of *The Thousand and One Nights* to enraptured audiences.

Cairo by night, its bright lights reflected in the calm waters of the Nile

particularly during Ramadan, there are often music evenings and theatre productions held at the **Beit Zeinab Khatoun** and the **Al-Ghouri Palace for Traditional Culture**, part of the historic Al-Ghouri Complex *(see pp91–2)*. It is worthwhile trying to attend one or more of the performances at the Al-Ghouri Complex even if it is only to savour the atmosphere of the superb historic setting.

INFORMATION

There is no shortage of entertainment guides in Egypt. Each month a glossy magazine called *Egypt Today* is published and includes extensive coverage of artistic and cultural events taking place throughout the country. It is available from bookstands and newsagents everywhere. The weekly English-language newspapers *Al-Ahram Weekly, The Middle East Times* and *The Cairo Times* also carry good listings information on what is showing at cinemas, galleries and the theatre, although their coverage is limited solely to Cairo. *The Big Croc*, a small, quarterly, pocket-sized magazine covering the city's nightlife and entertainment scene has now folded but may start up again in the future. Their website at www. ecroc.com is still operational.

There is no central booking office for shows and concerts, and it is generally necessary to buy tickets from the relevant theatre or concert hall box office. It is also a sensible precaution to book tickets several days in advance.

ARABIC MUSIC

Much of the programming at the **New Cairo Opera House** and Alexandria's **Sayed Darwish Theatre** involves live performances of Arabic classical music. In Islamic Cairo,

WHIRLING DERVISHES

The Al-Ghouri complex in Islamic Cairo stages whirling dervish performances Wednesdays and Saturdays, from 9pm. The shows are free. There is fairly limited seating, so get there early to avoid having to stand. It is permitted to take photos but not to film on video. More dance and musical events are held at the **Al-Sawy Culture Wheel**.

Whirling dervish putting on a spectacular performance in Cairo

Belly Dancing

Despite a heritage that dates back to Pharaonic times, modern-day belly dancing owes more to the European experience of Egypt in the 18th and 19th centuries. The sensual movements of the Egyptian dancers, who blended folk, gypsy and Ottoman dances, fired the imaginations of repressed Europeans. It is largely due to their descriptions that the dancing was associated with prostitution. Even dedicated, professional belly dancers, who prefer the term "oriental dancer", get tarred with this brush.

The advent of cinema put belly dancing on the big screen, increasing its popularity and making stars of the performers. Today, despite its popularity, belly dancing still carries a social stigma which discourages Egyptian women from entering the profession, and the gap is increasingly being filled by foreign dancers.

A belly dancer's backing musician

Dancers *played an important part in ancient Egyptian ritual and celebration. Their poses, as shown here, clapping or using castanets are very similar to modern Egyptian dancing.*

Salome, *in the Bible, asked Herod for the head of John the Baptist as reward for her dancing. Late 19th-century writers added eroticism to the story, resulting in a series of scantily-clad cabaret acts as depicted in this 1909 music sheet cover.*

Superstar Amira *dances at the Giza Pyramids. Although belly dancing's popularity has been hit by the rise of Islamic fundamentalism, its top stars are among Egypt's highest earners.*

Belly dancers *at nightclubs in Central Cairo perform before mainly male audiences, who look but most definitely do not touch.*

Orientalist painters *from America and Europe frequently depicted exotic scenes such as this French 1914 lithograph. However, here they ignored the fact that men would not have been allowed in the harem.*

View of the Cairo Opera House from the top of the 185-m (606-ft) Cairo Tower *(see p84)*

BELLY DANCING AND FOLKLORIC DANCE

While the best dancers perform at the nightclubs attached to Cairo's five-star hotels, such as the **Haroun al-Rashid Club** and **Auberge du Nil**, where a seat costs about US $50 a head (buffet included), for pure entertainment visit the much cheaper **Palmyra**. The main act generally does not appear until at least 1am and the band will not call it a night until the sun is rising. Dancers can be seen at most hotels and tourist restaurants in the country. Venues in Luxor and Aswan, such as the **Aswan Cultural Palace**, often feature Egyptian folkloric dance troupes.

SOUND AND LIGHT SHOWS

Every major site in Egypt feels compelled to present a sound and light show. These begin once the sun goes down, and involve the monument being illuminated by coloured floodlights while a recorded voice narrates snippets of history and mythology. The narration often leaves a lot to be desired, but it is worth going just to revisit some of Egypt's sights by moonlight. The Pyramids at Giza, Luxor, Karnak, Philae and Abu Simbel all offer several shows a night in various languages.

WESTERN CLASSICAL MUSIC

Egypt's main classical music venue is the **New Cairo Opera House**, on the island of Gezira. Its main hall hosts regular performances from a variety of visiting international artists. On such occasions a jacket and tie is compulsory for men. The small hall has nightly recitals by quartets, soloists and ensembles and is also used by the Cairo Symphony Orchestra, which gives concerts here every Saturday from September to mid-June. The Cairo classical music scene is well covered in *Al-Ahram Weekly*. In Alexandria, both the **Alexandria Conference Hall** and **Sayed Darwish Theatre** host classical concerts organized by the French, Italian or German consulates. Details of what's on are posted in the window of the Elite restaurant *(see p300)*. Otherwise, you are unlikely to hear much Western classical music in Egypt.

Billboards advertising forthcoming cultural events in Cairo

OPERA AND BALLET

The premises of the **New Cairo Opera House** are shared by both the Cairo Ballet Company and the Cairo Opera Company. The season is limited, and productions are few, although they are sometimes supplemented by visiting companies. There are also occasional dance performances at Cairo's **Gumhuriyya Theatre**. Almost every year now, the Ministry of Culture also mounts a grand production of *Aida*, the opera written in honour of the opening of the Suez Canal *(see pp60–61)*. Previous performances have been held at the temples of Hatshepsut and Karnak in Luxor, but most recently the venue has been the Pyramids. It is a very high-profile occasion, drawing opera-lovers from all over the world. Egypt's overseas tourist offices will be able to provide full details on when the next grand event takes place.

Inside a young and fashionable bar in upmarket Mohandiseen, Cairo

BARS AND DISCOS

Despite being predominantly Islamic, there are plenty of bars in Egypt beyond those in the hotels – look for signs for "cafeterias". Some of the best are to be found in Alexandria, notably the **Cap d'Or**, a beautiful old place that feels like a real Mediterranean taverna. In Cairo, nightlife centres on the upmarket neighbourhoods of Zamalek and Mohandiseen. Bars such as **Deals, L'Aubergine, Le Tobasco** and **Bull's Eye** cater mainly for young wealthy Egyptians, as well as the city's large expatriate community. Later on, those with the energy move on to the busy Downtown discos which play hip hop and dance music. These include **Space Disco**, Egypt's only purpose-built dance venue, part of a large, modern entertainment complex called Cairo Land.

Red Sea and Sinai resorts such as Sharm el-Sheikh, Naama Bay and Hurghada are also packed full of bars and discos. But the scene is constantly changing, so pick

A hotel disco at Agami, on the North Coast, west of Alexandria

up *Sinai Today* or *Red Sea Today* from bookshops or newsstands to get all the details on what's happening.

The resorts along the north coast have few good bars or discos. Typically these are attached to hotels like the **Summer Moon** at Agami, the so-called St Tropez of Egypt.

ROCK, JAZZ AND POP

Rock, jazz and pop concerts are virtually unheard of. A handful of artists, such as The Grateful Dead, Shirley Bassey and, at the Millennium celebrations, Jean-Michel Jarre, have played the Pyramids but such events happen very rarely. Egyptian pop stars don't do concerts either. Practically the only place to hear live contemporary music is in hotel lounges and bars. Every major five star establishment has a resident cabaret singer or jazz quartet, but don't expect to recognize any names. About the only dedicated live venue in the country is the **Cairo Jazz Club**, a small, suitably smoky joint, with a band every night, usually drawn from the tiny but enthusiastic local scene.

DIRECTORY

ARABIC MUSIC AND WHIRLING DERVISHES

Alexandria Conference Hall
International Conference Centre, Shatby, Alexandria.
Tel (03) 487 8093.

Al-Ghouri Palace for Traditional Culture
Sharia al-Muizz li-Din Allah, Cairo. **Map** 2 F5.
Tel (02) 510 0823.

Al-Sawy Culture Wheel
1 Sharia 26th July, Zamalek, Cairo. **Tel** (02) 736 8881.
www.culturewheel.com

Beit Zeinab Khatoun and Beit al-Harawi
Harat al-Azhar, Cairo.
Map 2 F5.
Tel (02) 735 7001.

New Cairo Opera House
Sharia at-Tahrir, Gezira, Cairo. **Map** 1 A5.
Tel (02) 739 8114.

Sayed Darwish Theatre
22 Tariq al-Horreyya, Alexandria.
Tel (03) 486 5106.

BELLY DANCING

Aswan Cultural Palace
Corniche, Aswan.
Tel (097) 313 390.

Auberge du Nil
Royal Nile Tower Hotel, Corniche el-Nil, Cairo.
Map 5 A5.
Tel (02) 362 1717.

Haroun al-Rashid Club
Semiramis Hotel, Corniche el-Nil, Cairo.
Map 5 A4.
Tel (02) 795 7171.

Palmyra
Just south of Sharia 26th July, between Sharia Sharif and Mohammed Farid, Cairo. **Map** 2 D4, 6 D2.

SOUND AND LIGHT SHOWS

For all sites
Tel (02) 386 3469.
www.sound-light.egypt.com

OPERA AND BALLET

Gumhuriyya Theatre
12 Sharia al-Gumhuriyya, Cairo. **Map** 2 D3.
Tel (02) 390 7707.

BARS AND DISCOS

L'Aubergine
5 Al-Sayyid al-Bakri, Zamalek, Cairo. **Map** 1 A3.
Tel (02) 738 0080.

Bull's Eye
32 Sharia Jedda, Mohandiseen, Cairo.
Tel (02) 761 6888.

Cap d'Or
4 Sharia Adib, Alexandria.
Tel (03) 487 5177.

Deals
Al-Sayyid al-Bakri, Zamalek, Cairo. **Map** 1 A3.
Tel (02) 736 0502.

Space Disco
Cairo Land, 1 Sharia Salah Salem, Cairo. **Map** 3 C4.
Tel (02) 365 6913.

Summer Moon
Summer Moon Hotel, Agami. **Tel** (03) 433 0367.

Le Tabasco
8 Midan Amman, Doqqi, Cairo. **Tel** (02) 336 5583.

ROCK, JAZZ AND POP

Cairo Jazz Club
197 Sharia 26th July, Mohandiseen, Cairo.
Tel (02) 345 9939.

The Cosmos cinema, one of many local movie houses in Cairo

CINEMA

In recent years, cinema in Egypt has had an overhaul. Large, modern multiplexes have been opened in Cairo and Alexandria and old movie houses have been refurbished. Programming is usually split between Arabic films and the latest Hollywood releases, with foreign films screened in their original languages and subtitled in Arabic. All films suffer censorship except those screened during the Cairo International Film Festival *(see p41)*, where the possibility of seeing exposed flesh on the big screen ensures packed houses.

A trip to the cinema is an experience in itself. Audiences are extremely animated, greeting screen events with cheers, boos or applause. In Downtown Cairo, particularly around the Sharia Talaat Harb area, there are many old, single-screen cinemas, several of which, including the **Metro**, **Miami** and **Radio**, show English-language films. Better equipped cinemas include the **Galaxy** and those located in shopping malls, such as **Stars** in Nasr City, **Horreyya I & II** in Heliopolis, the **Ramses Hilton I & II** and the **Renaissance**.

In Alexandria, the **Amir** and **Metro** are outstandingly beautiful period cinemas, which are worth a visit for the architecture alone. But by far the most luxurious cinema in Alexandria is the **Renaissance**, attached to the Smouha Mall, to the east of the city centre.

Up-to-date details of all the films currently being screened are published in *The Egyptian Gazette, Middle East Times* and *Al-Ahram Weekly*.

Colourful advertising for the Diana Palace cinema

THEATRE

The numerous local theatres in Cairo are testimony to a strong dramatic tradition in Egypt. Productions are performed in Arabic and are of local fare, typically slapstick comedy with a bit of belly-dancing thrown in. Cairo's Downtown area, particularly along Sharia Emad al-Din, is home to several small theatres including the **At-Talia**, as well as the **Gumhuriyya Theatre**. Non-Arabic speakers may wish to visit the **Wallace Theatre**. This venue stages a number of plays throughout the year which are performed in English by students of the neighbouring American University in Cairo *(see p72)*. Occasionally, a high-profile theatrical event takes place at the **New Cairo Opera House**. In the past, the Opera House has received visits from the likes of Britain's Royal Shakespeare Company.

Once a year, the International Experimental Theatre Festival *(see p41)* brings in a variety of acting troupes from all around the world to perform at venues throughout Cairo. The *Al-Ahram Weekly* newspaper is an excellent source of information on all such events. The newspaper also lists details of all the regular theatre performances taking place in Cairo.

CASINOS

Many of Egypt's five-star hotels have casinos, open to non-Egyptians only (passports must be shown at the door). All games are conducted in US dollars or other major foreign currencies, with a minimum stake of US $1. The dress code is smart casual. Hotels with casinos include the **Semiramis Intercontinental**, the **Marriott Cairo** and the **Nile Hilton** in Cairo and the **As-Salamlek Palace** in Alexandria. Note that in Egypt the word "casino" is sometimes used to denote a bar – this is usually the case when it is encountered outside a hotel.

Billboard advertising an Arabic theatre production

SPECTATOR SPORTS

Football rules in Egypt. A big match is one of the few times when the country is silent – at least until the final whistle, when the streets fill with flag-waving, horn-honking fans. Footballing life is dominated by Cairo, home to the country's two biggest clubs, Ahly and Zamalek. These clubs, along with Alexandria's Ittihad team, boast players of international standard. Games between Cairo's big clubs are the highlight of the sporting calendar and take place at the **Cairo Stadium** in Medinat Nasr. Tickets for all major games are in high demand and can be difficult to obtain.

Football fans cheering on the Egyptian national soccer team in Cairo

Media sports coverage focuses almost entirely on football, even in summer when there are no matches. Of other sports, the most prominent is squash. The annual August Al Ahram International Squash Tournament draws competitors from all over the world to play in glass-enclosed courts set up next to the Pyramids. The Pyramids also feature as the start and finishing point in the annual Pharaoh's Rally, a four-wheel-drive and trail-bike desert race in October. Other spectator sports include rowing races on the Nile every Friday between November and April, and horse racing at the **Gezira Sporting Club** and the **Alexandria Sporting Club** from October to May. Since the year 2000, there has also been an annual showjumping competition held in the second two weeks of February at the Alexandria Sporting Club. For something more unusual, watch local Bedouin participate in inter-tribe camel racing as part of the annual Sharm el-Sheikh festival (see p38).

Details of all sporting fixtures are in *The Egyptian Gazette* and *Al-Ahram Weekly*.

DIRECTORY

CINEMA

Amir
41 Sh aria Horreyya, Alexandria.
Tel (03) 391 7972.

Galaxy
67 Sharia Abd al-Aziz al-Saud, Al-Manial, Cairo.
Tel (02) 532 5746.

Horreyya I & II
Sharia al-Ahram, Heliopolis, Cairo. *Tel (02) 469 8025.*

Metro
35 Sharia Safiya Zaghloul, Alexandria.
Tel (03) 487 0432.

Metro
35 Sharia Talaat Harb, Downtown, Cairo. **Map** 1 C5, 5 C3.
Tel (02) 393 7566.

Miami
38 Talaat Harb, Downtown, Cairo. **Map** 1 C5, 5 C3.
Tel (02) 574 5656.

Radio
24 Sharia Talaat Harb, Downtown, Cairo. **Map** 1 C5, 5 C3. *Under renovation.*

Ramses Hilton I & II
Ramses Hilton Annex, Sharia al-Galaa, Downtown, Cairo.
Map 1 C4.
Tel (02) 574 7436.

Renaissance
World Trade Centre, 1119 Corniche el-Nil, Cairo. **Map** 1 B2.
Tel (02) 580 4039.

Renaissance
Smouha Mall, Sharia Victor Emmanuel, Smouha, Alexandria.
Tel (03) 424 2555.

Stars
Stars City Center, Ahmed Fakhry Street, Nasr City, Cairo.
Tel (02) 480 2012/ 13/14/15.

THEATRE

At-Talia Theatre
Midan Ataba, Downtown, Cairo. **Map** 2 E4.
Tel (02) 593 7948.

New Cairo Opera House
Sharia at-Tahrir, Gezira, Cairo.
Map 1 A5.
Tel (02) 739 8144 (info)
(02) 739 8132 (info)
(02) 739 8114 (box office)
www.cairoopera house.org

Gumhuriyya Theatre
12 Sharia al-Gumhuriyya, Cairo.
Map 2 D5, 6 D3.
Tel (02) 390 7707.

Wallace Theatre
Sharia Mohammed Mahmoud, Downtown, Cairo.
Map 1 C5, 5 B4.
Tel (02) 797 6935.

CASINOS

As-Salamlek Palace Hotel
Montazah Palace, Alexandria.
Tel (03) 547 7999.

Marriott Cairo
Sharia al-Gezira, Cairo.
Map 1 A4.
Tel (02) 735 8888.

Nile Hilton
Midan Tahrir, Cairo.
Map 1 C5, 5 B4
Tel (02) 574 4002.

Semiramis Intercontinental
Corniche el-Nil, Cairo.
Map 1 B5.
Tel (02) 795 7171.

SPECTATOR SPORTS

Alexandria Sporting Club
Mahatet al-Riada, Alexandria.
Tel (03) 542 0435.

Cairo Stadium
Medinat Nasr, Cairo.
Tel (02) 260 7863.

Gezira Sporting Club
Zamalek, Cairo. **Map** 1 A4.
Tel (02) 735 3914.

Coffee House Culture

Found on almost every street corner, the ubiquitous coffee house (*ahwa*) plays an important role in the everyday life of Egyptians. Like the cafés of continental Europe, *ahwas* are social places where Egyptians can meet to talk with friends, idle away an hour reading a newspaper, or watch football on TV. Frequented predominantly by men, coffee houses are busy at all hours of the day and many

Card players with *sheeshas* concentrate on their game

remain open around the clock. As well as tea (*shai*) and coffee (*ahwa*), most serve fresh lemon juice (*lamoon*), iced *karkade*, a refreshing crimson drink made from boiled hibiscus leaves, *zabaady*, a yoghurt drink and *sahleb*, a warm drink made with semolina powder, milk and chopped nuts. No coffee house would be complete without the *sheesha* (waterpipe) through which tobacco is smoked.

A typical coffee house, *such as Fishawi's in Khan al-Khalili, is often little more than a collection of old tables and chairs placed in a narrow alleyway.*

Chess *is not particularly common in Egypt but a few coffee houses are venues for fans of the game, including the popular Horreyya situated in Downtown Cairo.*

Backgammon *and dominoes are the most popular of the coffee house games with animated players slamming down their pieces.*

Sheeshas *(waterpipes) are offered in coffee houses as an accompaniment to drinks. The tobacco is soaked in molasses or sometimes apple juice.*

Coffee houses, *like Horreyya, are often all-male environments but foreign women are usually welcomed.*

CHILDREN'S ENTERTAINMENT

When the heat of Cairo becomes too much, **Dr Ragab's Pharaonic Village** can provide a welcome break and keep children thoroughly entertained. The village is an ancient Egypt theme park situated on the southern tip of Al-Qorsaiah Island which lies on the west bank of the Nile, 10 km (6 miles) south of the city centre. Visitors take small boats through the reed beds viewing scenes of Pharaonic daily life recreated by costumed actors. The park also boasts a replica temple.

The **Cairo Puppet Theatre**, just north of Midan Opera, gives performances of traditional tales like Sindbad and Ali Baba. The plays take place most mornings from October to May and although in Arabic, they are highly visual and easy to follow. Another alternative is the **Cairo Zoo** in Giza. The zoo is set in pleasant grounds on the west bank of the Nile opposite Rhoda Island. Although it has promised to concentrate on improving conditions, some may find the animal enclosures distressing.

On the outskirts of Cairo are several recently built amusement parks. **Dream Park**, northwest of Cairo, has Disney-type rides, go-karts and games arcades, as well as golf and tennis courts. **Aquapark**, 32 km (20 miles) east of Cairo, offers waterchutes, a wave pool and a playground area. The nearby theme park **Gero Land** also has rollercoasters, go-karts and other thrill rides.

Children enjoying themselves at the fairground of a local festival

Elsewhere in Egypt there are few concessions made to children's entertainment. However, activities are often laid on for children during *moulids* (saints' days) and other festivals. At the coast, many of the bigger resort hotels now run activity centres designed to keep younger guests amused.

COFFEE HOUSES

There is an abundance of coffee houses (*ahwas*) in Egypt, each one filling its own niche and frequented by its own particular clientele. Several of the more interesting coffee houses are tucked away down tight alleys and include the Downtown **Ash-Shams**, notable for its garishly painted walls. One of the oldest and most famous of all the coffee houses is **Fishawi's** (*see p90*). Buried in the narrow lanes of Khan al-Khalili, it is open 24 hours and is as much a

must-see sight for visiting out-of-town Egyptians as it is for foreigners. In Alexandria, coffee houses line the Corniche, while in Aswan and Luxor there are several dotted around the busy souq areas.

WEDDINGS

Thursday night is the end of the Muslim week and the traditional night for weddings in Egypt. Throughout the country celebrations are heralded with drums, tambourines, honking cars and women wailing. Weddings are very public affairs, where musicians, dancing processions and showers of rose petals fill the streets, and foreign spectators are often invited to join the celebrations.

A young child enjoying the beach at the resort of Dahab

OUTDOOR ACTIVITIES AND SPECIALIST HOLIDAYS

E gypt's varied terrain – from the expansive plains and oases of the Western Desert to the rugged hills of the Sinai, and from the clear waters and colourful coral reefs of the Red Sea to the unique wetlands of the Nile Delta – offers an exciting range of activities for outdoor enthusiasts.

Year-round clement weather makes Egypt the ideal destination for all outdoor sports, and many five-star resorts around Hurghada and Sharm el-Sheikh, as well as several luxury hotels in Cairo, offer world-class golf and tennis facilities. Elsewhere, the choice of activities ranges from scubadiving and water-skiing to hot-air ballooning; from horse and camel riding to four-wheel-drive safaris across the desert.

Starfish

Hot-air ballooning over the Sphinx, Cairo

ADVENTURE PACKAGES

Specialist holidays can be booked directly with tour operators such as **Abercrombie & Kent Travel**, **Explore Worldwide** and **Guerba Adventure & Discovery Holidays**, or in the US, **Overseas Adventure Travel**. Most adventure holidays can also be arranged on arrival through travel-agency desks at most large hotels, or through local tour operators, such as the Cairo-based **Egypt Exploration Society**.

Holidays off the beaten track can be arranged to suit all budgets and comfort zones: from desert safaris sleeping in tents, to airconditioned four-wheeldrive journeys with luxury accommodation.

The rugged interior of the Sinai Peninsula is popular for climbing and hiking tours, while the extreme

environment of the Western Desert offers a different type of adventure. An organized safari is the easiest way to experience the thrill of desert driving and camping, with experienced English-speaking guides and drivers, as well as a cook to prepare most meals. Trips into the desert from oases such as Kharga or Bahariyya are offered by many hotels and guesthouses in these areas.

The best season for a holiday off the beaten track is winter (Nov–Mar), when temperatures during the day are tolerable and nights are cool, even chilly.

Visitors intending to take an adventure holiday should ensure that their travel insurance offers adequate cover, including emergency medical evacuation.

BALLOONING

Hot-air balloon flights over the Valley of the Kings are run by several companies, such as

Balloons Over Egypt, **Hod Hod** and **Magic Horizon**. Flights generally lift off early in the morning and take in the ancient sites, the surrounding mountains and the Nile. They often end with a champagne picnic at the landing site.

DIVING AND SNORKELLING

Renowned for the clarity of its waters and the variety of its spectacular corals and fish, the Red Sea offers a wide range of submarine habitats – from remote seamounts that attract large open-water species such as sharks and barracuda, to inshore, shallow-water reefs.

All the larger resorts on the southern tip of the Sinai Peninsula, the Gulf of Aqaba and the coast near Hurghada have dive clubs. As well as short trips to nearby dive sites, specialist dive operators offer live-aboard cruises that allow divers to spend up to two weeks at sea.

An underwater encounter with a lion fish in the Red Sea

Many dive clubs also offer a variety of courses. Before signing up for these, make sure that the dive centre is certified by a reputable international organization such as **PADI** or the **British Sub Aqua Club (BSAC)**. Recommended dive centres can be found on the websites of either of these organizations. Information, availability and reservations for numerous dive centres at all Red Sea resorts can also be found at www.goredsea.com.

The prestigious El Gouna resort complex has nine diving centres offering courses at all levels, including junior open-water diving courses for children.

Windsurfing lesson at a beach on the Sinai Peninsula

For non-divers, snorkelling over shallow reefs is a great alternative. Most dive centres rent masks, fins and snorkels, but the masks are often old or leaky; bring your own, or buy a new one on arrival. For more on diving, see pp320–21.

WATERSPORTS

Both the Mediterranean and the Red Sea coasts offer excellent powered watersports. Water-skiing, jet-skiing and parascending are available at most beaches. All the major resort hotels have their own watersports centres. These may be a little more expensive than independent operations nearby, but they usually offer better-quality, more reliable equipment and trained English-speaking staff.

Wind and water conditions are reliably excellent for windsurfing at the Sinai resorts of

Feluccas gliding lazily on the Nile

Sharm el-Sheikh, Dahab, Taba and Nuweiba, with consistent cross-shore winds, shallow waters for novices, and larger swells further offshore that allow experts to use their jumping skills. Kite-boarding is also increasingly popular. Equipment for both sports can be rented at all resorts.

FELUCCA SAILING

The 160-km (100-mile) journey down the Nile from Aswan to Luxor by felucca takes five to six days. Boats with crew can be chartered at Aswan, where hundreds of feluccas are based and boat owners eagerly approach visitors to offer their services. In theory, prices are set by the government, and the trip to Luxor in a felucca for six passengers should cost E£450–E£500. In practice, however, many extra charges must also be negotiated.

Felucca travellers must bring necessities such as toilet paper, a torch and batteries, mosquito repellent and/or a mosquito net and alcoholic beverages if required. Boat owners provide food, water and soft drinks for an extra charge, which must also be negotiated. Felucca travellers can sleep on board under the stars or arrange hotel or guesthouse accommodation for each night along the way.

FISHING

The huge expanse of Lake Nasser, the world's largest artificial lake, offers anglers some of the best fishing in the world. The catch here is

likely to be tiger fish and the giant Nile perch. Fly-fishing can also be practised, as can bait fishing for catfish, including the giant vundu, one of the world's largest freshwater fish. Boats with crew may be hired in Aswan through **The African Angler**. Equipment can also be hired.

GOLF AND TENNIS

Many five-star resorts around Cairo and on the Red Sea boast superb golf courses, often flanked by floodlit tennis courts. One of the country's newest developments is the 18-hole Karl Litten-designed **Dreamland Golf Course**, at the Dreamland City leisure development on the outskirts of Cairo. It also has floodlit tennis courts for night play. Other recently built golf and tennis resorts around Cairo include **Katameya Heights**, with a 27-hole course and ten clay courts, and **Mirage City**, part of the JW Marriott, near the airport. Elsewhere, near Naama Bay, the **Jolie Ville Mövenpick Golf Resort** has a good international course.

The golfing green at Katameya Heights, not far from Cairo

BIRDWATCHING

Egypt is a rich environment for birdwatchers. There are around 150 resident bird species, but these are outnumbered by the 280 or more species that use one of the world's greatest migration corridors, between Eurasia and southern Africa. Millions of migratory birds traverse the Egyptian skies each year, with waves of storks, raptors and other migrants heading north from mid-February until April, and returning southward from August until early November. Organized birding package tours are available through **Sarus Bird Tours** and **Travel Egypt**.

HORSE AND CAMEL RIDING

Visitors to the Pyramids are usually approached by touts offering rides on mangy camels or flea-bitten nags. These are best avoided. Instead, rent a mount and guide in advance from a reputable livery stable, such as **Arabian Horse** or **Recoub Al Sorat**, both in Giza. The latter offers countryside trail rides as well as rides around the Pyramids of Giza and Saqqara. At Sharm el-Sheikh, the Hotel Sofitel (*see p280*) has a highly recommended stable offering desert rides.

SPAS

Thanks to a boom in luxury resort developments, Egypt now has hotels with deluxe spa, health and beauty facilities to match any in the world. The prime spots for such hotels are Sharm el-Sheikh, which has the **Four Seasons**, the **Ritz-Carlton** and the **Hyatt Regency**; the purpose-built luxury resort of **El Gouna**, with its cluster of world-class hotels; and the international brand hotels of Cairo and its suburbs, such as **Le Meridien Heliopolis** and the **Oberoi Sahl Hasheesh**. The new five-star **Angsana Spa** at the Mövenpick Resort & Spa El Gouna, is the first of its kind on the Red Sea. Managed by the award-winning Banyan Tree group, it offers an array of holistic and contemporary spa treatments. El Gouna's lavish golf clubhouse at the El Gouna resort complex (*see Directory, Golf and Tennis*) also houses a chic spa that offers Thai, Swedish and shiatsu massages, traditional Egyptian body-scrub treatments, a gym, sauna and Turkish baths. Hotels at all Egyptian destinations offer inclusive spa packages, and guests can also book spa, health and beauty treatments on an ad hoc basis on arrival.

Scarlet ibis stork

A yacht moored at the small harbour of Giftun Island

YACHTING AND MOTOR CRUISING

There are large marinas at ports such as Hurghada and El Gouna, where the Abu Tig Marina and Abydos Marina are rated the finest in the Red Sea. Sailing yachts – either crewed or on a bare-boat basis – can be chartered at both Hurghada and El Gouna.

OASIS AND DESERT SAFARIS

The Western Desert is an exciting destination for four-wheel-drive safaris using specially equipped desert vehicles with long-range fuel tanks, global satellite positioning (GPS), satellite communications equipment and trained drivers. The **Badawiya Safari Company** offers four-wheel-drive safaris through the White Desert. Oases easily accessible from the Nile corridor include Bahariyya, Farafra, Dakhla and Kharga, while longer-range desert safaris travel into the Great Sand Sea, and as far west as Siwa, or head for lesser-known oases such as Areg, Bahrein and Ain Della.

WALKING

Egypt offers walkers several spectacular walking routes. The St Catherine Protectorate region of southern Sinai peninsula is a hiker's paradise of jagged mountains, natural springs and forgotten ruins. Hikers must be accompanied by a local guide.

Sheikh Mousa organizes trekking tours led by Bedouins in the mountains of the Sinai. Treks include the well-trodden Mt Sinai, the summit of Jebel Abbas Pasha

Horse riding around the Pyramids at Giza

and gentler walks along dry river beds. Treks can also be arranged at St Catherine's village; for information, visit the Visitors' Centre at St Catherine's Monastery *(see pp222–5)*. A number of

specialist tour operators in the UK, mainland Europe and North America also offer escorted walking packages.

Another focus for walking holidays is the Bahariyya Oasis in the Western Desert.

Several specialist operators such as the Badawiya Safari Company *(see Oasis and Desert Safaris)* offer treks with Bedouin guides and accommodation in tents or village guesthouses.

DIRECTORY

ADVENTURE PACKAGES

Abercrombie & Kent Travel
Sloane Square House,
Holbein Place,
London SW1W 8NS, UK.
Tel 0845 0700 610.
www.abercrombiekent.
co.uk

Egypt Exploration Society
British Council,
191 Sharia el-Nil,
Agouza, Cairo, Egypt.
Tel (02) 747 6118.

Explore Worldwide
Nelson House, 55 Victoria Road, Farnborough,
Hampshire GU14 7PA, UK.
Tel (0870) 333 4001.
www.exploreworldwide.
com

Guerba Adventure & Discovery Holidays
Essex House,
40 Station Road,
Westbury, Wiltshire BA13 3JN, UK.
Tel (01373) 826 611.
www.guerba.com

Overseas Adventure Travel
Cambridge, Mass, USA.
Tel 1-800 493 6824.
www.oattravel.com

BALLOONING

Balloons Over Egypt
Luxor.
Tel (095) 370 368.

Hod Hod
Luxor.
Tel (095) 370 116.

Magic Horizon
Luxor.
Tel (095) 365 060.
www.magic-horizon.com

DIVING AND SNORKELLING

Blue Brothers Diving
www.bluebrothers
diving.de

BSAC
www.bsac.com

Colona Dive Centre and Live-Aboards
www.colona.com

The Dive Connection
www.diveconnection.com

The Dive Tribe
www.divetribe.com

Easy Divers Academy
www.easydivers-
academy.com

Euro Divers
www.euro-divers.com

Orca Diving Centre
www.turtles-inn.com

PADI
www.padi.com

TGI El Gouna
www.tgidiving.com

FISHING

The African Angler
PO Box 191, Aswan.
Tel (097) 230 9748.
www.african-angler.co.uk

GOLF AND TENNIS

Dreamland Golf Course
Dreamland City,
Alwahat Rd, Cairo.
Tel (02) 855 3164.
www.dreamlandgolf.com

Katameya Heights Golf and Tennis Resort
New Cairo City, Cairo.
Tel (02) 758 0512.
www.katameyaheights.com

Jolie Ville Mövenpick Golf Resort
Um Marikha Bay,
Sharm el-Sheikh.
Tel (02) 69 360 3200.
www.moevenpick-
hotels.com

Mirage City
JW Marriot Hotel,
Ring Road, Cairo.
Tel (02) 411 5588.

BIRDWATCHING

Sarus Bird Tours
12 Walton Drive,
Walmersley,
Bury BL9 5JU, UK.
Tel +44 (0) 161 761 7279.
www.sarusbirdtours.
co.uk

Travel Egypt (World Explorer Tours and Travel)
Suite 150,
4015 Nine McFarland Drive, Alpharetta,
GA 30004, USA.
Tel 877 778 3497.
www.travelegypt.com

HORSE AND CAMEL RIDING

Arabian Horse
Abo Sir, Giza.
Tel (02) 727 4714.
email
hanyabbas@hotmail.com

Recoub Al Sorat
Mamouneya Road, Giza.
www.alsorat.com

SPAS

Angsana Spa
Mövenpick Resort El Gouna, El Gouna.
Tel (065) 354 4501.
www.moevenpick.com

El Gouna Resort
Tel (02) 305 7843.
www.elgouna.com

Four Seasons Sharm el-Sheikh
1 Four Seasons Boulevard,
Sharm el-Sheikh.
Tel (069) 360 3555.
www.fourseasons.com

Hyatt Regency Sharm el-Sheikh Resort
Gardens Bay,
Sharm el-Sheikh.
Tel (069) 360 1234.
www.hyattintl.com

Le Meridien Heliopolis
51 El Orouba Street,
Heliopolis, Cairo.
Tel (02) 905 055.
www.starwoodhotels.
com

Oberoi Sahl Hasheesh
Safaga, Red Sea.
Tel (065) 3440 777.
www.oberoihotels.com

Ritz-Carlton Sharm el-Sheikh
Om el-Seed,
Sharm el-Sheikh.
Tel (069) 366 1919.
www.ritzcarlton.com

OASIS AND DESERT SAFARIS

Badawiya Safari Company
Flat 66,
22 Talaat Harb St, Cairo.
Tel (02) 5742 554.
www.badawiya.com

WALKING

Sheikh Mousa
St Catherine's, Sinai.
Tel (069) 3470 457.
www.sheikhmousa.com

Scuba Diving and Snorkelling

Clear waters and abundant sea life make the Gulf of
Sinai one of the world's finest dive destinations, with
something for every skill level: from inshore reefs and
submarine canyons to shipwrecks and blue holes. The
major resorts – Hurghada, Sharm el-Sheikh, El-Gouna
and Dahab – have numerous dive centres where you
can rent equipment. Many dive centres also offer
internationally recognized learn-to-dive courses.
Do a little research and ensure that your dive centre
of choice is approved by a reputable organization
such as PADI or the British Sub Aqua Club (BSAC).
Shallow reefs close to the shore, often in only a few
metres of water, offer ideal conditions for snorkelling.

The impressive colours of the Red Sea

**The Thistlegorm wreck at Sha'ab
Ali ①,** probably the Red Sea's most
famous wreck site, lies in 20–30 m
(65–100 ft) of water, on the bed
of the Straits of Gubal. Legendary
diver Jacques Cousteau discovered
this wartime wreck in the 1950s
but kept its location secret, and
it was not until 1992 that it was
rediscovered.

SINA

Gulf of Suez

Hurghada •
Port
Safaga •

Shaab Umm Qamar ⑥, a sloping
reef wall close to a tiny rocky islet
not far offshore from Hurghada, is
a magnet for marine life, especially
schools of pelagic and reef species,
all of which are accustomed to
divers and very approachable.
The wreck of a fishing boat at
25 m (80 ft) is an attractive focus
for divers, and there is plentiful
coral. Sharks are sometimes seen.

0 kilometres   140

0 miles   60

DIVE-SITE RATINGS

Dive sites here range from
novice-friendly shallow
reefs to deep-water dives
that should be attempted
only by experienced divers
with qualified guides.

	SNORKELLING	NOVICE DIVING	ADVANCED DIVING	EXPERT DIVING
THISTLEGORM ①			●	●
THE BELLS ②			●	●
THE ISLANDS ③	●	●	●	●
BLUE HOLE ④	●	●	●	●
SHARK BAY ⑤	●	●	●	●
SHAAB UMM QAMAR ⑥	●	●	●	●
THE BROTHERS ⑦			●	●
SAFAGA ⑧	●	●	●	●

Safaga (Kilo 32 North) ⑧ is a shore-entry dive
site south of Port Safaga, where bottlenose
dolphins, turtles and a wide variety of reef fish
may be seen in depths of 20–35 m (65–115 ft).
Reef walls pierced by crannies and caves
surround a shallow bay and are covered by
large coral heads and soft corals.

The Bells ② is located north of Dahab in depths from 25–50 m (80–160 ft). This is a site for experienced divers only, who descend into a 5-m (16-ft) wide chimney that extends into the open sea at 30 m (100 ft). As well as plenty of marine life, you are likely to see black and white coral, and plate and cabbage coral.

GETTING TO THE DIVE SITES

Dive centres offer boat trips to inshore reefs and wrecks, or minibus rides to walk-in dive sites. Some of the Red Sea's best dive sites can be reached only on a live-aboard dive cruise. Currents can be strong, and diving with a guide who knows the area well is highly recommended.
Getting there: Hurghada and Sharm el-Sheikh airports receive flights from Europe and from Cairo, Luxor and Alexandria. Access to Nuweiba and Dahab is by bus, minibus or taxi from Sharm el-Sheikh; Safaga is reached by road from Hurghada.

The Blue Hole ④ is a shore-entry dive close to Dahab. On a good day, the 102-m (335-ft) deep hole should yield jacks, barracuda and reef sharks. The outer slope of the reef enclosing the lagoon offers corals, fissures and shoals of numerous fish species. The Blue Hole also attracts snorkellers.

The Islands ③, a shore-entry, shallow-water dive near Dahab, is a great beginners' dive, in depths of 12–16 m (40–50 ft), with superbly preserved coral, spectacular scenery and wide-ranging marine life from turtles to barracuda. One of the most rewarding dives on this coast.

Snorkelling off the beach at Dahab

Shark Bay ⑤, just north of Na'ama Bay near Sharm el-Sheikh, is a novice-friendly dive in just 20 m (65 ft) of water. Superb soft corals line a sandy underwater canyon haunted by lyre-tail coralfish; eagle rays, barracuda and sharks are sometimes seen in the deeper water. Angelfish, parrot fish, grouper, wrasse and moray eels also inhabit the reef, while rays favour the sandy bottom.

Octopus found off the shores of the Sinai

The Brothers ⑦ is one of Egypt's most impressive dive sites. These two rocky islets are the tops of twin deep-water reefs, covered by magnificent corals, that attract huge numbers of reef and open-water fish, including large sharks. Features include a vertical wall, shallow reefs and two shipwrecks. Accessible only by live-aboard boat, the Brothers is never crowded; some cruises allow up to a week's diving here.

Turtle in a swim-through

NILE CRUISES

Nothing beats sitting on the deck of a slow-moving boat as it glides elegantly along the Nile. Cruising combines transport and accommodation to provide the most relaxing way of exploring the major cultural sites, as well as those that are otherwise difficult to get to. The on-board guides, many of them qualified Egyptologists, are on hand to explain the history of each site and outline their most important architectural features.

Hathor, Cow God, Temple of Dendara

The Nile is home to more than 200 cruise boats and hundreds of feluccas. Many tour operators offer cruises as part of a package holiday to the region. Flights arrive at Luxor airport, and direct transfers are laid on to get you to your cruise ship in Thebes.

View of the Nile from the deck of a cruise ship

WHEN TO GO

The best time for a Nile cruise is from December to February, when it is not too hot. However, this means that resorts like Luxor and Aswan tend to become unpleasantly overcrowded. It also means that prices are higher than at other times of the year, and the opportunities for bargains greatly reduced. From March to April and from October to early November, the weather is still pleasant, but there are fewer visitors, and prices drop. From May to October is the hottest season and not the best time to enjoy cruising. Having said that, if you are not bothered by the heat, this is when the best bargains can be found. At this time the Nile is at its lowest level because of the need to conserve water at the Aswan Dam; this can make it difficult for the boats to navigate. If locks on the Nile are closed, operators arrange boats on either side of the locks and you then transfer between them.

NILE CRUISING AS A PACKAGE DEAL

Romanticized by countless films and novels, cruising on the Nile has been a popular tourist pastime since the 19th century, when visiting Egypt's ancient sights was a highlight of the Grand Tour. Since then, cruising has developed into a hugely profitable industry, with an incredible selection of boats plying the river between Aswan and Luxor. The simplest way of organizing a Nile cruise is to book an inclusive

The elegant, luxurious interior of a cruise ship on the Nile

package holiday from home. This will include flights to Egypt, where you will join your cruise boat. Trips vary in length and may be one way from Luxor to Aswan or include the return journey.

A typical trip will start in Luxor and Thebes (see pp182–203), with visits to the Luxor Temple and the Temple of Amun at Karnak. Following a night on board the cruise ship, an organized excursion leaves the next morning for the Valley of the Kings and a few of the more famous tombs, including that of Tutankhamun and possibly those of Ramses VI and Tuthmosis III.

Another attraction on this trip is the magnificent Hatshepsut Temple, possibly the most visually appealing monument in Thebes. Set in a natural amphitheatre, the temple has been used in recent years for performances of Verdi's opera *Aida*. Some tours may also include a visit to the Ramesseum, the mortuary Temple of Ramses II. On your way back to the boat, you will stop at the two huge statues known as the Colossi of Memnon.

The cruise ship then leaves Luxor heading south towards Aswan and stopping en route to visit various ancient temples and settlements. As the boat sails slowly along the river, you can unwind by sitting under a sun shade on deck, reading a book or joining some of the many activities that are included in the price of your cruise. Or you can just relax while Egypt moves slowly past you. Fishermen in feluccas, old men on donkeys and small children on the river bank will all wave to you in much the same way as their ancestors would have done to the Pharaohs several millennia ago.

Since your accommodation, transport and meals are included in the price – as are on-board entertainment, entrance fees to the sites and the services of professional guides – most trips offer good value for money. There are always some excellent deals available on Nile cruising holidays, and it does pay to shop around. Before booking, check carefully exactly what is included in the price.

Cruises offered as part of package holidays are generally reliable and of a consistent standard. **Sonesta International Nile Cruises** is a tried and trusted American-based operator with offices in Cairo. Its modern fleet consists of five ships built between 1989 and 2006, ranging in size from 33 suites to 65 cabins. Sonesta's oldest vessel, the *Moon Goddess*, was completely renovated in 1995, bringing it up to the same standard as the latest ships. Depending on which vessel you choose, facilities include swimming pools, lounge bars and restaurants. Evening entertainment is provided in the form of discos, belly dancers and Nubian shows.

The Temple of Kom Ombo at sunset

Air-conditioned cabins are en suite and have satellite television, video players, mini bars and safety deposit boxes. On the more luxurious ships, you might also find a jogging track or a spa with gym, massage, sauna and Jacuzzi, and extras in the cabins like private telephones, wireless Internet access with laptop and private dining until midnight.

All five Sonesta ships sail between Luxor and Aswan and offer a variety of combinations including three-, four-, six- and seven-night cruises.

Falcon statue at the Temple of Horus, Edfu

The Luxor-shore excursions take in the Temples of Karnak and Luxor, the Valley of the Kings and Queens, the Hatshepsut Temple and the Colossi of Memnon.

During your cruise down the Nile, you are also likely to visit the Temple of Dendara *(see pp178–9)* in

Qena, the Temple of Horus in Edfu *(see p204)* and the Temple of Kom Ombo *(see p205)*. In Aswan *(see pp208–11)* the shore-based itinerary includes visits to the Aga Khan Mausoleum, the High Dam granite quarries and the Temple of Philae *(see p212)*.

CAIRO-BASED NILE CRUISING

It is no longer possible to cruise from Cairo to Aswan. If you are based in the capital but still want to enjoy the rest of the Nile, you can fly from Cairo or book a sleeper on the overnight train to Luxor or Aswan and join a cruise ship there.

River buses travel regularly up and down the Nile and are good for day trips to Qanater *(see p169)*. However, if you are based in Cairo, Alexandria or the Sinai Peninsula and want to visit the ancient monuments of the Nile Valley, you may decide that a cruise is the best way of doing this. Because of the proliferation of boats offering such excursions, cruises are easy to arrange through the major hotels, including the Sheraton, Oberoi and Hilton *(see pp268–71)*. The best deals, however, are generally found through local agents or by dealing directly with the boatmen in Luxor or Aswan. Prices vary greatly, depending on the level of luxury offered. Shop around and check out the facilities on board before confirming the booking. Always ensure that you know what is included in the fare.

The hustle and bustle of a port on the banks of the Nile

Enjoying a felucca trip on the Nile

FELUCCA TRIPS

No holiday in Egypt would be complete without a trip in a felucca, a working boat of a design that has been used by Nile fishermen for hundreds of years. These vessels are available for short trips or longer cruises. Most felucca trips, however, are fairly short and cannot be compared in any way to the luxurious cruises on what are really floating hotels.

Facilities on feluccas range between the primitive and the non-existent. You won't have a cabin and will have to sleep on the open deck, under the stars. This is an excellent way to get a true appreciation of the Nile.

The most popular felucca trips are between Aswan and Luxor. Travellers can sail from Aswan to Kom Ombo or Edfu, and continue on to Luxor by road. Some boats do travel further down the Nile to Esna (see p204) and Luxor, but this often depends on the security measures in operation along this stretch of water. In winter, when the weather is most favourable, the journey to Kom Ombo takes two nights, while the trip to Edfu and Esna takes at least three nights. Since the journey upstream from Luxor to Aswan depends heavily on the wind, most travellers start the journey in Aswan and travel downstream.

To arrange a day trip, simply walk along the banks of the Nile at Aswan and Luxor. You'll be hailed by boat skippers all looking for work. Decide on a felucca you like the look of, tell the skipper what you want, and then haggle over the price.

Another option in Luxor is to hire a felucca to take you across the Nile and pick up a taxi to tour the sites. The skipper may offer to make a taxi arrangement on your behalf. It is probably best to turn down all such offers politely but firmly – as soon as you dock, you will be besieged by waiting taxi drivers, so you can negotiate your own deal. Do not ask the skipper to wait until you return or to come back for you at a pre-arranged time either. That might prove costly, and there are plenty of boats about, or you can

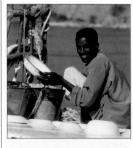

A member of the crew washing up onboard a felucca

take the ferry. Felucca cruises require a minimum of five people. If your group is smaller, enquire at the tourist office for others who may like to join you. The tourist office can also recommend good captains, as can hotels, although the latter may charge a commission. Tourist offices quote rates for all-inclusive cruises. Prices vary according to the season and demand, so these rates should be taken as a starting point for negotiation. Note that, in some cases, "all inclusive" may not guarantee that water, or even food, is included, so always check exactly what is on offer.

Ensure that your felucca is stocked with the following: a water container (such as a jerry can); a shade awning; a kerosene stove and lamp; utensils and cutlery; and a luggage hold with a lock. Nights are very cold on the river, so make sure that the felucca has plenty of blankets. Better still, take a sleeping bag with you. Also take some water and some back-up food with you just in case. Three litres of drinking water per person per day is the minimum; this does not include water for cooking. To ensure that you have a pleasant experience, hats, sunscreen and insect repellent are also essential.

Hygiene can be a serious issue on feluccas. Treat the Nile water used for washing up with sterilizing tablets and take extra care to wash your hands before handling any food. Burn all rubbish, and bury bodily waste to avoid polluting the banks of the Nile.

Do not – under any circumstances – swim in the Nile. There is the odd crocodile, but far more dangerous is the risk of bilharzia. The Nile is infested with parasitic worms, the larvae of which penetrate the skin, causing this disease. The resulting infection is sometimes called snail fever or swimmer's itch. Although the mortality rate is very low, the disease is extremely debilitating, so do keep out of the Nile.

DIRECTORY

NILE CRUISE TOUR OPERATORS

IN EGYPT

Abercrombie & Kent
18 Sharia Yusuf al-Gindi, Cairo. **Map** 5 C4.
Tel (02) 3936 255.
www.abercrombie
kent.com

Airlink Travel
23 Al Ahrar Street, Mohandiseen, Giza, Cairo.
Tel (02) 3377 511
or (02) 7609 716.
www.airlinktravelegypt.
com

Champion Tours
2 Petrol Buildings, Ahmad Orabi St, Mohandiseen.
Tel (02) 3053 930/950.
www.champion-
tours.com

Five Star Travel Group
49 Sharia Moheyel Dine Abul Ezz, Mohandiseen, Cairo.
Tel (02) 3360 255.
www.fivestar-egypt.com

KT Travel
15 Lebanon St, Mohandiseen, Cairo.
Map 5 C4.
Tel (02) 3028 486.
www.kt-travel.com

MyWay Travel
14 Abdel Ghafar St, Heliopolis, Cairo.
Tel (02) 7739 149.
www.egyptmyway.com

Nile Melody
3 El Khadrawi Street, El Tahrir Square, Cairo.
Tel (02) 5783 127
or (02) 5795 882.
www.egyptmelody.com

SafariEgypt.com
6 El Gamme St, El Agouza, Cairo.
Tel (02) 3936 727/728/
734 or (02) 3913 963.
www.safariegypt.com

Sonesta International Nile Cruises
120 Al Thawra Street, Heliopolis, Cairo.
Tel (02) 4183 540.
www.sonesta.com/egypt

Sonesta Nile Cruises
St George Hotel, Corniche el-Nile, Luxor.
Tel (095) 2382 575.
www.sonesta.com/
egyptluxor

Spring Tours
3 Sharia al-Sayed al-Bakry, Zamalek, Cairo.
Map 1 A3.
Tel (02) 7365 972.
www.springtours.com

Suneast Tours
El-Nasr Road, Nasr City, Cairo.
PO Box 78, Cairo Airport.
Tel (02) 2754 968.
www.suneasttours.com

Thomas Cook
17 Sharia Mahmoud Bassiouni, Cairo.
Map 3 B3.
Tel (02) 5743 955.
www.thomascook
egypt.com

Travcotels
19 Yehia Ibrahim St, Zamalek, 11211 Cairo.
Tel (02) 7354 890/895.
www.travcotels.com

IN THE UK

Acacia Adventure Holidays Ltd
23A Craven Terrace, Lancaster Gate, London W2 3QH.
Tel (020) 7706 4700.
www.acacia-africa.com

Amoun Travel & Tours Ltd
56 Kendal Street, London W2 2BP.
Tel (020) 7402 3100.
www.amountravel.co.uk

Andante Travel
The Old Barn, Old Road, Alderbury, Salisbury SP5 3AR.
Tel (01722) 713 800.
www.andantetravels.
co.uk

Archers Direct National Call Centre
Ground Floor, Dale House, Tiviot Dale, Stockport, Cheshire SK1 1TB.
Tel 0871 423 8425.
www.archersdirect.co.uk

Audley Travel
New Mill, New Mill Lane, Witney, Oxfordshire OX29 9SX.
Tel (01993) 838 000.
www.audleytravel.com

Bales Worldwide Ltd
Bales House, Junction Road, Dorking, Surrey RH4 3HL. *Tel 0845 057 1819.*
www.balesworldwide.com

Blue Water Holidays
The Old Mill, Firth Street, Skipton, North Yorkshire BD23 2PT. *Tel 0845 226 2475 or (01756) 639 609.*
www.cruisingholidays.
co.uk

Cox & Kings Travel Ltd
Gordon House, 10 Greencoat Place, London SW1P 1PH.
Tel 0871 871 2234.
www.coxandkings.co.uk

Discover Egypt
80 Borough High Street, London SE1 1LL.
Tel 0870 755 8466.
www.discoveregypt.co.uk

Exodus Travels Ltd
Grange Mills, Weir Road, London SW12 0NE.
Tel 0870 950 0039 or (020) 8675 5550.
www.exodus.co.uk

Explore Worldwide Ltd
Nelson House, 55 Victoria Road, Farnborough, Hampshire GU14 7PA.
Tel 0870 333 4001.
www.explore.co.uk

Hayes & Jarvis Worldwide
The Atrium, London Road, Crawley RH10 9SR. *Tel 0870 366 1636.* www.
hayesandjarvis.co.uk

Kuoni
Kuoni House, Dorking, Surrey RH5 4AZ.
Tel (01306) 743 000.
www.kuoni.co.uk

onthegotours
254–284 Sauchiehall Street, Glasgow G2 3EH.
Tel (0141) 353 2224.
www.trailfinders.com

Planet Holidays
Castle House, 21 Station Road, New Barnet EN5 1PA.
Tel (020) 7873 5000.
www.planet-holidays.co.uk

Soliman Travel UK
113 Earl's Court Road, London SW5 9RL.
Tel 0870 027 5230.
www.solimantravel.co.uk

Travelscope Holidays Ltd
Pioneer Avenue, Gloucester GL3 4AW.
Tel 0870 380 3333.
www.travelscope.co.uk

Voyages Jules Verne
21 Dorset Square, London NW1 6QG.
Tel 0845 166 7003.
www.vjv.co.uk

Worlds Apart Travel Ltd
15 Clarence Parade, Cheltenham GL50 3PA.
Tel (01242) 226 570.
www.worldsaparttravel.
co.uk

IN THE USA

Exodus Travels/ Explore Worldwide
Adventure Center, 1311 63rd Street, Suite 200, Emeryville CA 94608.
Tel (510) 654 1879;
toll free: 1 800 228 8747
www.exodus.co.uk
www.explore.co.uk

Misr Travel Company
630 5th Avenue, Suite 1460, New York.
Tel (212) 332 2600.
www.egypt-vacation.com

Sonesta International Nile Cruises
116 Huntington Avenue, Boston, MA 02116.
Tel 800 766 3782;
UK: 0800 898 410.
www.sonesta.com

Travel Egypt Inc
4015 Nine McFarland Dr, Suite 150, Alpharetta, GA 30004. *Tel (678) 319 9556;*
toll free (877) 778 3497.
www.pharaohsnile.com

SURVIVAL
GUIDE

PRACTICAL INFORMATION

Egypt has made significant progress in improving its tourist infrastructure and the provision of services and security to visitors. Nevertheless certain obstacles remain. Major cities usually have adequate signposting, but most of the monuments still lack proper on-site information panels, signs and labelling. One of ancient Egypt's gifts to the world was bureaucracy and modern-day

Sign for the Temple of Amun, Siwa

visitors must now contend with a sometimes bewildering and frustrating number of formal and informal procedures. With six millennia of history behind them, Egyptians are not in as much of a hurry as the rest of the world. Problems can often be avoided by allowing extra time for even the most minor tasks. However, patience and a good sense of humour are definite assets on a trip to Egypt.

A tourist sign providing general information at Saqqara

PASSPORTS AND VISAS

Visitors to Egypt should possess a passport valid for six months beyond their planned date of entry. All North Americans, Australians, New Zealanders and most Europeans need a tourist visa to enter the country. These can be obtained in advance from Egyptian consulates abroad, but it usually only takes a few minutes to buy one on arrival at Cairo, Hurghada or Luxor airport. Note that general visas cannot be purchased at the overland crossings of Rafah and Taba, nor can they be obtained at Aswan, Suez or Nuweiba.

Both the single-visit and multiple-entry types of visa allow visitors to stay in Egypt for one month; multiple-entry visas allow the bearer to go in and out of the country three times during that period.

Visas that are valid only for Sinai can be purchased at the border crossing at Taba, at Sharm el-Sheikh airport

and at the ports of Sharm el-Sheikh and Nuweiba. These visas last for only two weeks and restrict visitors to the Aqaba coastline as far as the main resort of Sharm el-Sheikh and the vicinity of St Catherine's Monastery.

Be prepared for individual officials to introduce new regulations or to be generally obstructive. In such an event, try to keep calm and friendly.

CUSTOMS AND DUTY-FREE ALLOWANCES

If you wish to bring personal supplies of cigarettes and alcohol into Egypt, it is best to purchase them when you arrive at either Cairo or Luxor airport. Both have duty-free shops, before and after the Customs checkpoint. The shops before Customs are generally better stocked and less crowded than those after.

Semiramis Hotel, Cairo, which offers duty-free facilities

Upon arrival, visitors can purchase 4 litres of alcohol, or 3 litres and a case of beer, and 200 cigarettes. If visitors elect not to purchase these items upon arrival, they have 24 hours to get to a duty-free shop elsewhere, where they can purchase 3 litres of alcohol and 200 cigarettes.

There are duty-free shops in Cairo at the Semiramis Hotel, the Giza Sheraton, the Stars City Center at Ahmed Fakhry Street in Nasr City, and at the end of Sharia Gamiat ad-Dowal al-Arabiyya in Mohandiseen. There are also duty-free shops in the centre of Luxor and Hurghada. Bring your passport, as you will be asked for it. You may also be approached by Egyptians asking if they can borrow your passport to visit the shop themselves.

The allowance for visitors bringing cigarettes or alcohol that have been purchased in another country is 1 litre of alcohol and 200 cigarettes.

If you bring a video camera or computer into Egypt, it must be declared on "Form D" upon arrival. If either of those items is stolen, be sure to obtain a police report. If not, when you leave, it will be assumed that you have sold them and a duty of 100 per cent will be levied.

LANGUAGE

Most urban and professional Egyptians speak a little English and sometimes some French as well. Egyptians working in the tourist sector are accustomed to visitors who cannot speak Arabic and will speak enough English to

Ticket kiosk at Philae – vendors usually understand some English

take care of your needs. It is still worth mastering a few Arabic words and phrases. Recognizing Arabic numerals can help in getting around and dealing with money, while being able to convey a polite greeting will inevitably delight the recipient. If you are planning to travel off the beaten tourist track, a little knowledge of basic Arabic can be useful, if not essential.

PUBLIC CONVENIENCES

Public toilets are rare in Egypt, although major tourist sites often have some type of provision. Facilities in petrol stations, bus and train terminals and cafés in the poorer quarters are likely to be unpleasant, squat toilets. Toilet paper is unlikely to be provided, so it is a good idea to carry tissues with you. Small packets are available from kiosks, stores and street vendors everywhere. Better hotels and restaurants usually have flush toilets. These are often staffed by an attendant who will provide toilet paper and turn on the tap for you. *Baksheesh* of 25–50 piastres is customary for this service.

Electric plug adaptor with two round pins

ELECTRICAL ADAPTORS

The electric current is 220V and sockets take two-pin plugs. A travel converter will enable you to use appliances from abroad. Brief power cuts are common, so it is a good idea to carry a torch with you.

TIME

As well as being two hours ahead of the standard GMT, Egypt often uses its own concept of time – what Egyptians and foreigners alike call "IBM" time, which stands for *Inshallah, Bokra, Maalesh*.

Inshallah (God willing) is a way of remembering Allah in every action, but sometimes, in the context of tourism, it suggests that something might or might not happen. *Bokra* literally means "tomorrow", but it might be used to mean two days, two weeks or perhaps never. It definitely means "not today". *Maalesh* means "Never mind, don't worry, forget about it."

Egyptians do not like to say no or disappoint guests, so you must be persistent and good-humoured in trying to establish when, or if, a desired outcome is likely to occur.

CONVERSION CHART

Imperial to Metric
1 inch = 2.54 centimetres
1 foot = 30 centimetres
1 mile = 1.6 kilometres
1 ounce = 28 grams
1 pound = 454 grams
1 pint = 0.6 litre
1 gallon = 4.6 litres

Metric to Imperial
1 millimetre = 0.04 inch.
1 centimetre = 0.4 inch
1 metre = 3 feet 3 inches
1 kilometre = 0.6 mile
1 gram = 0.04 ounce
1 kilogram = 2.2 pounds
1 litre = 1.8 pints

DIRECTORY

Tips for Visitors

Although practical information is sometimes hard to obtain from the Egyptian tourist board, the major offices are worth visiting as most of the staff usually speak good English and are knowledgeable about the sites. Travel agencies and hotel receptionists are often more helpful and can usually offer up-to-date advice on accommodation, transport and other practicalities.

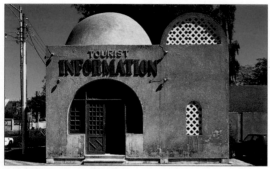

Tourist information office at Aswan with Nubian-style domes

OPENING HOURS

The major historic sites and museums are open daily from 9am until 5pm (6pm in summer). During Ramadan, they may open a little later than the advertised time and will close around 3pm.

Government and administrative offices generally close on Fridays, while shops and stores sometimes close on Sundays. Most stores are open from 9am until 2 or 3pm, then again from 5 to 9pm. However, shops in tourist areas usually stay open all day and late into the night. During Ramadan, offices and shops open later than normal and close around 3pm. They re-open around 8 or 9pm, and remain open until quite late.

VISITING RELIGIOUS SITES

Egypt generally welcomes non-Muslim visitors to its mosques (see pp32–3). It is, however, advisable to seek permission before visiting any mosque outside Cairo and Alexandria, where residents may be less accustomed to seeing tourists.

With the exception of the mosques of Al-Hussein and Sayyida Zeinab, most religious sites in Cairo are seen as historic monuments, open to non-Muslims from 9am until 4pm. However, tourists should not intrude in any way on worshippers and avoid visiting at prayer times.

Modest dress is essential at all mosques. In some places, women may be asked to cover their hair (a scarf will be provided). You must also remove your shoes before entering the mosque. There is sometimes a shoe custodian (who will expect a small baksheesh) or you can leave them outside the door. If you want to climb the minaret, carry your shoes, with the two soles pressed together.

Similar rules apply when visiting monasteries, though you will not have to remove your shoes. With the exception of St Catherine's, which is

Modestly dressed women visiting a mosque

Greek Orthodox, monasteries in Egypt are Coptic. All the monasteries quite readily admit visitors during the day, except during Lent.

DISABLED TRAVELLERS

Few tourist sites in Egypt are equipped for disabled visitors. Steep flights of stairs, deep sand and the poor condition of streets combine to make life difficult for those who are less able. On a more positive note, Egyptians are not embarrassed by disability and museum and hotel staff are always willing to help.

The Egyptian national travel company, **Misr Travel**, has tours and accommodation suited for disabled travellers, while **ETAMS Tours** organizes trips specifically for people with physical disabilities. For those who wish to experience the magic of swimming and diving in the Red Sea, the **Camel Dive Club** has facilities and training geared towards those with special needs.

STUDENTS

Full-time students can enjoy discounts at museums and historical sites, and reduced air, rail and bus fares with an International Student Identity Card (ISIC). If you arrive in Cairo without one, you can obtain a card at the Egyptian Scientific Centre, 23 Sharia al-Manial on Rhoda Island. A student card can also be purchased at several down-town hotels, but beware of shops offering forgeries.

International Student Identity Card

ETIQUETTE

Egypt is one of the most liberal Muslim countries in the Middle East, and its citizens are justifiably famous for their tolerance, generosity and warmth. However, the presence of five-star hotels,

Visitor about to engage in the ancient art of haggling in Aswan's souk

beach resorts, casinos and other trappings of Western culture, such as mobile phones, luxury cars and bars serving alcohol, may lead the casual visitor to conclude that Egypt is more open and liberal than it really is. At its heart, Egypt is still a deeply conservative country and the dominant values are Islamic. To get closer to a truly welcoming people, visitors need to be aware of these values and modify their dress and behaviour accordingly.

Modest dress is essential if one wishes to avoid giving offence or, for women, attracting undue attention. Shorts and swimwear are really only acceptable at beach resorts, primarily along the Aqaba coast on the Red

Sea, and the private beaches of certain hotels in Hurghada. In other areas, use your discretion, but remember that, for both sexes, bare shoulders are considered offensive.

Boorish behaviour, such as arrogance or bluntness, can create problems, so remain patient and polite when confronted with bureaucratic hassles or persistent touts. A gentle sense of humour helps to ameliorate difficult circumstances, and is the approach most often deployed by Egyptians themselves.

Egyptians of the same sex frequently hold hands and kiss in public, but open displays of affection between the sexes are rare and can cause deep offence. If invited to someone's home, a small gift of flowers or sweets is appropriate. For men, sitting with legs crossed and showing the sole of your foot is seen as rude. Shopkeepers will offer tea or soft drinks during negotiations, but this incurs no obligation to buy. When bargaining, however, once you have agreed a price, it is rude to refuse to purchase the item.

Egyptians are aware of their country's weaknesses but do not appreciate it when foreigners point them out.

Avoid criticizing religion or the president, and issues such as *baksheesh* or the condition of the streets or buildings.

PHOTOGRAPHY

Museums and major tourist sites charge for the use of video and still cameras. The use of a flash is often forbidden, so bring some fast film with you (400 ASA or higher) as it is hard to find in Egypt. Always ask permission before taking someone's photograph, especially of women or religious figures and in rural areas. Taking photographs that show Egypt as backward or poor may also cause offence. Visitors should remember that it is forbidden to take pictures of army bases, airports, government buildings, dams, bridges or anything considered vital to security.

Tourists photographing the Sphinx near the Pyramids of Giza

DIRECTORY

Security

In spite of the size and population density of its cities, Egypt is one of the safest countries in the world for travellers. The most serious crime that most visitors are likely to encounter is minor theft, which is rare, especially away from congested tourist areas. Visitors should, of course, take the usual precautions of wearing a money belt and keeping a close watch on cameras and bags. In fact, tales abound of taxi drivers, hotel personnel and ordinary citizens returning lost property and keeping a look-out for the welfare of guests.

POLICE

Visitors to Egypt are often surprised by the numbers of police posted on street corners, at intersections and outside government buildings and historic sites. This is not a sign of imminent or recent trouble, but has simply been the status quo since the 1960s.

Different police forces deal with different aspects of law and order. The Municipal Police handle crime and are recognizable by their uniforms – khaki in winter and tan or white in summer. Traffic Police wear similar uniforms, with the addition of striped cuffs. Both forces deal with accidents and can help in emergencies, but few speak English.

The Tourist Police are the agency visitors should turn to in times of trouble. Ordinary ranks wear khaki uniforms, while officers wear black in winter, white in summer. Easily identified by "Tourist Police"

armbands, they are stationed at ports, airports, stations, tourist sites and museums and usually speak some English.

The Central Security Police guard embassies, banks and highways. Dressed in black uniforms and armed with Kalashnikovs, their appearance can be very intimidating. In general they are no cause for concern, but if you do find yourself caught up in a demonstration, get right away immediately.

POLICE of ANTIQUITIES

Sign for police guarding antiquities

Unless drugs or espionage are suspected, foreigners are usually treated with extreme politeness by the police.

PETTY CRIME

Egypt is proud of its low crime rate and in general visitors should have little trouble as long as they take sensible precautions and avoid travelling alone when away from tourist areas. As in any large city, crowded areas, such as the Khan al-Khalili, provide the ideal conditions for pickpockets and petty thieves. Keep your money and passport in a money belt or pouch and your camera and other valuables out of sight. Security on camp sites, hostels and cheap hotels is likely to be poor, so leave valuables at the reception desk, or take them with you. If travelling by car, do not leave anything of value visible or accessible.

Crowded street near Khan al-Khalili, where it is wise for visitors to mind their valuables

TRAVEL AND TERRORISM

The area commonly known as Middle Egypt – which includes the cities of Minya, Asyut and Sohag and the historic sites of the Tombs of Beni Hassan, Tell al-Amarna, Abydos, Dendara and several monasteries – is a potential hot spot for trouble *(see p176)*. Because of this, the Egyptian authorities are reluctant to allow visitors into the area. There is heavy security and the movements of tourists are very tightly controlled.

It is possible to arrange day trips as part of a group from Cairo and Luxor, but only under strict security. If you try to go alone by local bus or by service taxi, you will eventually be discovered at one of the many police checkpoints and either given an escort into the sites or back to where you started from, depending on the situation. Information about the causes and extent of the unrest is hard to come by and often conflicting. The threat is not always directed at tourists, but visitors do run the risk of being caught up in local violence.

Terrorist attacks on tourists in general have ceased since the massacre at the Temple of Hatshepsut in Luxor, on 17 November 1997. Since then, the Egyptian government has expressed its determination to prevent further attacks on tourists and has increased security, particularly at the major historical sites.

Get up-to-date advice from your ministry of foreign affairs before travelling. In the UK, call the Foreign and Commonwealth Office or visit their website. US citizens should check the US State Department's website for current advice for travellers.

IN CASE OF FIRE

Hostels, cheap hotels and even some of the more expensive establishments are unlikely to have adequate fire exits or even fire extinguishers. Therefore, it is a good idea at

Distinctive Egyptian fire engine, equipped for the rough terrain

least to familiarize yourself with the layout of the building and possible escape routes in case a fire does occur.

WOMEN TRAVELLERS

Egypt has become more conservative in recent years, as witnessed by the increasing numbers of women wearing the *hijab* or head-scarf. Women tourists are not expected to wear scarves, but may feel more at ease doing so in mosques or rural areas.

The social norms for women in Egypt are very different from those in the West and this, combined with images of women in Hollywood films, creates misconceptions. For example, women travellers unaccompanied by a man are often regarded as morally loose. While serious sexual assaults are rare, verbal harassment and groping does occur. The risk of harassment can be reduced by dressing modestly. Wear long, loose, opaque clothes that cover your chest, shoulders, upper arms and your legs below the knees. Many single women wear wedding rings, which signal respectability. Sit with other women on trains and buses and in the front car of the Cairo Metro, which is reserved for women. Avoid eye contact and smiling at strange men as these can be misconstrued. If you are harassed, the best response is to ignore the offender. Using phrases such as *haram* (shame), or *sibnee le wahdi* (leave me alone) may bring help. Women in Islam are highly respected and help is frequently extended to female travellers in distress.

EMBASSIES

If you find yourself in trouble, contact your embassy or consulate who will give legal advice and replace lost passports. They are unsympathetic to drug offenders and will not lend you money to get home, although, as a last resort, they will arrange repatriation. It is as well to remember that although you are a welcome visitor to the country, you are still subject to Egyptian laws.

DIRECTORY

EMERGENCY SERVICES

Fire *Tel* 125.
Tourist Police *Tel* 126.

TRAVEL ADVICE

www.fco.gov.uk (in UK) or
Tel (0870) 606 0290.
http://travel.state.gov (in US).

EMBASSIES

Australia
World Trade Centre (11th floor),
Corniche el-Nil, Bulaq, Cairo.
Map 1 A3. ***Tel*** (02) 578 0650.

Canada
26 Sharia Kamel el Shenawi,
Garden City, Cairo. **Map** 5 A5.
Tel (02) 794 3110.

Ireland
3 Sharia Abu al-Feda,
Zamalek, Cairo. **Map** 1 A3.

Tel (02) 735 8264.

UK
7 Sharia Ahmed Ragheb,
Garden City, Cairo. **Map** 5 A4.
Tel (02) 794 0850.

USA
5 Sharia Amerika al-Latineya,
Garden City, Cairo. **Map** 5 B4.
Tel (02) 797 3300.

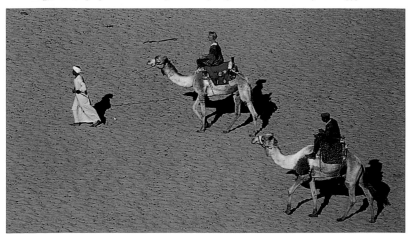

A police escort accompanying tourists taking a camel ride at Aswan

Health and Insurance

Distinctive Egyptian pharmacy logo

Although travelling in Egypt might be thought to pose serious health risks, these can be minimized by careful pre-planning, taking sensible precautions while in the country and by the reassurance offered by taking out appropriate travel insurance before leaving home. The most common problems are mild gastric disturbances – simply caused by bacteria in food and drink to which the traveller has yet to acquire immunity – plus the range of ailments induced by a careless attitude to extreme heat and sunshine.

Egyptian pharmacy shop front, with name in Arabic and English

GENERAL ADVICE

For most visitors to Egypt, stomach upsets and over-exposure to the sun constitute the greatest health risks. It is a good idea, however, to pack a first-aid kit with plasters, bandages, antiseptic ointment and some painkillers. Insect repellent is vital, especially in the Western Desert oases, on the Sinai coast, in the Delta, and for felucca rides at sunset. Include some oral rehydration salts in your kit: these will help replace lost minerals if you do suffer a bad bout of diarrhoea.

Pack supplies of prescription medicines and contact lens solution. Lens wearers may find that desert dust causes problems: it is advisable to wear glasses instead of lenses for at least part of the time to avoid constant irritation.

The sun is strong throughout Egypt, even in winter, and particularly in Upper Egypt, where there is very little shade. Wear a sunhat and sunglasses and use a sunscreen with a protection factor of at least 15.

VACCINATIONS

Visitors to Egypt do not require any vaccinations unless they are coming from an infected area. However you may like to ask your GP for the current World Health Organization (WHO) health bulletin on Egypt before travelling. As well as ensuring that your polio and tetanus cover is up to date, the most common recommendations include vaccinations against typhoid and Hepatitis A and B. A meningitis vaccination may also be advised.

Rabies is a serious problem throughout the country. Avoid touching any stray animals, including cats, dogs, bats and monkeys. If you think you have been exposed to the disease, seek help urgently.

PHARMACIES

Egyptian pharmacists are a good source of help for minor health complaints. They generally speak English and can be trusted to advise on remedies for most common ailments. Pharmacies carry a wide range of drugs, which are cheap and can often be dispensed without a doctor's prescription. Pharmacists can also help you find a doctor.

A dive trip in the Red Sea, with fierce sun, intense heat and lack of shade posing potential health hazards

STOMACH UPSETS

Mild diarrhoea is a common ailment for visitors to Egypt. However, a few simple precautions can reduce your chances of falling ill, or at least lessen the effects.

While tap water is generally safe, it is heavily chlorinated and rather unpleasant tasting. Bottled water is available everywhere – but make sure that the seal is unbroken when you buy it. Avoid raw vegetables and unpeeled fruit, or wash them thoroughly in purified water. Do not buy food from a street stall that has no running water, and beware of ice-cream that may have melted, then been refrozen. Choose budget restaurants with care and always check that meat has been cooked thoroughly.

Local brand of Egyptian bottled water

If you do feel unwell, bottled water with a little added fresh lime juice can help settle an upset stomach.

OTHER HAZARDS

Dehydration, sunburn and heat exhaustion are of particular concern, especially in Upper Egypt. Lack of shade at archaeological sites, plus wind-blown sand and dust, can make for an uncomfortable experience. Sweat evaporates quickly in these dry conditions and you may become dehydrated without realizing it. Drink plenty of bottled water and add a little extra salt to your food to replace salts lost in sweat. Wear a sunhat and loose-fitting clothes made of natural fibres, and wear a T-shirt when swimming.

Heatstroke is a potentially fatal condition that occurs when the body temperature rises to dangerous levels. Symptoms include flushed skin, severe headaches and confusion. Immediate medical attention is essential.

Bilharzia, or schistosomiasis, is another hazard in Egypt. This disease is transmitted by water-borne flukes that infest the stagnant water found in canals or in slower-moving stretches of the Nile. Do not wade or bathe in such water or walk barefoot on the muddy banks. Never drink water from such a source.

HOSPITALS AND EMERGENCIES

Private hospitals provide the best medical care in Egypt, but they still fall short of standards found in the West. The most reliable private hospitals are in Cairo and Alexandria, and those attached to universities are generally competent and well equipped. Irrespective of whether the patient is insured, both private and state-run hospitals will probably ask for a cash payment before providing treatment of any kind. If you do not have sufficient funds to cover this, contact your embassy who may be able to arrange for relatives or your insurance company to cover the fees in advance of your claim. Be sure to obtain receipts for all the expenses you incur, since these will be required by your insurance company to support your claim for reimbursement.

With the exception of the private service run by As-Salaam Hospital in Cairo, ambulances do not carry paramedics or life-support equipment. Since telephone lines in Egypt are seriously overloaded, it is best, in a real emergency, to take a taxi to the nearest hospital rather than trying to call an ambulance.

DIRECTORY

EMERGENCY NUMBERS

Tourist Police *Tel* 126.
Public Ambulance *Tel* 123.

CAIRO HOSPITALS

Anglo-American Hospital
Sharia al-Hada az-Zuhriya, Gezira. **Map** 1 A5.
Tel (02) 735 6162, 735 6163.

As-Salaam Hospital
3 Sharia Syria, Mohandiseen.
Tel (02) 302 9091 or (02) 303 0502.

As-Salaam International Hospital
Corniche el-Nil, Maadi.
Tel (02) 524 0250.

CAIRO PHARMACIES

Isaaf
38 Sharia 26 July, Downtown.
Map 1 C4, 5 B2. ○ *24 hours.*
Tel (02) 574 3369.

Ataba Pharmacy
17 Midan Ataba, Downtown.
Map 2 D4, 6 D2.

Victoria Pharmacy
6 Sharia al-Brazil, Zamalek.
Map 1 A3. ○ *until 11pm.*
Tel (02) 735 1628.

TRAVEL INSURANCE

Most travel policies cover you for lost belongings and cancellation as well as medical emergencies, and are strongly recommended. Be sure to inform the insurance company if you intend to take part in any dangerous sports, such as diving, otherwise your cover may be invalid. Keep the documents with you so that you can readily contact the company if necessary.

مستشفى قصر العيني التعليمي الجديد

اسعاف

A typical red and white Egyptian ambulance

Communications

Egyptian telephone and internet services have improved dramatically in recent years. An entirely new public card phone system is now in place and internet cafés are opening in the more tourist-orientated areas. Unfortunately the same cannot be said of the postal service. Overseas letters sent from Egypt can still take weeks to arrive, if they do at all. Egypt has eight television channels and many satellite channels, as well as several English-language newspapers and magazines.

Postage stamps celebrating Egypt, past and present

PUBLIC TELEPHONES

Three companies – Menatel, Nile Telephone and Ringo – offer public card phone services, replacing the decades-old coin-operated system. Menatel, identified by its green-and-yellow half-booths, is the more widespread of the three systems. Cairo is especially well served, with Menatel phones on most streets – a welcome relief in a city where not every house has a phone. Phonecards can be obtained from pharmacies, newspaper stands, tobacco shops and kiosks displaying the green-and-yellow Menatel sign. The LE 10 cards are for local calls and the LE 30 cards for international calls. Local calls cost 25 piastres for every three minutes. The Ringo telephone booths are silver, and they accept LE 10, 20 and 30 cards. The Nile Telephone booths, which are red and blue, are fewer. Their cards for calls within Egypt cost LE 10, while international cards come in LE 20 and 40 denominations. You can dial mobile phones from all three systems, and all booths have instructions in Arabic and English.

In spite of these improvements, the phone system as a whole remains overloaded and it can take numerous attempts to reach the person you are calling. Numbers change often

Nile Telephone and Menatel phonecards

and in such cases, a recorded message both in Arabic and English will provide you with the new number.

MAIL SERVICES

Most post offices in Egypt are open from 9am to 3pm daily, except Friday and Saturday. They are often overcrowded and difficult to use if you don't speak Arabic. Overseas postboxes are painted blue; the red ones are for domestic post. However, it is probably simpler to buy stamps and send mail from hotels. To send important letters or packages, it is strongly advised to use one of the

Typical blue and red postboxes for international and domestic mail respectively

international courier services, such as Federal Express or DHL. Both companies have offices in Cairo. This is a more expensive option but the only way of guaranteeing that items will reach their intended recipient quickly.

Receiving letters *poste restante* at the post office is not always reliable and it is a better idea to have letters sent to your hotel. In addition, the main American Express office in Cairo at 15 Sharia Qasr el-Nil holds mail for people who have American Express cards or Amex traveller's cheques. Receiving packages or over-stuffed envelopes from overseas is best avoided as all such parcels are inspected by customs and censors. Items such as compact discs, video tapes and computer games arrive very late or not at all. If they do arrive, expect to pay duty worth more than the package's contents.

USEFUL DIALLING CODES

- To dial locally: dial the 7-digit telephone number.
- To dial within Egypt: dial 0 + area code + telephone number.
- Area codes: Cairo and Giza: 2; Alexandria: 3; Aswan: 97; Fayoum: 84; Luxor: 95; Ismailia: 64; Hurghada: 65; Sharm el-Sheikh: 69.
- To dial internationally: dial 00 + country code + telephone number.
- Country codes: US and Canada: 1; France: 33; Germany: 49; Italy: 39; Netherlands: 31; Spain: 34; Switzerland: 41; UK: 44; South Africa: 27; Australia: 61.
- Mobile phone numbers are prefixed by 010; 012; 016; or 018.

TELEVISION AND RADIO

Television channels 1 and 2 are the national channels, with the latter broadcasting news in English and French. Channel 3 is the local Cairo channel. Channels 4 to 8 are broadcast from Ismailia, Alexandria, Tanta, Minya and Aswan respectively. All the channels broadcast foreign language programmes with Arabic subtitles, and the better hotels provide cable or satellite television.

Foreign-language radio programmes are rare outside Cairo and Alexandria. In Cairo, FM 95 broadcasts programmes in English and French and a few other stations mix Western classical and pop music with Arabic music and news. Check the *Egyptian Gazette* for TV and radio schedules or *Egypt Today* magazine for satellite and cable TV highlights.

A selection of English-language newspapers and magazines

NEWSPAPERS AND MAGAZINES

The daily *Egyptian Gazette* and the weekly *Middle East Times* and *Al-Ahram Weekly* cover international and domestic news; the latter two provide good coverage of television, films and cultural events. The weekly *Cairo Times* is a mix of local and regional news, features and reviews. Outside Cairo, the *Egyptian Gazette* is the only local English-language paper.

There are a number of English-language magazines. The monthly *Egypt Today* contains comprehensive

Newspaper stand selling foreign papers in Mahattat Ramla, Alexandria

cultural and restaurant listings. Other English-language magazines include *Egypt's Insight*, and *Egypt Today*'s sister publications *Business Today* and *Sports and Fitness*, which is useful for health clubs, sports and recreation listings. A broad range of Western newspapers is usually on sale the day after publication at street-side newspaper stands in affluent areas of large cities and at major hotels. *Time* and *Newsweek* are also available.

INTERNET AND FAX

Fax machines can be found in the business centres of most major hotels. However, rates are usually high. Faxes are also available in long-distance and international phone centres, but these machines have a reputation for being less reliable, if cheaper.

There is currently an internet boom taking place in Egypt and internet cafés are a fast-growing phenomenon, especially in the tourist centres of Cairo, Alexandria and Luxor. Most major hotels also offer internet access.

One of the latest Egyptian internet cafés: glob@l net Alexandria

DIRECTORY

MAIN POST OFFICES

Cairo
Midan Ataba. **Map** 6 E2.

Luxor
Sharia al-Mahatta.

INTERNATIONAL COURIER SERVICES

Federal Express
1079 Corniche el-Nil, Garden City, Cairo. **Map** 5 A5.
Tel (02) 795 0427.

DHL
20 Gamal ad-Din Abu Mahasid, Garden City, Cairo. **Map** 5 A5.
Tel (02) 795 7301.

INTERNET CAFES

Internet Egypt
Ground floor, 2 Midan Simon Bolivar, Garden City, Cairo.
Map 5 B4.
Tel (02) 796 2882.

Nile Hilton Cybercafé
Nile Hilton Shopping Mall, Cairo.
Map 5 B3.
Tel (02) 578 0444 x758.

Mohandiseen Cybercafé
Sharia Gamiat ad-Dowal al-Arabiyya, Cairo.
Tel (02) 305 0493.

glob@l net
6th floor, 29 Sharia al-Nabi Daniel, Elghonemy Bld, Alexandria.
Tel (03) 391 2889.

Rainbow Internet Café
Officers' Club, Corniche (N of Sharia as-Sayyed Youssef), Luxor.
Tel (095) 2387 938.

Banking and Currency

Egypt is still very much a cash economy. Both banks and exchange offices will change cash and traveller's cheques, but exchange offices usually offer better hours, shorter queues and more favourable rates. Credit cards, while accepted at most major hotels and some tourist shops, are not much use anywhere else. Automated Teller Machines (ATMs) are now often found outside many banks and can be used for cash withdrawals, although some credit cards charge heavily for this service. Egypt prohibits the exportation of its currency, which, in any case, is useless outside the country.

Logo of Banque de Caire

Standard ATM with instructions in a range of languages

BANKS

The usual opening hours for banks in Egypt are Sunday to Thursday 8:30am to 2pm. Exchange offices are also open in the evenings from 6:00pm to 9:00pm. Most banks are closed on Friday and Saturday. As well as Egyptian banks, which include Banque Misr, there are a few well-known international names such as Barclays and Citibank. The best time to go is just as the bank opens – to avoid crowds.

Thomas Cook exchange office on the Corniche, Luxor

EXCHANGE OFFICES

Exchange offices can be found throughout major cities and tourist areas and are preferable to banks, shops and hotels for changing money. The black market for hard currency is now in decline and scarcely worth the risk.

It is a good idea to change some money on arrival; both terminals at Cairo Airport have 24-hour exchange offices.

TRAVELLER'S CHEQUES AND CREDIT CARDS

Most banks and exchange offices accept American Express, Barclays, Citibank and Travelex traveller's cheques. Eurocheques are not recommended for use in Egypt. A passport is required to change traveller's cheques. Always keep the receipt and a record of the serial numbers separate from the cheques in case they are lost or stolen. It is difficult outside tourist areas to use either traveller's cheques or credit cards. The most widely used credit cards are Visa, MasterCard and American Express.

BAKSHEESH AND TIPPING

People demanding *baksheesh* without rendering a service can be irritating, but calm and good-humoured refusals will eventually meet with success. Most Egyptians are paid such low salaries that *baksheesh*, in the form of a tip for service, is a vital part of their income. It is usual, in restaurants, to round up the bill or give an extra 10 per cent directly to the waiter. Small tips, in the 25 pt to LE 1 range, should be given to people who help you in some small way, such as lavatory attendants, and the people who park cars, carry luggage or unlock tombs. Offers to bend the rules a bit, such as letting you into a site after hours or opening one supposedly closed, will cost a little more. However, don't assume money will buy you everything. Do not risk offence by refusing to pay small sums for even minor assistance, but also do not throw money at people to get your way.

DIRECTORY

BANKS

Banque Misr
151 Sharia Mohammed Farid, Cairo. **Map** 2 D5, 6 D4. *Tel (02) 391 2172.*

Barclays International
12 Midan al-Sheikh Yusuf, Garden City, Cairo. **Map** 3 B1, 5 A5. *Tel (02) 366 2600.*

Citibank
4 Sharia Ahmed Pasha, Cairo. **Map** 3 B1, 5 A5. *Tel (02) 794 7246.*

EXCHANGE OFFICES

American Express
15 Sharia Qasr el-Nil, Cairo. **Map** 1 C5, 5 C3. *Tel (02) 574 7991.*

Winter Palace Arcade, Luxor. *Tel (095) 237 8333.*

Thomas Cook
17 Sharia Mahmoud Bassiouni, Cairo. **Map** 1 C5, 5 B5. *Tel (02) 574 3955.*

Semiramis Hotel, Cairo. **Map** 3 B1, 5 A5. *Tel (02) 795 8544.*

Midan Saad Zaghloul, Alexandria. *Tel (03) 484 4073.*

Winter Palace Arcade, Luxor. *Tel (095) 237 2402.*

LOST OR STOLEN CREDIT CARDS

American Express
Tel (02) 567 2430 (570 3152 after 5pm).

Visa/MasterCard
Tel (02) 796 2850 or 796 2844.

CURRENCY

The basic unit of currency in Egypt is the Egyptian pound or *ginee*, written as £E or LE. The Egyptian pound is divided into 100 piastres (pt) or *irsh*. The 50 and 100 LE notes can sometimes be difficult to change, so always carry some smaller notes. It is also advisable to keep a separate supply of lower denomination notes for *baksheesh* and for taxis who invariably have no change. Avoid accepting ragged or mutilated notes because taxi drivers and vendors will also refuse to take them.

Coins

Coins come in denominations of 5, 10, 20 and 25 piastres, and are mainly used for tipping. There are two versions of the 10 piastres coin.

5 piastres (5 pt)

10 piastres (10 pt)

10 piastres (10 pt)

20 piastres (20 pt)

25 piastres (25 pt)

Banknotes

Banknotes are issued in 1, 5, 10, 20, 50 and 100 pounds denominations as well as 50 and 25 piastres. There are also notes worth 5 and 10 piastres, although these are getting rare. Smaller in size than pound notes, they are often refused by vendors and taxi drivers alike. Most smaller shops round prices up or offer sweets or matches in lieu of exact change.

50 piastres (50 pt)

25 piastres (25 pt)

1 Egyptian pound (LE 1)

5 Egyptian pounds (LE 5)

10 Egyptian pounds (LE 10)

20 Egyptian pounds (LE 20)

100 Egyptian pounds (LE 100)

50 Egyptian pounds (LE 50)

TRAVEL INFORMATION

Most visitors to Egypt fly to Cairo, but flights are also available to Luxor, Alexandria, Hurghada and Sharm el-Sheikh. A holiday in Egypt can also be combined with a visit to another Middle Eastern or North African country, but flying within the region is comparatively more expensive than flying direct from the US or Europe.

EgyptAir logo

Another popular method of entry into Egypt is overland from Jordan, via Israel, although this entails some extra effort and time because of having to cross two borders on the way. An easier route from Jordan is on the regular ferry or catamaran service that runs between Aqaba and Nuweiba on the Gulf of Aqaba coast of Sinai.

Cairo International Airport, to the northeast of the city

ARRIVING BY AIR

Direct flights to Egypt are regularly available from most European capitals. Both British Airways and EgyptAir fly daily from Heathrow (with a flight time of approximately 5 hours) while Air France flies daily from Paris (4.5 hours). Other daily flights include CSA from Prague, KLM from Amsterdam, Lufthansa from Frankfurt, Malev from Budapest, Olympic from Athens, TAROM from Bucharest and Turkish Airlines from Istanbul. Charter flights are available to Luxor, Sharm el-Sheikh and Hurghada.

EgyptAir flies direct to Cairo from New York's JFK airport five days a week. The flight time is approximately 12 hours. Currently, there are no American airlines operating flights to Egypt. EgyptAir also flies once a week to Los Angeles, with a flight time of 17 hours. There are no direct flights to Egypt from Canada.

Travellers from Australia and New Zealand usually get to Egypt via London, or add on Cairo as part of a Round the World Ticket. However, Singapore Airlines offers three flights a week from Sydney to Cairo, with a flight time of 19 hours. Fares vary according to the time of year.

TRANSPORT FROM CAIRO AIRPORT

Cairo International Airport is 20 km (12 miles) to the northeast of the city and has two terminals. Western European and US airlines use Terminal 2 (also known as the New Airport), while the Egyptian carriers, El-Al, and most Arab, African and Eastern European airlines land at the Old Airport – Terminal 1.

Both of these terminals are connected to the city centre by bus and minibus, but the fastest and most comfortable transfer is by taxi. (For more general information regarding buses and taxis, see pp343–7.)

There is no difficulty in finding a taxi at the airport, as drivers descend on new arrivals the minute they have cleared Customs. The time of day, number, gender and appearance of the passengers, amount of luggage, volume of traffic and bargaining skills all factor into the fare. A trip from the airport to downtown Cairo typically costs between LE 25 and 35 per car load, not per person. New arrivals may also be offered a "limousine" service – the fixed rate for the trip in a decent saloon is around LE 40 to 50.

Both terminals have duty-free and tourist shops, cafés offering meagre fare and currency exchange booths.

TRANSPORT FROM OTHER AIRPORTS

The airport in Alexandria is 5 km (3 miles) south of the city and is served by buses and minibuses. A taxi to the centre of town costs approximately LE 10 to 20. Most visitors arriving at Luxor are met at the airport by representatives from their hotels or cruise boats. If not, a taxi into town costs around

Black and yellow taxi serving Alexandria airport

LE 10 to 15. Similarly, most visitors to Sharm el-Sheikh are met by hotel transportation. Taxis from the airport, located north of Naama Bay, test the skills of the best bargainers. Expect to pay around LE 25 to 30 per trip. The situation at Hurghada airport is similar, but a taxi into town should cost only LE 15 to 20.

ARRIVING BY LAND FROM ISRAEL AND JORDAN

Buses run daily from Tel Aviv and Jerusalem to Egypt, crossing at Rafah or Taba. Taba is the gateway to the Sinai coast while Rafah is more convenient for getting to Cairo. The journey between Jerusalem and Cairo takes 12–14 hours, depending on how long it takes to cross the border. In recent years the process has been streamlined slightly at the Taba crossing, which serves both the Israeli resort of Eilat and Egyptian resorts on the Gulf of Aqaba and the rest of the Sinai.

It is also possible to enter Egypt by land from Jordan through Israel. The journey involves a 5-km (3-mile) taxi or "service" taxi from Aqaba to the border, followed by a short walk to the Israeli side. From there, visitors can take a taxi into Eilat. Buses and taxis

Cruise ship passing through the Suez Canal

run from the centre of Eilat to the border with Egypt at Taba. Departure taxes must be paid when leaving Jordan and Israel, even if one is just passing through the latter.

Bear in mind that having Israeli stamps in your passport may preclude you from visiting other Arab countries.

ARRIVING BY SEA

Although Egypt is served by several ports on both its Mediterranean and Red Sea coasts, the advent of cheap air fares and package holidays has inevitably seen the decline of passenger ferries bringing travellers to the country. There

is one exception to this – the crossing from Aqaba, in Jordan, to Nuweiba, in the Sinai. This route is served by both a ferry, which takes 3–5 hours, depending on the weather, and a high-speed catamaran service that does the trip in an hour.

There are no longer any direct ferries from Greece or Cyprus, but two cruise ships sail from Limassol to Port Said, taking passengers on a two-day group visa to Egypt.

Otherwise the only other arrivals by sea are passengers from the cruise ships in the surrounding waters, who come ashore on daytrips to visit some of the sights.

DIRECTORY

AIRPORTS

Alexandria
Tel (03) 427 1036.

Cairo
*Tel (02) 265 5000
(Terminal 1).*
*Tel (02) 265 2222
(Terminal 2).*

Luxor
Tel (095) 2374 655.

AIRLINE OFFICES IN CAIRO

Air France
2 Midan Talaat Harb.
Map 1 B5, 5 B3.
Tel (02) 575 8899.

Air Sinai
Nile Hilton, Midan Tahrir.
Map 1 B5, 5 B3. *Tel (02)
577 2949 or 576 0750.*

British Airways
1 Sharia Abd al-Salaam
Arif, Midan Tahrir.
Map 1 C5, 5 B3.
Tel (02) 578 0742.

EgyptAir
9 Talaat Harb.
Map 1 C5, 5 B3.
Tel (02) 393 2836.

Cairo International
Airport.
Tel (02) 634 1460.

KLM
Cairo International
Airport.
Tel (02) 418 2385.

Lufthansa
6 Sharia al-Sheikh al-Marsafi, Zamalek.
Map 1 A4.
Tel (02) 739 8339.

Cairo International
Airport.
Tel (02) 417 6419.

Malev
5 Sharia Talaat Harb.
Map 1 C5, 5 B3.
Tel (02) 392 0188.

Olympic Airlines
23 Sharia Qasr el-Nil.
Map 2 D5, 5 C3.
Tel (02) 393 1277.

Cairo International
Airport.
Tel (02) 290 5878.

Singapore Airlines
Nile Hilton, Midan Tahrir.
Map 1 B5, 5 B3.
Tel (02) 575 0526.

Cairo International
Airport.
Tel (02) 690 0798.

Swissair
4 Behler Passage,
Sharia Qasr el-Nil.
Map 2 D5, 5 C3.
Tel (02) 396 1737.

BUSES TO AND FROM ISRAEL

**East Delta Bus
Company**
4 Sharia El-Tayaran
Madinet Nasr, Cairo.
*Tel (02) 261 1886, 261
1882, 261 1889.*

Travco
13 Sharia Mahmoud
Azmi, Cairo.
Tel (02) 735 2224.
www.tourism.egnet.net/
travco
Buses leave from the
Abbassia Terminal daily.

Travelling in Egypt

The overall standards of plane and train travel in Egypt are pretty good, but both services can be frustrating in terms of booking and scheduling. The rail network links the Nile Valley, the Delta and the Canal Zone, while EgyptAir and Air Sinai, the national carriers, serve the major cities. Costs for air travel, however, are substantially higher than trains and long-distance buses, so it is not an option for budget travellers. The bus service in Egypt is extensive and, for short trips, often preferable to trains, both in cost and transit time. For longer journeys, night buses are often available.

Egyptian tour bus logo

Train bound for Aswan departing from Ramses station in Cairo

Sign for the Abu Simbel airport in the Nile Valley

DOMESTIC FLIGHTS

Flying within Egypt entails flying with EgyptAir as the company has a monopoly on air travel within the country. Air Sinai is part of the same company and was formed to serve Israel and the Sinai, thus protecting the mother carrier from losing its landing rights in other Arab countries. EgyptAir operates frequent daily flights between Cairo, Luxor, Hurghada and Aswan, and a slightly reduced service to Alexandria. All domestic flights leave from Terminal 1, the Old Airport, in Cairo. There are several flights a day between Aswan and Abu Simbel. Air Sinai offers daily flights between Cairo, Luxor, Hurghada, Sharm el-Sheikh and St Catherine's Monastery.

FLIGHT RESERVATIONS

Fares are average by international standards and are calculated in US dollars. It is possible to pay in Egyptian pounds, backed up by an exchange receipt. Reservations should be made as far in advance as possible, especially during winter or important Muslim festivals such as Eid al-Adha and Eid al-Fitr (see p39).

Overbooking is common on EgyptAir and Air Sinai: always confirm your flight reservation and make a note of the confirmation reference number. Delays are also common and Egypt's domestic airports are dreary places. It is a good idea to have something to read or to otherwise fill the time you may spend waiting. The baggage allowance for domestic flights is 20 kg (44 lb), but this rule is often flouted, especially with regard to hand luggage. It is important to arrive at the airport at least one hour before domestic flights and two hours before international flights.

TRAINS

Trains are the best option for long trips between major cities, offering a much more pleasant alternative to buses and taxis. For short journeys, however, trains tend to be slower and less reliable. Trains in Egypt fall into two

categories: air-conditioned (A/C), which includes the luxury wagons-lits, and non-A/C, or local stopping trains. A/C trains usually offer first- and second-class cars. First-class cars are less crowded and the seats are more comfortable. Second-class travel is not significantly worse and costs quite a bit less. Seats can be reserved up to a week in advance. Round-trip bookings are not possible, so it is best to book for the return journey when you arrive at your destination. There are 16 A/C trains a day between Cairo and Alexandria and five daily between Cairo and Luxor and Aswan. Two overnight express trains run between Cairo and Luxor and Aswan.

Wagons-lits provide a fast, comfortable, but expensive overnight service between Cairo and Luxor and Aswan. Carpeted compartments have

Façade of the Masr train station in central Alexandria

One of the buses used by the West Delta Bus Company

two bunks and a washbasin.
There is a lounge car, and
breakfast and dinner are
served in the compartments.
Wagons-lits must be booked at
least a day in advance: this is
best done through Thomas
Cook or American Express. In
Cairo, bookings can be made
at the Helnan Shepheard Hotel.

Non-A/C trains have only
second- and third-class seats,
the latter with open doors
and windows for ventilation.
Both classes are very dirty
and crowded and are rarely
used by foreign travellers.

Logo of the Superjet bus run by the
Arab Union Transport Company

LONG-DISTANCE BUSES

There are three main bus
operators in Egypt. The
Upper Egypt Bus Company
operates services to the Nile
Valley, Al-Fayoum, the Western
Desert oases and towns along
the Red Sea Coast down to
Quesir. It also runs a luxury
bus service every evening to
Luxor and to Aswan. The East
Delta Bus Company covers services to the Sinai beach towns
of Sharm el-Sheikh, Dahab,
Nuweiba and Taba, as well as
to St Catherine's Monastery and
the Suez Canal towns of Port
Said, Ismailia and Suez. Alexandria, Marsa Matruh, Siwa
Oasis and the Delta towns are
served by the West Delta Bus
Company. Travellers have a
choice between air-conditioned
(A/C) buses, which are usually
newer, and non-A/C vehicles

which are generally in worse
shape and can take much
longer to arrive at their destination. Be aware that just because
a bus is advertised as having
air-conditioning does not mean
that it will actually work; nor
will passengers necessarily
obey the "no smoking" signs.

The Arab Union Transport
Company operates the super-
comfortable Superjet and
Golden Arrow buses along
the main Cairo to Alexandria,
Luxor, Hurghada, Sharm el-
Sheikh and Aswan routes.
Superjet buses also serve Port
Said with around nine trips a
day. The buses are air-
conditioned, with toilets,
videos and hostesses offering
highly priced snacks.

All long-distance buses from
Cairo now depart from the
bus terminal behind Ramses
train station. In Alexandria,
Port Said and Ismailia several
different terminals are used.
Bus schedules, usually posted
in Arabic, are erratic
and change frequently
so it is advisable to
ask travel agencies,
hotels and tourist
offices to help check
the departure times.
Tickets are sold from
small kiosks at city
terminals, up to 24
hours in advance for
A/C and long-haul
services. In smaller
towns, tickets may
only be available an
hour or so before
departure. Ticket
prices vary according
to the type of service
and time of day you
want to travel. For
popular trips, it is
wise to book as early
as possible to be sure
of a seat and to catch
the bus at the main
departure terminal.

DIRECTORY

AIRPORTS

Alexandria
Tel (03) 427 1036.

Aswan
Tel (097) 3480 333.

Cairo
Tel (02) 291 4266.

Hurghada
Tel (065) 3442 831 or 3442 592.

Luxor
Tel (095) 2374 655.

Sharm el-Sheikh
Tel (069) 3601 140.

BUS COMPANIES

East Delta
Tel (02) 419 8533.

Superjet
Tel (02) 5/9 8188.

Upper Egypt
Tel (02) 431 6723.

West Delta
Tel (02) 414 1318.

TRAIN STATIONS

Alexandria
Masr Station, Midan al-
Gumhuriyya. *Tel (03) 392 3207.*

Cairo
Ramses Station, Midan Ramses.
Map 2 D3. *Tel (02) 575 3555.*

Imposing entrance to Ramses train station, on
Midan Ramses, Cairo

Road Travel in Egypt

Typical petrol pump

Driving in Egypt is not for the faint-hearted. Traffic in Cairo is continually busy and horrendous and the main roads out of the metropolis are hazardous. In Alexandria, traffic is no more orderly than in Cairo, but it is less dense, except for summer when millions of Egyptians relocate to Alexandria and the Mediterranean coast. Service (pronounced *servees*) taxis go just about anywhere in the country, providing a fast, cheap form of transport. However their relative discomfort and lack of safety limit their usefulness on all but a few routes. For day-trips, hiring a driver with car may be the best option.

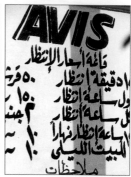

Parking sign for international car rental agencies in Egypt

SERVICE TAXIS

As in other Middle-Eastern countries, service taxis form an important part of Egypt's internal transport system, providing a fast and cheap method of getting around the country. Drivers congregate at recognized locations – usually near bus and train stations – and tout for passengers by shouting out their destination. They leave when their vehicle is full. They will not leave before unless the passengers are prepared to pay the extra fares. There is no need to book a seat: just show up at the "terminal" and look for a vehicle that goes to your destination.

Because the vehicles are always full to capacity, the ride can be hot and uncomfortable, especially over long distances. There is little room for luggage, though there is usually a roofrack where luggage can be stowed. More worryingly, the drivers are notorious for their reckless driving and their vehicles are often in poor condition.

Alternatively, you may like to hire a whole service taxi for your group if you wish to undertake a day trip to a destination that is not easily accessed by other means. This can be a cheaper option than hiring a car to drive yourself or using other forms of public transport.

In Cairo, Giza and Alexandria, a new taxi service called Radio Cab allows you to order a private car with a driver at any time of the day or night.

CAR RENTAL

International vehicle rental companies such as Hertz, Budget and Avis have offices at the airports and in major hotels in tourist areas. To rent a car, you must be between 25 and 70 years old and hold a valid International Driver's Licence. Cairo and the larger towns are well served by petrol stations but in rural and desert areas long distances can separate them, so always fill the tank to the limit. If driving off-road, always carry spare fuel, water and tools. Most petrol stations can perform minor repairs and Egyptian mechanics are quite good at solving problems, sometimes resorting to more creative or less orthodox measures.

DRIVING IN EGYPT

There are few fixed rules for driving in Egypt and in the cities anarchy prevails. Drivers ignore lane markings, drive the wrong way up one-way streets, back up in the face of oncoming traffic if they miss a turn and ignore red lights and non-signposted intersections. Drivers' intentions are often communicated by hand gestures rather than by conventional signals. A common gesture of drivers

Large estate car operating as a service taxi for longer trips

Minibus holding up to 12 passengers, operating as a service taxi

and pedestrians alike is raised fingers, tips pinched together. This means "Wait". A flip of the hand forward means "Pass". Drivers will sometimes signal turns by pointing with their whole arm out of the window. However, drivers and front passengers must wear seat belts, and indiscriminate honking of horns is now forbidden. Failure to observe either rule is an offence that will incur a fine.

Other hazards in the cities include people jumping from moving buses, overloaded motorbikes, donkey carts and flocks of sheep, and pedestrians who also do not follow any rules of road etiquette.

Hazards on roads between cities are even more serious and numerous. Cars and trucks routinely overtake in the face of oncoming traffic or on the hard shoulder. Roads are in poor condition, with potholes, rough patches and drifting sand. Children often play alongside and in the road, and all manner of livestock, including camels, wander across. Motorists will stack rocks or construction

Typical heavy traffic near Midan Ramses in Cairo

debris in the road in lieu of hazard warning signs when they have pulled in because of a breakdown.

Driving at night is best avoided. Egyptians tend not to use their lights at night, except to flash them at oncoming vehicles. Off-road driving without a local guide in the Sinai, along the North Coast near El-Alamein and in the Canal Zone can be especially dangerous because of the presence of land mines, left over from World War II and the Arab-Israeli wars.

Police checkpoints are a frequent occurrence. Foreign drivers are usually waved through, but be prepared to show your passport.

Hiring a private car with a driver can work out cheaper than renting a car. Check with travel agencies and hotels. Regular taxis can also be hired for the day at negotiable rates.

MAPS

The best general map of Egypt is one published by Freytag & Berndt, which is available in most major tourist areas. Mobil's *Motoring Guide to Egypt* is a good choice if you are going to drive. It is sold in Mobil stations and tourist bookstores. Egyptians themselves seldom refer to maps and map coverage of cities other than Cairo is poor.

Stop sign

Uneven road

No car horns

DIRECTORY

TAXI SERVICE

Radio Cab
Tel 19155 or 19730.

CAR RENTAL

Avis
Cairo International Airport.
Tel (02) 265 2429.

Nile Hilton, Corniche el-Nil, Cairo. **Map** 5 A3. *Tel* (02) 579 2400.

Budget Rent-a-Car
Cairo International Airport.
Tel (02) 265 2395.

Cairo Marriott, Sharia Saray al-Gezira. **Map** 1 B4. *Tel* (02) 735 8888.

Hertz
Cairo International Airport.
Tel (02) 265 2430.

Ramses Hilton, Corniche el-Nil, Cairo.
Map 5 A3.
Tel (02) 575 8914.

195 Sharia 26th July, Mohandiseen, Cairo.
Tel (02) 347 2238.

Kilo 28, Cairo-Alexandria Desert Road.
Tel (02) 539 1380/1383.

J-Car
Cairo International Airport.
Tel (02) 265 2340.

33 Sharia Mesiah, Dokki.
Tel (02) 335 0521.

MOTORING ORGANIZATIONS

Automobile Association (AA)
Fanum House, Basingstoke, Hants RG21 2EA.
Tel (01256) 201 123.

Automobile and Touring Club of Egypt
10 Sharia Qasr el-Nil, Cairo. **Map** 1 C5.
Tel (02) 574 3355.

Royal Automobile Club (RAC)
PO Box 100, RAC House, 7 Brighton Road, South Croydon, CR2 6XW.
Tel (020) 8686 0088.

MAP OUTLETS

In UK
Stanfords
12–14 Long Acre, London WC2E LP.
Tel (020) 7863 1321.

In Egypt
AUC Bookshop
AUC, Mohammed Mahmoud Gate, Cairo.
Map 1 C5, 5B4. *Tel* (02) 797 5929.

Getting Around Cairo and Alexandria

Metro sign at Midan Opera

The traffic in Cairo is notorious, both for its congestion and its chaos. Driving in the city is impractical for the visitor and many areas, such as the narrow streets and alleys of Islamic and Coptic Cairo, are best explored on foot. The city's public transport includes an extensive bus system, which is cheap but extremely overcrowded, and a clean and efficient metro, which is of limited use to visitors. Taxis are the easiest way to get around and are plentiful, inexpensive and simple to use once the fare system is understood.

Alexandria's main form of transport is its tram system which covers most areas around the city centre. Downtown is compact enough to negotiate on foot but while distances are short the area has not yet been properly mapped and street names appear in French and Arabic.

Tram in front of the Basilica in Heliopolis (see pp136–7)

WALKING

Walking in Cairo is the best way to experience the richness and diversity of this vibrant city. Tackling the streets for the first time, however, can be an intimidating prospect and care should be taken. Drivers do not obey lane markings, road signs or traffic lights. They will slow down to give you time to cross the street, but do not hesitate partway across as this confuses the dodge-and-dash flow of traffic and pedestrians and can increase the chances of an accident. Where possible, cross with groups of other people. Walking in the poorer quarters is remarkably safe, but be wary of petty thieves in crowded areas like the Khan al-Khalili.

Women may also encounter verbal harassment and gropers downtown, on the bridges and in the Khan al-Khalili.

TAXIS

To hail one of Cairo's black-and-white taxis, stand on the side of the road and signal with your hand. State your destination by district or landmark and be prepared for the driver to pick up other people travelling in the same direction.

By law, taximeters must be switched on but they are never used. Drivers will leave the fare up to you, so it is best to know the going rate in advance to avoid overpaying. In general, most trips within the Downtown-Doqqi-Mohandiseen-Zamalek area cost between LE 3–5. From Downtown to Heliopolis or Maadi charges are LE 10–15 and from Downtown to the airport, LE 25–35. Expect to pay a little more late at night.

Taxis at five-star hotels charge higher fares but are good for day hire as they are in better condition and the drivers speak some English. Radio Cab (see p344) is also an important service for tourists.

Single women passengers are generally safe, but should ride in the back of cabs and not talk or make eye contact with the driver, both of which can attract unwanted attention.

RIVER BUSES AND FELUCCAS

An alternative means of getting around is by river bus. These are inexpensive and run approximately every half-hour from near Coptic Cairo to the Arab Television Building north of the Egyptian Museum, stopping at Rhoda Island (see pp124–5). At weekends, the buses are full of revellers heading for the Nile Barrages (see p169) north of the city. River buses only run until 4pm.

Feluccas (sailing boats) are found along the river and can be hired out for short cruises (about LE 35–45 per hour). This is a great way to see Cairo from the Nile and cruises at sunset are particularly popular. One of the main departure points is in Garden City by the Meridien Hotel. Feluccas can also be hired out for longer cruises (see p322).

METRO

The Cairo Metro is clean, safe and inexpensive but visitors will find it useful for only a few stops, the most prominent of which is the

One of Cairo's ubiquitous black-and-white taxis

Felucca on the Nile in Central Cairo – a sedate mode of travel

Mar Girgis station opposite Coptic Cairo. There are two lines, identified by direction. The al-Marg to Helwan line follows the east bank of the Nile for most of its length and the recently opened Shubra to Giza line runs north to southwest, via Midan Tahrir. The last stop on the line is displayed on the front of each train and maps of the network can be found at each station.

Tickets are available at all stations and are valid for one trip, including transfers. Ticket-operated turnstiles control access to all platforms so you will need to keep your ticket in order to exit at your destination. The metro is extremely crowded during the morning and evening rush hours.

The first car on each train, and sometimes the second as well, is reserved for women only, but women can and do ride on any car.

BUSES

City buses are red, blue and white with route numbers displayed in Arabic on the front. The buses are often overcrowded and in poor condition and are not really recommended. However, they do cover almost all destinations and are extremely cheap. The city-run minibuses (orange and white) are a slightly more pleasant experience and also very inexpensive. These have

Local bus providing an authentic Cairo experience for the visitor

fixed routes and a flat fare, paid as you board. Buses leave from Midan Tahrir or from where you see metal shelters, signs mounted on lamp posts, or more commonly, crowds of people waiting alongside the road. Two useful minibus routes are numbers 82 and 83 which run from Midan Tahrir to the Pyramids at Giza. The city also has microbuses and service taxis that operate on fixed routes and stop on request. However, like the local buses, they are overcrowded and used mainly by workers and residents.

GETTING AROUND ALEXANDRIA

Alexandria still relies on an aged tram system. The cars are worn and the pace is slow, but fares are cheap. The service runs from 5:30am to midnight, and to 1am during the summer months. Ramla is the main downtown terminal, located east of the bus depot on Midan Saad Zaghloul. Trams headed east from Ramla are blue, while those travelling west are yellow. Note that on trams that are made up of three cars the middle car is normally reserved for women.

Useful tram routes for visitors include No.15 for the Mosque of Abu al-Abbas Mursi (see pp244–5) and Fort Qaitbey (see p245), and No.16 for Pompey's Pillar (see p246). Heading east, route No.2 travels two-thirds of the way to Montazah Palace (see p247). All tram and route numbers are in Arabic script only.

As in Cairo, buses are old and overcrowded. Minibuses are a better option, following most of the same routes and operating hours as the tram. City minibuses are white while private ones are blue or grey. Both cost under LE 1.

Useful minibus routes for visitors include No.706 and No.707 to Fort Qaitbey via the Corniche, No.703 and No.710 from Midan Orabi to the airport, and No.728 and No.729 from Masr Station to Abu Qir (see p250).

City taxis are black and orange, or yellow, and the rules that apply to taxis in Cairo (see p346) apply here.

Horse-drawn carriages, or caleches, ply the Corniche and Masr Station and can be a relaxing way of getting around the city, providing the traffic is light. The price, as elsewhere in the country, is negotiable. An hourly rate of LE 10–15 is reasonably equitable to all involved.

A westbound tram on a busy thoroughfare in Alexandria

General Index

Page numbers in **bold** type refer to main entries.

Acknowledgments

Dorling Kindersley would like to thank the following people whose contributions and assistance have made the preparation of this book possible.

Publishing Manager
Jane Ewart.

Managing Editor
Anna Streiffert.

Director of Publishing, Travel Guides
Gillian Allan.

Publisher
Douglas Amrine.

Production
Joanna Bull, Sarah Dodd.

Main Contributors
Jane Dunford, Dr Joann Fletcher, Carole French, Robin Gauldie, Andrew Humphreys, Kyle Pakka, Richard Williams.

Additional Contributors and Consultants
Mohammed Saad El-Essawy, David Stone, Hugh Taylor.

Additional Illustrations
Rebecca Milner.

Additional Photography
Jo Doran, Ian O'Leary, Rough Guides/Eddie Gerald, Clive Streeter.

Design and Editorial Assistance
Helen Foulkes, Dale Harris, Victoria Heyworth-Dunne, Samira Mahmoud, Collette Sadler, Rada Radojicic, Sands Publishing Solutions, Kareen Sharawy.

Proof Reader
Stewart J Wild.

Indexer
Helen Peters.

Special Assistance
Ben Faulks, Gamal, Peter Sheehan, Shehad, Hisham Youssif.

Additional Picture Research
Nicole Kaczynski.

Photography Permissions

The publisher would like to thank all the churches, museums, hotels, restaurants, shops, galleries and sights too numerous to thank individually, for their co-operation and contribution to this publication.

Picture Credits

t=top; tl=top left; tlc=top left centre; tc=top centre; tr=top right; cla=centre left above; ca=centre above; cra=centre right above; cl=centre left; c =centre; cr=centre right; clb=centre left below; cb=centre below; crb=centre right below; bl=bottom left; b=bottom; bc=bottom centre; bcl=bottom centre left; br=bottom right; (d)=detail.

The publisher would like to thank the following individuals, companies and picture libraries for permission to reproduce their photographs.

4CORNERS IMAGES: SIME/Fantuz Olimpio 10cla.

ALAMY IMAGES: Peter Bowater 318bl; Adam Butler 321cb; Peter Chadwick 318c; Carolyn Clarke 316cl; Gary Cook 11br; Dennis Cox 11cl; Dacorum Gold 323c; Nick Hanna 321ca; 321cr; Peter Horree 10br, 150cla; imagebroker/Manfred Bail 321br; Paul Ives 316br; Stan Kujawa 318tr, 344b; Celia Mannings 324bc; Barry Mason 322bc; Michele Molinari 289c; Patrick Syder Images 322tc; Wolfgang Pölzer 320tr; Profimedia International s.r.o./Jaroslav Hejzlar 320cl; SAS 289tl; Gordon Sinclair 317cl; WaterFrame 320crb; Andrew Woodley 323bl; WoodyStock/McPhoto 324tl.

AFP, LONDON: Amr Mammoud-STR 309cr; AMR NABEEL-STR 42t; Manoocher Deghati-STF 39clb; Marwan Naamani-STF 38cr; Mohammed al-Sihiti-STR 40bl, 38t, 41t, 313tr; Narwan Naamani-STR 40b; Patrick Hertzog-STF 42b; STR 39tr; STR-STR 41b.

AKG LONDON: 55tc; 183t, 240bl, 245ca; François Guenet 174b; Erich Lessing 24tl, 83cl, 175tr, 183t, 197bl, 238tr; Gilles Mermet 110bl.

ANCIENT ART & ARCHITECTURE COLLECTION: 22tr, 24cl, 26–27, 26br, 28tr, 29cl, 31tl, 45ca, 48br, 49b, 50crb, 51b,

52clb, 52bc, 56bc, 70cb, 77tl, 105tl, 132br, 168cr, 174tr, 175cl, 190br, 193cr, 193br, 195br; Dr. S Coyne 211tr, 211cl, 211br; Muhammed al-Agsarai 56crb; R Sheridan 20tl, 22br, 34br, 246b.

THE ANCIENT EGYPT PICTURE LIBRARY: 30bl, 74cl, 174cr, 175br, 177tr, 178bl, 194cra, 194bl, 239cl.

JON ARNOLD: 1c.

THE ART ARCHIVE: Egyptian Museum of Cairo 10tc; Mander & Mitcheson Theatre Col/ Eileen Tweedy 61ca; Museo Civico Revoltella Trieste/Dagli Orti 60–61c; Museum Correr, Venice/Dagli Orti 58cb, 215cra; Dagli Orti 58t; Museum of Islamic Art Cairo/Dagli Orti 79c; The Egyptian Museum, Cairo/Dagli Orti 3c, 27tr, 74clb, 76tl, 76br, 77bc.

AXIOM: Heidi Grassley 215bl, James Morris 31crb, 164br, 177cb, 177bl, 215tc, 239br, 260cb.

BILDARCHIV PREUSSISCHER KULTURBESITZ: Johannes Laurentius 54cl.

BRIDGEMAN ART LIBRARY, LONDON/NEW YORK: 30tr, 30cr, 32ca, 55tr, 57br, 59bc, *The Flight into Egypt* by Jean-Leon Gerome 123t, 128tr; Bargello, Florence 57bc; Magdelen College, Oxford 57br; Musée des Beaux-Arts, Beziers 54–5 c; Musée du Louvre 22cl, 22–23, 26bl, 178br; Stapleton Collection 24b, 65inset, 132bl, 214tr, 309bl; The British Library, London 58bc; The British Museum, London 46bl; Whitford & Hughes 123t.

ROB DEN BRAASEM: photographersdirect.com 152cla.

JEAN-LOUP CHARMET: 53bl.

BRUCE COLEMAN LTD: Franco Banfi 37bl; Charles and Sandra Hood 227br, 316br.

THOMAS COOKE ARCHIVE: 191cr.

CORBIS: 60tr; Yann Arthus-Bertrand 15b; Bettman 55ca; Bettmann 18c; Hulton Deutsch Collection 20br; Jose Fuste Raga 323tr; Reuters New Media Inc, 54c, 257cl;

Galen Rowell 261cbr; Stephane Compoint/Sygma 19t; Sygma 20/21c; Vanni Archive 118–119; Sandro Vannini 262–3; Julia Waterlow/Eye Ubiquitous 18b; KM Westermann 64–5, 314cl

G. DAGLI ORTI: 110cl; Graeco-Roman Museum, Alexandria 55tl, 242tl, 242clb, 243cra; Graeco-Roman Museum, Alexandria.

CM DIXON: 24tr.

DK PICTURE LIBRARY: 60b, 306tr, 306br; Alan Hills 306bl; Alistair Duncan 21t, 25b, 25cra; British Museum 23cb, 31br; British Museum/ Peter Hayman 122t, 122tr; Dave King 307br; Frank Greenaway 55cb; Geoff Brightling 21br, 31clb; Peter Hayman 30cbl; Philip Dowell 307br; Philip Enticknap 191cl.

DK PICTURE LIBARY/BRITISH MUSEUM, LONDON: 28cla, 28cl, 28cr, 28crb, 28br, 28bcl, 29tl, 29tr, 29cla, 29ca, 29crb, 29bl, 48t, 55bl.

JO DORAN: 115b, 201t.

EDIMEDIA FRANCE: 34c.

MARY EVANS PICTURE LIBARY: 56tc, 57tl, 59tr, 59cr, 59clb, 59br, 60cl, 191crb, 191br, 309cbl.

WERNER FORMAN ARCHIVE: 51ca, 134cr, 163tc, 164cl, 192tr, 195cb, 199crb; British Museum London 26tl, 30ca; Dr. E Strouhal 31bl, 31c, 198bl, 198tl, 199tl, 203tl; Graeco-Roman Museum, Alexandria 53tc, 242cl, 242bl, 243bl; J Paul Getty Museum, Malibu 169bc; Metropolitan Museum of Art, New York 77c, Musée du Louvre 31cla; Schimmel Collection New York 23tl, 122cl; The Egyptian Museum, Cairo 20clb, 50ca, 51cb, 74tl, 74bc, 75tr, 75cra, 75cr, 75cb, 76cr, 76cla.

KENNETH GARRETT: 194b.

GENESIS SPACE PHOTO LIBRARY: 10bl.

GETTY IMAGES: Photographer's Choice/Georgette Douwma 11tr; The Image Bank/Stuart Westmorland 288cl.

© J. PAUL GETTY TRUST: Guillermo Aldana 199br.

PATRICK GODEAU, EGYPT: 14fp, 114b.

RONALD GRANT ARCHIVE: 55b.

HILTON ALEXANDRIA GREEN PLAZA: 265b.

HEMISPHERE IMAGES: Arnaud Chicurel 316tc; Luis Orteo 317tr.

© MICHAEL HOLFORD: 23tr, 25crb, 117tc, 197br, 206–207.

ANGELO HORNAK LIBRARY: 34tl, 35ca, 93cr.

HULTON GETTY: Hulton Getty 54tr.

HUTCHISON LIBRARY: Liba Taylor 166–167.

JURGEN LIEPE: 5bl, 45bl, 46tl, 47tc, 47crb, 47bl, 49cb, 122bl, 132tc, 309cla.

KATAMEYA HEIGHTS GOLF & TENNIS RESORT: 317br.

MAGNUM: Bruno Barbey 63bc.

LEONARDO MEDIA LTD: 240cr; 284bl.

RICHARD T NOWITZ: 110tr, 114ca, 116bl, 125c, 184b, 185b, 187cr, 187br, 316c.

ORONOZ ARCHIVO FOTOGRAFICO: British Museum 22bl.

LESLEY ORSEN: 237cla.

CHRISTINE OSBORNE: 25tl, 31cra, 35cb, 92bl, 103br, 106tr, 106cl, 107t, 111bl, 114cb, 120bl, 121bl, 123b, 176tl, 176c.

OXFORD SCIENTIFIC FILMS: Mark Webster 216; Mike Brown 261tc.

PA PHOTOS: 61br; EPA European Press Agency 63cb, 63t.

PHOTOLIBRARY: JTB Photo 322cl.

POPPERFOTO: 20tr, 20cla, 20cl, 21cr, 60tl, 61bl, 62tl, 62cb, 63br, 122br, 125br, 135bc; Donald McLeish 73tr.

RANA EL NEMR PHOTOGRAPHY: photographersdirect.com 152bc.

RETROGRAPH ARCHIVE LTD: 191bl.

SCALA GROUP S.P.A.: 30tl, 116cr; Archaeological Museum, Palestine 44a; Coptic Museum, Cairo 114t, 116t; The Egyptian Museum, Cairo 15t, 45bc, 66crb.

TOPHAM PICTUREPOINT: 20bl.

ART DIRECTORS & TRIP: D Saunders 226tl.

WAWSON WOOD: 227t, 227cra, 227clb, 227bl.

JACKET
Front: THE ART ARCHIVE: Egyptian Museum Cairo/Dagli Orti clb; GETTY IMAGES: Stone/Diehm main image.
Back: ALAMY IMAGES: BL Images Ltd tl; DK IMAGES: Max Alexander bl, cla, clb.
Spine: DK IMAGES: Max Alexander b; GETTY IMAGES: Stone/Diehm t.

All other images © Dorling Kindersley.
For further information see:
www.dkimages.com

Phrase Book

The official language of Egypt is Arabic. While it is not an easy language for newcomers to learn, it is well worth taking the time to practise and memorize a few key words and phrases. Most urban Egyptians speak a little English but they will greet any attempt to speak Arabic with delight and encouragement.

The Arabic given here is the Modern Standard Arabic. This is the Arabic written in newspapers, spoken on the radio and recited in prayers in the mosque. This varies somewhat from the language spoken on the street (Egyptian Colloquial Arabic), which is in fact a dialect of the standard language. Nevertheless if you speak slowly and clearly, you should have no difficulty being understood.

Transliteration from Arabic script to the Roman alphabet is a difficult task. Although many attempts have been made, there is no satisfactory system and you will repeatedly come across contradictory spellings in Egypt.

In this phrase book we have given a simple phonetic transcription only. The underlined letter indicates the stressed syllable.

Pronunciation

a, -ah	as in "mad"
aa	as in "far"
aw	as in "law"
ay	as in "day"
e	as in "bed"
ee	as in "keen"
i	as in "bit"
o	as in "rob"
oo	as in "food"
u	as in "book"
A	pronounced as an emphasised "a" as in "both of us - you And me!"
D	a heavily pronounced "d"
gh	like a French "r" - from the back of the throat
H	a heavily pronounced "h"
kh	as in the Scottish pronunciation of "loch"
q	a "k" sound from the back of the mouth as
in	"caramel"
S,T	heavily pronounced "s", "t"
th	as in "thin"
Z	heavily pronounced "z"
'	this sounds like a small catch in the breath

When two different vowels occur together, for example Ae- and aA- each is pronounced separately.

In Emergency

Help!	an-najdah!
Stop!	qeff!
I want to go	oreed al zehab
to a doctor	lel tabeeb
I want to go to a	oreed al zehab lel saydaliya
pharmacist	
Where is the nearest	ayn yoogad aqrab telifoon?
telephone?	
Where is the hospital?	ayn toogad al mostashfa?
I'm allergic to...	Andee Hasaaseeyah men...
...penicillin/aspirin	penicillin/aspirin

Communication essentials

Yes/No	naAm/laa
Thank you	shokran
No, thank you	laa shokran
Please (asking for something)	min faDlak
Please (offering)	tafaDal
Good morning	sabaaH al-khayr
Good afternoon	as-salaam Alaykum
Good evening	masa' al-khayr
Good night	teSbaH Ala khayr
(when going to bed)	
Good night	maA as-salaamah or
(leaving group early)	as-salaam Alaykum
Goodbye	maA as-salaamah
Excuse me, please	min faDlak, law samaHt
today	al-yawm
yesterday	al-ams
tomorrow	ghadan
this morning	haza aS-sabaaH
this afternoon	al-yawm baAd aZ-Zohr
this evening	haza al-masa'
here	hona
there	honaak
what?	maza?
which?	ay?
when?	mata?
who?	man?
where?	ayn?

Useful Phrases

I don't understand	la afham
Do you speak	hal tatakalam
English/French?	engleezee/faransee?
I can't speak Arabic	la ataklam al Arabeya
I don't know	la aAref
Please speak more slowly	men faDlak tahadath bebote'
Please write it down for me	men faDlak ektob ala hazeehee al-waraqah
My name is...	esmee...
How do you do,	kayf Haalak,
pleased to meet you	tasharafna be-meArefatak
How are you?	kayf Haalak?
Sorry!	aasef
I'm really sorry	aasef jeddan
Can you help me, please?	min faDlak, momken tosaAednee?
Can you tell me...?	men faDlak qol lee...?
I would like....?	oreed...
Is there...here?	yugad...hona?
Where can I get...?	ayn ajed...?
How much is it?	kam thaman haza (m) hazeehee (f)?
What time is it?	as-saAh kam
I must go now	labod an azhab al-a'n
Do you take credit cards?	hal taqbal Visa, Access?
Where is the toilet?	ayn ajed al-hamam?
Go away!	emshee!
(for children only)	
Excellent!	momtaaz!
left	yasaar
right	yameen
up	fawq
down	asfal

Travel

I want to go to...	oreed al zehab le...
How do you get to...	kayef tazhab le...?
I'd like to rent a car	oreed asta'jer sayaarah
driver's licence	rokhSat qiyaadah
I've lost my way	ana Dalayt aT-Tareeq

Where is the nearest garage?	ayn yoogad aqrab warshet sayarat?
garage (for repairs)	garaaj meekaaneekee
petrol/gas	banzeen
petrol/gas station	maHaTTat banzeen
When is there a flight to..?	mata toogad reHalat tayaran ela...?
What is the fare to...?	kam thaman al tazkarah le...?
A ticket to...please	law samaHt, tazkarat zehaab le...
airport	maTaar
ticket	tazkarah
passport	jawaaz safar
visa	veeza
airport shuttle	baaS al-maTaar
When do we arrive in...?	mata nasel ela...?
When is the next train to..?	mata yaqoom al-qeTaar alzaheb le...?
What station is this?	hazehe ay maHaTTah?
train	qeTaar
first-class (train)	darajah oolah
second-class	darajah thaaneeyah
sleeping car	Arabat nawm
bus	otobees
bus station	mahatet el-otobees
boat	markeb
cruise	Jawlah baHareeyah
ferry	Abaarah
taxi	taaksee

Making a Telephone Call

may I use your telephone?	momken astaAmel teleefoonak
How much is a call to...?	be-kam al-mokaalamah le...?
Can I call abroad from here?	momken ataSel bel-khaarej men hona?
Hello, this is...speaking	alloo,...yatakalam
I would like to speak to...	oreed atakalam maA...
Could you leave him a message?	momken tatrok laho resaalah?
My number is...	raqamee...
telephone call	mokaalamah
emergency	Tawaare'
operator	sentraal

Post Offices and Banks

How much is a letter to...?	kam taklefat ersal kheTab ela....?
This is to go airmail	erselha bel-bareed al-jawee
I'd like to change this into...	oreed oghayyer haza ela
bank	bank
dollar (US)	dollar
exchange rate	seAr at-taghyeer
letter	kheTaab
postbox	sondooq bareed
package	tard
post	boosTah
postcard	beTaaqah bareedeeyah
post office	maktab al-bareed
stamp	TaabeA bareed
traveller's cheque	sheek siyaaHee

Staying in a Hotel

Have you got any vacancies?	hal yoogad ghoraf khaaleeyah?
I have a reservation	Andee Hajz
I'd like a room with a bathroom	oreed ghorfah be-Hammam
May I have the bill please?	momken al-hesab law samaHat
I'll pay by credit card	sa-asfaA al-fatoorah law Visa, Access
I'll pay by cash	sa-adfaA naqdan
hotel	fondoq
air-conditioning	takyeef
double room	ghorfa mozdawajah

single room	ghorfa be-sareer waaHed
shower	dosh
toilet	towaaleet
toilet paper	waraq towaleet
key	meftaaH
lift/elevator	mesAd
breakfast	foToor
restaurant	maTAm
bill	faatoorah

Shopping

I'd like...	oreed...
Do you have...?	hal Andak...?
How much is this?	be-kam haza?
I'll give you...	ha aAteek...
Two for...	ethnayn be...
Where do I pay?	ayn adfaA?
to buy	yashtaree
to go shopping	yatasawwaq

Sightseeing

mosque	jaamea
street, road	shaareA
house	bayt
square	mjdan
beach	shaaTee'
museum	matHaf
church	kaneesah
castle, palace	qasr

Eating Out (see also pp280–81)

A table for...one/two, please	ma'eda le-shakhS waHed/le-shakhSayn, law samaHt
I'd like...	oreed...
May we have the bill, please?	momken al-Hesaab, law samaHt?
May we have some more...?	momken al-mazeed mendfadlak...?
My compliments to the chef!	taheyaty le-Tahy!
beer	beerah
bottle	zojaajah
cake	kayk
coffee	qahwah
– no sugar	- saadah
– medium	- maZbooT
– sweet	- sukkar zeyaadah
– with milk	- bel-Haleeb
cup	fenjaan
glass	koob
plate	Tabaq
sandwich	sandwetsh
snack	wajbah khafeefah
sugar	sukkar
table	ma'eda
tea	shaay
mint	neAnaA
(mineral) water	miyaah (maAdaneeyah)
wine	nabeez

Food and Drink

soup	shorbah
fish	samak
aubergine salad	salaaTat baazenjaan
melon	shammaam
pickles	mekhallalaat
hummus	Hommos
falafel - fried balls of ground fava beans or chickpeas	falaafel
fried balls of ground fava beans with herbs	taAmeeyah
olives	zaytoon
stuffed vine leaves	waraq Aenab maHsee

aubergine and tahina paté | baaba ghanooj
cheese | jebnah
curd cheese | labnah
egg | bayDah
macaroni | makaroonah
noodles | sheAreeyah

Fish

grilled fish | samak mashwee
fried fish | samak maqlee
fish with rice | samak sayaadeeyah
smoked fish | samak medakhan
shrimp | jambaree
squid | Habaar
tuna | toonah

Meat and Poultry

beef | laHm baqaree
chicken | firaakh
chicken pieces | koftat dajaaj
duck | baTT
grilled lamb kebab | kebaab
lamb | laHm Daanee
meat | laHm
meatballs | koftah
mixed grilled meats | luHoom mashweeyah
pigeon | Hamaam
roast beef | roosbeef
sliced spit-roast lamb | shaawerma
steak | boftayk

Vegetables

aubergine | baazenjaan
avocado | abookaado
cabbage | koronb
celery | karafs
chillies | felfel Haamee
cucumber | khiyaar
lentils | Adas
lettuce | khass
okra | baamyah
onions | baSal
potatoes | baTaaTes
rice | rozz
tomatoes | TamaaTem
vegetables | khoDaar

Fruit and Nuts

almonds | looz
apricots | meshmesh
bananas | mooz
dried fruits | fawaakeh mojaffafah
figs | teen
fruits | fawaakeh
lemon | laymoon HaameD
pistachio nuts | fostoq
watermelon | baTeekh

Desserts

cake | kayk
baclava | baqlaawah
biscuits | baskooweet
dessert | Halawiyaat
fritters in syrup | zalaabeeyah
fruit salad | salaatet fawaakeh
ice cream | aays kreem
"Mother of Ali" | omm Alee
    milk pudding with raisins
pastry with nuts and syrup | konaafah
yoghurt | zabaadee

Methods of Cooking

baked | feel-forn
barbecued | mashwee Ala al-faHm
boiled | maslooq
fried | maqlee
grilled | mashwee
pickled | mekhaalil
spiced | metabbel
stewed | mesabbek
stuffed | maHshee

Numbers

0	sefr		30	thalaatheen
1	waaHed		31	waaHed wa thalaatheen
2	ethnayn		32	ethnayn wa thalaatheen
3	thalaathah		40	arbaAeen
4	arbaAh		50	khamseen
5	khamsah		60	setteen
6	settah		70	sabAeen
7	sabAh		80	thamaaneen
8	thamaaneeyah		90	tesAeen
9	tesAh		100	me'ah
10	Asharah		110	me'ah wa Asharah
11	Hedaash		200	me'tayn
12	etnaash		300	thalaathme'ah
13	thalaathaash		400	arbaAme'ah
14	arbaAtaash		500	khamsme'ah
15	khamastaash		600	setme'ah
16	settaash		700	sabAme'ah
17	sabaAtaash		800	thamaanme'ah
18	thamaantaash		900	tesAme'ah
19	tesAtaash		1,000	alf
20	Aeshreen		2,000	alfayn
21	waaHed wa Aeshreen		10,000	Asharat aalaaf
22	ethnayn wa Aeshreen		1,000,000	malyoon

Days, Months and Seasons

Sunday | yawm al-aHad
Monday | yawm al-ethnayn
Tuesday | yawm ath-tholatha'
Wednesday | yawm al-arbeAa'
Thursday | yawm al-khamees
Friday | yawm al-jomAh
Saturday | yawm as-sabt
January | yanaayer
February | febraayer
March | Maars
April | ebreel
May | maayo
June | yoonyo
July | yoolyo
August | aghosTos
September | sebtember
October | oktoober
November | noofember
December | deesember
spring | al-ar-rabeeA
summer | aS-Sayf
autumn | al-khareef
winter | ash-sheta'

Things You'll Hear

enshaallah | God (Allah) willing
tasharafna | you're welcome
esmak eh? | What is your name?
bel-hanaa' wash-shefaa' | Enjoy your meal